The Melting Pot Book of

BABY NAMES

2nd EDITION

Connie Lockhart Ellefson

BETTERWAY PUBLICATIONS, INC.
WHITE HALL, VIRGINIA

Published by Betterway Publications, Inc.
P.O. Box 219
Crozet, VA 22932
(804) 823-5661

Cover design by Rick Britton
Typography by Park Lane Associates

Cover photograph © 1987 John Sunderland/Photostaff, Inc.

The children in the cover photograph (from left to right) are: Farah
Farahmandi, Amber Stroud, Lindsay Widmark, and April Coleman

Library of Congress Cataloging-in-Publication Data

Ellefson, Connie Lockhart
    The melting pot book of baby names / by Connie Lockhart Ellefson.
-- 2nd ed.
      p. cm.
    ISBN 1-55870-178-8 : $8.95
     1. Names, Personal--United States--Dictionaries. 2. United States-
-Emigration and immigration.   I. Title.
    CS2375.U6E44 1990
    929.4'0973--dc20   90-39085
                                                   CIP

Printed in the United States of America
0 9 8 7 6 5 4 3 2

To Elaine . . .
who told me to get on with this idea,

And to my family . . .
Jerry, Ben, and Ian who suffered privation while I did.

PRONUNCIATION GUIDE

I have included the pronunciation for names most English-speaking Americans might have trouble pronouncing and general pronunciation guides for most chapters. With few exceptions (carefully noted in the pronunciation guides at the end of each chapter), vowels should be pronounced as shown below:

a = "ah" as in ball   o = "oh" as in hope
e = "eh" as in late   u = "oo" as in moon.
i = "ee" as in keep

ABBREVIATIONS USED

A.S.	= Anglo-Saxon	OE	= Old English
Celt	= Celtic	OGer	= Old German
Fr	= French	ONorse	= Old Norse
Gael	= Gaelic	Scand	= Scandinavian
Ger	= German	Span	= Spanish
Gr	= Greek	Teut	= Teutonic
H	= Hebrew	Ukr	= Ukranian
L	= Latin		

comb.	= combination of	ref.	= reference
dim.	= diminutive of	var.	= variation of
fem.	= feminine of		

CONTENTS

INTRODUCTION

A few years ago when I was pregnant I looked for a list of Norwegian names for Baby to go with my husband's Norwegian name. Though I found books with thousands of names, I never found a list of just Norwegian names.

In the end Baby was named Ian, which is Scottish for John, and I have to admit I got the idea from the credits of a movie. But I still wondered if that Norwegian name list was out there somewhere. I decided to track it down as well as some others in case there were other prospective parents who were as interested in their ethnic heritage as I was.

What I found was the stunning array of contributions made by America's immigrants, which was humbling but exhilarating. How lucky we are to have this huge diversity of languages and values contributing to the essence of the American.

I was in awe of the stories of astonishing hardship borne by some of the immigrants to get here, the further hardships of discrimination against newcomers and unfamiliarity with the language, and the bravery they must have possessed to face the journey at all.

My favorite immigrant story, however, was not one of hardship. A Greek couple came to the United States for their honeymoon, arriving just as World War II began. Not wanting to return to war-torn Greece they decided to wait it out. But the war lasted seven years in Greece, and by the time it was over this couple had established a nice little business in Chicago, so they decided to stay.

The myth of the melting pot has come under attack, given that almost every ethnic group arriving in large numbers has encountered mistrust, discrimination, harassment, and worse. But I can't help but notice that the immigrant groups which have been here more than one generation seem to be fully accepted as part of mainstream America.

So perhaps it is only the initial shock of a new ingredient to the melting pot that is uncomfortable. We certainly haven't melted into one homogeneous liquid, but have each retained good-sized chunks of our original ethnic character, which is as it should be.

As for the name lists, I have gathered names from many sources, including immigrants, foreign students, language professors, and the hundreds of ethnic organizations which exist in the U.S. today to keep alive their respective cultures. I have tried to search for the names that are contemporarily popular in those countries, so if you want to give Baby an authentic name from the culture of your ancestors you can rest easy in the knowledge that your choice won't be out of date!

I have also included some names which older people might bear in those countries, so if you're a spy novelist seeking the perfect name for your East European undercover agent, you'll be able to find it here, too!

Please let me know if I've left out your favorite ethnic name or if you want to straighten me out on what's really popular in that country now. I'll need the input to keep this book up to date.

AFGHANISTAN

Originally populated by Pushtun (Pathan) tribal peoples, Afghanistan was the crossroads for the Central Asian invaders of India and the western Islamic world. Its heterogeneous modern population of twelve to fifteen million people reflects the various groups that have invaded and passed through it; approximately sixty percent of Afghans are Pushtuns, fifteen percent are Tadzhiks, and the remainder are a mixture of Turkomans, Uzbeks, Hazarahs, Baluchi, and others.

By 1980 there were only 2,500 Afghans living in the U.S. Many of the recent immigrants were students who stayed, especially after the Soviet invasion of Afghanistan in 1978. Family loyalty is often of highest priority in Afghanistan and ninety-nine percent of the present population is Muslim. Dari (Afghan Persian) is spoken by over eighty-five percent of the people as either a first or second language. Pashto and Dari are among the official languages of Afghanistan and many other languages and dialects are spoken.

Afghans are living in almost every state in the Union with the largest concentration around Washington, DC and the east and west coasts. Professional fields such as medicine, engineering, education, anthropology, and other technical fields tend to be among the most common occupations among Afghan-Americans.

AFGHANISTAN FEMALE NAMES

Asma sky

Badria moonlike

Fowzia (FOW-zyuh) productive

Frebah (FREE-bah) illusive

Frogh (FE-rosh) light

Gulalai (guhl-LA-lay) fresh

Gulmakai (guhl-MA-kay) flower

Mallalai (Pashtu) beautiful

Nahid (NA-heed) a star

Omaira (Arabic) red

Palwasha spark of light

Pashtoon Afghan

Roxanna (rokh-SHA-nuh) sparkling

Seema sky, profile

Shahla (SHEH-luh) beautiful eyes

Shaima (SHAH-ee-mah) (Arabic) having a mole or beauty spot

Soraya a star

Souriya a smile

Wajjmah whisper

AFGHANISTAN MALE NAMES

Ajmal (AZH-mehl) good-looking

Arsallah messenger

Babur joy, peace, happiness

Daoud (dah-WOOUD) (H) beloved

Fakoor thinker

Iskander (Gr) defender of mankind

Matteen disciplined, polite

Mirwais name of famous Afghan king (ca. 900 A.D.), amir=king

Nadir scarce

Osman (Turk) founder of Ottoman Empire; or (A.S.) servant of God

Paieendah (pa-YEN-dah) durable

Timour (H) stately, tall; or (Russian) conqueror

Wali (Arabic) all-governing

Yasir humble, one who takes it easy

Zahir (ZAH-hir) (Arabic) evident, splendid

Zalmai (ZEHL-may) young

Zelgai (ZEHL-gay) heart

Zemar (ZE-mahr) loin

Zerak (ZE-rak) shroud

ARABIC COUNTRIES

The Arabic world today extends from Morocco on the western side of North Africa east through Algeria, Libya, Egypt, Saudi Arabia, Syria, Iraq, and several smaller countries around the Saudi Arabian peninsula. Although one might think all Arabs are followers of the Muslim religion, there are numerous Christian and Jewish sects in the Arab world.

In fact the earliest Arabic immigrants were primarily Christians from Syria who began immigrating about 1876 in search of economic opportunity. They came from a semi-autonomous province of the Turkish Ottoman empire called Mt. Lebanon (part of present-day Lebanon). Exceptionally sketchy immigration records make it impossible to determine accurately the number of Syrian immigrants. However, the figure rose from a few hundred in 1887 to 4,000 in 1898 to over 9,000 in 1913.

In Arab society the honor and status of one's extended family is one of the supreme, inviolable values. The elevation of one's family status by attaining wealth (the basis of status in the United States) has produced a competitive spirit and work ethic which put the Syrians directly in line with American values. Thus, from extremely dissimilar backgrounds has come an ideal mold for assimilating into American society.

Many Syrians began their economic life as peddlers, first clustered in New York City and then spreading to the most remote parts of the U.S. As their businesses grew they often recruited new Syrian immigrants or fellow countrymen to work for them. Through this unique network many Syrian immigrants were absorbed quickly into the ranks of the employed.

A total of 115,000 Arabs are said to have immigrated to the U.S. through 1945. In an era, however, when North African Arabs might be classified as "other Africans" and non-Syrian Arabs as "other Asians" for the immigration record, the number is probably an underestimate.

Of the more than one million Arabs that live in the U.S. today, ninety percent are Christian and ten percent Muslim. Over half are the descendants of the Arabs who arrived between 1875 and 1948. Of the approximately 100,000 Muslims in the United States, drawn from all the present-day Arabic countries, most arrived after 1948.

After World War II several Arabic nations began sending students to Europe and the U.S. to be trained in essential skills needed to help their home countries modernize. However, continued ideological and territorial wars drained economies as well as the students' desire to return. Many students simply stayed away.

Many Arab immigrants came as Palestinian refugees, especially after the Arab defeat in the Arab-Israeli war of 1967. After 1967, there were more more than 104,000 Arab immigrants, out of a total 154,000 who came between 1949 and 1976 primarily from Egypt, Jordan, Lebanon, Syria, and Iraq.

The names in the Arabic list are primarily of the Muslim religion (called Islam, or "submission to God"), reflecting the main religion of the Arab world. Believers hold that Mohammed, a seventh century Arab, was the last in a long line of prophets from God, which included Moses and Jesus. Islam is similar to Judaism and pre-Reformation Christianity in that religion, politics, and society are inseparable.

The revelations of Mohammed are contained in the Holy Quran (Koran) and govern every activity in the lives of the believers. It is considered desirable to have at least one boy named Mohammed in every extended family. Other names may be shared in an extended family, although not among siblings. Choices for names include the names of Allah (God) or one of His divine attributes, the name of another prophet, or a Quranic term describing an Islamic value.

The most popular names for girls are the names of Mohammed's wives and daughters. Naming customs vary from country to country. One custom in the North African countries of Libya, Tunisia, and Morocco is the practice of using the father's first name for the baby's middle name, regardless of the child's sex. Occasionally the suffix -adeen, meaning "of the faith" (Islam), is added to the middle name.

The pronunciation of most of the names in the list is included; however keep in mind that the same name might be pronounced various ways in different parts of the Arabic world. Also, names may be "telescoped" in unfamiliar ways. For instance the name Sofia in pronounced "so-FEE-ah" in European languages, but pronounced "SOF-yah" in Arabic.

ARABIC FEMALE NAMES

A'ishah (ah-ee-SHAH) living; prosperous; wife of Muhammad

Abia great

Abida worshiper

Abir (AH-beer) fragrance

Ablah (AH-blah) perfect

Abra example, lesson

Adara (AH-drah) virgin

Adiba cultured, polite

Adila (AH-dee-lah) equal, like — Adilah

Adiva pleasant, gentle

Adlai just

Afaf (AH-fahf) chastity

Afifah (ah-fee-FAH) chaste

Afra earth colored

Ahd knowledge

Aida (ah-ee-dah) reward, present

Ain (ah-EEN) eye, thus "precious"

Aisha ** (ah-EE-shah) living — Ayisha

Akilah (AH-kee-lah) (N. Africa) intelligent, one who reasons

Alima * (AH-lee-mah) wise

Aliye noble

Alma learned

Altair bird

Amal * hope — Amala

Amany * aspiration

Amatullah (ah-mah-TOO-lah) female servant of Allah

Amber semiprecious stone

Ameerah * princess — Amira, Meerah, Mira

Aminah (a-MEEN-ah) trustworthy, faithful

Anan * (a-NAHN) clouds

Anisah * (an-EE-sah) friendly; of good company

Anwar (AHN-wahr) rays of light

Ara opinions

Arub (ah-ROOB) woman loving to her husband

Asima protector

Asma ** daughter of Abu Bakr

Atia old

Atifa * affection, sympathy

Atiya gift

Azhar (AHS-rah) blossoms; flowers

Azizah * (a-ZEE-zuh) esteemed, precious, cherished

Badriyyah (ba-DREE-ah) resembling full moon

Bahira (ba-HEER-ah) dazzling, brilliant

Banan * (ba-NAHN) finger tips

Baraka white one

Bari'ah (bah-ree-AH) excelling

Bashiyra joy

Basimah * (BAH-see-mah, or bah-SEE-mah) smiling

Batul (bah-TOOL) ascetic virgin

Buthaynah (boo-TAH-ee-nah) of beautiful and tender body

Cala castle

Cantara small bridge

Dahab gold

Duha (doo-HAH) forenoon

Fadilah * (fah-DEE-lah) virtue

Fadwa (fad-WAH) name derived from self-sacrifice

Faizah * (FAH-ee-zah) (N.Africa) victorious

Falak (fa-LAHK) star

Faridah * (fa-REE-dah) unique

Farihah (fah-REE-hah) happy; joyful

Fatima ** (FAH-tee-mah) (N.Africa) daughter of the Prophet

Fatin (FAH-teen) captivating — Fatinah (FAH-tee-nah)

Firyal (feer-YAHL) name (popular in Egypt)

Fukayna (foo-KEH-ee-nah) (N.Africa) knowledgeable, scholarly

Ghadah (GAH-dah) beautiful — Ghayda

Ghaliyah (gah-LEE-yah) fragrant

Ghusun (goo-SOON) branches of a tree

Habibah (hah-BEE-bah) (N.Africa) beloved

Hadiya (HAH-dee-yah) guide to righteousness

Hafsah (HAF-sah) (N.Africa) wife of the Prophet

Hafthah (HAF-thah) (N.Africa) preserved, protected

Halah (HAH-lah) aureole

Halimah * (hah-LEE-mah) gentle, patient

Hamidâh (hah-MEE-dah) praiseworthy

Hana * (hah-NAH) happiness

Hanan (hah-NAHN) mercy

Hanifah (hah-NEE-fah) (N.Africa) true believer

Haniyyah (hah-NEE-yah) pleased; happy

Haqikah (hah-KEE-kah) (N.Africa) truthful

Hasna (has-NAH) beautiful

Hayat * (hah-YAHT) life

Hayfa * (hah-ee-FAH) slender, of beautiful body

Hind (HEEND) proper name (popular in Saudi Arabia)

Huda * (hoo-DAH) right guidance

Hurriyyah (HOO-ree-yah) angel

Husn (HOOSN) beauty

Husniyah (hoos-NEE-yah) (N.Africa) beautiful

Ibtihaj (eeb-TEE-hazh) joy

Ikram (ee-KRAHM) honor, hospitality, generosity

Ilham (EEL-hahm) intuition

Iman* (ee-MAHN) faith, belief

In'am (een-AHM) act of kindness; benefaction; bestowal

Inas (een-AHS) sociability

Inayah (een-NAH-yah) concern, solicitude

Intisar (een-tee-SAHR) triumph

Izdihar (ees-dee-HAHR) flourishing; blossoming

Jala' (jah-LAH) clarity; elucidation

Jamilah* (ja-MEE-lah) beautiful

Janan (ja-NAHN) heart or soul

Jumanah (joo-MAH-nah) silver pearl

Kalila beloved

Kamilah* (kah-MEE-lah) (N.Africa) the perfect one

Karimah* (kah-REE-mah) (N.Africa) generous

Kawthar (kaw-THAHR) river in Paradise

Khadijah** (kah-dee-YAH) name of Muhammad's wife

Khalidah (ka-LEE-dah) immortal

Khulud (koo-LOOD) immortality

Lama (lah-MAH) darkness of lips

Lamis (la-MEES) soft to the touch

Lamya (LAHM-yah) dark-lipped

Lateefah* (lah-TEE-fah) (N.Africa) gentle, pleasant

Leila born at night — Laila, Layla

Lina (LEE-nah) tender

Ma'isah (mah-EE-sah) walking with a proud swinging gait

Madihah (ma-DEE-hah) praiseworthy

Maha (ma-HAH) wild cow

Maizah (MAH-ee-zah) (N.Africa) discerning

Majidah (ma-JEE-dah or MAH-jee-dah) glorious

Makarim (ma-KAH-reem) of good and honorable character

Makarramma (moo-kah-RAH-ma) (N.Africa) honored, respected

Malak** (MAH-lak) angel

Manal* (ma-NAHL) attainment, achievemant

Manar (ma-NAHR) guiding light (lighthouse)

Maram (ma-RAHM) aspiration

Maryam* (mahr-YAHM) name of mother of Jesus

Mawiyah (MAH-wee-yah) (N.Africa) the essence of life

May (MAH-ee) old Arabic name

Maysa (mah-ee-SAH) to walk with a proud swinging gait

Maysun (mah-ee-SOON) of beautiful face and body

Mufidah* (moo-FEE-dah) useful

Muhjah (MOO-jah) heart's blood-soul

Muminah (MOO-mee-nah) (N.Africa) pious believer

Muna (moo-NAH) wish, desire

Munirah (moo-NEE-rah) illuminating, shedding light

Mushirah (moo-SHEE-rah) giving counsel, advising

Muslimah (moos-LEE-mah) (N.Africa) devout believer

Na'imah* (na-EE-mah) living a soft, enjoyable life

Nabihah (na-BEE-hah) intelligent

Nada* (na-DAH) generosity; dew

Nadidah (na-DEE-dah) equal to another person

Nailah (NAH-ee-lah) (N.Africa) one who succeeds

Najah (na-ZHAH) success

Najat (na-ZHAHT) safety

Najibah (na-ZHEE-bah) of noble birth

Najiyah (na-ZHEE-yah) safe

Nathifa (nah-THEEF-ah) (N.Africa) clean, pure

Nawal* (na-WAHL) gift

Nawar (nah-WAHR) flower

Nazihah* (na-ZEE-hah) honest

Nazirah (na-ZEE-rah) like-equal

Ni'mah (nee-MAH) blessing, loan — Ni'mat

Nibal (nee-BAHL) arrows

Nida* (nee-DAH) call

Nudar* (noo-DAHR) gold

Nur (NOOR) light

Qubilah (KWUB-ee-lah) (N.Africa) concord

Ra'idah (rah-EE-dah) leader

Rabab (ra-BAHB) white cloud

Rabi'ah (rah-bee-AH) garden

Radeyah (rah-DEH-yah) content; satisfied

Radwa (rahd-WAH) name of mountain in Medina

Rafa (rah-FAH) happiness, prosperity

Raja* (rah-JAH) hope

Rana* (rah-NAH) to gaze; look

Raniyah (rah-NEE-yah) gazing

Rasha (rah-SHAH) young gazelle

Rashidah* (rah-SHEE-dah) wise, mature

Rayya (rah-YAH) sated with drink

Rima (REE-mah) white antelope — Rim

Rukan (roo-KAHN) steady, confident

Ruqayyah* (roo-KEE-yah) name of the Prophet's daughter

Ruwaydah* (roo-WAH-ee-dah) walking gently

Sabah* (sah-BAH) (N.Africa) morning

Sabirah* (sah-BEE-rah) patient

Safa* (sah-FAH) clarity, purity, serenity

Safiyyah* (sah-FEE-yah) untroubled, serene, pure

Sagirah (SAH-gee-rah) (N.Africa) little one

Sahar dawn

Sahlah (sah-hee-lah) smooth, soft ground

Saidah* (sah-EE-dah) (N.Africa) happy, fortunate

Sakinah God-inspired peace of mind; tranquility

Salihah (N.Africa) correct, agreeable

Salimah* (sah-LEEM-ah) safe, healthy

Samah* (sa-MAH) generosity

Samar evening conversations

Samihah (sa-MEE-hah) generous

Samirah* entertaining companion (woman)

Samiyah* elevated, lofty

Sana* (sa-NAH) to gaze; look

Sawsan lily of the valley

Selma* (N.Africa) secure

Shadha* (shahd-HA) aromatic

Shadiyah singer

Sharifah* noble

Siham* (see-HAHM) arrows

Suha* (soo-HAH) name of a star

Suhailah* (soo-HAH-ee-lah) (N.Africa) gentle, easy

Suhayr proper name

Sumayyah proper name

Tahirah (tah-HEE-rah) pure, chaste

Takiyah (tah-KEE-yah) (N.Africa) pious, righteous

Talibah (tah-LEE-bah) (N.Africa) seeker after knowledge

Tarub (tah-ROOB) merry

Thana (THAH-nah) thankfulness

Thara (ta-hee-rah) wealth

Thurayya (thoo-RAH-ee-yah) star

Umayma* (oo-MAH-ee-mah) (N.Africa) little mother

Umm (OOM) (N.Africa) mother

Wafa* (wah-FAH) faithfulness

Wafiqah (wah-FEE-kah) successful

Wafiyyah* (wah-FEE-yah) loyal, faithful

Wajihah* (wa-ZHEE-hah) eminent, distinguished

Walidah (wah-LEE-dah) (N.Africa) new-born

Widad* love, friendship

Wijdan* (wij-dahn) ecstasy, sentiment

Wisal (wee-SAHL) communion in love

Wordah (war-dah) rose

Yaminah (yah-MEE-nah) (N.Africa) right and proper

Yasmin* (yahs-MEEN) jasmine

Yusra (yoos-RAH) proper name

Zafirah victorious, successful

Zahirah shining, luminous — Zahrah

Zahra* (zah-RAH) white

Zakiyyah* (za-kee-yah) pure

Zaynah beautiful

Zubaidah (zoo-BAH-ee-dah) (N.Africa) excellent

---

* Popular
** Very popular

ARABIC MALE NAMES

Aban (ah-BAHN) old Arabic name

Abbas* description of a lion

Abbud (ah-BOOD) worshipper

Abd al bari* (ahbd-ahl-bah-REE) servant of the Creator

Abd al hadi* (hah-DEE) servant of the Guide

Abd al hakim* servant of the Wise

Abd al hamid* servant of the Praiseworthy

Abd al jabbar* servant of the Mighty

Abd al matin* servant of the Firm; Strong

Abd al mu'izz* servant of the Giver of Might and Glory

Abd al qadir* (ahbd-ahl-kah-DEER) servant of the Capable

Abd al rahman** servant of the Mercifully Gracious

Abd al rashid* servant of the Rightly Guided

Abd al samad* servant of the Eternal

Abd al sami* servant of the All-hearing

Abd al'alim* servant of the Omniscient

Abd al'azim* servant of the Mighty, the Powerful

Abdel (AHB-duhl) or (ahb-DOOL) servant of ...

Abdullah** servant of God

Abu al khayr* one who does good

Abu bakr** the companion of Prophet Muhammad

Adil* (A-deel) just

Adnan* proper name

Ahmad** (AH-mahd) commendable, praiseworthy

Akil (ah-KEEL) intelligent, thoughtful

Akram* most generous

Aliyy** (ah-LEE) excellent, noble

Altair flying eagle

Amin* faithful, trustworthy

Amir* (AH-meer) populous

Amjad* (ahm-ZHAHD) more glorious

Ammar the Builder, Constructor

Arif (AH-reef) acquainted; knowledgeable

Asadel (A-sa-del) most prosperous

Ashraf* more honorable

Asim (ah-SEEM) (N.Africa) protector, defender

Aswad (ahs-WAHD) black

Ata (ah-TAH) gift

Atif (ah-TEEF) compassionate, sympathetic

Ayyub* a Prophet's name

Aza comfort

Azhar (ah-ZAHR) the Most Shining, Luminous

Azim, (A-zeem) defender

Azzam determined, resolved

Badr al din* (bahdr-ahl-DEEN) full moon of the faith

Bahir dazzling, brilliant

Barakah blessing

Bashshar* bringer of glad tidings

Basil (BAH-seel) brave

Bassam (bah-SAHM) smiling — Basim (bah-SEEM)

Bilal* (bee-LAHL) (N.Afr.)a black man, first convert of Prophet, Muhammad

Bishr* joy

Burhan proof

Coman (ko-MAHN) noble

Dabir (dah-BEER) (used in Algeria and Egypt) secretary, or teacher

Dawud* (dah-OOD) (H) beloved

Diya al din (dee-yah-ahl-DEEN) brightness of the faith

Fadahunsi (FAH-dah-hoon-see) (N.Africa) royalty has favored me

Fadi (FAH-dee) redeemer

Fadil* (FAH-deel) generous

Fahd* lynx

Fakhir (FAH-keer) proud, excellent

Fakih (fah-KEE) (N.Africa) legal expert; one who recites the Qu'ran

Farid* (fah-REED) unique

Faris* (FAH-rees) horseman, knight

Faruq* (fahr-OOK) he who distinguishes truth from falsehood

Fath (FAT-h) victory

Fatin (fah-TEEN) clever, smart

Faysal* decisive

Ferran baker

Firas perspicacity

Fudail (foo-DAH-el) (N.Africa) excellent in character

Ghalib (gah-LEEB) victor

Ghassan* (gah-SAHN) old Arabic name

Ghazi conqueror

Gilad camel hump — Gilead, Giladi

Habib (hah-BEEB) (N.Africa) beloved

Haddad smith

Hadi (HAH-dee) guiding to the right

Hakeem ruler

Halim (HAH-leem) mild, gentle, or patient

Hamal (HA-mal) lamb

Hamid the praised one — Hammad, Humayd, Hamdrem

Hamza* (HAHM-zah) (N.Africa) historically significant personage

Hanbal (HAHN-bahl)
(N.Afr.) purity (founder
of an Islamic school of
thought)

Hanif (HAH-neef) true believer (in Moslem reli-
gion) — Hanef

Harb war

Harith* (HAH-reeth)
(N.Africa) cultivator

Haroun (hah-ROON) lofty
or exalted — Harun

Hasan* beautiful — Hassan

Hashim (HAH-shem)
(N.Africa) destroyer or
crusher [of evil]

Hassan* handsome —
Hasan

Hatim* judge

Hibah (hee-BAH) gift

Hilel the new moon

Hisham (hee-SHAHM)
generosity

Hud (HOOD) a Prophet's
name

Humam* courageous and
generous

Husain* little beauty

Husam* sword

Husam al din sword of the
faith

Husayn* beautiful

Ibrahim** (H) father of a
multitude

Idris a Prophet's name

Ihsan (ee-SAHN) benefi-
cence

Ikrimah female pigeon

Imad* (ee-MAHD) support,
pillar

Isa* (ee-SAH) a Prophet's
name (Jesus)

Isam* (ee-SAHM) safeguard

Ishaq* (ee-SHAHK) a
Prophet's name

Isma'il (ees-mah-EEL) a
Prophet's name

Izz al din* might of the
Faith

Ja'far ribulet

Jabir* (zhah-BEER) consoler, comforter

Jamal* beauty

Jamil (zhah-MEEL) beautiful

Jawhar (jah-oo-HAR)
(N.Africa) jewel; essence

Jed the hand

Jibril* (jih-BREEL)
archangel of Allah
[cf.Hebrew: Gabriel]

Jihad holy war

Jumah (JOO-mah) born on
Friday

Kadar (KAH-dahr) powerful — Kedar

Kadin (kah-DEEN) com-
panion, friend, or confi-
dante

Kadir (KAH-der) green, or
green crop

Kaliq (KAHL-eek) creative

Kamal* perfection — Kamil

Kamil (kah-MEEL) perfect

Kardal (KAHR-dahl) mus-
tard seed

Karif (kah-REEF) born in
autumn — Kareef

Kasib (KAH-sib) fertile

Kasim (kah-SEEM) divided
— Kaseem

Kateb writer

Khaldun (khal-DOON)
(N.Africa) eternal

Khalid* (KHAH-leed)
(N.Africa) eternal

Khalil (ka-LIL) a friend

Khayri charitable, beneficent

Khoury priest

Labib sensible, intelligent

Lateef (lah-TEEF)
(N.Africa) gentle, pleas-
ant

Lukman (look-MAHM)
(N.Africa) prophet

Lutfi* (LOOT-fee) kind and
friendly

Ma'd* (MAH-d) old Arabian
tribe's name

Ma'mun trustworthy

Ma'n benefit

Mahdi* guided to the right
path

Mahir skilled

Mahmud* praised

Maimun (MI-moon) lucky

Majdi* (MAHZH-dee) glorious

Makin (mah-KEEN) strong,
firm

Malik (MAH-lik) (Moslem)
master, angel, king

Mansur* (man-SOOR) divinely aided

Marid (MAH-rid) rebellious

Marwan* (mar-WAHN)
(N.Africa) historical personage

Marzuq blessed by God,
fortunate

Mas'ud happy, lucky

Mazin proper name

Misbah lamp

Mousa* (H) saved from the
water (Moses)

Mufid (moo-FEED) useful

Muhammad** the praised
one — Mahmud, Mehmet,
Mohamet, Mahmoud,
Amed, Ahmad

Muhannad sword

Muhsin* beneficent, charitable

Muhtadi rightly guided

Mujahid (moo-zhah-
HEED) fighter in the way
of Allah

Mukhtar* (mook-TAHR)
chosen

Munir brilliant, shining

Mus'ad unfettered camel

Muslim (MOO-slim)
(N.Africa) believer, sub-
mitting himself to God

Mustafa* chosen (name for
Muhammad)

Muti obedient

Nabhan noble, outstanding
— Nabih

Nabil* (nah-BEEL) noble

Nadim friend

Nadir* (nah-DEER) dear,
rare

Naeem (nah-EEM)
(N.Africa) benevolent

Naji* (NAH-zhee) safe

Najib* (nah-ZHEEB) of noble descent

Nasim fresh air

Nasser* (NAS-ser) (Muslim) victorious

Nazih pure, chaste

Nizam (nee-ZAHM) (N.Africa) discipliner, arranger

Numair (noo-MIR) panther

Nur al din* brightness of the Faith

Nuri* (NOO-ree) shining

Omar** (O-mar) (N.Africa) the highest [one of the followers of Muhammad]

Qasim (kah-SEEM) divider

Qudamah (koo-dah-MAH) courage

Ra'id (rah-EED) leader

Rabah gainer

Rabi (ra-BEE) breeze

Rafi exalting

Rafiq* (rah-FEEK) kind, friend

Raghib* (rah-GEEB) desirous

Rahman (rah-MAHN) (Moslem) compassionate

Rakin respectful

Ramadan* (Muslim) ninth month of Muslim year

Rashad* (rah-SHAHD) integrity of conduct

Rashid* rightly guided, having true faith

Reda satisfaction — Ridha

Reyhan favored by God

Rida favor

Riyad (ree-YAHD) gardens

Sa'id* (sah-EED) happy; rivulet — Saeed

Sabih beautiful

Sabir patient

Sahir wakeful

Salam* (SAH-lam) lamb

Salih* (SAH-lee) (N.Africa) good, right, proper

Salim* (sah-LEEM) safe — Salman

Samir* entertaining companion (man)

Samman grocer

Saqr falcon

Sariyah clouds at night

Sarsour bug

Sayyid master

Seif (SI-eef) sword of religion

Shadi singer

Shakir* (SHAH-ker) (N.Africa) thankful

Sharif* (shah-REEF) honest

Shawki (SHAH-oo-KEE) (N.Africa) yearning for right conduct

Shihab (shee-HAHB) blame, blaze

Shuaib (shoo-AH-eeb) (N.Africa) Qur'anic prophet

Shunnar pheasant

Siraj (see-RAZH) lamp, light

Sofian (SOH-fee-an) devoted

Su'ud good luck

Subhi (soo-BEE) early morning

Suhail* (soo-HAH-el) (N.Africa) gentle, easy

Suhayb* of reddish hair or complexion

Sulaiman* (soo-lah-ee-MAHN) (N.Africa) peaceful [cf.(H) Solomon, Shelomon]

Tabari (TAH-bah-ree) (N.Africa) famous Muslim historian

Tahir* (TAH-heer) (N.Africa) clean, pure

Talib* (TAH-lib) (N.Africa) seeker

Tamir one who owns date palm trees

Tarafah kind of tree

Tarif rare, uncommon

Tarik* (TAH-rick) (N.Africa) Muslim general who conquered Spain

Taysir facilitation

Thabit (TAH-bit) (N.Africa) firm

Ubadah (oo-BAH-dah) servant of God

Ubaid (oo-BAH-eed) (N.Africa) faithful

Umar old Arabic name — Omar, Omer

Umarah (oo-MAH-rah) old Arabic name

Usamah* description of a lion

Uthman* (oot-MAHN) (N.Africa) one of the companions of the Prophet

Wahid* (wah-HEED) single, exclusively unequalled

Waleed* (WAH-leed) (N.Africa) new-born — Walid

Wasim graceful, good looking

Yahya a Prophet's name

Yaman (yah-MAHN) proper name

Yasin* (yah-SEEN) name for Muhammad

Yasir wealthy

Yazid (YA-zid) God will increase — Zaid

Yushua God saves

Yusuf** a Prophet's name (Joseph)

Zafir victorious

Zahid (za-HEED) self-denying; ascetic

Zahir* bright, shining

Zaid* (ZAH-eed) (N.Africa) increase, growth

Zakariyya* a Prophet's name

Ziyad* (zee-YAHD) (N.Africa) an increase — Zayd

Zuhayr* bright

---

* **Popular**
** **Very popular**

ARMENIA

Armenia, part of the U.S.S.R located east of Turkey, was once a nation that reached from the Caspian Sea to the Mediterranean Sea. Its territory is now divided between Iran, Turkey, and the Soviet Union. To curb a nationalist movement in the late 1800's Turkey's Sultan (Armenia had been under Turkish control for nearly 400 years) in 1894 ordered a massacre, in order to drive Armenians out of their homeland. Immigration to the U.S. jumped from sixty-nine in 1870 to nearly 15,000 in 1899.

After arriving in New York City most immigrants moved to take factory jobs in the Northeast and Midwest. A significant community of Armenians developed in Worcester, Massachusetts. Many Armenian immigrants were able to open small businessses, such as groceries, restaurants, general stores, and tailor shops. Manufacture and sale of affordable domestic Persian rugs became an Armenian specialty.

Many Armenian immigrants with dreams of owning their own farms were drawn to the San Joaquin Valley of California, especially Fresno, in part because the climate was so similar to that of their homeland. One Armenian became the "melon king of America," another was the first to market native-grown figs, but the most widespread enterprise was cultivating grapes for raisins.

In A.D. 301 Armenia was the first state to adopt Christianity as its offical state religion (Armenian Apostolic Church). The religion and the Armenian language (Indo-European) help maintain unity among Armenians throughout the world. Roughly half a million Armenians live in North America.

ARMENIAN FEMALE NAMES

Anahid (Diana) (L) goddess of the moon

Ankine valuable, precious, costly, priceless

Anoush sweet — Anush

Aram father of King — Ara

Arax the daughter of an Armenian king — Araxie (Armenian river)

Armenouhie Armenian woman

Astrid (Persian) star

Elmas (Persian) diamond — Elmast

Gadar (Katherine) apex, top of a mountain, perfect, pure — Gadarine

Gayane a Christian martyr

Gosdantina (L) constant — Gosdantia

Heghine (Gr) light

Lucine moon — Lusine

Mihranoush (Persian) good, sweet sun

Nairi land of canyons; old name for ancient Armenia

Nevart (Persian) new rose — Neuvart, Nouvart, Nuvart

Ohanna (H) God's gracious gift

Perouze (Persian) turquoise — Perooz

Serpuhi sacred or holy woman — Sirpuhi, Srpouhi, Surpoohie

Shake (Arabic) open window (to let light in)

Shoushan lily

Siran lovely — Siroun

Sirvat dear rose, lovely rose

Vartouhi beautiful as a rose

Voshkie gold

Zagir flower — Zaghir, Zaghig

ARMENIAN MALE NAMES

Antranig the oldest, first-born

Ara legendary Armenian king (Plains of Ararat and Armenia=namesakes)

Armen Armenian

Avedis good tidings, bringer of good tidings

Bedros (Peter) (Gr) stone

Dareh (Persian) possessing wealth

Dickran a great king of Armenia (95-55 B.C.) Dicran, Dikran

Gevork (George) (Gr) a farmer — Kevork

Hagop (L) God's gracious gift — Hoven, Hovhaness, Ohan, Ohannes

Haig legendary Armenian Patriarch

Jirair strong and active working man

Khachig small cross — Khatchig

Krikor (Gregory) (Gr) vigilant

Magar young man accompanying a groom — Magarious

Nishan cross, sign, mark

Parounag one who gives glory or thanks to God — Parounak

Raffi a famous writer of the 19th century — Rafi

Shabouh a Persian king

Vartan rose giver, rose producer

Yervant an Armenian king

Zeroun a wise, repected old man

BASQUE REGION

According to an old French saying about the Basque people of the Pyrenees (northern Spain and southern France) "One who speaks Basque speaks Catholic." Indeed so strong is the Catholic influence that Jeanne d'Albert, a Protestant missionary working in the Middle Ages was said to have converted only eleven people in the Basque region, although he was much more successful in neighboring areas.

Recent travelers to the Basque region say the Catholic influence is still strong hundreds of years later. A girl might be named Mate Jose (Mary Joseph) and a boy might be named Jose Mate (Joseph Mary). A glance at the Basque name list shows numerous references to the Virgin Mary. Each of these are the local versions of Our Lady of _____ from the different towns and regions of the Basque area.

However, there is definitely a trend there today to give older, purely Basque names to babies. This trend is part of the growing movement towards Basque separatism that has gained momentum since 1978, when a forty-year-old prohibition against teaching the Basque language and culture was lifted. It had been dictated by President Franco as punishment to the Basque people for siding against him in the Spanish Civil War.

Now some 80,000 students are learning Basque. It is typical of the independent nature of the Basques that forty years of repression has been quite unable to stamp out their culture in any significant way.

The nature of the Basque language itself is also a tribute to the enduring nature of the culture. Scholars are unable to determine any relation between the Basque language and any other language in the world, concluding it is a very primitive language which has survived thousands of years without being supplanted. Even the Romans were unable to stamp it out, and indeed appear to have given up on invading the region altogether.

A look at the emmigration pattern from Spain shows a fascinating fact. By far the greatest number of immigrants to the United States from Spain is from the Basque provinces and Catalin, another Spanish province.

Basque immigrants have been in the New World for hundreds of years. At least four sailors and perhaps a captain in Columbus' entourage were Basque. Basque mercenaries fought with Cortes in his conquest of Mexico, then later moved north into what is now New Mexico. They started the first European colony in the Southwest in 1598.

When the California Gold Rush occurred in 1849, Basques were there and soon began raising sheep and cattle to feed miners when the supply of gold proved to be less than expected.

From California, Basque shepherds gradually spread from the coast to settle eventually in twelve Western states. They became the backbone of the long flourishing sheep-raising industry.

Large numbers of Basque also immigrated during the 1900-20 period, settling primarily in the Rocky Mountains. So renowned were the Basque shepherds that in the 1950's, special laws were passed to let Basques enter the U.S., despite immigration quotas, when there was a shortage of shepherds. A little over 5,000 herders immigrated under this law between 1957 and 1970. However, rising wages in the Basque homeland as well as increased work opportunities in Peru, Mexico, and southern Spain appear to have brought the Basque immigration to an end.

Pronunciation

Basque pronunciation is similar to Spanish, except that each syllable is supposed to be pronounced with the same emphasis, and there are some letter combinations with unexpected pronunciations:

a = "ah" as in ball
e = "eh" as in late
i = "ee" as in keep
o = "oh" as in hope
u = "oo" as in oops

j = "h" as in hope, or "y" as in you
x = "sh" as in share
tx = "ch" as in church
tz = "ts" as in rats
ts = "tsh" as in itch

BASQUE FEMALE NAMES

Abarrane (H) fem. of Abraham, father of a multitude — Abarne

Agate (Gr) good or kind

Agurtzane (Ah-goorts-ah-neh) Ref. to the Virgin Mary

Ainhoa (ah-een-o-ah) Ref. to the Virgin Mary

Aintzane (ah-een-tsah-neh) glorious

Aitziber (ah-ee-tsee-behr) Ref. to the Virgin Mary

Alazne (ah-las-neh) miracle

Alesandese (Gr) fem. of Alexander — defender of mankind

Aloña (ah-lo-nyah) Ref. to the Virgin Mary

Amaia end

Amalur motherland

Amarande (Gr) immortal, flower name

Anamari (H) grace; Ana Maria

Andere fem. of Andrew

Andoniñe (ahn-do-nee-nyeh) (L) beyond praise — Andone

Ane (H) grace

Apirka (Gael) pleasant

Arama Virgin Mary

Arene (Gr) very holy one

Argi light

Arrate (ahr-rah-teh) Ref. to the Virgin Mary

Arrosa (L) rose

Aurelne (L) gold

Aurkene (ah-oor-keh-neh) Presentation

Bakarne solitude

Balere (bah-lah-reh) (L) strong

Begoña (beh-go-nyah) Ref. to the Virgin Mary

Bibiñe (bee-bee-nyeh) (L) lively

Birkita (Celt) strength

Bittore (L) victorious

Bixenta (bih-shen-tah) victorious

Catalin (Gr) pure

Danele (H) God is my judge

Deiene (Span) religious holiday of Annuniciation — Deikun, Deina

Delbin (Gr) flower name or dolphin

Dominica (L) of the Lord

Donata (L) gift

Dorbeta (dor-beh-tah) Virgin Mary

Dorote (do-ro-teh) (L) gift of God

Edurne (eh-door-neh) snow

Eguskiñe (eh-goo-skee-nyeh) sunny

Ehunate (eh-oo-nah-teh) Ref. to the Virgin Mary

Elisa (H) consecrated to God

Elizabete (H) consecrated to God — Elisa

Erdotza (ehr-do-tsah) Ref. to the Virgin Mary

Errita (Gr) (from Margarita) — Irta

Errukine (eh-roo-kee-neh) merciful

Eskarne (ehs-kar-neh) (Span) merciful

Espe (ehs-peh) (L) hope

Estibalitz (ehs-tee-bah-leets) Ref. to the Virgin Mary

Floria (L) flower — Florella, Floris, Florica, Flori, Lore

Garabi (L) clear — Garbi, Kalare

Garaitz (gar-ah-eets) victorious

Garbiñe (gar-bee-nyeh) (Span) purification

Gardotza Ref. to the Virgin Mary

Gechina grace

Gildas (Celt) servant of God — Kermeilde

Gizane (gee-sah-nee) Incarnation of Christ

Godalupe (Span) Virgin Mary or valley of the wolf

Gorane (go-rah-neh) (Span) Holy Cross

Gotzone (go-tso-neh) angel; messenger

Graciana (L) graceful

Idoia (ee-doy-ah) Ref. to the Virgin Mary

Idurre (ee-doo-reh) Ref. to the Virgin Mary

Igone (ee-go-neh) ascension

Ikerne (ee-kehr-neh) visitation

Iratze (ee-rah-tseh) Ref. to the Virgin Mary

Irmina daughter of Venus and Mars

Irune Trinity

Itsaso (ee-tshah-so) sea

Itxaro (ee-chah-ro) hope

Itziar (ee-tsih-ahr) Ref. to the Virgin Mary

Izar (ee-sahr) (Span) star — Izarra

Izazkun (ee-sah-skun) Ref. to the Virgin Mary

Jaione (hah-ee-o-neh) Nativity

Jakinda (yah-keen-dah) (Span) hyacinth

Jasone (hah-so-neh) assumption

Jokiñe (yo-kee-nyeh) (H) God will establish

Jone (yo-neh) (H) God's gracious gift

Josune (yo-soo-neh) Jesus (for female)

Joxepa (yo-sheh-pah) (H) God will add — Josebe

Julene (huh-leh-neh) (L) youth

Kalare (L) bright, clear — Garbi

Karmele (L) song

Katalin (kah-tah-leen) (L) pure

Katarin (Gr) pure — Kattalin

Kepa (keh-pah) (Gr) stone — Kepe

Kermeilde (OE) guilded — Gildas

Kesare (keh-sah-reh) (Span) fem. of Cesar

Koldobike (kol-do-bee-keh) (Teut) famous holiness

Kolete (ko-leh-teh) (Gr) victory of the people

Kontxesi (kon-cheh-see) Immaculate Conception

Koru Ref. to the Virgin Mary

Kosma (Gr) order, universe

Landa name for Virgin Mary

Legarra name for Virgin Mary

Leire (leh-ih-reh) Ref. to the Virgin Mary

Lide (lee-deh) (L) life

Lorda shrine of the Virgin Mary

Lore (lo-reh) flower — Flora

Lukene (loo-keh-neh) (L) bringer of light

Lur earth

Madalen (H) woman from Magdala — Maialen, Malen

Maitane (OE) beloved — Maite, Maitena

Maite (Span) love; name for Virgin Mary — Maitea

Matea (ma-teh-ah) (H) gift of God

Matxalen (mah-chah-leen) (H) woman of Magdala

Mendi name for Virgin Mary

Mikele (mee-keh-leh) (H) who is like God?

Milia (Teut) industrious

Mirari (mih-rah-reh) miracle

Miren (H) bitter (variation of Maria)

Molara ref. to Virgin Mary

Naiara ref. to the Virgin Mary

Nekane (neh-kah-neh) (Span) sorrows

Nerea mine (pronoun)

Nora (Gr) light

Oihane (oy-ah-neh) forest

Olatz Ref. to the Virgin Mary

Osane (o-sah-neh) health

Pa(n)txike (pahn-chee-keh) (L) free

Pauli (pah-oo-lee) (L) little

Pellkita (L) happy

Sabiñe (sah-bee-nyeh) (L) Sabine woman (ancient tribe of central Italy)

Sebastene (seh-bahs-teh-neh) (Gr) venerable

Sorkunde (sor-koon-deh) Immaculate Conception — Sorne

Terese (teh-reh-seh) (Gr) harvester

Tote (TO-teh) ancient Visigoth name

Ula name for Virgin Mary — Uli

Usoa (oo-so-ah) dove

Yanamari comb. Jean and Marie

Yera Virgin Mary

Yoana (Span) God's gracious gift

Yordana (H) descendant

Yosebe (yo-seh-beh) (H) God will add

Yulene (yoo-leh-neh) (L) youth — Julene

Zezili (seh-see-lee) (L) blind, gray eyes

Zuria (soo-rih-ah) (Fr) white, fair — Zuri

Zuriñe (soo-ree-nyeh) white

BASQUE MALE NAMES

Abarran (H) father of a multitude

Adiran (ah-dee-rahn) (L) of the Adriatic

Ager (H) gatherer

Aingeru (ah-een-gehr-oo) messenger — Gotzon

Akil (Gr) name of a river

Anatoli (Gr) from the East

Ander (Gr) manly

Andoni (L) beyond praise — Antton

Asentzio (ah-sehn-tsee-o) Ascension

Balasi (Gr) flat-footed

Balendin (bah-lehn-deen) (L) strong, brave

Bardol (Aramaic) ploughman — Bartol

Beñat (beh-nyaht) (OGer) courage of a bear

Benin (L) blessed

Benkamin (H) son of the right hand

Bingen (L) conqueror

Bittor (bee-tor) (L) conqueror

Dabi (H) beloved

Damen (Gr) taming

Danel (H) God is my judge

Deunoro (deh-oo-no-ro) All Saints

Domeka (L) like the Lord

Domiku (L) like the Lord

Dunixi (doo-nee-shee) (Gr) god of wine

Edingu (Ger) famous ruler

Edorta (OE) wealthy guardian

Edrigu (Teut) famous ruler

Edur snow

Elazar (H) God helps

Erramun (Teut) mighty protector — Erroman

Errando (Ger) bold venture

Errapel (H) divine healer

Erroman (L) Roman

Estebe (Gr) crowned with laurels

Etor (Gr) steadfast

Fermin (L) solid

Fortun (Fr) lucky

Gabirel (H) God is my strength — Gabin

Gaizka (gah-ees-kah) Saviour — Garikoitz

Garai (L) conqueror

Gentza (gehn-tsah) peace

Gilamu (Teut) resolute soldier

Gilen (Teut) illustrious pledge

Gillen (Teut) resolute soldier

Gorka (Gr) farmer

Gotzon (go-tson) angel; messenger

Gurutz Holy Cross

Iban (H) God's gracious gift — Jon

Ibon (Teut) archer

Iker (ee-kehr) visitation

Ilari (L) cheerful

Illan (L) youth

Imanol (H) God is with us

Iñaki (ee-nyah-kee) (L) fiery — Iñigo

Ixaka (H) (ee-shah-kah) laughter

Ixidor (ee-shah-dor) (Gr) a gift of ideas

Jacobe (yah-KO-beh) (H) supplanter — Jagoba, Yakue, Jakes (yah-kehs)

Jakome (yah-ko-meh) St. James — Xanti (shahn-tee)

Javier (hah-vee-ehr) owner of the new house

Jeremi (yehr-eh-mee) (H) God will uplift

Jerolin (L) holy name

Jokin (ho-keen) (H) God will establish

Jon (YON) (H) God's gracious gift

Joseba (yo-seh-ba) (H) God will add

Josu (yo-soo) (Jesus) (H) God saves — Yosu

Julen (hoo-lehn) (L) youthful

Karmel (H) vineyard

Kasen (L) protected with a helmet

Kauldi (L) lame

Kelmen (L) merciful

Kemen strength

Kerbasi (Teut) warrior

Kerman (Fr) germane

Kindin (L) fifth

Koldobika (Teut) famous in battle; famous holiness

Korneli (L) horn

Kuiril (Gr) lord

Lander (Gr) lion man

Laurentzi (lo-rehn-tsee) (L) crowned with laurel — Lauran, Lorentz, Loren

Lon (L) lion

Lopolda (Teut) patriotic

Luken (L) bringer of light — Luk

Luki (OGer) renowned warrior

Maren (L) sea

Matai (H) gift of God

Mikel (mee-kehl) who is like God?

Mikolas (Gr) victory of the people

Narkis (Gr) daffodil

Ortzi (sky)

Palben (Sp) blond, yellow

Patxi (pah-chee) (Teut) free

Paul (L) little — Paulin

Peli (L) happy — Zorion

Pello (Gr) stone — Peru, Pi-arres

Prosper (L) fortunate

Sabin (L) Sabine (ancient tribe of central Italy)

Salbatore (Sp) saviour

Satordi (Fr) Saturn

Sebasten (Gr) venerable, revered

Sein (S) innocent

Tibalt (Germ) people's prince

Todor (Gr) gift of God

Txanton (chahn-ton) Joseph Anthony

Txomin (cho-meen) (L) like the Lord

Ugutz John the Baptist

Unai shepherd

Urtzi (oor-tsee) sky

Xabat (shah-baht) (Sp) savior

Xabier (shah-bee-ehr) owner of the new house

Xalbador (shahl-vah-dor) (Sp) saviour — Xalvador

Xarles (shar-lehs) (OFr) full-grown, manly

Xavier (sha-vee-ehr) owner of the new house

Ximen (shee-mehn) (H) God is heard — Ximon, Ximun

Yuli (L) youthful

Zadornin (tsah-dor-neen) Saturn

Zigor (see-gor) punishment

Zorion (so-ree-on) (L) happy

BULGARIA

Bulgarian-Americans immigrated from present-day Bulgaria and the surrounding areas in the Balkan Mountains, particularly from the historic region of Macedonia, primarily before World War I. Economic hardship and overpopulation were the spurs for immigration, as well as reprisals from a failed Macedonian revolt against ruling Turks in 1903.

An estimated 50,000 Bulgarians immigrated between 1900-10. Almost exclusively they were single men, unskilled laborers seeking to earn enough money to return home and buy land or open a small business. Most of those who stayed settled in the Midwest; the largest number of Bulgarian-Americans is in Michigan (10,000) and nearby states.

Between 1910 and 1929 the number of returnees exceeded the number of new immigrants. Recent immigrants included refugees and political opponents of the Communist government in Bulgaria. Approximately 70,000 Bulgarians and their descendants live in the U.S. today. Most Bulgarian-Americans are Eastern Orthodox Christians and the church remains a center of community life. Social events are held at churches and some parishes sponsor schools where Bulgarian and English are taught.

BULGARIAN FEMALE NAMES

Elena (Gr) light

Elisveta (H) consecrated to God

Irina (Gr) peace

Iulia (L) youthful

Katerina (Gr) pure

Khrustina (Gr) Christian

Lora (L) crown of laurels

Lucine (L) light

Maria (H) bitter

Marketa (Gr) a pearl

Nataliia (Fr) born at Christmas

Pavlina (L) little

Sofia (Gr) wisdom

Tereza (Gr) harvester

Viktoria (L) victorious

BULGARIAN MALE NAMES

Aleksandur (Gr) defender of mankind — Alekko, Sander

Andres (Gr) manly — Andrey, Andrei

Danil (H) God is my judge

Foma (H) twin

Grigori (Gr) vigilant — Gruev, Grigorov

Ioan (H) God's gracious gift — Ivan

Matei (H) gift of God

Mihail (H) who is like God?

Nikolas (Gr) victory of the people — Nikita

Pavel (L) little

Piotr (Gr) stone — Petr

Stefan (Gr) a crown

Veniamin (H) son of the right hand

Vilhelm (Teut) resolute protector

BURMA

The people of Burma (now known as the Republic of Myanmar) are divided into five major groups, each with its own language, history, and lifestyle. Burmans make up about half the population. Other sizable groups include the Shans, the Karems, the Kachins, and the Chins; each group except the Karems lives in a specific state in Burma. The presence of so many ethnic groups and the fact that loyalty to the group is often stronger than loyalty to the nation has led to difficulty in uniting Burma into a cohesive nation.

Similar conficts are felt between traditional Buddhist beliefs denouncing wordly ambitions and materialism, and modern beliefs that there should be progressive economic betterment in the life of the citizens. A centuries-old tradition of democracy has been abolished by a Marxist regime in place since 1962.

In traditional society, anyone, no matter how modest his family, could become a monk and go on to be a person of great moral influence even at court. Royalty was achieved and not automatically passed on to the offspring. The king was regarded with awe, but more as a symbolic upholder of the faith than as a dictator of everyday affairs. There was no great class of feudal lords and ordinary Burmans ruled themselves under a board of elders (called a "circle") for a little region composed of five neighboring villages or hamlets.

Immigration from Burma has been very small. Immigrants began arriving in the 1960's and totaled approximately 6000 by 1971; 500-1000 per year have immigrated since then. Most Burmese immigrants come in family groups, the men in the families being predominately technical, white-collar, and professional workers, especially craftsmen and engineers.

In Burma a child is named according to the day of the week he or she is born on. The days have letters associated with them, and the child's name begins with one of those letters. There are no "last names" in Burma, and boys and girls may have the same name. A little girl born on Sunday (vowel begins name) might be called

"Ma" (Little Sister) "Aye" (cool temperament). As she grows up her name might change to "Daw" (roughly, "aunt"). She would remain Daw Aye, even after marriage. Similarly, a little boy might go from "Maung" (Little Brother) "Aye" to "U" ("uncle") "Aye." Former United Nations Secretary-General U Thant was born on a Friday, so his name began with "th" as does the name for all Friday-born children.

The spoken language of the Burmans came from near Tibet, while the written language system probably developed via Sri Lanka (Ceylon) from India's alphabet. (This is common in several Southeast Asian cultures where the languages come down from the North, but the written systems are adapted from ancient India's.) The Burmese alphabet is similar to our Roman alphabet in theory and function, but in appearance looks like strings of little circles dancing across the page ("bubblewriting").

BURMESE FEMALE NAMES

Aung success
Aye cool
Khin lovable
Kyaw overcome
Kyi clear
Meit affection
Mima woman
Mya emerald
Myint affection; high
Ne Htun sunsine
Nu tender
Thaw noisy
Thin learned
Tin above
Warwar yellow
Yon rabbit

BURMESE MALE NAMES

Ba Tu like his father
Htoo distinctive
Lin bright
Min king
Myo city
Ngwe Khain silver spring
On coconut
Po Mya grandfather emerald
Po Sin grandfather elephant
Saw early
Tan million
Than million
Thaung ten thousand
Thet She long life
Win bright
Yo honesty

CAMBODIA

In traditional Cambodian society, as in many Southeast Asian cultures, women were on equal footing with men. They didn't give up property or even change their names when they married. Daughters could inherit and dispose of property as easily as sons, and women owned as much land as men did.

Great segments of the Cambodian population lead lives different from each other. The largest group is the Cambodians, or Khmer, but there are also sizable numbers of Chinese, Vietnamese, Cham-Malays (a Moslem group), and hill people.

Previous fighting among several of these groups has been largely replaced by struggles of several other groups to regain control of the country, which has been held by a Vietnamese-backed puppet government since 1975. One of the groups consists of supporters of Prince Norodom Sihanouk, the enigmatic monarch in power from 1941 to 1970. Another is the Khmer Rouge, a brutal dictatorship responsible for the mass killings reported by Cambodian refugees during its rise to power in the early 1970's and continuing even now.

Before 1975 the number of immigrants was too few to be classified separately. Roughly 8,000 Cambodians fled to the U.S. after the April 1975 collapse of the South Vietnamese government and similar upheavals in Cambodia. Hundreds of thousands more fled to temporary resettlement camps throughout Southeast Asia, and many are still awaiting asylum. Very few countries other than the U.S. are willing to accept the refugees.

One problem Cambodian immigrants have had in integrating into American society is that family groups of up to twenty-five people may stay together, and voluntary sponsor groups prefer to help smaller groups. However, churches and other private organizations are continuing to sponsor incoming Cambodian refugees and help them resettle.

CAMBODIAN FEMALE NAMES

Boupha (BO-fa) like a flower

Chan sweet-smelling tree

Channary girl faces like a full moon

Chantou flower

Chantrea (CHAN-thee-ay) moonshine or moon

Kalliyan (KEL-lee-ehn) best

Kannitha (KEN-nee-tha) angels

Kolab rose

Kunthea (KUN-thee-eh) good smell

Mliss (MLEES) name of a Southest Asian flower

Pheakkley (FAK-kleh) loyalty

Sopheary beautiful girl

Soportevy (so-PER-teh-vee) a beautiful girl like an angel

Tevy (TEH-vee) angel

Vanna golden color

Veata (ve-EH-teh) the wind

CAMBODIAN MALE NAMES

Arun (AH-run) the sun

Bourey (BU-ree) county

Chankrisna (CHEHN-krees-neh) name of a sweet-smelling tree

Dara (deh-reh) stars

Kiri (kee-ree) mountain

Munny (MOH-nee) wise man

Nhean know what one is about

Phirun (FEE-rum) rain

Pich (PEECH) diamond

Rangsey (REHNG-seh-ee) seven kinds of colors

Rithisak (REETH-ee-sak) powerful

Sakngea (SAK-ngee-ay) dignitary

Sovann (SOH-ven) gold

Veasna (veh-EH-sneh) luckily

CHINA

Chinese people have been in the New World since the 16th century and possibly earlier. They appeared as servants of Spanish sailors in 1565, and arrived in 1635 as shipbuilders in Acupulco and colonists in Mexico City. Documented cases of Chinese sailors, carpenters, smiths, students, and others show their presence in the first half of the 19th century, but it wasn't until mid-century that they began to arrive in large numbers.

Drought in the Canton province of China between 1847 and 1850 sent over 41,000 Chinese to America. Some came later to seek their fortune in the "gold rush." They were among the first to stake their claims in California, but as their numbers grew, legislation was enacted to exclude them. They then followed new gold strikes in other western states, migrating as far east as Black Hills, South Dakota, often gleaning gold from abandoned lean claims.

The rise of so many Chinese laundries had its roots in the gold rush for the shrewd reason that in offering a service white men considered "women's work," Chinese could make the leap between hired hand and "boss." Although doing laundry in those days was hard work, it was less hazardous than digging railroad tunnels.

An estimated 12,000 to 14,000 of their countrymen were put to work between 1858 and 1869, building California railroads, and later the Central Pacific Railroad, which formed the western link of the transcontinental railroad. Chinese workers made up nine out of ten workers for the railroads constructed in this part of the country. They often worked under slave-like conditions, doing the most dangerous work, for low wages. Their strike for wages equaling the Caucasian workers was unsuccessful.

Completion of the railroad opened up the West for development of its other resources. A 1868 treaty with China ensured a steady supply of Chinese laborers for agricultural work. Their efforts converted the swamps of the San Joaquin Valley into rich farmland. Chinese were also employed in the cigar, shoe, and garment industries and in woolen mills which developed in California.

Immigration averaged more than 12,000 each year during this period resulting in a Chinese population of 105,000 by 1880, mostly in California.

Other Chinese were hired to work in silver and coal mines throughout the West and in the canneries of the Northwest. Chinese developed shrimp and abalone fishing around San Francisco, as well as starting their own cigar, shoe, and garment enterprises.

Hard times in the 1870's, combined with the fact that the U.S. westward expansion had finally arrived in California, resulted in an oversupply of Caucasian workers needing jobs held by Chinese. Public clamor to get rid of the Chinese culminated in the passage of the Chinese Exclusion Act of 1882, which prohibited immigration of Chinese laborers for ten years. The law was extended for another decade in 1892 and 1902. A policy of almost total exclusion of Chinese continued until 1943, when wartime manpower shortages again made jobs available for them. A number of war brides and fiancees of G.I.s began to immigrate after 1945. From then until 1970, women outnumbered men among Chinese immigrants, whereas 19th century immigrants were almost exclusively men.

After immigration restrictions were lifted in 1965 Chinese immigration increased dramatically as families long separated were reunited. From less than 1,000 annually in the 1950's their numbers increased to 12,000 annually in the 1970's and 20,000 to 30,000 per year in the 1980's.

Because of the extreme difficulty in transliterating Chinese names into English words the Chinese name list is very small. It's meant to be a representative sampling of the kind of names that might be chosen, because in the Chinese culture, names are designed to be unique. Each child is given a carefully conceived name and its meaning may be known only to the parents.

A person may be given new names at later stages of life such as starting school, getting married, or beginning a career. Traditionally, Chinese took a generational name as part of their names, which was one word of a poem with no repeating words. Each generation in turn would take the next word in the poem.

Religious names are rare, and a girl is often given a more flowery, elegant name than a boy. Boys' names may be very plain or attempt to appear that his presence is a matter of indifference, in order to trick the devils into leaving the (preferred) male child alone.

Throughout the Orient, Chinese characters are mutually intelligible to literate people, regardless of dialect or language. Each language attaches its own pronunciation to the characters and may change the meaning slightly. Compared to English in which the language of 600 years ago is almost completely different from today, Chinese works written 4,000 years ago can be read by modern-day Chinese.

CHINESE FEMALE NAMES

Ah Cy lovely

Ah Kum good as gold — Gum

Ah Lam like an orchid

An (AHN) peace

Bik jade

Bo (BAU) precious

Chao-xing (chau-TSEENG) morning star

Chow summer

Chu hua (choo-KHWAH) chrysanthemum

Chun (CHWEN) spring

Chyou (CHYOH) autumn

Da Chun long spring

Da-Xia (dah-SHAH) long summer

Dai-tai leading a boy (in hopes boy will follow)

Eu-fùnh playful Phoenix

Eu-meh (YOO-meh) especially beautiful

Fang (FAHNG) fragrant

Far flower

Fung bird

Guan-yin (kwahn-YEEN) goddess of mercy

Howin a loyal swallow

Hu (HOO) tiger

Hua flower

Hùifang (hweh-FAHNG) nice fragrance

Hwei-ru (WHEH-roo) wise, intelligent

Jiahui (jah-HWEI) nice

Jing-wei (tcheeng-WEH) small bird

Jun (TCHOON) truth

Kuai hùa (kwigh-KHWAH) mallow blossom

Kue ching (goy-CHEENG) piano-reach=sounds good

Kwong broad

Lee plum

Lì húa (lee-WHAH) pear blossom, beautiful flower

Lian (LEE-AHN) the graceful willow

Lien hua (lee-en-HWAH) lotus flower

Lien (LEE-EN) lotus

Lihwa (lee-HWAH) a Chinese princess

Lin beautiful jade

Ling (LEENG) delicate and dainty

Lìxúe (lee-SHWEH-EE) beautiful snow

Marrim (MAH-reem) tribal name among Purim Kukis in Manipur State

Méh-è beautiful posture

Méh-fùnh pretty or beautiful Phoenix

Mei can mean beautiful, plum, sister or rose

Meiying (MEH-yeeng) beautiful flower

Meizhen (meh-CHE-UHN) beautiful pearl

Ming-húa tomorrow's flower

Mu lan (moo-LAHN) magnolia blossom

Mu tan (moo-TAHN) tree peony blossom

Nuwa (noo-WAH) mother goddess

Ping duckweed

Qiànrú (CHYAN-roo) nice smile

Rúfen (roo-FEN) nice fragrance

Sheu-fùnh elegant Phoenix

Syà (SYAH) summer

Sying (SYEENG) star

Tao (TAU) peach (symbol of long life)

Tè (TEH-AH) special

Tu jade (earth element in generational cycle, as in air, water, etc)

Ushi (OO-shee) the ox

Xiu Mei (shoo-MEH-ee) beautiful plum

Yáng (YAHNG) sun Tiayang

Yet Kwai beautiful as a rose

Yín (YEEN) silver

Yow feminine

Yu-jun (yoo-TCHOON) from Chongching

Yuèhai (yoo-eh-DEE) beautiful moon

Yuèqín (yoo-e-CHEEN) moon-shaped lute

Yuet moon

Yuk moon

Yuke jade (esteemed in the Orient)

Yüying (yoo-YEENG) jade-flower

Yüzhen (yoo-CHEN) jade-gem

CHINESE MALE NAMES

An (AHN) peace

Angúo (AHNG-WAH) protect country

Chen vast or great

Cheung good luck

Chi the younger generation

Chung intelligent

Délì (DE-UH-LEE) virtuous

Déshì (DE-UH-SHEE) a man of virtue

Déwei (DE-UH-WEH) highly virtuous

Dìngbang (DEENG-BAHNG) protect country

Fai (FAH-EE) growth, beginning or fly

Gan (GAHN) dare, adventure

Guotin polite, firm, strong leader

Ho the good

Hop agreeable

Huang Fu rich future

Hulin only people of the Marrim clan may use this name in China

Hung great

Jaw-long like a dragon

Jin gold

Jun (JOON) truth

Keung universe

Kong glorious, sky

Lì (LEE) strenth

Liang (lee-AHNG) good, or excellent

Liko (LEE-koo) protected by Buddha

Lok happiness

Manchu (MAHN-choo) pure

Ming-hóa brilliant, elite

Ming-tun intelligent-heavy

On peace

Park the cypress tree

Quon bright

Shàoqiáng (SHAU-chyahng) strong and profound

Shen (SHEN) spirit, deep thought

Shìlín (shee-LEEN) intellectual

Shing (SHEENG) victory

Shoi-ming life of sunshine

Shu-sai-chong happy all his life long

Sueh-yén continuity, harmonious

Sying star

Tsun-chùng tsun=village, chung=middle or second brother

Tung all, universal

Wang (WAHNG) hope, wish

Wing glory

Yu universe

Zhìhuán (chee-KHWAHN) ambitious

Zhìxin (chee-SHEEN) a man of ambition

Zhìyuan (chee-YWA-en) ambition

CZECHOSLOVAKIA

Both Czechs and Slovaks immigrated to America in vast numbers in the late 19th and early 20th centuries. (400,000–500,000 from each group during that time.) Czechoslovakia's western part (Bohemia and Moravia) is inhabited by Czechs, and its eastern part (Slovakia) by Slovaks, each with a distinct but often similar language. Czechs and Slovaks were united once before in one country (Great Moravia) in the 9th and 10th centuries, but later, because of wars and other upheavals Slovakia was annexed by Hungary, and Moravia and Bohemia became part of the Austro-Hungarian empire. After World War I the regions were reunited as Czechoslovakia.

Most of the Czech immigrants who arrived in the 1850's through 1880's were cottagers who had sold their small plots of land and set out for Texas or the Midwest. In the next two decades cottagers were outnumbered by skilled laborers such as tailors, miners, carpenters and shoemakers.

In the Slovak region the population had risen from one million in 1720 to 2.4 million in 1840; in four eastern counties the population had increased sevenfold. Hungary, which ruled the area, instituted no industrialization or land reform to absorb the increase, and many Slovaks were forced to emigrate to survive.

Meanwhile, in the U.S. after the Civil War a surge of industrialization led to a labor shortage. Agents of American coal mines and railroads recruited cheap labor in Eastern Europe, and thousands of Slovaks responded.

A new wave of immigration from Czechoslovakia occured after the 1948 Communist coup. An estimated 25,000 made their way to America, including large numbers of professional and highly skilled workers. Some 10,000 more Czechs arrived in the ten years after the Soviet invasion of Czechoslovakia in 1968.

The Czech and Slovak languages (along with Polish and Sorbian) are classified as West Slavic.

CZECH FEMALE NAMES

Alzbeta (AHLZH-byeh-tah) (H) consecrated to God

Anezka (AH-nezh-kah) (Gr) gentle, pure (name of medieval queen)

Anna (AH-nah) (H) grace — Anicka (AH-nyich-kah), Anca (AHN-tchah)

Bozena (BOH-zhe-nah) unknown, may be dim. of Elizabeth, Bozka (BOZH-kah)

Dana (DAH-nah) fem. of Daniel (H) God is my judge

Emilie (Teut) industrious — Milka (MILL-kah), Mila (MEE-lah)

Eva (EH-vah) (H) life

Frantiska (FRAN-tyish-kah) (Teut) free — Fanka (FAHN-kah)

Jana (YA-nah) (H) God's gracious gift

Jirina (YEER-zhih-nah) (Gr) farmer

Karla (OFr) strong

Libuse (LIB-oo-sheh) figure from old fable (popular)

Ludmila (LOOD-mill-ah) love of the people

Marie (MAR-yeh) (H) bitter — Marenka (MAR-zhen-kah), Mana, Maruska

Miroslava (MEER-oh-slah-vah) peace-glory — Mirka (MEER-kah)

Otilie (OH-teel-yeh) (OGer) lucky heroine — Otka

Pavla (PAHV-lah) (L) little

Ruzena (ROO-zhee-nah) (L) rose — Ruza (ROO-zhah)

Vlasta (VLA-stah) figure from old fable (popular)

Zdenka (ZDEHN-kah) (Phoenician) from Sidon, ancient Phoenician city

CZECH MALE NAMES

Alois (AHL-ois) (OGer) renowned warrior — Lojza (LOI-zhah)

Antonin (AHN-ton-yin) (L) inestimable — Tonda

Bohumil (BOH-hoo-mil) God's peace Bohous (BOH-howsh)

Bohuslav (BOH-oo-slahv) (Slavic) God's glory

Cestmir (CHEST-meer) (Slavic) fortress

Eduard (EH-doo-ahr) (OE) wealthy guardian — Eda (EH-dah)

Evzen (EHV-zhen) (Gr) well-born, noble

Ferdinand (FEHR-dee-nahnd) (Teut) adventurous, brave — Ferda (FEHR-dah)

Frantisek (FRAHN-tee-shek) (Teut) free — Franta

Gustav (Teut) staff of the gods

Ivan (EE-vahn) (H) God's gracious gift

Jan (YAHN) (H) God's gracious gift — Jenda (YEHN-dah), Honza

Jaroslav (YAHR-oh-slav) glory of spring; figure in Czech fable — Jarda

Jiri (YIR-zhee) (Gr) farmer — Jirka (YIR-kah)

Josef (YO-sef) (H) God will add — Jozka (YOHZH-kah), Pepik (PEP-ik)

Karel (KAHR-ell) (OFr) strong and manly (Slovak: Karol)

Ladislav famous ruler — Lada (LAD-yah), Laco (LAHT-soh)

Miloslav (MEEL-oh-slav) love of glory — Milda (MEEL-dah)

Miroslav (MEER-oh-slav) peace, glory — Mirek (MEE-rek)

Ota (Teut) prosperous — Otik (OHT-yeek)

Richard (RIK-hahrd) (OGer) powerful ruler — Risa (REE-shah)

Rostislav unknown meaning, (-slav means glory) — Rosta (ROHST-yah)

Stanislav (STAHN-yih-slav) glory of the camp — Standa

Tomas (TOH-mahsh) (H) twin — Tomik

Vaclav (VAHT-slav) (Slavic) wreath of glory — Vasek (VAH-shek)

Zdenek (ZDEH-nyeek) (OFr) a follower of St. Denis

DENMARK

The total number of Danish immigrants (360,000 from 1820-1975) has been relatively small compared to that of other Scandinavian countries (1.3 million Swedes and 855,000 Norwegians in the same time period) but they have scattered widely, assimilated quickly, and always been welcome.

The first Danish immigrants joined the Dutch in New Amsterdam in the late 1600's. In 1629 Jonas Bronck arrived and purchased a large tract of land which later became known as the Bronx. Still, by 1675 only about 100 Danes had immigrated.

In 1735 a colony of Danish converts to the Moravian religion established themselves in Bethlehem, Pennsylvania. A hundred years later Baptist converts in Denmark immigrated to the U.S. to escape religious persecution at the hands of the Lutheran state church.

In the 1850's Mormon missionaries were more successful at acquiring converts in Denmark than any other country except England. Many of them (3,700 total) immigrated to the Midwest and Utah, more to be with their fellow Mormons than because of excessive persecution in their homeland. Between 1860 and 1930 Danes were the second largest ethnic group in Utah, after the British.

In general, conditions were better in Denmark than in the rest of Scandinavia in several areas. A liberal constitution adopted in 1849 allowed freedom of religion and widespread suffrage, so there was less impetus to search for greater freedom by emigrating. Industrial development in Copenhagen occurred faster than in Sweden, which allowed more displaced agricultural workers to find jobs. Practical governmental land policy prevented farms from being subdivided below subsistence level.

Thus, the push towards emigration lagged behind that of other nearby countries, including Germany. However, in the 1860's a series of disasters hit Denmark, including the loss of one-fourth of its territory to Prussia and Austria in 1864. A conservative government, which assumed power in 1868, repealed some of the earlier reforms, and population growth outstripped Denmark's capacity to absorb new workers.

Unemployment, a rising crime rate, and, in the southern area that had been lost to Germany, repression and forced military service caused Danes to look to America in hope of a better life. Between 1850 and 1900 the total number of Danish immigrants to the U.S. was 245,000, one-tenth of Denmark's population in 1900.

Danes settled in the Midwest, especially Iowa. In 1910 more than ten percent of the Danes in America lived in Iowa though they made up only two percent of that state's population. Immigrants from Denmark also settled in California, which has had the largest Danish population since 1920, although they have been in every American state and territory since 1870.

In 1917 Denmark sold the Virgin Islands to the U.S., and ten years later, the 3,200 Danes who lived there became U.S. citizens along with the other Islanders.

Immigration from Denmark has continued at a rate of about 500 per year since 1970, averaged 1,000 annually in the 1950's and 1960's, and was much lower during the Depression and War years.

The most popular baby names in Denmark have a decidedly Danish flavor and are very similar to the most popular names in Norway. Double names such as Anne-Metta and Metta-Lise are very popular for girls in Denmark now. Comparison of the Swedish, Norwegian, and Danish names shows the similarity of languages. In fact they are all off-shoots of the root Germanic language, other branches of which are the German, English, and Dutch-Flemish languages.

Pronunciation

a = "ah" as in ball

e = "eh" as in late, "e" as in bet at the end of a word and some times "ee" as in keep

i = "ee" as in keep

o = "oh" as in hope

o = "er" as in work (rough approximation)

u = "oo" as in moon

j = "y" as in yes

DANISH FEMALE NAMES

Äase (Norse) tree-covered mountain

Abellona (Gr) manly

Ailsa form of Elisabet (H) consecrated to God

Anne (AHN-e) (H) grace – Anna

Anne-lise* comb. name

Anne-mette* comb. name

Arvada eagle

Asta (Gr) a star

Astrid (ONorse) divine strength

Bente* (L) blessed

Bette (BEHT-e) (H) consecrated to God

Bitten unknown meaning

Britta (Celt) strength – Birgit

Clady (KLAH-dee) (L) lame

Dagmar glory of the Danes

Dagny (ONorse) Dane's joy

Dana from Denmark

Dania (H) God is my judge

Dorothea (L) gift from God

Ebba (OGer) strong

Elisabet (H) consecrated to God

Ellen* (Gr) light

Elna (Gr) light

Else (EHL-seh) (H) consecrated to God Elsa

Gerda (GEHR-dah) (Ger) protection

Grette* (Gr) a pearl

Gudrun divine wisdom

Hanne* (HAHN-uh) (H) gracious

Helga (Russian) holy

Helsa dim. Elizabeth (H) consecrated to God

Inga-lise* comb. name

Ingeborg (ONorse) Ing's protection (Ing was god of fertility)

Inger (Teut) hero's daughter – Inga

Iola (Welsh) lord-value

Jensine (yehn-seen) (H) God is gracious

Jette* (YUH-tuh) (L) coal black

Johanna (yo-HAHN-ah) (H) gracious

Kaia lise comb. of Kaia (Gr) earth; and Elizabeth (H) consecrated to God

Kamma meaning unknown; perhaps from Kamilla (L) ceremonial attendant

Karan (Gr) pure

Kasen (Gr) pure

Kathrine (Gr) pure

Kirsten* (KEER-sten) (Gr) Christian

Krista (Gr) Christian

Kristina (Gr) Christian

Laila (LAH-ee-la) (H) night

Leta (L) gladness

Lillian (H) lily

Lisbet* (LEES-bet) dim. Elisabet

Lise (LEE-suh) dim. of Elisabet (H) consecrated to God

Magarethe (Gr) a pearl

Magda (H) woman of Magdala

Marianne (mahr-YAHN-e) (H) rebellious; form of Mary

Meta dim. of Margarethe

Metta-lise* comb. name

Mette (Gr) a pearl – Meyta

Nadia (Slavic) hope

Ovia (L) egg

Ragnild (RAHNG-ild) (ONorse) warrior goddess

Rigmor (REE-mor) name of a Danish queen

Saffi (Gr) wisdom

Sena (L) blessed

Sigrid (ONorse) victorious counselor

Sorine unknown meaning; possibly (ONorse) Thor, thunder god

Stinne nickname for Kristina

Vibeke (Low German) little woman

---

* Currently popular

DANISH MALE NAMES

Äage (AHG-e) (Norse) ancestors

Aksel (H) father of peace

Anker (Gr) manly

Anton (L) inestimable

Aren (AH-rehn) eagle or rule

Argus watchful or vigilant — Gus

Arlan (Celt) pledge

Arne (OGer) eagle

Axel (H) father of peace

Bardo (Aramaic) ploughman

Bent* (L) blessed

Berde glacier

Bjarne (BYUHRN) (ONorse) bear

Bjorn (BYORN) (ONorse) bear

Bo* commanding

Bodil commanding

Brede (BREH-deh) glacier

Christian* (Gr) Christian

Clemens (L) gentle or kind

Cort (Teut) bold speech

Dan* (H) God is my judge

Dane (DAHN-e) from Denmark

Egon (EE-gon) (Teut) formidable

Erhardt (OGer) honor

Erik* (EE-rik) (ONorse) ever powerful

Finn* from Finland; or (Norse) he who finds

Flemming (OE) Dutchman; Flanders

Georg (Gr) farmer — Joren

Gerard (OE) spear hard

Gerold (Teut) mighty with the spear

Gert (GEHRT) (Teut) fighter

Gregos (Gr) vigilant

Gustaof (Teut) staff of the gods

Hans* (H) God's gracious gift

Harald (HAHR-ald) (ONorse) war chief

Helge (Russian) holy

Hendrik (Teut) ruler of an estate — Henrik

Henerik* (Teut) ruler of an estate

Henning (Teut) ruler of an estate

Hjalmar (HYAHL-mar) meaning unknown; old Danish name

Homerus (Gr) pledge

Ian (EE-an) (Scottish, H) God's gracious gift

Ib (Phoenician) oath of Baal

Ivar (Teut) archer

Jakob (YAH-kob) (H) the supplanter

Jan (YAHN) (H) God's gracious gift — Johan, Hans, Hanschen

Jens* (YEHNS) (H) God's gracious gift — Jen

Jeremias (yehr-uh-MEE-as) (H) God will uplift

Joen meaning unknown, perhaps form of John (H) God's gracious gift

John* (H) God's gracious gift (pronounced as in English)

Jorgen (YOR-gehn) (Gr) farmer

Jorn (YORN) (Gr) farmer

Kaj (KAH-ee) (Gr) earth — Kai

Karel (OFr) full-grown, manly

Karl (OFr) full-grown, manly

Kim* (OE) ruler, or chief; made popular by an English book

Klaus* (Gr) victory of the people (from Nicolaus) — Claus

Knud* (K'NOOD) (Norse) knot, kind

Lars* (L) laurel

Leonhard (Teut) bold lion

Lief* (LIFE) (Norse) descendent

Lorens (L) crowned with laurel

Loritz (L) laurel — Lauritz

Marius (L) warlike

Martinus (L) warlike

Matthews (H) gift of God — Mads

Mette (Gr) a pearl — Almeta

Michael* (MEE-chehl) (H) who is like God? — Mikael

Mikkel (MEE-kel) (H) who is like God?

Mogens unknown meaning; possibly "power" from Dutch

Nicolaus (Gr) victory of the people — Nikolai, Kolinka

Niels* (Celt) champion — Niel

Niles son of Neil — Nils

Nils (Celt) champion

Olivier (L) olive tree

Peter* (Gr) stone — Peder

Poul (L) little

Preben (Gr) stone

Rasmus (RAHS-moos) (Gr) amiable

Sakeri (H) remembered by the Lord

Samson (H) the sun's man

Soren unknown meaning; perhaps from (ONorse) Thor, thunder god

Steen (Teut) stone

Svend (Norse) young man

Tage (TAHG-e) (Teut) day

Thor (ONorse) thunder god

Torquil (Teut) Thor's caldron

Vilhelm (Teut) resolute protector

***** **Currently popular**

ENGLAND

During the earliest immigration of English to America in 1628-42 approximately 58,000 arrived in North America or the Caribbean, settling mainly in Maryland, Virginia, Massachusetts, Connecticut, and Rhode Island.

Indentured service was introduced by 1620, bringing many English and Irish farm laborers, domestic servants, and artisans. Between 1635 and 1705 an estimated 2,000 to 2,500 indentured servants arrived in America each year. Roughly one-half to two-thirds of the migration occurred south of New England, primarily to Virginia and Maryland.

In the 18th century an estimated 20,000 convicts were transported to America and either sold as servants or released on their own recognizance. A massive wave of immigration occurred in the early 1770's. From December, 1773 to April, 1775 more than 6,000 immigrated from England to the U.S., many of whom were skilled artisans or property owners.

Ninety percent of the American mainland colonists in 1690 were of English birth or descent. By 1790 the figure had been reduced to forty-nine percent of the population.

The American war for independence brought an abrupt halt to English immigration, which languished for thirty years. After the War of 1812 ended in 1815, a massive wave of English immigration began. U.S. immigration records put the number of immigrants at 61,000 between 1825 and 1850, but one source considers this extremely low and suggests a number nearer 400,000. By 1850 280,000 English natives were reported in the U.S. census. Another 630,000 immigrated between 1850 and 1890.

In the first half of the 19th century the largest share of immigrants came from the more rural and less developed southern and western area of England. In a reversal of the pattern of most immigrant populations, the largest group of English immigrants was pre-industrial craftsmen, followed by industrial workers such as weavers and metal workers.

Also more farmers than farm laborers immigrated during this period and most of the English immigrants (inspired by Jefferson, perhaps) had a strong urge to acquire farms, even if they had to work at their former trades part time until they were established. As the century advanced, laborers, miners, and workers in the building trades became the largest group. Most immigrants in the latter half of the 19th century settled in either the mining, farming, and cattle-raising areas west of the Mississippi or in the oldest industrial and mining areas in New Jersey, Ohio, Pennsylvania, and Massachusetts.

Beginning in 1893, when an economic downturn hit the U.S., English immigration to the U.S. also began a permanent decline. Although emigration continued out of England, after 1905 increasing numbers went to Canada instead. Dropping from an average of 65,000 per year in the 1880's, immigration from England now averages about 10,000 each year.

Although Old English and Anglo-Saxon names arising out of English number in the hundreds, only a relative few are popular in England now. The favorites now are the perennial, traditional names which have been popular for the last 200 years and, thus have withstood the test of time. Names like Robert, James, Anna, and Charlotte (and not nicknames) are being chosen by British parents today. Occasionally Scottish names may be selected, but on the whole, the simple, strictly traditional names win.

The most popular names in England are noted in the name list below. A few, more elaborate, old-fashioned names that would have been in use earlier in the century are included.

ENGLISH FEMALE NAMES

Abigail (H) a source of joy

Adrian (L) of the Adriatic — Adriana, Adriane

Agatha (Gr) kind and good

Agnes (Gr) gentle, pure — Agna

Alberta (OGer) noble, bright

Alexandra (Gr) defender of mankind — Sandy, Sondra

Alexis (Gr) defender of mankind — Ali, Aleki

Alice (OGer) noble, kind

Alison (OGer) noble, kind

Althea (Gr) wholesome — Thea

Amabel (L) lovable

Amanda* (L) beloved, lovable — Manda, Mandy, Amandine

Amelia (L) industrious, persuasive — Emily, Millie

Amy* (OFr) beloved — Aimee, Ami, Esme

Anabel (L) lovable, beautiful — Mabel

Andrea fem. Andrew (Gr) manly

Angela* (Fr) angel — Angie

Anne* (H) grace — Anna, Nancy, Netta, Nan

Antonia (L) inestimable — Toni, Antoinette

April (L) when earth opens for growth of spring

Ashley (OE) from the ash-tree meadow

Audrey (OE) noble strength — Audra, Audie, Audre

Augusta (L) venerable — Augustina, Austina, Tina, Gussie

Avril (OE) born in April

Barbara (L) the stranger

Beatrice (L) she makes happy or blesses — Trixie, Bea, Beatrix

Becky dim. Rebecca (H) servant of God

Berenice (Gr) bringer of victory

Beth dim. Elizabeth — Betsy, Bess, Betty

Beverly (OE) from beaver meadow

Blythe (A.S.) glad, joyous

Bonnie (L) sweet and beautiful

Brenda (Norse) fem. Brand: sword

Bridget (Celt) strength

Brooke (OE) stream

Candace (Gr) glittering, glowing white — Candy, Candice, Candis

Carol (Fr) song of joy — Carole

Carolyn* fem. Charles — Caroline, Carrie, Carly

Cassandra (Gr) prophetess — Cass, Cassie, Sandra*

Catherine* (Gr) pure

Cecilia (L) gray eyes, blind — Cecily, Cicely, Cecile

Celia (L) heavenly — Celeste, Celina, Celinda

Charity (L) charity

Charlotte* (Fr) petite and feminine — Carla, Lotte, Lola, Sharyl

Chelsea (A.S.) port

Cherry (OFr) cherrylike

Chloe* (Gr) blooming

Christine* (Gr) Christian — Chrissy, Chris, Christy

Claire* (L) bright, clear — Clare, Clarissa

Claudia (L) lame

Colette (Fr) dim. Nicolas (Gr) victory of the people

Constance (L) constant — Connie

Courtney (L) court

Cynthia (Gr) the moon

Dagmar (Danish) glory of the Danes

Dana (Scand) from Denmark

Danielle (H) God is my judge

Daphne (Gr) bay tree or laurel

Darcie (OFr) the dark

Darlene (OE) beloved

Dawn (OE) dawn

Deborah (H) a bee — Debrah, Debbie

Deirdre* (Celt) mythological heroine; young girl

Diana* (L) goddess of the moon — Diane, Deanna, Dee, Di

Dominica (Fr) of the Lord

Donna (L) lady

Dorian (Gr) child of the sea

Doris (Gr) from the sea

Dorothy (Gr) gift of God

Dory (Fr) golden-haired

Drew (Gr) vision

Edith (Teut) rich gift

Elaine (Gr) light

Eleanor (Gr) light — Nora, Nell, Aileen, Alena

Elizabeth* (H) consecrated to God — Eliza, Liza, Liz, Elisa, Betsy, Bess

Ellen* (Gr) light

Emily (Teut) industrious

Emma* (OGer) universal — Emily, Emmy

Erica (ONorse) ever powerful

Esme (A.S.) gracious protector

Eugenia (Gr) well-born, noble

Eve (H) life — Evelyn, Eva

Faith (L) trust — Faye

Felicity* (L) fortunate, or lucky — Felicia, Felise

Fiona* (Celt) white, fair

Flora (L) flower

Florence (L) blooming, flourishing — Flo

Frances* (Teut) free — Fran, Franny, Fanny*

Frederica (OGer) peaceful ruler

Gail (OE) lovely — Gale, Gayle

Gay (Fr) merry

Gemma (JEM-muh) (Fr) precious stone

Genevieve (Fr) white wave

Georgia fem. George (Gr) farmer — Georgina

Gill (JILL) (L) youth

Gillian* (JILL-ee-an, or GILL-ee-an) (L) youth

Gladys (L) gladiolus, sword

Glenna (Irish) of the glen or valley

Guinevere (Celt) fair lady — Gwenevere, Gwen

Gwen (Welsh) white

Gwendolyn (Celt) white brow

Hannah (H) gracious

Harriet (Teut) mistress of the home

Hayley (OE) from the hay meadow

Heather (OE) heather

Helen* (Gr) light — Ellen, Nellie, Elaine, Elinor

Hermione daughter of Venus and Mars

Hilary* (L) cheerful — Hillary

Holly (OFr) shrub

Hope (OE) hope

Ianthe (Gr) violet-colored flower

Irene (Gr) peace — Rena

Iris (Gr) rainbow

Isabel (H) consecrated to God

Ivy (OE) plant name

Jacqueline (Fr) fem. Jacques (H) God's gracious gift

Jane* (H) God's gracious gift — Jan, Janice, Janie, Jean, Jana

Janet* (H) God's gracious gift

Janis* var. Jane

Jean* (H) God's gracious gift

Jemima* (Arabic) dove

Jennifer* (Celt) white wave

Jessamine (OFr) jasmine

Jessica* (H) grace of God — Jessie

Jill* var. Gillian — Jillian

Jinny (L) virgin maiden

Joan* (H) God's gracious gift — Joanne, Joanna

Jodie (H) praised

Jolie (zho-LEE) (Fr) pretty, merry

Joscelin (L) just

Joy (OFr) jewel, delight

Judith (H) praised

Julie (L) youth — Julia, Juliet

Justine (L) just

Karen (Gr) pure — Karin, Caren

Katherine* (Gr) pure — Kathie, Cathie, Cathy, Kathryn, Karen, Kay, Kelly

Katie (Gr) pure

Kelly (Teut) farm by the spring

Kerrie (OE) name of a king — Kerry

Kimberly (OE) from the royal fortress meadow — Kim, Kimbra

Kirsty (Gr) Christian

Laura (L) crown of laurels — Laurel, Lori, Laurie

Laurel (L) crown of laurels — Laurie

Leanne comb. of Lee and Anne

Leigh (OE) meadow

Leslie (Gael) from the gray fortress — Lesley

Letitia (L) gladness — Lettie, Letty

Libby var. Elizabeth

Lily (L) lily flower — Lilian, Lil

Linda (Span) beautiful

Lindsay (OE) from the linden-tree island

Lisa dim. Elizabeth

Livia (L) short for Olivia — Livie

Lola (Span) dim. Carlota

Lorraine (Fr) from Lorraine, in France

Louise fem. Louis (Teut) renowned warrior — Louisa

Lucy* (L) bringer of light — Lucia, Lucille, Lucie

Lydia (Gr) ancient province in Asia Minor

Lynn (A.S.) from the waterfall — Lynne, Linn

Madeline (H) woman from — Magdala Madeleine

Maggie (Scot) dim. Margaret

Mandy dim. Amanda

Marcia (L) warlike — Marcella, Marsha, Marcie

Margaret* (Gr) a pearl — Margot, Marjory, Peg, Peggy*

Mariam (H) bitter — Marion

Marianne (H) rebellious; form of Mary

Marie (H) bitter

Marilyn var. Mary (H) bitter

Marina (L) sea maid

Marjorie var. Margaret

Mary* (L) star of the sea (H) bitter — Marie, Mariette, Marise

Maude (Teut) heroine

Maureen (OFr) dark-skinned — Moreen, Maurine

Maxine (L) greatest

May (Scot) shortened Margaret

Megan (A.S.) strong

Melanie (Gr) black

Melissa (Gr) honeybee — Lisa, Melisse, Melita

Meredith (Celt) sea protector

Meryl (Arabic) myrrh

Michelle (H) who is like God?

Miranda (L) miraculous

Moira (Celt) great

Molly (H) bitter

Mona (Irish) noblewoman

Monica* (L) advisor

Nadine (Fr) dim. Bernadine

Nancy (H) grace — Nan, Nanette, Nana

Naomi (H) pleasant, sweet

Natalie (Fr) born at Christmas

Nicola (Gr) victory of the people — Nicole

Nicole (Gr) victory of the people

Nina (H) grace

Noelle (Fr) born at Christmas — Noel

Nona (L) ninth — Noni

Nora (Gr) light — Norah

Octavia (L) eighth

Olivia (L) olive tree — Livy, Livia, Nollie

Paige (Fr) attendant on noble — Page

Pamela* (Gr) entirely of honey — Pammie, Pammy, Pam

Patricia* (L) noble — Patty, Tricia, Trisha

Paula (L) little

Peggy dim. Margaret (Gr) a pearl

Penelope* (Gr) weaver — Penny

Philippa (Gr) lover of horses

Phoebe (Gr) shining, brilliant

Phyllis (Gr) foliage — Philis

Polly nickname for Mary

Portia heroine of *Merchant of Venice*

Priscilla (L) from the former times

Prudence (L) prudent

Rachel (H) innocence of a lamb

Rebecca* (H) binding, servant of God — Becky, Reba

Regina (L) queen — Gina, Reina, Rina

Rhea mother of the gods in Greek mythology; from the earth — Rea

Rita (Gr) a pearl

Roberta fem. Robert (Teut) of shining fame — Robin, Robyn

Rose (L) rose — Rosalie, Rosanne

Rosemary comb. Rose and Mary — Rosemarie

Rowena (Celt) white mane

Roxanne (Persian) bright dawn

Ruby (L) red; jewel name

Ruth (H) beauty, friend

Sally (H) princess

Samantha (H) name of God

Sandra* (Gr) defender of mankind

Sarah* (H) princess — Sara*, Sally, Sarita

Selena (Gr) moon — Selina

Sharon (H) of the land of Sharon

Shawn (Irish from Hebrew) God's gracious gift

Sheila (L) blind

Shelley (A.S.) ledge meadow

Sherry (OE) white meadow — Shirley

Shirley (OE) shining meadow

Sibyl (Gr) the prophetess

Sidonie (OFr) a follower of St. Denis — Sidonia, Sydney

Simone (H) God is heard

Sonia (Gr) wisdom — Sonya

Sophia (Gr) wisdom — Sophie

Stacey (Gr) resurrection — Stacie, Stacy, Anastasia

Star (L) star — Starr

Stella (L) star

Stephanie (Gr) a crown

Susan (H) lily — Sue, Susanna, Suzy

Suzanne (H) lily

Sylvia (L) from the forest — Sylvanna, Silvia

Tabitha (Aramaic) gazelle Tabby

Taite (A.S.) cheerful — Tayte, Tate

Tamara (H) palm tree

Tara (Celt) tower

Teresa (Gr) harvester — Theresa, Tess, Tessie, Resa

Terry nickname for Teresa

Thea (Gr) goddess

Tina short for Christina

Tory short for Victoria

Tracy (Gr) harvester

Ula (Celt) jewel of the sea

Una (L) one

Ursula (L) little bear

Valerie (L) strong — Valery

Vanessa (Gr) butterfly — Vania, Vanny, Vanna

Vera (L) true

Veronica (L) true image

Victoria* (L) victorious — Vicky, Vicki

Virginia (L) pure

Vivian (L) lively — Vivien

Wallis (OE) wall

Wenda (OE) fair

Wendy made-up name first in *Peter Pan* in 1904

Whitney (A.S.) white island

Wilhelmina fem. Wilhelm (Teut) resolute protector

Winifred (Teut) friend of peace — Winnie, Winnifred

Yvone (OFr) archer

Zoe (Gr) life

---

* Most popular

ENGLISH MALE NAMES

Aaron (H) teaching; mountaineer

Adam (H) son of the red earth

Adrian (L) of the Adriatic

Alan (Gael) handsome, cheerful — Allan, Allen

Alaric (OGer) noble ruler

Alban (L) white

Albert (OGer) noble, bright

Alexander (Gr) defender of mankind — Alec

Alfred (OE) wise counselor

Algernon (OFr) with whiskers

Alistair (Gr) defender of mankind

Ambrose (Gr) the divine, the immortal one

Andrew* (Gr) manly — Andy

Anthony (L) inestimable — Tony

Archibald (OGer) noble and bold — Archie, Arch, Archer

Arthur (Celt) noble

Austen (L) the exalted, sacred, sublime — Gus, Augustus

Averil boar-like

Avery var. of Alfred

Barclay (OE) from the birch tree meadow

Barnaby (H) son of prophecy — Barnabas, Barney

Barry (Celt) good marksman

Bart (H) farmer's son

Barth son of the earth

Basil (Gr) kingly or magnificent

Benjamin (H) son of the right hand — Ben

Bernard (OGer) bold as a bear

Bert (L) bright raven — Bertram, Bertrand, Bart, Berty, Bertie

Bishop bishop

Blaise stammerer — Blaze

Blake (OE) pallid, fair-complected

Brad (OE) from the broad valley — Brady

Braden from the wide valley — Bradan

Bradley from the broad meadow

Brandon sword — Bran, Brand

Brendan (Gael) little raven

Brent steep hill — Brentan

Brian (Celt) strong — Bryan

Brook from the brook — Brooks

Bruce (Fr) from the brushwood thicket

Byron (Fr) from the cottage

Cameron (Celt) crooked nose

Carey (OWelsh) from the castle — Cary

Carter cart driver — Cart

Cecil (L) blind

Chad from the warrior's town

Charles* (OFr) strong and manly — Carl, Carroll

Chester from the fortified camp

Christian (Gr) Christian

Christopher* (Gr) Christbearer — Chris, Kris

Clarence (L) bright, famous

Clifford dweller in the ford near the cliff — Clifton

Clive* from the cliff

Colin* (Gr) victor — Collin, Colan

Cooper barrel maker

Corbin (L) the raven — Corwin

Corey (A.S.) chosen one

Cosmo (Gr) well-ordered

Courtney (OFr) from the court — Cort

Craig (Celt) crag dweller

Crispin (L) curly-haired

Curtis (OFr) the courteous

Cyril (Gr) lordly one — Cy

Damien (Gr) constant one — Damon

Daniel* (H) God is my judge

Darren* (Gael) great

David* (H) beloved — Davin, Davis, Davey

Davis (OE) David's son

Dean (OE) from the valley — Deane, Dene, Dino

Dennis (Gr) god of wine Denys

Devin (Celt) poet

Dominic (L) of the Lord — Dominy, Nicky

Donald (Celt) ruler of the world — Don

Dorian (Gr) child of the sea — Dore

Douglas (Celt) from the black stream

Dudley (OE) from the people's meadow

Duncan (Gael) dark warrior

Dustin (OGer) brave fighter

Eaton from the state on the river — Eatton

Edmund (OE) prosperous protector — Edmon

Edward* (OE) wealthy guardian — Ed, Ted, Ted

Egan (Irish) ardent

Ellery (Teut) of the alder trees

Elliot (H) Jehovah is God — Eli, Ellis

Elton (OE) from the old town — Alden, Alton

Emory (OGer) joint ruler — Emery

Eric (ONorse) ever powerful — Rick

Eugene (Gr) noble — Gene

Evan (Welsh) a youth

Felix (L) happy

Fitzgerald (OE) son of the spear-mighty

Fitzhugh (OE) son of the intelligent one

Fitzpatrick (OE) son of a nobleman

Fleming (A.S.) from Flanders

Fletcher (OFr) arrow featherer

Foster (L) keeper of the woods

Frank (Teut) free — Francis

Frederick (Teut) peaceful ruler — Freddy, Ricky

Garrett (A.S.) powerful with the spear — Gareth

Gary (OE) spear carrier — Garey

Gavin (OWelsh) hawk of the battle

Geoffrey* (A.S.) gift of peace — Jeffrey, Geoff, Jeff

George* (Gr) farmer — Georgie, Jorge

Gerald (Teut) mighty with the spear — Garold, Jerold, Gerry

Gerard (OGer) spear hard

Gervase (Teut) spear vassal; honorable — Jervis, Jarvis, Gervais

Gideon (H) feller of trees

Giles (Gr) shield bearer

Gordon (A.S.) from the cornered hill

Graham (L) grain — Graeme, Gram

Gregory (Gr) vigilant

Grosvenor (GROV-ner) (Fr) mighty huntsman

Guy* (OFr) guide

Harley (OE) the stag's meadow — Harleigh, Arleigh

Harold (ONorse) war chief — Herrick, Harry, Hal

Harrison (OE) son of Harry — Harris

Harry* (Teut) ruler of an estate

Henry (Teut) ruler of an estate — Harry, Hal, Hank

Hilary (L) cheerful

Howard (Teut) chief guardian

Hugh (Teut) intelligence, spirit

Hunter (OE) huntsman

Ian (H) God's gracious gift

Ivor (Teut) archer — Ivo, Iver

Jack (H) God's gracious gift

James* (H) the supplanter

Jared (H) descendant, ruler — Jordan, Jori

Jarvis (OGer) sharp spear

Jason (Gr) healer — Jasun, Jay

Jasper (Persian) treasurer

Jay (Fr) blue jay

Jeffrey (A.S.) gift of peace

Jeremy (H) God will uplift — Jerry

Jerome (L) holy name

Joel (H) Jehovah is the Lord

John* (H) God's gracious gift — Jack

Jonathon* (H) God gives

Joseph (H) God will add — Joe

Judd (H) praised

Judith (H) praised — Judy

Julian (L) youth

Justin* (L) the just — Justus, Justis

Karl (OFr) strong and manly

Keith (OWelsh) from the forest

Kendrick (A.S.) royal ruler — Kenric, Ric

Kenneth (OE) royal oath — Ken

Kent (OWelsh) white, bright

Kenton (OE) from the king's estate — Kent

Kevin (Celt) kind, gentle

Kim (OE) ruler or chief

Kipp (OE) from the pointed hill — Kippar, Kippie

Kit (Gr) (from Christopher) Christ-bearer

Kyle (Gael) handsome

Lance (A.S.) spear

Laurence (L) crowned with laurel — Lawrence, Lawron, Lawrie, Laurie, Lorin

Lee (OE) from the meadow — Leigh, Leo

Leighton (OE) from the meadow farm — Layton, Leigh, Lay

Leo (L) lion

Leonard (Teut) bold lion — Len

Leslie (Gael) from the gray fortress — Lesley

Lewis (OGer) renowned warrior — Lew, Lou, Louis, Lewes, Clovis

Lloyd (Welsh) gray-haired one

Lorimer (L) harness-maker — Lorrie, Lorrimer, Lorry

Louis (OGer) renowned warrior — Lewis

Lucas (L) bringer of light — Luke, Lucian

Lynn (A.S.) from the waterfall — Lyn

Mark* (L) warlike

Martin (L) warlike

Matthew* (H) gift of God — Matt

Maurice (L) dark-skinned — Morie, Morris, Maury

Maxwell (OE) from the influential man's well — Max

Merrick (Teut) industrious ruler

Michael* (H) who is like God? — Mickey, Mike

Miles (Gr) millstone — Milo, Myles

Montague (Fr) from the pointed mountain — Monte

Montgomery (OE) from the rich man's mountain — Monte

Morley (OE) from the meadow on the moor — Morlee, Morly

Nathaniel (H) gift of the Lord

Neil (Celt) chief — Niel, Neale

Nelson son of Neil — Nilson

Neville (OFr) from the new town

Nicholas* (Gr) victory of the people — Nicolas, Colan, Nick

Nigel (L) dark, or black

Noel (L) Christmas

Norman (OFr) Norseman — Normand, Norm

Nyle (OE) island

Octavio (L) eighth — Octavian, Octavius, Tavey

Oliver* (L) olive tree — Olvan

Parry (Welsh) son of Harry

Patrick (L) noble

Paul* (L) little

Perry (A.S.) pear tree

Peter (Gr) stone — Perrin

Philip* (Gr) lover of horses

Quentin (L) fifth child

Quinn (Celt) the wise

Ray (L) the radiant

Reed (OE) red-haired

Reginald (OGer) strong ruler — Reggie, Reg

Richard* (OGer) powerful ruler — Rick, Rich

Robert* (Teut) of shining fame — Robin, Rob, Bob

Robin (Teut) of shining fame

Roderick (Teut) famous ruler — Rod, Roddy, Rory

Roger (Teut) famous warrior Rogers

Rory (Teut) famous ruler

Roy (OFr) king

Russell (A.S.) like a fox

Ryan (Gael) little king; strong

Samuel* (H) God hears — Sam

Scott (L) a Scotsman

Sheldon (OE) shield town

Sidney (OFr) a follower of St. Denis — Sid, Sydney

Simon (H) God is heard

St. Alban place name

Stan (OE) from the rocky meadow — Stanley

Stephen (Gr) a crown

Stuart (A.S) steward — Stewart

Terry (L) smooth — Terence

Theodore (Gr) gift of God — Ted, Teddy

Thomas (H) twin — Tommie, Tom, Tommy

Timothy (Gr) honoring God — Tim

Todd (Scottish) fox

Tomlin (OE) little twin

Vaughn (OWelsh) small one

Victor (L) conqueror

Walter (Teut) powerful ruler — Walt

Wayne (OE) wagon-maker

William* (Teut) resolute protector

Zachary (H) remembered by the Lord

Zane (H) God's gracious gift

---

* Most popular

ETHIOPIA

Immigration from Ethiopia to the U.S. has only numbered in the several hundred each year starting in the early 1970's. In the 1970's and 1980's there have been hundreds of thousands of refugees from famine and civil strife, who fled to neighboring African countries. Over ninety percent of Ethiopia's population lives in rural areas. Seventy known languages are spoken there, but the dominant one is Amharic.

The country consists roughly of a large, temperate central plateau surrounded by fiercely hot deserts. The province of Eritrea on the northeastern coast is one of the hottest and driest areas in Africa. One of its coastal cities, Massaua, has an average annual temperature of eighty-six degrees Fahrenheit.

Eritrea has been a part of Ethiopia since 1952, but in recent years Eritreans as well as Tigres (another ethnic group living southeast of Eritrea) have been battling to secede from Ethiopia. Many roads to the mountainous interior have been destroyed in the fighting. Food supplies to relieve famine in the interior, channeled through Eritrea (where Ethiopia's only ports are located) have been blockaded and confiscated for use by Eritrean troops and citizens.

Ethiopia is one of the oldest Christian nations. About half of Ethiopians are Christians (Ethiopian Orthodox), forty percent are Muslims, and a small minority are Ethiopian Jews (called Falash), who believe in a mixture of Judaic and traditional African ideas.

ETHIOPIAN FEMALE NAMES

Afework golden month
Alam world
Desta happiness
Fannah fun
Genat heaven
Louam sleep well
Maharene forgive us
Makda (H) woman from Magdala
Melesse eternal
Retta won
Seble autumn
Selamawit make as peace
Semhar country
Senaiet happy
Tsage happiness

ETHIOPIAN MALE NAMES

Assefa (ah-seh-FAH) enlarge
Atoberhan sunny
Beniam (H) son of the right hand
Berhanu his light
Dawit (H) beloved
Fethee judgment
Gebereal (H) God is my strength
Hagos happy
Iskander (Gr) defender of mankind
Kelile protection
Mengesha kingdom
Ogbay don't take from me
Semere (Gr) farmer
Tefere seed
Tekle plant

FINLAND

Legend has it that Finns were the first to build log cabins in the New World (settling here as early as the 1630's and 1640's in Delaware, Pennsylvania, and New Jersey). However, large-scale immigration to the U.S. didn't begin until the 1860's, reaching a peak between 1899 and World War I. U.S. immigration figures were not taken separately on Finns until later, but 274,000 received passports to leave Finland to travel to the U.S. and elsewhere between 1893 and 1920.

Laborers needed to develop copper mines in the Keweenan Peninsula of northern Michigan were recruited from Finland and Norway (where Finns had settled earlier). Others seeking land settled in St. Peter and Red Wing, Minnesota.

Although small in number, the 700 to 1,000 Norwegian Finns immigrating in 1864-85 introduced Michigan and Minnesota to the thousands from Finland who followed. Most settled in the thirteen northern states from the Northeast to the Pacific Coast, taking jobs in copper mines, steel and textile mills, granite quarries, and construction projects. Many were farmers, and often the women were the real farm operators since the men would hold part-time jobs as well as farming.

Women were most commonly employed as domestic servants. Finnish immigrants tended not to intermarry with other groups even though in 1900 there were 182 Finnish men for every 100 Finnish women.

Although Finland is considered a Scandinavian country its language is of the Uralic and Altaic language families, in which Hungarian, Turkish, Mongol, Manchu, and most of the languages spoken in the Asian part of Russia are included. All consonants and vowels are pronounced very distinctly in Finnish.

FINNISH FEMALE NAMES

Annikki (AHN-nee-kee) (H) bitter

Ansa (L) constant

Dorotea (Gr) gift of God

Eeva (EH-vuh) (H) life

Elli (H) consecrated to God — Elisa, Liisa

Helli (Gr) light

Inkeri (Teut) hero's daughter — Ingria

Janne (YAH-nuh) (H) God's gracious gift

Kalwa heroic

Katri (Gr) pure — Kaisa, Katrina

Kerttu (Teut) fighter (an old name)

Kristina (Gr) Christian

Kyllikki (KOO-leek-kee) character from Finnish national epic; strong woman

Laina (Gr) light

Lilja (LEEL-yah) (H) lily

Maija (MIGH-yah) (H) bitter — Maiju, Maikki, Maijii

Marjatta (mahr-YAH-tah) (Gr) a pearl

Mielikki pleasing

Mirja (MEER-yah) (H) bitter

Rikka (RREEK-ah) (Teut) peaceful ruler — Fredericka

Ruta (H) beauty, friend (not common)

Ruusu (L) rose

FINNISH MALE NAMES

Antti (Gr) manly

Eikki (ONorse) ever powerful

Jani (YAH-nee) (H) God's gracious gift — Johan, Jussi, Jukka, Juha

Joosef (YOO-sef) (H) God will add — Jooseppi

Kaarlo (OFr) strong and manly — Kalle, Kaarle

Kalevi a hero

Lasse (Gr) victory of the people

Mikko (H) who is like God?

Paaveli (L) little Paavo

Pekka (Gr) stone

Rikard (OGer) powerful ruler

Risto (Gr) Christ-bearer

Taaveti (H) beloved — Taavi

Taneli (H) God is my judge

Tapani (Gr) crowned with laurels — Teppo

Tuomas (H) twin

Viljo (Teut) resolute protector — Vilho

Yrjo (EURR-yuh) (Gr) farmer — Jorma

FRANCE

The earliest immigrants from France were trappers who headed into the untamed interior of the U.S. to trade with the Indians. In the 17th and 18th centuries they established trading outposts at present-day Detroit, St. Louis, and New Orleans.

Beginning in 1538, reaching a peak in 1685, and continuing until the 1760's, a total of 14,000 French Huguenots (Protestants forbidden to practice their religion in officially Catholic France) immigrated to the U.S., settling in all thirteen colonies, especially South Carolina and Massachusetts.

In striking contrast to other immigrant countries, France has sent America immigrants at a stable, almost non-varying low rate since records were first kept in 1820. Before then, an estimated few hundred French migrated here each year in the 17th and 18th centuries. Since then, it has ranged from a low of 39,000 in the 1940's to a high of 77,000 in the 1840's. The peak immigrant year was 1851 during the California Gold Rush when 20,000 came here.

The 1840's, when Germany, Ireland, and others were beginning large-scale immigration to America, brought a down-turn in population in France as well as a rise in the standard of living. Many of the people who did immigrate were from border areas such as Alsace, Savoy, and the Pyrenees (Basque), which had at different times been traded back and forth as the spoils of war or were not always culturally integrated with the mainstream of French life. For ordinary Frenchmen, when times got bad they usually migrated to Paris or stayed home.

Another unique feature about France that kept emigration at low levels was the amazing stability of population. In 1850 it was thirty-six million; in 1940 it was forty million. If it hadn't absorbed more immigrants compared to its size than the U.S., at some periods, the population might actually have declined. Also, the rate of industrial growth in France was always modest so there was not a rapid dislocation of society.

The immigrants from France have come almost exclusively as

individuals rather than as groups. Since 1820 an estimated 740,000 French have immigrated to the U.S. with possibly 30,000 to 40,000 before that. However, these figures are extremely hazy; the numbers of genuine French immigrants may be as little as half the amounts. The method of recording immigration to the U.S. by country of last domicile resulted in many refugees from Germany and Eastern Europe who had stopped briefly in France, to be counted as French.

In earlier times it was the custom in France to name a child after the saint who was celebrated on the child's day of birth. So rigid was this custom that a birth registration clerk might record the child's name as the saint name regardless of what name the parents had chosen. Needless to say this custom has loosened up!

There appears to be a definite stratification in French society regarding which names are most popular in the different social classes. The upper class selects mostly traditional names that have withstood the test of time, such as Anne, Cecile, Helene, Pierre, Vincent, Francois. Farmers also pick traditional names, but they stay away from "upper class" names. Favorites include Sylvie, Beatrice, Nadine, Maryse, Sebastien, Joel, Jerome, and Damien.

It is among the middle class and blue-collar workers that trendy names, nowadays characterized by the Anglo-American influence, are popular; such as Cindy, Jennifer, Vanessa, Anthony, Gregory, Jonathan, and Kevin (all pronounced the French rather than the English way).

In the 1990's the predominance of "ie"-ending names for girls is expected to fade, and be replaced with -"ine" names such as Pauline, Marine and -"ene" or -"aine" sounds like Charlene, and Laurene. For boys the -"ien" ending, as in Fabien, Sebastien, Julien, and Cyprien should be popular.

Pronunciation

a = "ah" as in ball

ai = "e" as in peck

ain, aim, ein, in, im = "anh" as in thank, but final sound is nasal, as if an "n" is pronounced without touching the tongue to the roof of the mouth

an, am, en, em = "onh" as in gong, pronounced nasally

au = "oh" as in note

e, e, e, = "e" as in peck

e = "eh" as in late

eu = "u" as in hurt

i = "ee" as in keep, or "y" as in yes

oi = "wa" as in wangle

ue = "u" as in curb

gn = "ny" as in canyon

ch = "sh" as in chandelier

g = "zh" as in azure, before e, i, y

g = "g" as in gun, before all others

FRENCH FEMALE NAMES

Abelia (H) breath − Abella

Aceline (ahs-LEEN) (Teut) noble − Asceline

Adèle (ah-DEHL) (OGer) noble, of good cheer − Adelaide

Adeline (ahd-LEEN) (OGer) noble, kind − Adelinda, Adette

Adrienne (L) of the Adriatic

Agathe (AH-guh-tuh) (Gr) good

Agnès (ah-NEHS) (Gr) gentle, pure

Aida help

Aimee (eh-MEH) beloved − Aimè, Ami, Amy

Alexandre (a-leks-ANDR) (L) defender of man − Alexine, Alexis, Alexandrine

Algiane (Teut) spear

Alice (OGer) noble, kind

Aline (Teut) all

Alix (Teut) noble − Alex, Alissandre, Lissandre

Amalie (L) industrious, persuasive − Ameline, Amèlie, Emeline

Amandine (L) beloved

Amarante flower name

Amédée (ah-meh-DEH) love God

Anaïs* (H) grace

Andrée fem. Andrew (Gr) manly

Ange angel − Angèle, Angeline, Angelique

Angèle (ahnh-ZHEHL) (Gr) messenger

Anne (H) grace − Annelle, Anouche, Annelore, Anneliese, Annie

Antoine (L) inestimable − Antoinette, Toinette, Antonine

Ariane (Gr) very holy one − Ariana

Asceline (Teut) noble

Aude (OFr) old, rich − Auda

Audrey (OE) noble strength

Augustine (L) venerable − Austine

Aure (Gr) soft air, breeze

Aurelie (L) gold

Aurore (L) dawn − Aurora

Aveline (OFR) nut − Avelaine

Axelle (H) father of peace

Babette dim. of Barbara (L) the stranger

Béatrice (L) she blesses

Beline (OGer) goddess

Belle (L) beautiful − Bell, Bellette

Bénédicte (L) blest − Bee

Bernadette (OGer) courage of a bear − Bernardine, Bernardina, Bernette

Bertille (Teut) heroine

Bibiane (L) lively

Blanche (L) white, fair

Blanchefleur white flower

Blandine (L) seductive

Brigitte (Celt) strength

Callia (Gr) beautiful

Camille* (L) ceremonial attendant

Candide (L) pure white

Capucine (kah-poo-SEEN) cape

Carine dear

Carol song of joy − Carole

Caroline fem. Charles

Catherine** (Gr) pure − Cathelle, Catia

Cecile (L) blind, gray eyes − Cecilie, Ceciliane

Celeste (L) heavenly − Celestine, Celia

Celine fem. Marcel (L) hammer

Cerise cherry

Chantal song

Charlotte* petite, feminine − Charla, Charlene, Charlaine

Christelle (Gr) Christian

Christine (Gr) Christian − Christiane, Kit, Christel, Christelle, Kristell

Claire* (L) bright, clear

Claude (L) lame − Claudette, Claudine

Clémence (L) merciful − Clementine

Clotilde (OGer) heroine

Colette (Gr) victory of the people − Coline, Nicoline

Constance (L) constant

Coralie coral − Coralee

Corine (Gr) maiden − Corrine

Cybele (Gr) wise old woman − Sibille, Sibyl

Cyprien (L) from Cyprus − Cyprienne, Sabria

Damien patron saint of surgeons − Damiane, Damiana, Damia

Danae (H) God is my judge

Danielle (H) God is my judge

Delphine (Gr) flower name − Delfine

Denise (Gr) Greek god of wine − Denice, Denyse

Désireé desire − Désir, Désirat

Dominique (L) of the Lord − Dominica, Domitiane, Dina

Dorine golden

Dorothée (L) gift of God

Édith (Teut) rich gift

Edwige (Teut) refuge in battle

Elena (Gr) light

Eléonore (Gr) light − Aliénor, Helene, Enora

Eliane (H) Jehovah is God

Élisabeth (H) consecrated to God

Elise (H) consecrated to God — Elisee, Lise, Lison, Elizé, Liese

Emeline (Teut) industrious

Émilie (Teut) industrious — Emilianne, Emilienne

Emma (OGer) universal — Emmélie

Emmanuelle (H) God is with us

Estelle (L) star

Eugénie (yew-zheh-NEE) (Gr) wellborn, noble — Genie, Genia

Eulalie (yew-la-LEE) (Gr) well-spoken

Fabienne (L) bean grower

Fanette dim. Stephanie (Gr) crowned with laurels

Fantine childlike

Félicité (L) fortunate, or lucky — Felicienne, Filicie

Fidèle (fi-DEHL) (L) faithful

Fleur flower — Fleurette

Floriane (L) flowering — Florence

France France

Francoise ** (fran-SWAHZ) (Teut) free — Francine, France, Francique, Fanchon

Gabrielle (H) God is my strength — Gaby, Gabi, Gabie

Gaëlle (Ger) stranger, foreigner

Gaétane (gah-eh-TAN) from Gaete in central Italy

Galatée white

Gallia Gaul — Galla, Gala

Gemma (ZHEH-mah) precious stone

Geneviéve (Celt) white wave

Ghislaine (zhees-LAYN) (OGer) sweet pledge — Guilaine

Gisèle (Teut) pledge

Gladys (L) lame

Hélène (Gr) light

Henriette (onh-ree-EHT) (Teut) ruler of an estate

Honorine (L) honor

Hortense (or-TAHNHS) (L) gardener

Hyacinthe (Gr) hyacinth

Inès (ee-NEHS) (Gr) gentle, pure

Ingrid (Teut) hero's daughter

Iphigenie (if-uh-zhe-NEE) (Gr) mythological figure

Irénée (ee-reh-NAY) (Gr) peace

Isabelle ** (ee-sa-BEHL) (H) consecrated to God — Iseline (ees-LEEN)

Jacinthe (zhah-SINTH) (Gr) hyacinth — Hyacinthe

Jacqueline ** (H) God's gracious gift — Jacquette, Jacquine, Jacotte

Janine ** (H) God's gracious gift

Jeanne ** (ZHAWN) (H) God's gracious gift — Janique, Johanne, Janine

Jocelin (zhoss-LANH) (H) supplanter — Joceline, Jocelyn

Joelle (H) Jehovah is God — Joelliane

Jordane (H) descendant

Josee (zho-SAY) (H) God will add

Joséphine (zho-seh-FEEN) (H) God will add — Fifi, Fifine

Josette pet — Josephine

Judith (H) praised

Julie (L) youthful — Julienne, Juliette, Julitte

Justine (L) just

Kristell var. Christine (Gr) Christian

Laure* (L) crown of laurels — Laura*, Laurence, Laurentine, Laurelle

Léa (H) weary

Léonore (Gr) light

Lise (LEEZ) dim. Elizabeth (H) consecrated to God — Lisette

Lorraine from Lorraine in France

Louise (OGer) famous warrior woman

Louisiane (OGer) famous warrior woman — Louise, Heloise, Eloise

Lucie (L) bringer of light — Lucienne, Lucille, Luce

Lydie (Gr) ancient province in Asia Minor

Madeline (H) woman from Magdala — Madeleine, Mado

Mäite dim. Marie-Thérèse

Manon (ma-NONH) (H) bitter

Marcelle (L) warlike

Margaux (mahr-GO) (Gr) a pearl — Margo, Marguerite, Margarita

Marguerite (Gr) a pearl

Marie ** (H) bitter (Number one name in France, 1986)

Marie-Madeleine comb. of Marie and Madeleine (saint name)

Mariette (H) bitter

Marine* (L) sea maid

Marion* (H) bitter

Marjolaine flower name

Marthe (MAHRT) (H) bitter

Martine (L) warlike — Marciane, Marcelle, Marcie, Marcelline

Mathena comb. of Marie and Thérèse

Mathilde* (Gr) brave in battle

Maude (Teut) heroine

Melanie (Gr) black

Melodie melody

Michelle (H) who is like God? — Micheline, Michaela

Mignon (me-NYONH) darling

Mimi (Teut) resolute, strong

Mireille (mee-REHY) miraculous

Monique** (L) advisor

Morgance (Celt) sea dweller — Morgane

Nadége (Slavic) hope

Nadette dim. Bernadette (OGer) courage of a bear — Nadine

Natacha (Gr) born at Christmas

Nathalie** born at Christmas — Natalene, Nowlle, Natalie

Nicole (Gr) victory of the people — Nicoletta

Nicolette (L) victory of the people — Nicole, Nichelle

Nina (H) grace

Ninon (nee-NONH) (H) grace

Odile (Ger) rich — Odelina, Odiane, Odette

Olga (Russian) holy

Olympe (Gr) Olympian

Ophelie (Gr) help, wisdom

Orane rising

Orlena gold — Orlene

Pascale Easter — Pascaline

Patricia (L) noble, well-born — Patriciane

Pauline* (L) little — Paule, Paulette

Perrine (Gr) stone — Pierrette, Petronelle

Prisca (L) the ancient

Raquel (H) innocence of a lamb

Rébecca (H) servant of God, binding

Régine (L) queen — Reine (RAYN)

Reneé (L) reborn — Renelle

Rollande (Teut) fame of the land — Rolande

Rosalie comb. Rose and Lily

Rose (L) rose — Rosine, Rosette

Rose-Marie comb. Rose and Mary

Roseline (L) rose — Rosine

Sabine (L) Sabine (ancient tribe of central Italy)

Salina (L) solemn

Sandrine (Gr) defender of mankind

Sarah* (H) princess

Sébastienne (Gr) venerable

Sidonie (OFr) a follower of St. Denis — Sidaine, Sidoine

Simone (H) God is heard

Solange solemn, dignified — Silana, Solaine

Sophie (Gr) wisdom

Stephanie (Gr) crown

Suzanne (H) lily — Susanne

Sylvie** (L) from the forest — Sylvianne, Sylvette, Silvia, Silvaine

Tatiana (Russian) fairy queen

Thérèse (tehr-ESS) (Gr) harvester — Theresa, Teressa

Tienette (Gr) crowned with laurel (from Stephanie)

Tiphanie (Gr) divine manifestation

Valerie (L) strong

Véronique (Gr) true image

Victoire (L) victorious

Violette (L) violet — Violaine, Viole, Violet

Virginie (veer-zhee-NEE) (L) pure — Virgine, Virge

Vivien (L) lively — Vivienne, Viviane

Xavière (zah-vee-EHR) (Basque) owner of the new house

Yolande (OFr) violet

Yseult (OGer) ice rule

Yvette (OFr) archer

Yvonne (OFr) archer — Yveline, Ivonne

Zoé (Gr) life — Zoelie, Zoë, Zoelle

---

* Predicted to be popular in the 1990s
** Currently in top ten

FRENCH MALE NAMES

Abel (H) breath

Adrian* (L) of the Adriatic

Alain** (uh-LANH) (Celt) handsome, cheerful

Alexandre (Gr) defender of mankind

Alfred (OE) wise counselor

Ambroise (am-BRWAHZ) (Gr) immortal, divine

André** (Gr) manly

Anselme (Teut) divine helmet — Anthelme

Antoine (L) inestimable

Armand (Teut) army man

Arnaud (OGer) eagle, power — Arnot, Arnoll, Arnott, Arnet, Arnald

Arsène (Gr) strong

Artur (Celt) noble, bear man

Audric old and wise ruler — Aldrick, Aldrich

Augustin (L) venerable — August

Aurélien* (L) gold

Avent Advent

Baptiste (Gr) baptizer

Barnabé (H) son of prophecy

Barthelemy (Aramaic) ploughman

Basile (Gr) kingly

Bellamy beautiful friend — Bell

Benjamin (H) son of the right hand

Benôit (behn-WAH) (L) blessed — Bénédicte

Bernard** (behr-NAHR) (OGer) courage of a bear — Bernon, Bernot, Barnard

Bertrand (behr-TRANH) brilliant

Blaise (L) stammerer — Blaize

Brice (A.S.) son of a nobleman

Bruce from the brush wood, thicket — Bruis

Bruno (Ger) brown

Charles (SHAHRL) (OFr) full-grown, manly

Christian (krees-TYANH) (Gr) Christian

Christophe (Gr) Christbearer — Christobal

Claude (L) lame — Claudian, Claus

Clément* (L) merciful

Conrad (OGer) honest counselor — Conradin

Constant (L) constant — Constantin

Courtney from the court — Curt, Court

Curtis courteous — Curtice

Cyprien (L) from the island of Cyprus

Cyril (Gr) lordly one — Cy, Cyrillus

Damien (Gr) taming

Daniel** (dan-YEHL) (H) God is my judge

David (H) beloved — Davin, Dani, Davey

Denis (Gr) god of wine

Didier (di-DYEH) desired, beloved

Dimitri (Gr) from Demeter, goddess of the harvest

Donald (Celt) proud chief

Donatien (do-nah-TYENH) gift

Edmond (OE) prosperous protector — Edmont

Édouard (OE) wealthy guardian

Emile (Teut) energetic

Eric (ONorse) ever powerful

Ernest (OGer) serious

Etiénne* (Gr) crowned with laurels

Eugène (Gr) noble

Evelyn (H) life

Fabrice (fah-BREES) (L) craftsman

Félix (L) fortunate, or lucky

Fernand (Teut) adventurous, brave — Ferdinand

Florentin (L) flowering — Florent

Florian* (flo-RYEHNH) (L) flowering

Fortuné (for-too-NEH) lucky

Francois (fran-SWAH) (Teut) free — Franchot

Frédéric (Teut) peaceful ruler

Gaétan from Gaete in central Italy

Gautier (go-TYEH) (Teut) powerful ruler — Gauthier

Geoffroy* (OFr) heavenly peace — Jeoffroi

Geórges (ZHORZH) (Gr) farmer — Georget, George

Gérald (Teut) mighty with the spear — Geraud, Giraud

Germain from Germany

Ghislain (OGer) sweet pledge

Gilbert (zheel-BEHR) (OE) trusted — Guilbert

Gildas (OE) gilded

Gilles (Gr) shield-bearer

Grégoire (Gr) vigilant — Grégorie, Grégor

Guillaume (gee-YOM) (Teut) resolute soldier

Gustave (Teut) staff of the gods

Guy (OFr) guide

Harold (ONorse) war chief

Henri (awnh-REE) (Teut) ruler of an estate

Herbert (ehr-BEHR) (Teut) bright warrior

Hervé (Teut) army warrior

Hubert (oo-BEHR) (Teut) bright mind

Hugues (Teut) intelligence, spirit

Hyacinthe (Gr) hyacinth

Isaak (H) laughter

Isidore (Gr) a gift of ideas

Jaques** (ZHAHK) (H) supplanter — Jacot, Coco (nicknames)

Jay blue jay — Jaye

Jean** (ZHAHNH) (H) God's gracious gift — Jeannot

Jean-Baptiste* John the Baptist

Jérémie (zhehr-eh-MEE) (H) God will uplift

Jérôme (L) holy name

Joël (H) Jehovah is God

Joseph (H) God will add

Jules nickname for Julius (L) youthful

Julien (joo-LYENH) (L) youthful

Justin (L) just — Juste

Kévin* (keh-VANH) (Celt) kind

Landry (lanh-DREE) (A.S.) ruler

Laurent (L) crowned with laurel

Léo (L) lion — Léonce, Léocadie

Léon (L) lion — Léonard

Louis (OGer) renowned warrior

Lowell little wolf — Lovell, Lowe

Luc (L) light

Luce (L) bringer of light — Lucius, Lucien

Lyle from the island — Lisle

Marc (L) warlike — Martin, Marcel, Martinien, Marceau, Marcellin

Marius (L) warlike — Martial

Marlon little falcon — Marlin

Marshal steward — Marsh, Marshal

Matthieu (maht-YEU) (H) gift of God — Matthias, Matthew

Maurice (L) Moorish

Maxime* (L) greatest

Michel** (top name, 1986) (mee-SHEHL) (H) who is like God? — Michon, Machau

Narcisse (Gr) daffodil

Neville from the new town

Nicolas (Gr) victory of the people — Nicole, Colas

Noel born at Christmas — Natale

Norbert (ONorse) brilliant hero

Octavien (L) eighth

Olivier (L) olive tree

Parfait (pahr-FAY) perfect

Pascal Easter — Pascual

Patrice (pah-TREES) (L) noble

Paulin (pow-LANH) (L) little — Paul

Philippe** (fee-LEEP) (Gr) lover of horses

Pierre*** (Gr) stone

Prosper (L) fortunate

Quentin (kanh-TANH) (L) fifth

Raoul (Teut) strong, wise counsel

Raymond (Teut) mighty protector

Remi from Reims, France

Renaud (ruh-NOH) (Teut) wise power

René** (reh-NAY) (L) reborn

Richard (ree-SHAHR) (OGer) powerful ruler

Robert (ro-BEHR) (Teut) of shining fame — Robers, Robin, Robinet

Rodrigue (Teut) famous warrior

Roland (Teut) fame of the land

Romain (ro-MANH) Roman

Rudolph (Teut) famous wolf

Samuel (H) God hears

Saül (H) longed for

Sébastien (Gr) venerable, revered

Serge (L) the attendant

Séverin (L) severe

Silvain (L) forest — Silvie, Silvestre

Simon (H) God is heard

Stanislas (Slavic) stand of glory

Sylvestre (L) from the woods

Tanguy (Celt) warrior

Théodore (Gr) gift of God

Théophile (Gr) divinely loved

Thibault* people's prince

Thierry (TEE-i-ree) (Teut) people's ruler

Thomas (H) twin

Ulrich (OGer) ruler of all

Urbain (oor-BANH) (L) of the city

Valentin (va-lenh-TANH) (L) strong, brave

Victor (L) conqueror — Victorin, Victorien

Vincent (vanh-SAHNH) (L) conqueror — Vincien (vanh-SYEHNH)

Yves (EEV) (OFr) little archer

---

* Predicted to be popular in the 1990s
** Currently in top ten

GERMANY

Since 1820 Germans have constituted more of the immigrants to America than any other ethnic group; a total of nearly seven million have arrived since then. The number of Americans with German ancestry is estimated at twenty to thirty-three million.

The peak decade for German immigration was between 1881 and 1890 when nearly one and a half million arrived. In 1870 and 1890 German immigrants made up four percent of the entire U.S. population.

The first German settlement began in 1683 when thirteen Quaker and Mennonite families from the Rhine valley, inspired by speeches of William Penn, founded Germantown, Pennsylvania.

In 1709 about 13,000 people from southwestern Germany immigrated to England to escape heavy taxation, overpopulation, and devastation from a recent war. Later, about 3,000 of them immigrated to the U.S. Their success inspired other groups to immigrate, often in search of religious freedom. Their most common destination was Philadelphia. Benjamin Franklin estimated one-third of the population of Pennsylvania was German. Maryland, New Jersey, and New York also received large numbers of immigrants. Altogether, 65,000 to 75,000 or more German immigrants probably arrived before the American Revolution.

In addition to the Eastern settlements there was also considerable westward migration, even in the 18th century. By 1721 there were three small German villages on the Mississippi River north of New Orleans.

Because of warfare on both the European and American continents, German immigration, for almost fifty years after the Revolution, was very small. Mass immigration started again in 1816-17 when disastrous harvests and economic turmoil after the Napoleonic wars sent thousands of Germans, mostly from the southwest part of the country, out of their homeland.

Religious freedom was the lure for several groups from Germany in the first half of the 19th century. An unsuccessful democratic revolution in 1848 and the resulting disillusionment and uncertainty were perhaps the catalysts that sent nearly 750,000 Germans to America in the next six years.

However, the greatest impetus to immigration in the 19th century were social conditions that gradually made it harder to maintain familiar lifestyles. These new conditions included increasing rural population, creeping industrialization which displaced many craftsmen, and rural reform that raised the number of landless rural workers.

German immigrants were often craftsmen − bakers, weavers, brewers, or carpenters. Many were also farmers, and in communities where high German populations reinforced traditional German values of thrift, hard work, and persistence, they stayed and prospered.

German immigration dropped sharply in the 1890's and continued to decline until the 1920's brought a surge of industrial workers in search of high wages. Because Germany had had the highest number of foreign-born citizens in the U.S. in 1890 (the year chosen to set immigration quotas for 1924) there was far less restriction on German immigration than on other countries. The German quota was 26,000 per year.

The last sizable immigration occurred in the 1950's when relatives of American servicemen and East German refugees swelled the numbers to nearly 480,000 in the decade.

Although Teutonic and Old German names have been the source for hundreds of names used in English-speaking and other parts of the world, the most popular names in Germany now include primarily names of French origin. The top ten names in Germany have been indicated in the name list, with other popular names noted as well.

When the Nazis controlled Germany, it was illegal to give a child a name that was not on an approved name list. Jewish people were compelled to give their children "Jewish-sounding" first names and surnames. Nicknames were forbidden except for a few that had developed into independent names, such as Klaus and Hans. If a child was given two names the parents had to designate which was to be used. Fortunately, these restrictions are no longer in effect!

Pronunciation

a = "ah" as in ball, but pro-
    nounced short (not
    drawn out)

e = "eh" as in late or "e" as in set

i, ie = "ee" as in keep

short i = "i" as in sit

o, oo = "oh" as in hope

a = "ai" as in air, or "e" as in set

o = "eh" as in late, but pro-
    nounced short

u = "ee" as in keep, but pro-
    nounced with rounded lips

ei, ai = "i" as in side

au = "ow" as in cow

au, eu = "oy" as in toy

ch = "kh" a guttural sound pro-
    nounced back in the throat

d = "d" as in door, or if final, "t"
    as in mat

j = "y" as in yes

qu = "kv"

s = "z" as in zoo before a vowel,
    "ss" as in less if final

sch = "sh" as in shoe

sp = "shp" if at beginning of
    word, or "sp" otherwise

st = "sht" if at beginning of
    word, or "st" otherwise

v = "f" as in father, usually, or
    "v" as in vase

w = "v" as in vest

z = "ts" as in cats

GERMAN FEMALE NAMES

Ada prosperous, happy

Adela (OGer) noble, of good cheer

Adelheid noble, kind – Adela, Adelle, Della, Edeline, Heidi

Agathe (Gr) good – Agapet

Agnes (Gr) gentle, pure

Alberta (OGer) noble, bright

Alexandra (Gr) defender of mankind

Alice (OGer) noble, kind

Alida (OGer) antiquity – Aleda, Alyda, Alda

Aloysia (OGer) famous warrior woman – Aloisia

Amalie (Teut) industrious – Amalia, Amelie

Amanda (L) beloved

Amara immortal, steadfast – Mara, Ararinda

Andrea* fem. Andrew (Gr) manly – Andreas

Angelika* (Fr) angel – Angela

Anna (H) grace – Anita, Anke, Annette

Anneliese (H) grace

Annemarie comb. Anne and Marie

Antje* (AHNT-yeh) (H) grace

Antonie (L) inestimable

Ariane (Welsh) silvery

Asta (Gr) star

Astrid (ONorse) divine strength

Barbara (L) the stranger – Babette, Barbel

Bathilda heroine, bold

Beatrice (L) she blesses, or makes happy – Beate, Beatrix

Benedikta (L) blessed

Berta (OGer) bright, glorious – Bertha, Bertina

Betti (H) consecrated to God – Betty, Bettina

Blanka (L) white – Bianca

Brita (Celt) strength – Brigitte, Birgit

Brunhilde (OGer) heroine

Caecilia (L) blind – Cecilie, Cacilie, Cilly

Carmen (H) garden

Carola (Fr) song of joy

Charlotte (Fr) petite and feminine

Christiana (Gr) Christian – Christie, Christa, Kristen, Krista, Kristina

Christiane** (krees-tee-AHN-e) (Gr) Christian – Christel

Clara (L) bright, clear – Klare

Claudia* (L) lame – Claudette*, Klaudia

Clementine (L) gentle, merciful

Clotilda fem. Clovis: King of the Francs

Constanze (L) constant – Stanzi

Cora (Gr) maiden

Dagmar (Teut) Dane's joy

Daniela* (H) God is my judge

Didrika (Ger) people's rule

Domino* (DO-mee-no) (L) Lord (newest popular name in Germany, 1986)

Dorothea (do-ro-TEH-ah) (L) gift of God – Dörte, Dörthe, Dora

Edeline (OGer) noble, of good cheer – Edda

Edith (Teut) rich gift

Eleonore (Gr) light – Lenore, Lore, Lora, Nora, Ellen

Elga (Russ) holy – Olga, Helga, Elgiva

Elisabeth (H) consecrated to God – Elise, Else, Ella, Liese, Lise, Betti, Ilse

Elke (Teut) industrious

Elsbeth (H) consecrated to God

Else (OGer) noble – Elsie, Elsa, Ilse, Ilyse, Elyse

Emelie (Teut) industrious

Emma (OGer) universal – Erma, Irma

Erika (ONorse) ever powerful

Erna (Teut) earnest – Ernestine

Esther (H) star

Eugenie (Gr) well-born

Eva (H) life – Eveline, Evelyn

Fania (L) free – Fanny

Farica (Teut) peaceful rule

Felise (L) fortunate, or lucky

Flora (L) flower – Florentine

Franziska** (frahn-SEES-kah) (Teut) free – Franze, Zissi, Ziska, Fran

Friederike (Teut) peaceful ruler – Frieda, Fritzi, Rike, Friedegard

Gabriele (H) God is my strength

Galiena (gah-lee-EH-nah) (OGer) lofty

Georgine (Gr) farmer

Geraldine (Teut) powerful soldier

Gerda (GEHR-dah) guarded, protected – Gerde

Gertraud (Teut) fighter – Gertrude, Gerta, Trude, Trudy

Gisele (Teut) pledge – Gisela, Gisa

Gitta from Brigitte (Celt) strength

Gretchen (Gr) a pearl – Gretel, Gretal

Grete (Gr) a pearl

Gudrun (GOO-druhn) divine wisdom – Gudruna

Hannele (H) grace – Hanna

Hannelore comb. of Hannah (Anne) and Lore

Hedwig (HEHD-vehg) (Teut) refuge in battle — Hadwig, Hedda, Hedy

Heidi* (OGer) noble, kind — Heida, Hilde, (from Adelheid)

Helene (heh-LEHN-uh) (Gr) light — Ellen, Ilona

Helga (Russian) holy

Henrika (Gr) mistress of the home — Rike

Herta earth — Hertha

Hida warrior — Gilda, Heidi, Hilde

Hildegarde (Teut) protection in battle — Hilde

Ida (EE-dah) (OGer) she who is active — Idna, Idaia, Idalie, Adeline

Idette (ee-DET-tuh) (OGer) industrious

Ilse (H) God's oath

Inga (Teut) daughter — Inge, Inger, Ingeborg

Ingrid (Teut) hero's daughter

Irene (ee-REH-nah) (Gr) peace

Irma (OGer) war god — Irmine, Erma, Irmgard

Isa (EE-sah) (Teut) (H) consecrated to God — Isabella

Isolde (OGer) ice rule

Itta work

Jennifer** (Celt) white wave — Jenny

Jette (YEHT-tuh) from Henriette (Teut) mistress of the home

Johanna (yo-HAH-nah) (H) gracious — Johanne

Judith (H) praised — Jutta

Julia* (L) youthful — Julie, Juliane, Liane

Käethe (KAH-tuh) (Gr) pure — Käte

Kamilla (L) ceremonial attendant

Karin (Gr) pure — Karen

Karlotta (Fr) petite and feminine

Karola fem. Karl — Karolina, Karla

Karoline (kahr-o-LEE-nuh) fem. Karl — Lina, Line

Katharina** (kah-tah-REE-nah) (Gr) pure (most popular name in Germany, 1986)

Katja* (KAHT-ya) (Gr) pure

Kirsten (L) Christian

Konstanze (L) constant — Stanzi, Constanze

Laura (L) crown of laurels — Lore

Liesbeth (H) consecrated to God — Lisbeth, Liesa, Lisa, Lisette, Lilli

Lieselotte comb. Elisabeth and Charlotte — Liselotte, Lilo

Lilian (L) pure as a lily

Loni from Apollonia (Gr) Apollo

Lucie (L) bringer of light — Lucia

Luise (loo-EE-suh) (OGer) renowned warrior — Louise

Lydia (Gr) ancient province in Asia Minor

Magda (MAHG-dah) (H) woman of Magdala — Magdalena

Margarete (mahr-gahr-EHT-uh) (Gr) a pearl — Marga, Margit, Margot, Meret, Gesche

Marie (H) bitter — Maria, Maike, Maja, Maren, Mieze, Mizi, Mia

Mariel (H) bitter — Marike

Marlis comb. of Maria and Elisabeth

Martha (MAHR-tah) (H) bitter

Martina (L) warlike

Matilde (Teut) brave in battle — Mattie, Tilda, Maud

Maude (Teut) heroine

Melanie (Gr) black

Meta (Gr) pearl

Michelle* (H) who is like God?

Mina dim. Wilhelmina

Minna (Teut) resolute, strong — Minnette, Minne

Mirjam (MEER-yam) (H) bitter

Mitzi little bitter one (H) — Mieze, Marie

Monika* (L) advisor — Monike

Nadine** (nah-DEEN) (Fr) from Bernadine (OGer) courage of a bear

Nastasia* (Gr) resurrection

Nicole (Gr) victory of the people

Odile (o-DEEL) rich — Odila, Oda

Olga (Russian) holy

Otthild (o-TEELD) (OGer) lucky heroine — Ottila

Patricia* (L) noble

Paula (pah-OO-lah) (L) little — Paulina, Pauline

Petra* (Gr) stone

Ragnild (rah-NYILD) (Teut) wise power — Reinheld, Renilde, Renilda

Rebekka* (H) binding, servant of God

Renate (L) reborn — Renata

Rita (Gr) a pearl

Rosalinde (L) rose — Rosabel, Rosalie, Rosanne, Rosamunde

Ruth (H) friend, beauty

Sabine (L) Sabine woman (ancient tribe of central Italy) — Bina, Binchen

Sandra (Gr) defender of mankind

Sara (SAH-rah) (H) princess

Senta (OGer) assistant

Sidonie (OFr) a follower of St. Denis

Sigrid (ONorse) victorious counselor — Siegrid, Siegfrida, Sigritt

Silke from Cecilia (L) blind

Silvia (L) forest — Sylvia

Sophie** (Gr) wisdom — Sophia, Sofie

Stefanie** (Gr) crown

Sunhild (Teut) swan girl

Susanna (H) lily — Susanne

Sybilla (Gr) prophetess — Billa

Tamara* (H) palm tree — Thamar

Tatiana (Russian) fairy queen — Tanja

Thekla (Gr) divine fame

Therese (tehr-EHS) (Gr) harvester — Tessi, Resi

Tilda (Teut) heroine

Toni from Antonie (L) inestimable

Ulla will

Ulrike (OGer) ruler of all — Ulrica, Ulka, Rica, Uli

Ursula (L) little bear — Ulla, Ursel

Valerie (L) strong — Walli

Vera (L) true — Wera

Verena (Teut) protecting friend — Verina

Veronika (L) true image — Beronika, Vroni

Viktoria (L) victorious — Vicky

Virginie (L) pure

Viviane (L) lively

Wanda (OGer) wanderer

Wiebke (VEEB-kuh) the young woman

Wilhelmine fem. Wilhelm (Teut) resolute protector — Elma, Vilma, Helmina

Winifred (Teut) friend of peace — Winfrieda, Winefred, Wina, Winnie

Yvonne (OFr) archer — Yvette

GERMAN MALE NAMES

Adal nobel — Adel

Adam (H) of the red earth

Adelbert noble bear — Adel, Bert

Adrian (L) of the Adriatic

Alexander* (Gr) defender of mankind — Alexis, Alex, Axel

Anson Son of John

Anton (L) inestimable, beyond praise

Archibald nobly or genuinely bold

Aric ruler — Arick

Armin (Teut) soldier

Arndt (OGer) eagle, power

Arnold (OGer) eagle, power — Arnd, Arend, Arno

Artur (Celt) noble, bear man

Aurick protecting ruler

Austin (L) majestic dignity — August

Baldwin bold friend — Balduin

Barrett bearlike

Bartel (Aramaic) ploughman — Bartholomaus

Bastien from Sebastien (Gr) venerable, revered

Benedikte (L) blessed

Berg mountain

Bern bear — Berne

Bernhard (OGer) courage of a bear — Bernd, Berend

Boris (Russ) fight, warrior

Brandeis dweller on a burned clearing

Brendan* a flame — Bren, Brendis

Bruno dark or brown

Christian** (krees-tee-AHN) (Gr) Christian (top name in Germany for ten years)

Christoph (Gr) Christbearer

Claas from Nikolaus (Gr) victory of the people — Claus

Conrad (OGer) honest counselor — Cord, Cort

Daniel** (dah-nee-EHL) (H) God is my judge

David (H) beloved

Dennis (Gr) god of wine

Dieter the people's ruler — Dirk, Derek

Dieterich (Teut) ruler of the people — Dierck, Dietz

Dominik (L) of the Lord

Eberhard boar-strong — Eward, Evrard

Eduard (OE) wealthy guardian

Edwin (OGer) happy friend

Eginhard sword strength — Einhard, Egon, Enno

Ellery (EL-er-ee) dweller by the alder tree

Emery (Teut) industrious ruler — Amery, Emmerich, Emory, Emmo

Emil (Teut) energetic

Erik (ONorse) ever powerful

Ernst (Teut) seriousness, steadfastness

Eugen (Gr) well-born

Fabian (FAH-byan) (L) bean grower

Fedor (Gr) divine gift

Felix (L) fortunate, or lucky

Florian (L) flowering

Folke* (Teut) people's guard — Volker

Franz (Teut) free — Franziskus (frahn-TSEES-kus)

Fredi (Teut) peaceful ruler — Friedel, Fritz, Friedrich

Friederich (Teut) peaceful ruler

Friedhelm (Teut) true peace

Gabriel (H) God is my strength

Garrick (Teut) spear king — Garek

Georg (Gr) farmer

Gerhard (OE) spear-hard — Gerd, Gerrit

Gerlach spear thrower

Gilbert (OE) trusted — Giselbert

Gottfried (Teut) God's peace

Gregor (Gr) vigilant — Grigor

Günther (Teut) battle army

Gustav (Teut) staff of the gods — Gustaf

Guy (Teut) warrior

Hagan (Teut) strong defense

Halden (Teut) half-Dane

Hamlin (Teut) ruler of an estate

Hans (H) God's gracious gift — Hanno

Hartwig (Teut) strong adviser — Hasso

Helmut courageous

Hendrik (Teut) ruler of an estate — Heinrich, Heike, Harro, Hinrich

Heribert (Teut) bright warrior

Hermann (Teut) warrior — Harm, Harms

Horaz (L) timekeeper

Hubert (Teut) bright mind

Hugh (Teut) intelligence, spirit — Hugo

Humfried (Teut) peaceful Hun

Isaak (H) laughter

Jakob (YAH-kob) (H) supplanter

Jan (YAHN) (H) God's gracious gift — Hans

Jens* (YEHNS) (H) God's gracious gift — Jen

Johann (YO-hahn) (H) God's gracious gift — Jan, John, Hanno, Anno

Jörg (YOERG) (Gr) farmer — Jungen, Jeorg, Jürgen

Jörn (Gr) vigilant

Josef (YO-sehf) (H) God will add — Joseph

Julian* (L) youthful

Justus (L) just — Jobst, Jost

Karl (OFr) strong and manly — Kalman

Kaspar (Persian) a treasured secret

Klaus from Nikolaus (Gr) victory of the people — Klaas

Klemens (L) kind, gentle

Konrad (OGer) honest counselor — Conrad, Cord, Konni, Kunz, Kord

Konstantin (L) constant

Krischan (Gr) Christian — Christel

Kurt (OGer) honest counselor — Kuno

Leo (L) the lion

Leonhard (Teut) bold lion

Leopold (Teut) bold for the people — Leo, Leupold, Luitpold, Poldi

Lorenz (L) crowned with laurel

Lothar (LO-thar) famous warrior

Louis (OGer) renowned warrior

Ludwig (OGer) renowned warrior — Lutz

Lukas (L) bringer of light

Magnus (L) large

Manfred (OGer) man of peace

Markos (L) warlike

Markus* (L) warlike one — Martel, Marius

Martin (L) warlike

Mathe (MAH-te) (H) gift from God

Mathias* (mah-TEE-ahss) (H) gift of God — Mathi, Matthaus

Matz (H) gift of God; newly popular in Germany

Mauritz (L) Moorish, dark-skinned — Moritz, Mauritius

Max (L) greatest

Meinhard strong firmness — Meinke, Meino

Meinrad strong counsel

Michael** (mee-KHAH-ehl) (H) who is like God? — Michel

Moritz (L) dark-skinned (Moorish)

Nikolas (Gr) victory of the people — Klaus, Nicolaus, Nicol, Claus, Nilo

Norbert (ONorse) brilliant hero

Norman (OFr) Norseman

Oliver* (L) olive tree

Osker (Celt) warrior — Oskar

Oswald (Teut) divine power — Osvald, Oswaldo

Otto (Teut) prosperous — Odo

Ottokar happy warrior

Patrick** (L) noble

Paul (L) little — Paulin

Paulin (L) little

Paxton (Teut) traveling trader — Paxon

Peter (Gr) stone — Pit, Pitter

Philipp (Gr) lover of horses

Rafe (Teut) house wolf

Raimund (Teut) mighty protector

Rainart strong judgment — Rainhard, Reinhard, Renke

Rainer counsel — Reiner

Raul (Teut) strong, wise counsel — Rudolf, Randolf, Ralph

Richard (OGer) powerful ruler — Rick, Rik, Rich

Robert (Teut) of shining fame — Rupert, Ruprecht, Robar, Rubert

Roch glory — Rochus

Roderick (Teut) famous ruler — Rurik, Rod, Roddy

Roger (Teut) famous warrior — Rudiger, Rotger

Roland (Teut) fame of the land

Rolf (Teut) swift wolf

Roth red-haired

Rudi (Teut) famous wolf

Sander (Gr) defender of mankind (from Alexander)

Sebastian** (Gr) venerable, revered

Severin (L) severe

Siegfried (Teut) conquering peace — Seifred, Sigfrid

Siegmund (Teut) conquering protection

Sigurd (ONorse) victorious guardian

Stannes (Slavic) stand of glory — Stanislaus

Stefan** (STEH-fahn) (Gr) crown — Steffen

Stoffel from Christopher (Gr) Christ-bearer

Sylvester (L) from the woods

Tedor (Gr) divine gift

Theo from Theodor (Gr) divine gift

Theobald (Teut) people's prince — Dietbold

Thoma (H) twin

Thomas (H) twin — Tom

Till from Dieterich (Teut) people's ruler — Tilmann, Timm, Thilo, Til

Tobias** (H) God is good

Toni from Anton (L) inestimable

Torsten (Teut) Thor's rock

Traugott (Teut) God's truth

Ulf (ONorse) wolf

Ullric (OGer) ruler of all — Uli, Ulz

Urban (L) of the city

Uwe (OO-uh) dim. Ullric (Teut) ruler of all — Udo

Valentin (Fr) strong, brave

Varick (Teut) protecting ruler — Warrick

Viktor (L) conqueror — Victor

Vincens (L) conqueror — Vinzenz

Vital (L) living — Vitus, Veit

Volker people's guard

Walden (OE) from the forest valley — Waldo, Waldi, Welti

Wallace (OE) Welshman — Walsh, Wallis

Walther (Teut) powerful warrior — Valter, Walt, Walder, Wat

Warrick (Teut) protecting ruler

Werner (Teut) guard — Warner, Wernhar

Wilfred (Teut) resolute peace

Wilhelm (VEEL-helm) (Teut) resolute protector — Willi, Willy, Wilm

Wilmot (Teut) resolute mood

Winfried (Teut) friend of peace

Wolf (Teut) wolf — Wulf

Wolfgang (Teut) wolf's progress

---

* Currently popular
** In top ten

GHANA

The immigration from Ghana was involuntary, and by American standards, early. Most of the slaves arrived in America between 1741 and 1807, before Congress banned importation of slaves in 1808. (Although another estimated 54,000 were smuggled into the country between 1808 and 1860.) During the peak slave trade period arrivals averaged 5,000 per year.

The total number of slaves brought to the Americas has been variously estimated at ten to twelve million, with perhaps an equal number dying in the process. Only seven percent of the slaves were brought to the United States. Far greater numbers were destined to go to Brazil and the Caribbean.

The development of the sugar cane, cotton, and tobacco trades in the American Southeast created an insatiable demand for labor; particularly for strong workers who could withstand not only heat but tropical disease. The African Negroes were, to their misfortune, relatively resistant to malaria and yellow fever, as well as conspicuous in their skin color (therefore it was easy to spot as runaways).

Approximately one-eighth of the 650,000 Africans brought to America were from various regions of Ghana, known until 1957 as the Gold Coast. Since the early 1970's immigration from Ghana has gradually increased from about 300 each year to about 900.

As with most regions of Africa, Ghana is comprised of several tribes and languages. Among them are the Ewe, Ga, and Twi languages, which are sister languages to Akan. Other forms of Akan are Ashanti and Fante.

The naming traditions are similar among the tribes who speak these dialects. A baby is given two names; the soul's name and the name given by the father. The soul's name comes from the deity associated with the day the child is born and is conferred on the child at the hour of its birth by the birth attendant. Seven days later in a naming ceremony the father gives the baby a name of a distinguished relative in the father's family. The child is taught early on that he or she has a responsibility to bring honor to the names chosen and exhibit the exemplary qualities of the namesake.

Kinship ties are thus knit early for African children, not only to the immediate family, but to the extended family of aunts, uncles, grandparents, etc., and to the larger community as well. Because of the harsh climate and prevalence of disease in West Africa only one in two babies reaches adolescence, and a strong, surviving child is welcomed and loved by all. The naming ceremony is an occasion of celebration in which the entire community takes part.

Although this sense of community, of being part of a "seamless web," made the shattering effect of enslavement doubly harsh on Africans, the Creole population (American-born blacks) flourished after the end of the slave importation, and the mortality rate among American slaves was considerably lower than among Caribbean slaves.

GHANAN FEMALE NAMES

Aba (ah-BAH) (Fante) born on Thursday

Abam (ah-BAHM) (Twi) second child after twins

Abena (ah-beh-NAH) (Fante) born on Tuesday

Abla born on Tuesday

Adwoa (ah-dwo-AH) (Fante) born on Monday

Afafa (ah-FAH-fah) (Ewe) first child of second husband

Afi (ah-FEE) (Ewe) born on Friday

Afryea (ah-FREE-yah) (Ewe) born during good times

Afua (ah-FOO-ah) (Ewe, Ashanti) born on Friday

Akosua (ah-KOO-soo-ah) (Ewe) born on Sunday

Akua (ah-KOO-ah) (Ewe) born on Wednesday

Akwete (ah-KWEH-teh) (Ga) elder of twins

Akwokwo (ah-KWO-kwo) (Ga) younger of twins

Ama (AH-mah) (Ewe) born on Saturday

Antobam (ahn-to-BAHM) (Fante) posthumous child

Baba (BAH-bah) (Fante) born on Thursday

Boahinmaa (bwa-HEEN-mah) (Ewe) one who has left her own community, expatriate

Do (DO) (Ewe) first child after twins

Dofi (DO-fee) (Ewe) second child after twins

Efia (eh-FEE-ah) (Fante) born on Friday

Enyonyam (EN-yo-nam) (Ewe) it is good for me

Kakra (kah-KRAH) (Fante) younger of twins

Kessie (Fante, Ashanti) fat at birth

Kukua (koo-KOO-ah) (Fante) born on Wednesday

Kunto (KOON-to) (Twi) third child

Lumusi (loo-moo-SEE) (Ewe) born face downwards

Mama (mah-MAH) (Fante) born on Saturday

Mawusi (mah-woo-SEE) (Ewe) in the hands of God

Morowa (mo-RO-wah) (Akan) queen

Nanyamka (nah-YAHM-kah) (Ewe) God's gift

Nyankomago (ng'yank-o-MAH-go) (Twi) second child after twins

Ozigbodi (oh-ZE-gbo-dee) (Ewe) patience

Panyin (pahn-YEEN) (Fante) elder of twins

Serwa (sair-WAH) (Ewe) noble woman

Sisi (see-SEE) (Fante) born on Sunday

Tawiah (TAH-wee-ah) (Ga) first child after twins

Thema (TAY-mah) (Akan) queen

Yaa (YAH-ah) (Ewe) born on Thursday

Ye (YEH-eh) (Ewe) elder of twins

GHANAN MALE NAMES

Abeeku (ah-BAY-koo) (Fante) born on Wednesday

Addae (ah-DAH-eh) (Akan) morning sun

Adeben (ah-deh-BEN) (Akan) the twelfth born

Adika (ah-dee-KAH) (Ewe) first child of a second husband

Adofo (ah-DO-fo) (Akan) warrior

Adom (ah-DOM) (Akan) help from God

Adusa (ah-DOO-sah) (Akan) thirteenth born

Afram River Afram

Agyei (ahd-JAY-ee) (Akan) messenger from God

Agyeman (ahd-JAY-man) (Akan) fourteenth born

Agymah (ahd-jee-MAH) (Fante) one who leaves his community, expatriate

Akwetee (ah-KWAY-teh) (Ga) younger of twins

Ametefe (ah-meh-teh-FEH) (Ewe) child born after father's death

Ampah (AHM-pah) (Akan) trust

Anane (ah-NAH-neh) (Akan) the fourth son

Ankoma (ahn-KO-mah) (Akan) last born of parents

Anum (AH-noom) (Akan) fifth born

Ashon (ah-SHON) (Ochi, Ga) seventh-born son

Ata (ah-TAH) (Fante) twin

Atsu (at-SOO) (Ewe) younger of twins

Atu (ah-TOO) (Fante) born on Saturday

Atwotwe (ah-TWO-tweh) (Akan) eighth born

Badu (bah-DOO) (Akan) tenth born

Bobo (bo-BO) (Fante) born on Tuesday

Bodua (bo-DOO-ah) (Akan) an animal's tail

Bour (BO-oor) a rock — Obo, Obour

Coblah (ko-BLAH) (Ewe) born on Tuesday

Coffie (ko-FEE) (Ewe) born on Friday

Commie (KO-mee) (Ewe) born on Saturday

Coujoe (ko-JO) (Ewe) born on Monday

Donkor (don-KOR) (Akan) humble person

Ebo (eh-BO) (Fante) born on Tuesday

Essien (ehs-se-EHN) (Ochi, Ga) sixth-born son

Fenuku (fay-noo-KOO) (Fante) born after term

Fifi (fee-FEE) (Fante) born on Friday

Fram ofram tree

Fynn the River Offin

Gyasi (JAH-see) (Akan) wonderful child

Jojo (jo-JO) (Fante) born on Monday

Kesse (KEH-suh) (Fante, Ashanti) fat at birth

Kodwo (ko-DWOH) (Twi) born on Monday

Kofi (ko-FEE) (Twi) born on Friday

Kojo (ko-JO) (Akan) born on Monday

Kontar (Akan) an only child

Kpodo (kpo-DO) (Ewe) elder of twins

Krobo several rivers and mountains have this name in Ghana

Kufuo (koo-FOO-o) (Fante) father shared birth pangs

Kwabena (KWAH-beh-nah) (Akan) born on Tuesday

Kwakou (kwah-KOO) (Ewe) born on Wednesday

Kwame (KWAH-meh) (Akan) born on Saturday

Kwasi (KWAH-see) (Akan) born on Sunday

Lumo (LOO-mo) (Ewe) born face downwards

Manu (mah-NOO) (Akan) the second born

Mawulawde (mah-woo-lah-weh-DAY) (Ewe) God will provide

Mawuli (MAH-woo-lee) (Ewe) there is a God

Mensah (MEN-sah) (Ewe) third son

Minkah (MEN-kah) (Akan) justice

Msrah ('m-SRAH) (Akan) sixth born

Nkrumah ('n-KROO-mah) (Akan) ninth born

Nsoah ('n-so-AH) (Akan) seventh born

Nyamekye ('nyah-MEH-kee-eh) (Akan) God's gift

Odom oak tree

Oko (o-KOH) (Ga) elder of twins

Oluoch (o-loo-OCH) (Luo) born on a cloudy day

Osei (o-SEH-uh) (Fante) noble

Prah the River Prah

Quaashie (kwah-SHEE) (Ewe) born on Sunday

Sisi (see-SEE) (Fante) born on a Sunday

Sono (Akan) elephant

Tano river Tano

Tse (TSEH) (Ewe) younger of twins

Tuako (twah-KO) (Ga) eleventh born

Twia (TWEE-ah) (Fante) born after twins

Yafeu (yah-FEH-o) (Ibo) bold

Yao (YAH-o) (Ewe) born on Thursday

Yawo (YAH-wo) (Akan) born on Thursday

Yoofi (yo-o-FE) (Akan) born on Friday

Yooku (yo-o-KOO) (Fante) born on Wednesday

Yorkoo (yor-KO-o) (Fante) born on Thursday

GREECE

The first Greek in America is said to have been a man named Theodoros who sailed with the Spaniards in 1528.

Apart from one small unsuccessful colony began in Florida in 1767 with a group of 1,400 Greeks and Italians, there was no large scale Greek immigration until the 1890's, when hundreds of Greeks began arriving each year. They were primarily young men looking for temporary employment who intended to return to their families. Between 1890 and 1920 nearly 370,000 Greeks immigrated, compared to just 13,000 in the prior thirty years.

Immigration was spurred by exorbitant taxes and interest rates (up to seventy and eighty percent), and crop failures. Many farmers had destroyed their olive trees to raise more profitable currants. After the bottom dropped out of that market in the 1890's farmers had to wait years for olive trees to bear marketable fruit.

Very few immigrant Greeks became farmers because it was their intention to make their fortunes and return home as soon as possible. Instead they became laborers and peddlers of fruits, flowers, cigars, vegetables, and candy. Very little cash outlay was required to begin these types of businesses, and a surprising number became successful restaurateurs. A number of Greek islanders immigrated to Florida to fish and dive for sponges.

Only direst poverty among the Greek immigrants stopped the flow of money home. A study by the Greek government in 1906 showed regions that had had greatest emigration became the wealthiest, because of money sent from America. Money was sent to pay debts, provide dowries, pay passage of other family members, or invest in the home neighborhood.

The massive Greek immigration came to a halt in 1924 when the quota was set at 308 Greeks per year. However, between 1946 and 1960 56,000 Greeks were allowed to immigrate as refugees from the enormous civil strife in Greece after World War II. Many of the newer immigrants were skilled workers, shipowners, merchants, teachers, and students rather than peasant farmers.

More than 122,000 Greeks entered the U.S. between 1967 and 1975 to escape the oppressive political climate of a ruthless military dictatorship. Altogether some 600,000 Greeks have immigrated, for primarily economic reasons, although the percentage of political refuges is unusually high. Nearly forty percent of the immigrants arriving between 1890 and 1920 returned to Greece, but most post-War immigrants came to stay. The current rate of immigration is about 4,000 each year.

First- and sometimes second-generation Greek immigrants attempt to maintain the Greek tradition of naming the first-born child after the paternal grandparent of the same sex. Subsequent children are named after grandparents until all four grandparents have been covered, and then an "outside" name may be chosen. The names for many generations have been chosen from the saints most revered by the Greek Orthodox Church, and, with this naming pattern of skipping generations, they continue to be the favorites. Thus, although the Greek language has been a source of hundreds of names that have found their way into use in other countries, very few Greek people bear these names, unless they also happen to be saint names.

The Greek name list below includes, for interest, many of the names from Greek antiquity, but it should be noted that the authentic name for a Greek child is much more likely to be a saint name among the ones listed as most popular.

Pronunciation

a = "ah" as in ball
e = "eh" as in late
i = "ee" as in keep

o = "oh" as in hope
g = "h" as in hope

GREEK FEMALE NAMES

Adara beauty; or variation of Andrianna

Adonia fem. Adonis; beautiful young man loved by Aphrodite (myth.)

Agalia (ah-gah-LEE-ah) brightness, joy

Agathi (ah-YAH-tee) good — (St.)

Akilina (L) eagle (St.)

Aleka from Alexandra (Gr) defender of mankind

Alethea truth — Alethia, Alithea

Anastasia* (ahn-ahs-stah-SEE-uh) resurrection (St.)

Anatola from the East

Andrianna fem. of Andrew (Gr) manly

Angele (ahn-YEHL-e) messenger — Angela

Angeliki (ahn-yehl-ih-KEE) angelic — Angelica

Anna** (H) grace — (St.)

Anthea flowerlike

Antonia (ahn-ton-EE-uh) (L) inestimable

Arete (ah-RAY-teh) graceful, lovely

Aretha nymph, orchid — Arethusa, Oretha

Ariadne very holy one

Artemisia* perfect

Aspasia* (ahs-pah-SEE-uh) lily — Asphodel

Asta star — Astra

Athanasia immortal

Athena* goddess of wisdom

Baptista baptizer

Berdine bright maiden

Calandra lark

Calantha beautiful blossom

Calida most beautiful — Calli, Calla, Callista

Calligenia (kah-lee-hehn-EE-ah) daughter of beauty

Calypso sea nymph

Candace glittering, glowing white — Candice, Candis, Candie

Cassandra prophetess — Cass, Cassie

Cassia champion

Celena daughter of a mythological figure — Selena

Charis (KAHR-is) love — Charissa

Chloe blossoming

Chloris pale

Christina (Gr) Christian (St.)

Cleopatra glory of the father

Clio celebrate

Cloris goddess of flowers

Cosima order, universe

Cyma flourish — Syma

Cynthia name for Artemis, goddess of the moon

Damara gentle girl — Damaris, Maris, Mara, Mari

Damia godess of forces of nature

Delia goddess of the moon

Delphine flower name

Dionne daughter of heaven and earth — Dione, Dionis, Diona

Dominica (L) of the Lord (St.)

Dora* gift (St. Theodora)

Echo sound

Elaine* light

Electra bright, amber hair

Elefteria* freedom

Elena* light — Ellena, Eliae

Eleni** (eh-LEH-nee) light or torch — Elenitsa, Nitsa

Elpida (ehl-PEE-thuh) hope

Erianthe sweet as many flowers

Eudosia esteemed (St.) — Eurocia, Eudokia

Euphemia* (yoo-fehm-EE-ah) well-known (St.)

Eurydice mythological figure

Eva* (H) life

Evadne mythological figure — Ariadne

Evangelia (eh-vahn-yeh-LEE-ah) one who brings good news — Lia, Litsa, Angel

Evangeline (eh-vahn-yeh-LEE-neh) brings good news

Evania (eh-vahn-EE-ah) tranquil

Evanthe flower

Evgenia* (ehv-hehn-EE-ah) well-born, noble (St.)

Fedora divine gift

Filia* friendship

Fotina (Teut) free

Galatea white

Georgia* (yor-HEE-ah) (Gr) farmer

Gryta a pearl

Hedia pleasing — Hedyla

Helena** light — (St.)

Helia sun

Hera (heh-RAH) goddess Juno, of womanhood and maternity

Hermione daughter of Venus and Mars (St.)

Hesper evening star

Ianthe violet-colored flower

Ilithya goddess of women in labor

Io daughter of a river god in Greek mythology

Ioanna* (YO-ah-nah) (H) gracious

Iona purple jewel — Ione, Ionia, Ioessa

Iphigenia (if-ih-hehn-EE-ah) Greek mythological figure

Irene* (ee-REHN-uh) peace (St.)

Isaura soft air — Aura, Isaure

Ismini* sister of Antigone

Jocasta mythological figure

Junia (L) June (St.)

Justina (L) just (St.)

Kairos goddess born last to Jupiter

Kalliope* (kahl-ee-O-pee) beautiful voice (St.) — Callia

Kalonice beauty's victory

Kalyca (kah-LEE-kah) rosebud — Kaly, Kali, Kalika

Katherine* pure — Catherine (St.), Katy

Kolina pure

Kora maiden; daughter of Jupiter and Venus

Koren maiden

Kynthia moon

Lalage talkative

Lana (Gr) light

Leda mythological figure

Lelia fair speech

Lena* light

Lia one who brings good news — Evangelia

Ligia silver voice

Lilika (L) lily flower

Lucia (L) bringer of light (St.)

Lycoris twilight

Maria* (H) bitter (St.) — Mary

Marianne (H) comb. Mary and Anne (St.)

Marina (L) sea maid (St.)

Martha* (H) bitter (St.)

Medea part goddess, part sorceress

Melania black (St.)

Melantha dark flower

Melina (L) canary-yellow color

Metea gentle

Monica (L) advisor (St.) (rare)

Nani (H) grace — Noula, Anna

Nerissa of the sea

Nike victory

Niki* pet form of Nikoleta (Gr) victory of the people — Nikolia

Niobe fern

Nitsa* dim. of Irene: peace

Nysa goal — Nyssa

Odele melody

Pallas name for Athene

Panagiota* (pah-nah-YO-tah) All Holy

Pandora gifted

Panthea of all the gods

Parthenie maidenly

Paula (L) little (St.)

Pelagia sea dweller (St.)

Persephone goddess of spring

Petrina a stone

Phaedra* mythological figure

Philothea lover of God (St.)

Rena (REH-nah) peace — Eirene, Ereni, Eirni, Nitsa

Resi (REH-see) from Tresa (Gr) harvester

Rhea mother of the gods, in Greek mythology; from the earth

Rhoda rose

Ritsa pet form of Alexandra (Gr) defender of mankind

Salome (H) peaceful (St.)

Selena moon

Sibyl the prophetess

Sofi wisdom — Sofia, Sophron, Sophie

Sofronia wise

Sophia* wisdom (St.) — Sophie

Stacie dim. of Anastasia

Stefania* (steh-fah-NEE-ah) crown

Tassos harvester

Tatiana* (Russian) fairy queen (St.)

Teresa harvester

Tessa fourth

Thea goddess

Thekla divine fame (St.) — Thecla, Tecla

Theodora* gift of God (St.)

Theodosia* (teh-o-do-SEE-ah) gift of God (St.)

Theophania divine manifestation

Theophilia divinely loved

Thetis mythological figure

Timothea (tee-mo-TEH-ah) honoring God

Vanessa butterfly

Varvara* (vahr-VAHR-uh) the stranger (St.)

Voska (L) the stranger

Xenia hospitality (St.)

Zena (ZAY-nah) hospitable — Polyxena, Zenia

Zephyr west wind

Zoe* life

---

* Popular
** Very popular

GREEK MALE NAMES

Achillios name of a river — (St.)

Agapios (ah-YAH-pyos) good (St.) — Agapetos

Agler (AHG-lair) gleaming

Alekos helper and defender of mankind

Alexander* defender of mankind (St.)

Alexios defender of mankind (St.)

Altair a star in constellation Lyra

Anatolios from the East (St.)

Andonios (L) inestimable, manly — Andonis, Tonis, Antonios

Andreas strong and manly — Evagelos

Andrew* (Gr) manly (St.)

Angelo (AN-juh-lo) angel or saintly — Ange, Angel

Anthony* (L) inestimable (St.)

Apostolos* apostle (St.)

Appollo manly beauty — Apolo, Polo

Argus watchful or vigilant

Aristeides son of the best

Aristokles the best (St.)

Arri seeking the best results — Aristotelis, Telis

Artemas safe and sound — Arty

Athanasios* immortality (St.) — Thanasis, Thanos

Augustine (L) venerable (St.)

Avel breath; mortality of man

Baltsaros Balthazar

Baruch doer of good

Basil** kingly — Vasilios (St.)

Carolos (OFr) strong and manly

Christian (Gr) Christian — Kristian, Cretien, Chris, Christiano, Kit, Kris

Christopher Christ-bearer (St.) — Christophoros

Christos* Christ (St.) — Khristos

Claudios (L) lame (St.)

Clement (L) merciful (St.)

Cletus summoned

Constantine* (L) constant — (St.) — Dean, Constantios

Cornelius (L) horn (St.)

Cosmo well-ordered — Cosimo, Cosme, Cos

Cyprian (L) from the island of Cyprus (St.)

Cyril lord (St.)

Cyrus sun — Cy, Russ, Ciro

Damaskenos from Damaskos (St.) — Damaskinos

Damian taming (St.) — Damon, Damae

David (H) beloved

Demetrios* goddess of the harvest (St.) — Demetri, Demetrius, Dimetre

Denys god of wine

Dhimitrios goddess of the harvest — Mitsos, Mitros

Dinos firm and constant — Costa, Kastas, Gus, Konstandinos, Kostas, Kostis

Dion (DEE-on) divine

Dionysios god of wine (St.)

Eleutherios* freedom (St.) — Eleftherios

Elias (H) Jehovah is God — Elijah (St.)

Emmanuel* a title of Christ (H) God is with us (St.)

Eneas (eh-NEH-us) praised one — Aeneas

Erasmus (er-AS-mus) lovable

Eugen (yoo-HEHN) noble — Eugenios

Eusebius pious (St.)

Felix (L) fortunate, or lucky (St.)

Feodor (Gr) gift of God

Flavian (L) blond, yellow — (St.)

George** farmer (St.) — Georgios, Gordios

Gregory vigilant (St.) — Gregorios, Gregor

Gus nickname for Constantinos

Hali (HAH-lee) sea

Haralambos* meaning unknown (St.)

Hercules glorious gift — Herakles

Hesperos evening star (St.)

Hieremias (H) God will uplift

Hieronymos (L) sacred name

Homeros pledge

Iakovos (H) supplanter — James (St.)

Ignatios (L) fiery

Ilarion (L) cheerful (St.) — Hilarion

Illias (e-LEE-as) (H) Jehovah is my God — Elias, Elijah

Ioannes (H) God's gracious gift — Giannes, Jannes, Nannos, Yanni, John

Ioannikios (yahn-ee-KEE-os) (H) God's gracious gift (St.)

Iorgos (Gr) farmer

Isaakios (H) laughter (St.) — Isaak

Isidore a gift of ideas (St.) — Isadorios

Jason healer (St.)

Jeremiah (H) God will uplift (St.)

Joacheim (H) God will establish (St.)

John** (H) God's gracious gift (St.)

Joseph (H) God will add (St.)

Justin (L) just (St.)

Karsten anointed

Kiril lordly one — Cyril, Kyrillos

Klemenis (L) kind, gentle — Clement

Korudon (ko-ROO-don) helmeted one

Kostas nickname for Constantinos (L) firm and constant

Kristo (KREES-to) nickname for Khristos: "Christ-bearer"

Kyros (KIH-ros) master (St.)

Laurentios (L) crowned with laurel (St.)

Leontios (L) like a lion (St.) — Leander, Leandros, Leo

Loukas (L) bringer of light — Luke

Lucian (L) light (St.) — Lukianos

Luke a person from Lucania — Lucais, Lukas, Lucas

Lysander liberator — Sander

Makarios happy, blessed

Makis (H) who is like God? Mahail, Mikhail, Mikhalis, Mikhos, Maichail

Marinos (L) warlike one — Markos, Martinos

Mark (L) warlike (St.)

Martin (L) warlike (St.)

Matthias (H) gift of God (St.) — Matthew

Maximos (L) greatest

Meletios unknown meaning (St.)

Michael* (H) who is like God? (Archangel) (St.)

Milos (Slav) pleasant (St.)

Mimis (MEE-mees) from Dhimitrios, goddess of harvest

Moris (L) son of the black one

Moses (H) saved from the water — Moyses

Nectarios* a recent saint (St.)

Nestor (Gr) traveler, wisdom (St.)

Nicholas** victory of the people (St.)

Nicodemus conqueror of the people

Nikita victory of the people (St.)

Nikolos (nee-KO-los) victorious army — Nicholas, Nikolaos, Nikos

Nilos dim. of Nikolos (Gr) victory of the people (St.)

Orestes mountain man — Oreste

Orion son of fire

Panagiotis* (pah-nah-HYO-tis) All Holy

Panteleimon All Merciful (St.)

Parthenios Virgin (St.)

Paul (L) little (St.) — Pavlos

Pericles* classical name (St.)

Peter stone (St.) — Petros, Panos

Philip lover of horses (St.)

Prokopios (l) declared leader (St.)

Prophyrios purple stone (St.)

Romanos (L) Roman (St.)

Rouvin (ROO-veen) (H) behold, a son

Sebastian venerable, revered (St.)

Seraphim (H) seraph (St.)

Sergios (SEHR-yos) (L) the attendant (St.)

Silas (L) forest (St.)

Silvanos (L) forest (St.)

Simon (H) God is heard

Socrates meaning unknown (St.)

Soterios* savior (St.)

Spyridon* round basket (St.)

Stamatios meaning unknown (St.)

Stavros* crowned with laurels (St.)

Stefanos* crown (St.)

Symeon (H) God is heard; (Gr) sign (St.)

Takis dim. of Panagoitis (All Holy) Panos, Panayotis

Taxiarchai (TAHKS-ee-ahr-heh) the Archangels

Thanos (TAHN-os) noble or bear man — Thanasis, Athanasios

Theodosios (teh-o-DO-syos) gift of God (St.)

Thomas* (H) twin

Titos of the giants (St.)

Vasilis (vah-SEE-lees) kingly — Vasos, Vasileios

Venedictos (L) blessed — Benedict

Vernados (OGer) courage of a bear

Verniamin (H) son of the right hand

Yannis (YON-nees) (H) gracious gift of God — Ioannis, Yannakis

Zachaios (H) remembered by the Lord (St.) — Zacheus

Zeno Zeus

Zotikos meaning unknown (St.)

---

* Popular
** Very popular

HAWAII

The original Hawaiians were Polynesian voyagers who traveled to Hawaii about 1,500 years ago from the Marquesas Islands nearly 2,000 miles to the south. They were later joined by immigrants from Tahiti. By 1778, when Captain Cook arrived in Hawaii from Europe, the native population numbered approximately 300,000.

In the next seventy-five years their numbers were sadly depleted, largely due to their contact with European diseases, from which they had no immunity. The first official census in 1853 counted only 71,000 native Hawaiians, less than one-fourth their population in 1778.

Beginning in the last decade of the 19th century, such large numbers of foreigners, especially Japanese and Korean, were hired to work in the sugar cane fields, that native Hawaiians gradually became a smaller and smaller proportion of the total population of Hawaii; by 1900, they represented only twenty-five percent.

Other notable immigration movements to Hawaii included six shiploads of Spaniards from Andalusia in southern Spain who were recruited to work in the Hawaiian sugar cane fields between 1907 and 1913. A much larger contingent of Portuguese from Madeira (see Portuguese chapter) immigrated for the same reason between 1878 and 1898. A total of 13,000 Portuguese immigrated in this period, and by 1930 the nearly 28,000 of their descendants made up seven and a half percent of the total population.

The Japanese were by far the largest immigrant group, however. Between 1861 and 1940 over 300,000 Japanese immigrated to Hawaii, with the peak time period being 1901 to 1907 when 108,000 Japanese immigrants entered the island. In 1900 Japanese people represented forty percent of the population of Hawaii. However, with the influx of Caucasians (called "haoles" in Hawaiian) their percentage declined to twenty-eight by 1970.

In line with their easygoing attitude toward life, Hawaiians have intermarried with immigrants much more freely than has occurred in other areas. The resulting cosmopolitan population includes not only the groups mentioned above but Europeans, Chinese, Filipinos, and Puerto Ricans.

In 1959, when Hawaii became part of the United States, over 600,000 citizens of this beautiful, benign region became a part of the melting pot.

The Hawaiian language consists only of five vowels and seven consonants. It is usually written with vowels and consonants alternating; however multiple vowels occur, in which case each is pronounced as a separate syllable. Hawaii, thus is pronounced "hawah-ee-ee."

Hawaiian names often include several words joined together to form a name, which may then be shortened to nicknames. An experience significant to the parents might be described fully in the long name, which would then be shortened.

The beauty and delicacy of images wrought by some of the Hawaiian names is evident in the name list below. Nature is a frequent source for names, as well as Hawaiian versions of American/English/Biblical names. Many names can be used interchangeably for boys and girls. Some names are created by the parents by combining elements such as Lani ("sky" or "heavenly"), Lei ("wreath" or "child"), Kapu ("sacred"), or Nani ("beautiful").

Pronunciation

a = "ah" as in ball   o = "oh" as in hope
e = "eh" as in late   u = "oo" as in moon
i = "ee" as in keep

HAWAIIAN FEMALE NAMES

Alamea ripe, precious

Alana an offering

Alani orange tree

Alaula light of early dawn

Aleka (uh-LEH-kuh) (Alice) (OGer) noble, kind

Alika (Gr) truthful

Aloha greetings, friendship, and farewells

Alohi shining, brilliant

'Alohilani bright sky

Amaui a thrush

Ana (Anne) (H) graceful Ane, Aneka (Annette)

Anabela graceful, or beautiful

Anakela (Angela) (Fr) angel

Anuhea* cool, soft fragrance

Aolani heavenly cloud

'Aukai* (AH-oo-KAH-ee) seafarer

'Aulani royal messenger

Aulii (ah-oo-LEE-eee) dainty

Derya ocean

Ekika (Edith) (Teut) rich gift

Elenola (Eleanor) (Gr) light

Elikapeka (eh-lee-kuh-PEH-kuh) (Elizabeth) (H) consecrated to God — Peke

Emalia (Emily) (Teut) industrious — Emele

Eme (EH-meh) (Amy) (Fr) beloved

Ewalina (ee-vuh-LEE-nuh) (Evelyn) (H) life

Haimi the seeker

Hau'oli* (hah-oo-OH-lee) happy

Haunani** (hah-oo-NAH-nee) beautiful dew

Healoha (heh-uh-LOH-huh) a loved one

Helena (Helen) (Gr) light

Hiwahiwa (hee-vuh-HEE-vuh) precious

Hoku star

Hokulani star in the sky/heaven

'Ihilani* (ee-hee-LAH-nee) heavenly splendor

'Ilima* (ee-LEE-muh) name of a yellow flower

Inoa name, or name chant

Io'ana (ee-oh-AH-nuh) (Joan, Joanne) (H) God's gracious gift

Ioi (ee-OH-ee) (Joy) (OFr) jewel, delight

Ipo sweetheart

Iulia (ee-oo-LEE-uh) (L) youthful

Iwalani* (ee-vuh-LAH-nee) heavenly sea bird

Iwone (ee-VOH-neh) (Yvonne) (OFr) archer

Ka'ohe* (kuh-OH-heh) the bamboo

Ka'ohu (kuh-OH-hoo) mist

Kahoku (kuh-HOH-KOO) the star

Kai'mi (kah-EE-mee) (Polynesian) the seeker

Kai (KAH-ee) sea or sea water

Kaili (kah-EE-lee) a Hawaiian deity

Kainoa* (kuh-ee-NOH-uh) the name

Kaipo* (KAH-ee-poh) the sweetheart

Kakalina (Gr) pure

Kala (Sarah) (H) princess

Kalama (Polynesian) the flaming torch

Kalea (kuh-LEH-uh) (Claire) (L) bright, clear

Kaleki (kuh-LEH-kee) (Grace) (L) graceful

Kalena (KAH-leh-nuh) (Karen) (Gr) pure

Kalola (KAH-loh-luh) (Carol) (Fr) song of joy

Kama (Gr) nursling

Kamika from English Smith

Kanani* (Polynesian) the beauty

Kani (KAH-nee) (Connie) (L) constant

Kanoa (Polynesian) the free one

Kapono* the righteous

Kapua (Polynesian) the blossom

Kapule (Polynesian) a prayer

Kau'i (KAH-oo-ee) the beauty

Kaula (Polynesian) prophet

Kaulana (kah-oo-LAH-nah) fame

Kawailani* (kuh-WAH-ee-LAH-nee) the heavenly water

Kawena* (kuh-VEH-nuh) the glow

Ke'ala* (keh-AH-luh) the fragrance

Keahi* (keh-AH-hee) the fire

Keakalina (keh-ah-kuh-LEE-nuh) (Jacqueline) (H) God's gracious gift

Kealoha* the loved one

Kehaulani (KEH-HAH-oo-LAH-nee) heavenly dew

Kekai (keh-KAH-ee) sea

Kekipi the rebel

Kekona second-born child

Kekupa'a (keh-koo-PAH-ah) the steadfast one

Kelekolio meaning unknown; probably seahorse Kele

Kepola (Deborah) (H) a bee

Kiele (kee-EHL-ee) gardenia, fragrant blossom

Kikilia (Cecilia) (L) blind, gray eyes

Kiliwia (kee-lee-VEE-uh) (Sylvia) (L) forest

Kini (H) God is gracious

Kolika (Doris) (Gr) from the ocean

Kololeke (koh-loh-LEH-keh) (Dolores) (L) sorrows

Kona (Donna) (L) lady

Konane (ko-NAHN-neh) bright as moonlight

Ku'uipo* (koo-oo-EE-poh) my sweetheart

Ku'ulei** (koo-oo-LEH-ee) my lei, my child

Kukana (koo-KAH-nuh) (Susan) (H) lily — Kuke

Kuulei** (koo-oo-LEH-ee) my lei: kuu=my; lei=lei

Lahela (Rachel) (H) innocence of a lamb — Rahela

Laka goddess of the hula

Lana buoyant, to float

Lanakila victorious

Lani* sky, heaven

Laniuma geranium

Lawai'a (luh-VAH-ee-uh) fisherman

Lehua** (leh-HOO-uh) ohi'a blossom

Lei** flower wreath, child, nickname for Leina'ala

Leialoha** (leh-ee-uh-LOH-huh) beloved child

Leihulu feather lei

Leilani** heavenly child

Leimomi pearl necklace

Leina'ala (leh-ee-NAH-ah-lah) path of leis (lei=lei, na=of, by ala=path)

Leinani* beautiful lei

Leolani* (leh-oh-LAH-ee) heavenly voice

Lepeka (Rebecca) (H) binding, servant of God — Peka (Becky)

Lilia lily flower — Liliana

Lokelani* small red rose

Luana** enjoyment

Luke (Lucy) (LOO-keh) (L) bringer of light

Lulani (Polynesian) highest point in heaven

Mahealani mahea=where, lani=heaven

Mahina (Polynesian) moon

Maile** (MAH-ee-leh) myrtle vine

Makamae (mah-kah-MAH-ee) precious

Makana gift, present

Makani the wind

Makelina (mah-keh-LEE-nuh) (Madeline) (H) woman from Magdala

Malia (muh-LEE-ah) (H) bitter — Mele, Mere

Malu (MAH-loo) peace

Malulani heavenly calm

Mamo saffron flower; yellow bird

Mana'o'i'o (MAH-nuh-oh-EE-oh) (Faith) (L) trust

Mana'olana (MAH-nuh-oh-LAH-nuh) (Hope) (L) hope

Mana (Polynesian) supernatural power

Mapela (L) lovable

Mapuana** (mah-poo-AH-nuh) wind-blown fragrance

Mei (MAY) (L) great one

Mele** (MEH-leh) song, poem

Mikala (Michelle) (H) who is like God?

Mililani heavenly caress

Moana* ocean

Moani* (moh-AH-nee) fragrance

Mokihana name of a fragrant plant

Momi** (MOH-mee) pearl

Nalani (nah-LAH-nee) the heavens

Namilani nami=beautiful; lani=heaven

Naneki (nuh-NEH-kee) (H) grace

Nani** beautiful

Napua the flowers

Noelani** heavenly mist

Nohea** (noh-HEH-uh) loveliness

Okalani of the heavens

Oliana oleander

Oliwia (oh-lee-VEE-uh) (L) olive tree

Onaona (oh-NAH-oh-nuh) sweet fragrance

Palaneke (puh-luh-NEH-keh) (Blanche) (Fr) white one

Palapala (Barbara) (L) the stranger

Palila bird

Peni (PEH-nee) (Penny) (Gr) weaver

Pi'ilani (pee-ee-LAH-nee) to go up to heaven: pii=ascend, climb; lani=heaven

Pikake (pee-KAH-keh) jasmine

Pilialoha (pee-lee-uh-LOH-huh) beloved relation

Pilikika (Bridget) (Celt) strength

Pilis (Phyllis) (Gr) lover of horses

Pokii (poh-KEE-ee) younger sister

Pua** (POO-uh) flower

Pualani** (poo-uh-LAH-nee) heavenly flower

Punani** (poo-uh-NAH-nee) pretty flower

Roselani (Polynesian) heavenly rose

Ulani cheerful

Ululani* (oo-loo-LAH-nee) heavenly inspiration

Uluwehi (oo-loo-WEH-hee) growing in beauty

Wainani (vah-ee-NAH-nee) beautiful water

Wanika (Juanita) (H) God's gracious gift

Wehilani (veh-hee-LAH-nee) heavenly adornment

Wikolia (vee-KOH-lee-uh) (L) victorious

Wilikinia (vee-lee-KEE-nee-uh) (Virginia) (L) maidenly

***** Popular
****** Very popular
******* Extremely popular

HAWAIIAN MALE NAMES

Aka (AH-kah) (Arthur) (Celt) noble

Akamu (Adam) (H) son of the red earth

Akoni (L) inestimable

Alena (ah-LEH-nuh) (Alan) (Gael) handsome, cheerful

Alika (Alec, Alexander) (Gr) defender of mankind

Analu (ah-nuh-LOO) (Andrew) (L) manly

'Aukai* (AH-oo-KAH-ee) seafarer

Ekewaka (eh-keh-WAH-kuh) (Edward) (OE) wealthy guardian

Eli (EH-lee) (H) Jehovah; the highest

Elika (Eric) (ONorse) ever powerful

Hakulani star in heaven

Hale (HAH-leh) (Harry) (ONorse) army ruler

Hanale (hah-nuh-LAY) (Henry) (Teut) ruler of an estate — Haneke (Hank)

Haoa (HAH-oh-ah) (Howard) (Teut) chief guardian

Hau'oli* (hah-oo-OH-lee) happy

Havika (David) (H) beloved

Hiu (HEE-oo) (Hugh) (Teut) intelligence, spirit

Iokepa (ee-oh-KEH-puh) (Joseph) (H) God will add — Keo (keh-OH) (Joe)

Ionakana (EE-oh-nuh-KAH-nuh) (Jonathon) (H) God gives

Iukini (ee-oo-KEE-nee) (Eugene) (Gr) noble — Kini (Gene)

Ka'eo (kuh-EH-oh) the victory

Kahale the home

Kaholo the runner

Kai (KAH-ee) sea or sea water

Kaili (kah-EE-lee) a Hawaiian deity

Kainoa* (kuh-ee-NOH-uh) the name

Kaipo* (KAH-ee-poh) the sweetheart

Kala* (kuh-LAH) the sun

Kalaiwa'a (KAH-LAH-ee-WAH-ah) canoe carver

Kalama the torch

Kalani** the heavens

Kale (KAH-lee) from Charles (OFr) strong and manly

Kaleonahe (kuh-LEH-oh-NAH-heh) the soft voice

Kali (KAH-lee) (Gary) (OE) spear carrier

Kamaka* the face

Kamakani* the wind

Kamuela (kah-moo-EH-luh) (Samuel) (H) God hears

Kanaiela (kuh-nah-ee-EH-luh) (Daniel) (H) God is my judge — Kana

Kane (KAH-neh) man; the eastern sky

Kanoa (Polynesian) the free one

Kapono* the righteous

Kawika (David) (H) beloved

Ke'ala* (keh-AH-luh) the fragrance

Keahi* (keh-AH-hee) the fire

Keaka (keh-AH-kuh) (Jack) (H) God's gracious gift

Keawe (keh-AH-veh) the strand

Kekapa the tapa cloth (made from mulberry tree bark, or other plant)

Kekipi the rebel

Kekoa* (keh-KOH-uh) the courageous one

Kele* (KEH-leh) the navigator

Kele (KEH-leh) (Jerry) (H) God will uplift

Kelekolio (keh-leh-KOH-lee-oh) (Gregory) (Gr) vigilant

Keli'i (keh-LEE-ee) the chief

Keli (KEH-lee) (Terry) (L) smooth

Keoki (keh-OH-kee) (George) (Gr) farmer

Keola* (keh-OH-luh) the life

Keoni (keh-OH-nee) (H) God's gracious gift

Kiele (kee-EH-leh) gardenia

Kika (Keith) (OWelsh) from the forest

Kilikikopa (KEE-lee-kee-KOH-puh) (Christopher) (Gr) Christ-bearer

Kimo (KEE-moh) (James, Jim) (H) the supplanter

Kimokeo (Timothy) (Gr) honoring God

Kini king

Koka (Scott) (L) a Scotsman

Koma (Thomas) (H) twin

Konala (Donald) (Celt) ruler of the world — Kona (Don)

Konane (ko-NAH-neh) bright as moonlight

Koukalaka (koh-oo-kuh-LAH-kuh) (Douglas) (Celt) from the black stream

Laban white

Lani (LAH-nee) (Polynesian) sky

Lavi lion Lieb, Liebel

Lawai'a (luh-VAH-ee-uh) fisherman

Lei (Ray) (Teut) wise protector

Likeke (Richard) (OGer) powerful ruler

Liko (LEE-koh) bud

Lio form of Leo (L) lion

Loe (LOH-eh) from Roy (Fr) king

Lokela (LOH-keh-luh) (Roger) (Teut) famous warrior

Lono god of peace and agriculture

Lopaka (Robert) (Teut) of shining fame — Lopine (loh-PEE-neh) (Robin)

Lui (LOO-ee) (OGer) renowned warrier

Lukela (loo-KEH-luh) (Russell) (A.S.) like a fox

Mahi'ai (mah-hee-AH-ee) farmer

Makaio (mah-KAH-ee-oh) (Matthew) (H) gift of God

Makani the wind

Maleko (mah-LEH-koh) (Mark) (L) warlike

Mamo (MAH-moh) saffron flower; yellow bird

Manu bird

Mauli (mah-OO-lee) dark-skinned

Meka eyes

Mika'ele (mee-kuh-EH-leh) (Michael) (H) who is like God?

Mililani heavenly caress

Mokihana name of a fragrant plant

Nahele (nah-HEH-leh) forest; grove of trees

Namaka the eyes

Nikolao (nee-koh-LAH-oh) (Nicholas) (Gr) victory of the people

Nohea handsome

Oliwa (oh-LEE-vuh) (L) olive tree

Onaona (oh-NAH-oh-nuh) sweet fragrance

Pakelika (pah-keh-LEE-kuh) (Patrick) (L) noble

Palaina (puh-LAH-ee-nuh) (Brian) (Celt) strong

Palani (Frank) (L) free man

Paulo (PAH-oo-loh) (Paul) (L) little

Pekelo (peh-KEH-loh) (Gr) stone

Peleke (peh-LEH-keh) (Fred) (Teut) peaceful ruler

Peniamina (PEH-nee-uh-MEE-nuh) (Benjamin) (H) son of the right hand — Peni

Pilipo (Philip) (Gr) lover of horses

Wikoli (vee-KOH-lee) (Victor) (L) the conqueror

Wiliama (wee-lee-AH-muh) (William) (Teut) resolute protector — Wile, Pila

---

* Popular
** Very popular
*** Extremely popular

HUNGARY

Social and economic laws that developed in Hungary in the 1860's to modernize the country served to loosen family and home ties and inspire the growth of individual aspirations. Hungarians began migrating within their country in search of better opportunities, and eventually began to look farther afield.

Before that era, small numbers of Hungarian merchants, travelers, and explorers had come to the United States. Some even fought in the American Revolution.

A poor farming year in Hungary in 1880 led many to immigrate to America. Within about five years a substantial stream of returnees brought the fortunes they had made in America back to Hungary, settled old debts, and began a much-improved lifestyle. Others who stayed also sent money home, further fanning the enthusiasm for emigration. In 1903, for instance, the Hungarian city of Veszprem received over half a million dollars from their emigrants to America.

Between 1899 and 1914, when World War I halted immigration, more than 450,000 Hungarians immigrated to the U.S. Those who came merely to seek their fortunes and return to Hungary were called "sojourners." They often found work in the rapidly expanding coal and steel industries in Pennsylvania, Ohio, West Virginia, Illinois, and Indiana. Because many were men under thirty who didn't plan to put down roots, the unsteady nature of mining didn't bother them; they merely moved to wherever jobs were available, even switching to mill work if necessary.

The Immigration Act of 1924 severely limited the immigration of southern and eastern Europeans, and the sojourner era ended. However, between 1925 and the 1940's another 15,000 Hungarians immigrated to the U.S., mainly professional and business people.

After World War II, because the Hungarian immigration quota was so small, nearly 24,000 Hungarians were on waiting lists for years to immigrate as refugees from the Communist regime in Hungary. During the Hungarian revolt in 1956 some 200,000 fled

Hungary. Eventually over 35,000 of them were admitted as refugees to the United States. In recent years immigration has averaged about 800 each year.

Literacy among Hungarian immigrants has always been unusually high. Around the turn of the century, for instance, the literacy rate was eighty-nine percent when the rate for Hungary in general was just fifty-nine percent. Many of the 1956 refugees were college students and professionals. They usually settled with the help of earlier immigrants in the industrial towns favored by the sojourners, and moved on to higher paying jobs fairly quickly.

The most popular names in Hungary now tend to be old-fashioned Hungarian names. Although the Hungarian language (called Magyar) and Polish look equally remote to Americans, they are actually from two entirely different root languages. Magyar is of the Uralic and Altaic family, which also contains Finnish, Turkish, and Mongolian. Polish is a Balto-Slavic language, which is in the same family as Russian, Czech, and Slovak.

Sources for names in Hungary have included saints (more than fifty percent of Hungarians are Catholic) and kings and queens of the Magyar dynasty that has occupied the Danube basin for over a thousand years. Several unusual (to Americans) letter combinations make Hungarian pronunciation very distinctive, though also very consistent.

Pronunciation

a = "o" as in hot
a = "ah" as in ball
c = "ts" as in hats
e = "e" as in met
e = "eh" as in late
gy ="d" with tongue pressed thickly against upper gum ridge
i = "ee" as in keep, but with lips opened more narrowly

i = same as above but longer
j = "y" as in yet
o = variety of sounds from short to long
s = "sh" as in shoe
sz = "s" as in sow
z = "z" as in zoo
zs = "zh" as in azure

HUNGARIAN FEMALE NAMES

Ágnes (AHG-nesh) (Gr) gentle, pure

Ágotha (Gr) good — Agota, Agi

Alberta (OGer) noble, bright

Alexandra (Gr) defender of mankind — Alexa

Alisz (AH-leezh) (OGer) noble, kind — Aliz (AH-leez)

Amália (Teut) industrious — Emilia, Mali, Malika, Malcsi (MAHL-chee)

Anastasia (ah-nahsh-TAH-shee-ah) (Gr) resurrection — Anasztaizia

Angyalka (AHN-dahl-kuh) (Gr) messenger — Angelina (AHN-gehl-ee-nah)

Anikó* (H) grace — Anci (AHN-tsee), Annus, Annuska (AHN-noosh-KAH), Nina

Anna* (H) grace — Hajna (HAH-ee-nah), Anyu

Aurelia (L) gold — Aranka, Aranyu

Bella nobly bright, or beautiful — Bela, Belle

Berta (BEHR-tah) (OGer) courageous — Bertus, Bertuska (behr-TOOSH-ka)

Borbàla (L) the stranger — Borsala, Bora, Boriska, Borsca, Borka

Bözsi (BO-zhee) (H) consecrated to God — (Betty) Boske, Erzsi (EHR-zhee)

Cili (TSEE-lih) (L) blind

Csilla (CHEE-luh) (H) protection

Darda a dart

Dorika (Dolly) dim. Dorothy (L) gift of God

Dorottya (do-RO-tah) Dorothy (L) gift of God — Doris, Dora

Duci (DOO-tsee) rich gift — Edith (EH-deet), Edit

Edith (EH-deet) (Teut) rich gift — Edit, Duci (DOOT-see)

Edna (H) rejuvenation

Eliz (EH-leez) (H) consecrated to God

Erika (ONorse) ever powerful

Erna (OGer) from Ernestine (L) serious

Ernesztina (EHR-nehs-tee-nah) (OGer) serious

Erzsébet (EHR-zhee-beht)(H) consecrated to God — Erzsi, Erssike, Erzsok,Beti

Eszter (EHS-ter) (H) star — Eszti

Etel (H) noble — Etilka

Éva (H) life — Evike, Evacska (eh-VAHCH-ka)

Fani (L) free — Fanni

Felicia (L) fortunate, or lucky

Flora (L) flower — Florentyna, Florka, Firenze, Virag

Franci (FRAHN-tsee) (Teut) free — Fereng, Franciska, Ferike

Franciska (FRAHN-tseesh-ka) (Teut) free — Franci (FRAHN-tsee)

Frederica (Teut) peaceful ruler — Frida

Frida (Teut) peaceful ruler — Frederica, Frici (FREE-tsee)

Gabriell (H) God is my strength — Gabi

Gertrud (Teut) fighter

Gisella (Teut) pledge

Gizi (GEE-zee) (Teut) pledge — Gizike, Gizus (GEE-zoosh)

Gyöngyi (DON-dee) (OFr) juniper

Györgike (DOR-gee-kuh) (Gr) farmer

Hajnal (HAH-ee-nahl) (L) dawn

Henrietta (Teut) mistress of the home

Ibolya (L) violet

Ida (OGer) she who is active

Ildikó* (Teut) warrior

Ilka (Gr) light

Ilona* (Gr) light — Ica (EE-tsah), Ilay, Ili, Ilka, Ilon, Ilonka, Ilu, Iluska (ee-LOOSH-ka), Lenci (LEHN-tsee)

Irén (Gr) peace — Irenke

Irma (OGer) war god — Irmus, Irmuska (EER-moosh-ka)

Izabella (H) consecrated to God — Izabel, Bella

Izsó (EE-zho) (H) salvation of the Lord

Janka (YAHN-kah) (H) God's gracious gift — Johanna (yo-HAHN-ah)

Jolán (YO-lahn) (OGer) country — Jolanka, Joli

Jozsa (YO-zhah) (H) God will increase

Judit (YOO-deet) (H) praised — Juci, (YOO-tsee), Jucika, Jutka

Julinka (L) youthful

Juliska (yoo-LEESH-ka) (L) youthful — Juli, Julianna, Julcsa (YOOL-chah)

Kamilla (L) ceremonial attendant

Karolina fem. Karl — Karola, Lina, Linka, Karla

Károly (Fr) song of joy — Karcsi (KAHR-chee), Kari

Katalin (Gr) pure — Kata, Katinka

Katarina (Gr) pure — Katerina, Katakin

Kati (Gr) pure

Katoka (Gr) pure — Katica (kah-TEE-tsah), Katus (KAH-toosh), Koto

Klára (L) clear — Klárisza (KLAH-reezh-uh), Klari

Kláríka (L) brilliant, or illustrious — Klára

Klotild (OGer) heroine

Kornelia (L) horn

Krisztina (KREEZH-tee-nah) (Gr) Christian – Kriszta, Kriska (KREESH-kah)

Lilike (L) lily flower

Liza (LEE-zah) nickname for Erzsebet – Liszka (LEES-ka)

Lucia (LOO-tsyah) (L) bringer of light

Lucza (LOO-tsah) (L) bringer of light

Lujza (loo-EE-sah) (OGer) famous warrior woman – Lujzi, Lujzika

Magdolna (H) woman of Magdala – Magda

Margit (Gr) a pearl – Margo, Gitta, Rita

Maria* (H) bitter – Mari, Marcsa, Mara

Marianna comb. Maria and Anna

Marika (H) bitter

Mariska (mah-REESH-ka) (H) bitter

Marja (MAHR-yah) (H) bitter

Márta (H) bitter – Martuska (mahr-TOOSH-ka)

Mathild (Teut) brave in battle

Monika (L) advisor

Nancsi (NAHN-chee) (H) grace

Natália (Fr) born at Christmas

Neci (NEH-tsee) (L) fiery

Ninácska (NEEN-ach-kah) (H) grace – Nusi

Nusa (H) grace

Nusi (H) graceful – Aniko, Anci, Annuska, Nin, Ninacska

Olga (Russian) holy – Olgacska (ol-GAHCH-ka)

Olivia (L) olive tree

Onella (Gr) light

Orzsébet (OR-zhee-beht) (H) consecrated to God

Paula (L) little – Pali, Paliki

Perzsike (PEHR-zhee-kuh) (H) consecrated to God – Perke, Perzsi

Piroska (pee-ROSH-ka) (L) the ancient (form of Priscilla) – Piri

Rebeka (H) servant of God

Réz (REHZ) copper-colored hair

Rezi dim. of Tereza (Gr) harvester – Riza

Rozália comb. of Rose and Lily – Roza, Rozsika (ro-ZHEE-ka)

Rozsa (RO-zha) (L) rose – Rozsi

Sári (SHAH-ree) (H) princess – Sarolta, Sarika, Sasa (SHAH-shah), Sara

Sofia (Gr) wisdom

Sziszi (SEE-see) nickname for Erzsebet – Zizi, Zsizsi (ZHEE-zhee), Zsoka

Teca dim. of Tereza (TEH-tsah)

Teréza (tehr-EH-zah) (Gr) harvester – Treszka (TREHS-ka), Terez, Tercsa

Teri (Gr) harvester – Terike, Terus (TEHR-oosh), Rezi

Tünde unknown meaning

Vera (L) true

Vica (VEE-tsah) (H) life – Vicus, Vicuka, Vicuska (vee-CHUSH-ka)

Viktoria (L) victorious

Zigana gypsy girl

Zita (Arabic) mistress

Zizi (ZEE-zee) (H) consecrated to God

Zsofia (zho-FEE-ah) (Gr) wisdom – Zsofi, Zsofika

Zsuzsanna* (zhoo-ZHAH-nah)(H) lily – Zsuzsa, Zsuzsi, Zsuzsika, Zsuska, Zsuzska

* Currently popular

HUNGARIAN MALE NAMES

Ábel (H) breath

Ábraham (H) father of a multitude

Ádam (H) man of the red earth

Adelbert (Teut) noble, bright – Béla, Adel

Adolf (OGer) noble-wolf

Adorján (AH-dor-yan) (L) of the Adriatic – Adi

Ágoston (L) venerable – Gusztav (GOOS-tahv)

Alajos (AH-lah-yos) (Teut) famous holiness – Lojze (LOY-zee)

Albert (OGer) noble, bright – Bela

Alfréd (OE) wise – Fredi (FREH-dee)

Ambrus (AHM-broosh) (Gr) immortal, divine

Anasztáz (AH-nahs-taz) (Gr) resurrection

Andor (Gr) strong and manly – Andras, Endre, Andi, Andris, Bandi

András (Gr) manly – Andor, Endre

Antal (L) inestimable

Arisztid (AHR-ees-teed) (Gr) son of the best

Aron (AH-ron) (H) enlightened

Árpád (AWR-pahd) a Magyar national hero who founded a dynasty in 890 A.D.

Artur (ahr-TOOR) (Celt) noble, bear man

Attila old mythological name

Bálint (L) strong and healthy – Baline

Ballas (BAHL-ahzh) (L) stammerer – Balázs

Barna (H) son of prophecy

Barta (Aramaic) ploughman – Bartalan, Berti

Béla dim. Albert

Benci (BEN-tsee) blessed — Benedik, Benedek, Benek

Benedek (L) blessed — Benke, Bence, Benci

Benjamin (BEHN-ya-meen) (H) son of the right hand

Bernát (OGer) courage of a bear

Bertók (Teut) bright raven

Bodi (BO-dee) may God protect the king

Boldizsár (BOL-dee-zhahr) Balthasar

Boris (Slav) battler; or stranger

Buni old mythological name

Cézar (L) Caesar

Clement (L) gentle, kind

Csaba (CHAH-buh) ancient Hungarian mythological name

Dániel (H) God is my judge — Daneil, Dani

Dávid (H) beloved

Demeter (Gr) goddess of the harvest — Domotor

Dénes (Gr) god of wine — Dennes

Dezsö (DEH-zho) (L) desired

Domokos (L) of the Lord — Domonkos, Domo, Dome, Dedo

Donát (Celt) world ruler

Dorján (DOR-yawn) (L) dark man; black man

Edgard (A.S.) happy warrior

Edvard (OE) wealthy guardian — Ede

Elek short form of Alexander (Gr) defender of mankind — Eli, Lekszi

Elemér (Teut) famous

Elias (H) Jehovah is God — Illes

Emánuel (H) God is with us — Mano

Emil (Teut) energetic

Ernö (OGer) serious

Ervin (EHR-vin) friend of the sea

Ferdinánd (Teut) adventurous, brave — Nandor

Ferenc (fehr-EHNTS) (L) free — Feri, Ferke, Ferko

Fredek from Frederick (Teut) peaceful ruler; or Alfred (OE) wise counsel

Frigyes (FREE-dehs) (Teut) peaceful ruler — Frici (FREE-tsee)

Fülöp (Gr) lover of horses

Gábor (H) God is my strength — Gabi

Gáspár (Persian) treasure master — Gazsi (GAH-zhee)

Gellért (Teut) powerful soldier

Gergely (Gr) vigilant — Gergo

Gottfrid (Teut) God's peace

Gusztáv (GOOS-tahv) (Teut) staff of the gods

Gyala (L) youth

György (DOR-dee) (Gr) farmer — Gyoergy, Gyuri, Gyurka

Gyula (DOO-lah) (L) youth — Gyuszi (DOO-see)

Harold (ONorse) war chief — Henrik

Henrik (Teut) ruler of an estate

Herbert (HEHR-bert) (Teut) bright warrior

Ignác (EEG-nahch) (L) fiery — Neci (NEH-tsee)

Imre (Teut) industrious

Ince (EEN-tseh) (L) innocent

István (EESHT-vahn) (Gr) crowned with laurels — Pista (PEESH-tah), Pisti

Iván (ee-VAHN) (H) God's gracious gift

Izidor (Gr) gift of ideas

Izrael (H) soldier of the Lord

Izsák (EE-zhahk) (H) laughter

Jancsi (YAHN-tsee) (H) God's gracious gift

János (YAH-nos) (H) God's gracious gift — Jani, Jankia, Janko

Jenö (YEH-no) (Gr) well-born — Jenci (YEHN-tsee)

József (YO-zhehf) (H) God will add — Joszef (YO-sehf), Joska (YOSH-ka), Jozsi

Jozsua (YO-zhua) (H) God saves

Kálmán (KAHL-man) (OFr) strong and manly

Karl (OFr) strong and manly

Károly (OFr) strong and manly — Kari, Karcsi (KAHR-chee)

Kazmér (KAHZ-meer) (Polish) he announces peace

Kelemen gentle, kind — Kellman

Klement (L) merciful

Konrád (OGer) honest counselor — Kurt

Kornél (L) horn — Soma (TSO-mah)

Kristóf (KREESH-tof) (Gr) Christ-bearer

Kurt (OGer) honest counselor

Lajos (LAH-hos)(Teut) famous holiness — Lajcsi (LAH-ee-chee), Laji,Lali

László (LAHS-lo) (Slav) famous ruler — Laci (LAH-tsee), Lacko, Lazlo

Lázár (H) God will help

Lenci (LEHN-tsee) (L) crowned with laurels

Lipót (Teut) patriotic — Poldi

Loránt (lo-rawnt) (L) crowned with laurels

Loreca (lo-REH-tsah) (L) crowned with laurels

Lorencz (LO-rehnts) (L) crowned with laurel — Lorenc

Lörinc (LO-reents) (L) crowned with laurel – Lenci (LEHN-tsee)

Lúkács (LOO-kahch) (L) bringer of light

Marci (MAHR-tsee) (L) warlike one – Marcilka (mahr-TSIL-kah), Marcilki

Márton (L) warlike – Marci (MAHR-tsee), Marcilka, Martino

Máté (H) gift of God

Mátyás (H) gift of God

Mihály (H) who is like God? – Miska (MEESH-ka), Misi (MEE-shee), Mika

Miklós (Gr) victory of the people

Miksa (MEEK-shah) (L) greatest

Miska (MEESH-kah) (H) who is like God?

Moricz (MOR-eets) (L) Moorish, dark-skinned

Mózes (H) saved from the water

Ödön (A.S) wealthy protector – Odi

Orbán (OR-bahn) (L) born in the city

Oszkar (OS-ker) (Celt) warrior

Otto (Teut) prosperous

Pál (PAWL) (L) little – Pali, Palika

Péter (Gr) stone – Peti, Peterke

Rendor policeman

Réz copper (boy with reddish hair)

Rezső (REH-zho) (Teut) strong, wise counsel – Rudolf

Rikárd (OGer) powerful ruler

Róbert (RO-behrt) (Teut) of shining fame

Robi (RO-bee) (Teut) of shining fame

Rudi (Teut) famous wolf – Rudolf, Rezso (REH-zho)

Salamon (SHAH-lah-mun) (H) peace

Sámuel (SHAH-myoo-ehl) (H) God hears – Samu, Samuka, Samie

Sándor (Gr) defender of mankind

Sebestyén (sheh-BEHSH-tehn) (Gr) venerable, revered – Sebo (SHEH-bo)

Simon (SHEE-mon) (H) God is heard

Tabor (TAH-bor) camp

Tamás (TAW-mahsh) (H) twin – Tomi

Tass ancient Hungarian mythological name

Tibor (Slavic) holy place

Todor (Gr) gift of God – Tivadar

Toni (L) inestimable – Tone, Toncse (TON-cheh)

Vencel (VEHN-tsehl) wreath, garland

Vidor (L) conqueror

Viktor (L) conqueror – Geza (GEH-zah)

Vilmos (VEEL-mosh) (Teut) resolute soldier – Vili

Vincze (VEEN-tseh) (L) conqueror – Vinci

Walter (Teut) powerful warrior

Zacharias (H) remembered by the Lord

Zoltán (Gr) life

Zsigmond (ZHEEG-mond) (Teut) conquering protection – Zsiga (ZHEE-ga)

---

* Currently popular

INDIA

Two significant waves of immigration have arrived from East India. The first occurred in the early 20th century.

A drought in the Punjab (northwestern India) between 1898 and 1902 sent nearly 5,000 Sikh men (mostly farmers) out of their country between 1900 and 1910. Most settled in California where they put their agricultural skills to work in vineyards and fig orchards around Fresno, and in the rice fields around Sacramento. Thousands also worked on the Western Pacific Railroad in northern California.

No significant immigration occurred from India before that, perhaps because of the high price of a boat passage to the United States and extreme differences in Eastern and Western culture. Only seven East Indian women came to the U.S. before World War I.

Sikhs comprised over half of India's immigrants to the U.S. during the early immigration period and Muslims made up a third. Hindus made up the smallest group of immigrants, perhaps because they had to give up so many of their old ways of life and religion (i.e., the caste system was not a viable way to live in the U.S.). Also, most Hindus are vegetarians, with the eating of meat (sacred cows) being most objectionable to them. Thus, only the most independent, adaptable, and energetic Indians were able to make the change.

Although the Sikhs now make up thirty to forty percent of the East Indian population in California they represent only two percent of the population in India. The Sikh religion was founded in the 15th century by a religious teacher who tried to combine the best aspects of the Hindu and Moslem religions, dedicated to one God.

Restrictive exclusion rulings against East Indians in 1917 and 1923, combined with the 1924 Immigration Act, effectively brought East Indian immigration to a halt until 1946, when the Asian quota was relaxed somewhat. About 6,000 East Indians immigrated between 1947 and 1965.

After the 1965 immigration laws eliminated national quotas, East Indian immigration increased dramatically. According to the 1970 census, there were 51,000 foreign-born East Indians in the U.S. By 1980 it was closer to 200,000. The largest concentration of immigrants lives in the New York City area; more than 30,000 live within fifty miles of New York. Other popular destinations include Chicago and California.

When the quota laws were abolished preference was given to highly trained professionals and their families. Almost 46,000 scientists, teachers, engineers, and business people immigrated in the decade following the new law, with an equal number of spouses and children. English-speaking and well-educated, these families tend to have little trouble assimilating into the American society, although they attempt to maintain aspects of their own culture as well.

The majority of East Indians in India and America are Hindu. Moslems make up five percent of the East Indian population and less among their immigrants here.

Hindus believe God is manifested in everything. They may name a child after a household object because every time they say the name they are pronouncing the name of God, which is a step toward salvation. Other sources of names are Nature, a made-up name, the name of one of the seven sacred Indian rivers, or one of the hundreds of names for Hindu gods, which are said to be manifestations of One God. The god of destruction, Siva, has 1,008 qualities, any of which can be used as a name. Occasionally, a child may be given an unpleasant name to trick the gods into not taking the child away.

Grandparents are often given the honor of choosing a name for a child.

ABBREVIATIONS USED:
Hin = Hindi
San = Sanskrit

INDIAN FEMALE NAMES

Aditi (Hin) goddess

Adya born on Sunday

Ahimsa (Hin) non-violence

Ajaya (Hin) invincible, intoxicating

Alka (Hin) girl between 8 and 18 years old; girl with long hair

Ambar (Hin) sky, horizon

Ambika (Hin) name for goddess, Sakti, of power and destruction

Amma a mother goddess (others: Mata, Amba, Mahamba, Bimba, El+ma)

Amritha (Hin) name of a god

Anala (Hin) fire — Agni

Ananda (Hindu) bliss

Anila (Hin) wind god

Anusha (Hin) name of a god; also one of 27 stars in Hindu astrology

Arhana (Hin) worship

Arpana (Hin) a present, dedication

Aruna (Hin) radiance; name of god

Asoka (Hin) non-sorrow flower

Asvina (Hin) born during lunar month corresponding to Libra

Avasa (Hin) independent

Baka (Hin) crane (longevity)

Bakula (Hin) a mythological plant

Bela (Hin) Jasmine flower or violin

Bharati (Hin) India

Bhavna (Hin) wish, fancy, desire

Chaitra (Hin) lunar month corresponding to Aries

Chandi (Hin) angry (name for goddess, Sakti) — Chanda

Chandra (Hin) moon, or moon god

Changla (Hin) active girl

Channa chickpea

Chitra (Hin) name of a god; also star in astrology

Corona (Hin) politeness, kindness

Daru (Hin) pine, or cedar

Deepa (Hin) name of a god; lamp

Deva (San) divine

Devaki black

Devi (DAY-vee) (Hin) name for Sakti, goddess of destruction

Divya (Hin) divine, heavenly Divia

Drisana (San) daughter of the sun Drisa

Durga (Hin) wife of Siva, god of destruction

Durva (Hin) durva grass

Ellama (Hin) mother goddess

Ganesa (guh-NAY-shuh) (Hin) god of good luck and wisdom

Ganga (Hin) holy river Ganges

Garuda (Hin) sun-bird that god Vishnu rides

Gauri (GO-ree) (Hin) yellow or fair

Gauri (Hin) yellow

Geetha (Hin) song; especially Hindu lyric Bhagarat Geetha

Girisa (gee-REE-shah) (Hin) mountain lord; name for god, Shiva

Guri (Hin) goddess of abundance

Hanita (Hin) divine grace

Hara (HAH-rah) (Hin) seizer, name for Siva, the destroyer

Hema (Hin) name of a god, daughter of the mountains

Indi (Hin) Indian

Indra (Hin) god of power

Jambu (Hin) rose apple tree

Jarita (Hin) legendary bird mother

Jaya (Hin) name of a god; victory

Jayne (JIN) (Hin) victorious

Jivanta to give life

Jyotis sun's light

Kala (Hin) black; time; name for god Siva

Kali (San) energy; black goddess; mother god Sakti

Kalinda (Hin) sun; from mythical Kalinda mountains

Kamala (Hin) lotus

Kantha (Hin) wife

Kanya (Hin) the Virgin; another name for goddess, Sakti

Kapila (Hin) ancient Hindu prophet

Karka (Hin) the crab (born during zodiacal month Cancer)

Karma action; destiny

Kasi (Hin) one of the seven holy Hindu cities

Kaveri (Hin) one of the seven sacred rivers of India

Kavindra (Hin) mighty poet — Kawindra

Kerani (Todas) sacred bells

Kesava (Hin) having fine hair

Kiran (Hin) ray

Kirsi (Todas) amaranth — Kiri

Klesa (Hin) pain (given to ward off evil spirits)

Kona (Hin) born under Capricorn

Kumuda (Hin) lotus

Kurma (Hin) tortoise; name for god Vishnu

Kusa (Hin) sacred kusa grass

Lajila shy, coy

Lakini (Hin) name of a god

Lakshmi (Hin) goddess of good fortune

Lakya born on Thursday

Lalasa (Hin) love

Lalita (Hin) name for goddess Sakti

Latika (Hin) name of a god; a small creeper

Leya (Tamil) constellation Leo

Lila (Hin) free will of God

Lota (Hin) portable drinking cup

Madhur (Hin) sweet

Magha (Hin) born during Aquarian lunar month

Mahesa (Hin) name for god, Siva, the destroyer

Mahila (San) woman

Makara (Hin) born during Capricorn lunar month

Malini (Hin) name of a god; a gardener

Manda (Hin) name for Saturn, god of the occult

Mandara (Hin) a mythical tree

Manidatta (San) pearl given

Matrika (Hin) mother; name for goddess, Sakti

Maya (Hin) God's creative power

Meena (Hin) a blue-colored precious stone; a bird

Mehadi flower

Mela (Hin) a religious gathering

Mesha (Hin) born during lunar month Aries

Mina (Hin) born in lunar month of Pisces

Mithuna (Hin) born in solar month Mithuna

Mitra (Hin) god of daylight

Mutu pearl

Mythili (Hin) name of a god

Nandini (Hin) name of a god Siva, the destroyer

Narmada (Hin) gives pleasure

Narmada (Hin) holy Indian river Warmada

Nata (Hin) rope dancer

Natesa (Hin) name for god Siva, of destruction

Neerja (Hin) lily

Nipa (Todas) stream

Nirveli (Todas) water child

Nishkala (Hin) name of a god; innocent

Nitara (Hin) deeply rooted

Nitya (Hin) name of a god; universal

Padma (PAHD-mah) (Hin) lots

Pandita (Hin) scholar

Pausha (PO-sha) (Hin) child born during lunar month Pausha (Capricorn)

Pavithra (Hin) name of a god; pure

Pinga (PEEN-gah) (Hin) dark, tawny (name for goddesss, Sakti)

Pipal (PEE-pahl) (Hin) a mythical tree with its branches in heaven

Pollyam (Hin) goddess of the plague (given to ward off evil spirits)

Prabha (Hin) light

Radha (Hin) a mythological woman who was a favorite of the god, Krishna

Rajni (Hin) night

Ramya (Hin) name of a god; beautiful, elegant

Rana (San) royal — Rani, Rayna

Rani (RAH-nee) (Hin) queen

Rashmika very sweet

Ratna (Hin) name of a god; a precious jewel

Ratri (Hin) night; name for goddess, Sakti

Rekha (Hin) fine

Reva (Hin) name for Narmada, a sacred river in India

Risha (Hin) born during solar month of Vrishabha

Rohana (Hin) sandalwood

Rohini (Hin) woman

Ruana (Hin) musical instrument similar to a viol

Ruchi (Hin) a love growing into a wish to please

Rudhra (Hin) name of a god

Rudra (Hin) rudraksha plant, whose berries are used for rosaries

Sagara (Hin) ocean

Sakari (Todas) sweet

Sakti (Hin) energy, a major goddess in Hindu belief

Sakujna bird

Sala a sacred Hindu tree that brings blessings and peace

Sandhya (Hin) name of a god; sunset time

Sanya born on Saturday

Sarisha (Hin) charming

Sarita (Hin) stream, river

Saroj (Hin) like a lotus

Saura (SOW-rah) a Hindu sect which worships the sun

Sesha (Hin) symbol of time

Sevti the white rose

Shanata (Hin) peaceful

Shanta (Hin) the daughter of King Dasratha

Sharan (Hin) protection

Shashi (Hin) moonbeam

Sindhu (Hin) name of a holy Indian river

Sita (Hin) furrow; mother earth goddess

Sitara (San) morning star

Soma (Hin) moon (born during lunar month Cancer)

Subha (Hin) nectar, beauty

Sunita (Hin) good conduct

Supriya (Hin) greatly loved

Sur (Todas) knife, one with sharp nose

Surata (Hin) blessed joy

Surya (Hin) born in lunar month Leo

Tira (Hin) an arrow

Tirtha (Hin) ford

Trina (Hin) sharp points of the sacred kusa grass

Trisha (TREE-shah) (Hin) thirst, a classification of love

Tula (Hundi) born in lunar month Libra

Tulsi (Hin) sacred tulasi plant

Uma (Hin) the goddess Parvati

Upala the opal

Usha (Hin) name of a god; sunrise time

Valli (Hin) a native plant in India

Vamana (Hin) incarnation of god Vishnu

Varaza boar

Varouna (Hin) goddess of the waters

Varuna (Hin) god of the sea

Vasudha (Hin) name of a god

Veda (Hin) sacred writings

Vibha (Hin) name of a god; also one year of a 60-year cycle; night

Vidya (Hin) knowledge and education

Vijaya (Hin) Durga, the name of Krishna's rosary; victory

Vina a stringed instrument carried by goddess of wisdom

Vineeta simple, straightforward, unassuming

Vinithra (Hin) name of a god

Vrinda a woman in Hindu mythology

Yamuna (Hin) after holy Indian river

Yamuna sacred river in India

Yasmine jasmine — Jasmine, Yasiman

Zudora (San) laborer

INDIAN MALE NAMES

Achir new

Aditya the sun

Adri (Hin) rock

Agni (Hin) god of fire

Aja (ah-jah) (Hin) a goat

Akshay (Hin) name of a god and a year (part of 60-year cycle)

Almiron (AHL-mee-ron) clothes basket

Anand (Hin) happiness

Anish without a master

Arun (Hin) sun

Ashwin (Hin) name of a star

Atman (Hin) the self

Balin (BAH-len) mighty soldier — Bali, Valin

Bhagwandas servant of God

Bharani (Hin) one of 27 stars in Hindu astrology

Bharat (Hin) saint name

Bhaskar (Hin) the sun

Bhavta an object of love, beloved person

Champak (Hin) name of a god; a tree bearing yellow fragrant flowers

Chander (Hin) the moon

Chinja a son

Dalal (dah-LAHL) bearer's or father's profession is a broker

Dandin (Hin) holy man

Darshan (Hin) a god

Deven for God

Gajra a thick woven garland of flowers

Ganesh (Hin) son of Shiva and Parvati

Girish (Hin) name of a god

Gulab the rose

Haidar (Muslim) lion — Hirsuma, Asad, Lais

Halim (HAH-leem) (Moslem) mild, gentle or patient

Hansh (Hin) name of a god

Hanuman (hah-noo-MAHN) (Hin) monkey

Hara (Hin) seizer (name for god Siva, the destroyer)

Hari (Hin) tawny

Hasin (hah-sen) laughing

Hastin (Hin) elephant

Inay (Hin) name of a god

Inder (Hin) name of a god

Ishan a direction

Jafar (jah-fahr) a little stream

Jalil (Hin) name of a god

Jatinra great Brahmin sage

Javas (JAH-vahs) swift and quick

Jivin to give life — Jivanta

Josha (JO-sha) satisfaction

Jyoti (Hin) light; name of a god — Jyotsua

Jyotish moon

Kabir name of a Hindu mystic

Kakar (KUH-kuhr) (Todas) grass

Kala (KAH-lah) (Hin) black; or time (name for god, Shiva)

Kalkin (kahl-KEEN) (Hin) tenth incarnation of the god Vishnu

Kamal (Hin) name of a god; lotus

Kami (KAH-mee) loving

Kantu (KAHN-too) happy; name for Kama, god of love

Kapil (Hin) name of a god; sage

Kapila ancient Hindi prophet

Karthik (Hin) name of a god; also one of 27 stars in astrology

Karu the cousin of Moses

Kavi a poet

Kedar (KEH-dahr) mountain lord (name for Hindu god, Shiva)

Kers (Todas) a plant name

Kesin (keh-SEN) (Hin) long-haired beggars

Kijika do; walks quickly

Kil (KEEL) (Todas) name comes from a prayer

Kintan (Hin) wearing a crown

Kiritan (kee-ree-TAHN) (Hin) wearing a crown

Kistna (Hin) an Indian river

Krishan (Hin) incarnation of Vishnu, protecting god

Kulen (Todas) short form of Kulpakh (meaning unknown)

Kumar prince

Lais (LAYS) (Muslim) lion — Haidar

Lal (LAHL) (Hin) beloved

Linu a lily

Loknath (Hin) name of a god

Lusila one possesses leadership ability

Madhar (Hin) name of a god

Malajit garland of victory

Manoj Cupid

Manu (Hin) name of person who wrote code of conduct for Hindus

Marut (Hin) name for god, Vayu, who controls the wind

Mayon (MI-yon) [short] (Hin) ancient equivalent of Krishna

Mehtar (meh-tahr) prince

Mohan (Hin) delightful

Mukul bud, blossom, the soul

Murali (Hin) Lord Krishna

Nadisu a beautiful river

Nandin (NAHN-deen) name for Hindu god, Siva, the destroyer

Narain (Hindu) (nah-RIN) name for god, Vishnu, protector of the world

Narayan (Hin) name of a god

Natesa (Hindu) dance lord (name for god Siva, the destroyer)

Natesh Shiva

Nehru canal

Nila blue

Niranjan (Hin) name of a god

Omparkash the light of God

Onkar (Hin) name of a god; indicative of attributes of the pure being

Palash a flowery tree

Paramesh (Hin) name of a god; superlative

Pavit pious, pure

Poshita cherished

Pumeet pure

Purdy (Hin) recluse

Qimat value, price

Rajak cleansing

Raktim colorfully red

Ram (Hin) name of a god

Ramanan (Hin) name of a god

Ranjan to delight, gladden

Ravi (Hin) sun god, Surya

Rishi a sage

Rohan (Hin) salndalwood

Rohin (ro-HEEN) on the upward path

Rohit a large beautiful fish

Roi (Fr) king

Sahen (shah-hehn) above

Sahir a friend, secretary

Sainath (Hin) saint name

Sajag vigilant, watchful

Salmalin (Hin) taloned

Samaresh Lord Shiva

Sanat (Hin) ancient

Sani (sah-NEE) (Hin) personification of the planet Saturn

Sanjiv long-lived

Sankar (Hin) name of a god

Sarad (Hin) born in the autumn

Sarngin (Hin) name for god, Vishnu, the protector

Sarojun (sah-ro-jeen) (Hin) lotuslike

Shalya throne

Shami husband

Shashida ocean

Siddhartha a name of Buddha

Siva (SHI-vah) (Hin) name for Siva, the destroyer

Srinath (Hin) name of a god

Srinivasan (Hin) name of a god

Sunreet one whose means are pure

Taj crown

Tayib (TAYB) good or delicate

Thaman (Hin) name of a god

Timin (tee-MEEN) (Arabic) huge fish in Hindu mythology

Uja to grow

Ultman (Hin) name of a god

Vadin (VAH-deen) (Hin) speaker

Valin (Hin) a monkey king — Balin

Varun (Hin) rain god

Vasin (VAH-seen) ruler or lord

Venkat (Hin) name of a god

Vijay (Hin) name of a god; victory

Vishnu (Hin) protector

Vivek wisdom

Yogesh (Hin) name of a god; the chief ascetic

IRAN

There was very little immigration from Iran before the 1950's and after 1979. Many immigrants were students or tourists who stayed and their families then followed. For instance, fifty-seven percent of all Iranian immigrants in the years 1958-76 were given permanent resident status after entering the U.S. on a temporary basis. From 1966-76 twenty percent of Iranian immigrants were tourists who became permanent residents and seven percent were students, many of whom married U.S. citizens.

Many are well-educated and highly-skilled. (There are about 2400 Iranian doctors in the American Medical Association.) By the end of the 1970's an estimated 25,000 Iranians were permanent residents of the U.S. Iran is about ninety-eight percent Muslim, and most speak Persian, although Arabic, Turkish, Kurdish, Baluchi, and a variety of Iranian dialects are also spoken.

PERSIAN FEMALE NAMES

Azar red
Farah (fah-RAH) happiness
Farideh (fahr-ee-DEH) glorious
Golnar center of flame, red flower (old name)
Jaleh (ZHAH-leh) rain
Laleh tulip
Marjan (MAHR-zhan) coral
Minau heaven
Mitra name of an angel
Nahid (NAH-heed) Venus
Pari (pah-REE) fairy eagle
Parvaneh butterfly
Shabnan (SHAHB-nahn) raindrop (old name)
Shahdi happy
Shahin eagle
Sholeh flame
Simin silver
Soraya ancient princess
Taraneh melody
Zohreh happiness

PERSIAN MALE NAMES

Amir (ah-MEER) king
Bahram ancient king
Behrooz lucky
Cyrus (KOORSH) king, sun
Darioush ancient king
Feroz (FEE-roos) fortunate
Jamsheed Persian
Kaveh ancient hero
Majeed great, one of the gods
Majnoon historical figure
Mehrdad gift of the sun
Nasim (NAH-seem) breeze
Saeed happiness — Said
Sohrab ancient hero
Soroush, happiness

IRELAND

An Irishman sailed with Columbus to the New World, another lived in the colony at Jamestown, Virginia in 1607, and another sailed with Henry Hudson. During the 1600's and 1700's thousands of Irish immigrated as indentured servants (working several years to pay off their transatlantic passage), religious refugees (primarily Catholics), transported political prisoners, and voluntary immigrants.

Of 200,000 Irish-born immigrants in the U.S. by 1760 an estimated 40,000 were true Irish, the rest being Scotch-Irish (see Chapter on Scotland). Many Scotch-Irish settled in deep southern backwoods areas in order to be as far from the English as possible.

Between 1820 and 1840 one-third of immigrants to America were born in Ireland; during the 1840s, just over forty-five percent of the arrivals were Irish. After about 1815 landlords had been gradually increasing rents to exorbitant rates as well as summarily turning out their tenant farmers in order to expand their own farming operations.

This practice, combined with the potato famine of 1845, caused a constant state of near starvation among peasant farmers. Between 1845 and 1851 approximately one million Irish died of starvation and disease, and other one million emigrated to escape the deprivation. After the famine was over Irish continued to emigrate. Emigration became for many a predictable life event, to be fit in between birth and death.

Irish immigration reached a peak in the 1850's, when over 900,000 arrived in the U.S. Large numbers continued to arrive through the 1920's although the percentage of the total immigrants gradually declined. A total of 4.7 million Irish immigrated to the U.S. between 1820 and 1982.

Most Irish immigrants settled in the Northeast, although significant numbers then migrated to the West Coast states after staying in the Eastern cities for a while. In 1870 Irish were the largest foreign-born group in California, and from the early 19th century Irish were always among the first groups in the drive west.

However, they were less likely to homestead than some other immigrant groups, because in Ireland they had been used to working small plots of established ground during the day, and joining their near neighbors in the evening for friendly gossip and relaxation. The lonely life of a sodbuster, miles from the closest neighbor, did not suit the Irish temperament. As a result, four out of five Irish immigrants settled in cities working as laborers, domestics, and factory workers.

After World War I Irish emigration resumed, however the destination then was much more likely to be England than America. Immigration from Ireland was very low during the 1930's and 1940's (as from all countries). After World War II it averaged about 5,000 each year in the 1950's, and has now dwindled to about 1,000 per year.

Old Irish names are very popular in Ireland now. The Irish language is a Celtic language closely related to Scottish Gaelic, and spoken now only in certain areas along the western seaboard. In attempting to decipher the Irish pronunciation one can come to appreciate the difficulty people must have in learning English. It's been pointed out that the letters "ough" can be pronounced five different ways in English with no real clue as to which one goes where (plough, trough, thought, rough, and though). The Irish language has similar irregularities as well as a different syntax.

Several purely Irish names have been included in the name list as well as the Anglicized versions of them that have developed in Ireland. Many of these names are very ancient Irish and many are names of Irish saints and martyrs not well-known in other countries (ninety-five percent of the Irish people are Catholic) so an authentic Irish name should be available from this list! Since it is so difficult to generalize on the pronunciation it has been included in the entries of names not easily pronounced by American readers.

IRISH
FEMALE NAMES

Abaigeal (AB-i-gel) (H) father of joy — Abigail, Abaigh, Abbie

Affrica (Gael) pleasant

Agata (Gr) good — Agatha

Aghna (EH-nuh) Irish for Agnes (Gr) gentle, pure — Ina

Aifric (A-frik) (Celt) pleasant — Afric, Africa, Aphria

Aignéis (AG-nesh) (Gr) gentle, pure — Agnes

Ailbhe (AL-vyuh) (OGer) noble, bright — Alvy, Elva (boy's name, too)

Aileen (Gr) light — Ellen

Ailidh (A-lee) (OGer) noble, kind — Alley

Ailís (A-lish) (OGer) noble, kind — Alicia, Elsha, Ailis, Ailse

Aimilíona (a-mil-EE-nuh) (Teut) industrious — Amelia

Áine (AN-yuh) (Celt) joy — Anne

Aingeal (AN-gel) (Gr) messenger — Angela

Aisling (ASH-ling) vision, dream — Ashling

Aithne (ATH-nyuh) (Celt) fire — Aine, Ena, Ethne

Alastríona (al-is-TREE-nah) (Gr) defender of mankind — Alastrina, Alexandra

Alma (Celt) good

Ánna (H) grace (differs from native Aine) — Anne

Annstás (AN-stahs) (Gr) resurrection — Anastasia

Aodhnait (EH-nat) ancient Irish name — Enat, Ena, Eny

Aoibheann ((W)EE-vuhn) ancient Irish name — Eavan

Aoife ((W)EE-fyuh) (H) life — Eva

Arienh (A-reen) (Gael) pledge

Arlana (Celt) pledge

Báb (BEHB) Babe; pet name

Báirbre (BAR-bruh) (Gr) a stranger — Baibin (BAB-een), Barbara

Bébhinn (BEH-vin) melodious lady — Bevin

Benvy Lady of Meath Bean Mhí (BEN-vee)

Bernadette fem. of Bernard (OGer) courage of a bear

Blair (Celt) from the plain

Blanche (L) white

Bláthnaid (BLA-na) blossom, flower-bud — Florence

Blinne dim. of Moninne, an Irish saint

Brenna (Celt) dark hair

Bretta (Celt) from Britain — Bret, Brit, Brite, Brittany, Brita

Briana (Celt) strong

Bride (Celt) strength — Briget, Bridget, Brietta

Bríghid (BRIDE) (Celt) strength — Brid (BREED), Bride, Breeda, Brigid

Brigid (Celt) strength — Bridget

Brina (Celt) protector

Brit (Celt) speckled

Cait (KATE) (Gr) pure — Caiti (KAT-ty)

Caitlin (KAT-leen) (Gr) pure — Caitilin

Caitrín (KAT-reen) (Gr) pure — Caitríona (kat-TREE-nuh), Catherine

Caoilfhionn (KEE-lin) (Celt) slender, fair — Keelin

Caoimhe (KEE-vy) gentleness, beauty, grace — Keavy

Cara (Celt) friend — Carrie, Carry

Carmel (H) vineyard

Christine (Gr) Christian

Ciannait (KEE-nat, or KIN-nat) ancient — Kinnat, Keenat

Ciar (KEER) saint name — Ciara, Ceire, (KEHR), Keara

Cinnie (Celt) beauty

Clare (L) bright, clear

Clodagh (KLOH-dah) name of a river in County Tipperary

Cordelia (Celt) jewel of the sea

Cristín (KRIS-teen) (L) Christian — Cristiona (kris-TEE-nuh)

Damhnait (DEV-nat) poet — Devnet, Downet, Dymphna

Dana (Celt) from Denmark

Darcy (OFr) from Arcy

Dearbháil (DER-vahl) true desire — Derval

Deirdre ancient Irish name, mythological heroine; young girl — Derdre

Derval true desire

Devnet poet — Downet

Doireann (DOR-en) sullen; or dim. of Dorothy (Gr) gift of God — Dorren

Doreen (Celt) moody

Duana (Gael) song

Éadaoin (eh-DEEN) fem. of Edwin (OGer) happy friend — Edwina

Edana (Celt) ardent, flame

Eibhilín (eh-y-LEEN) (Gr) light — Eveleen, Eileen, Aileen, Ellen

Eileánóir (EL-eh-nohr) (Gr) light — Eleanor, Léan (LEHN)

Eileen (Gr) light — Eleanore, Ellen, Elen, Helen, Eily, Ellie

Eilís (EH-leesh) (H) consecrated to God — Eilise, Elizabeth

Eimíle (EM-i-lee) (Teut) industrious — Emily

Eithne (ETH-nuh) kernel — Ethna, Etney

Elizabeth (H) consecrated to God — Eliza, Lizzie, Bessie, Betsey, Betty

Emily (Teut) industrious

Ena (Celt) fire

Erin (Gael) peace

Erlina (Gael) girl from Ireland

Etain shining

Fainche (FAN-chuh) Irish saint name — Fanny

Fanny Irish saint name

Feenat deer

Fianait (FEE-nat) deer — Feenat

Fiona (FEE-nuh) (Celt) white, fair

Fionnuala (fi-NOO-la) fair shoulders — Finola, Nuala

Gemma (JEM-ma) (Fr) precious stone

Glynis (Gael) valley

Gormghlaith (GOR-emlee) blue lady — Gormly

Gráinne (GROH-nyuh) grace; ancient name borne by sixteenth century queen

Guennola (Celt) white

Gwendolyn (Celt) white brow

Gweneth (Celt) fair

Helen (Gr) light — Nell, Lena, Neill

Hilde (Teut) battle maid; name of Irish abbess — Hildy

Íde (EED-uh) (Old Irish) thirst — Ida, Ita

Isibéal (ISH-a-behl) (H) consecrated to God — Isabel

Juliane (L) youthful — Jill, Jillian, Gill, Gillian, Sheila

Kathleen (Gr) pure — Katharine, Kathryn, Kathie, Kate

Keara saint name

Keavy gentleness, beauty, grace

Keelin (Celt) slender, fair — Keely, Keelia

Kelly (Gael) warrior woman — Kellie

Kennocha (ken-OH-kuh) (Celt) beauty

Kerry (Gael) dark, dark-haired — Keriann

Kinnat ancient — Keenat

Labhaoise (LAU-ee-shuh) (Teut) famous holiness — Louisa, Louise

Lasairíona (las-a-REE-nuh) flame-wine — Lassarina

Lavena (Celt) joy

Lil pet form of Elizabeth — Líle (LIL-ee), Lilly, Lelia

Lucy (L) bringer of light

Luighseach (LOO-seh) (L) bringer of light — Lucy

Máda (MEH-duh) from Mathilde

Madailéin (MAD-e-lehn) (Gr) Magdalene — Madeline, Maighdlin (MEHD-leen)

Maeve (MEHV) (Celt) fragile — Meave, Meaveen

Máire (MEH-ree) (H) bitter — Mary, Mairin (MEH-reen)

Máiréad (MAW-reed) (Gr) a pearl — Margaret, Maighread (MEH-reed)

Mairsil fem. of Marcel (L) warlike — Marcella, Mairsile

Maitilde (Teut) battle maiden — Matilda, Maiti, Matty

Mallaidh (MAL-ee) (H) bitter — Molly, May

Margaret (Gr) a pearl — Maggie, Meg, Meggy

Marsali (Gael) (Gr) a pearl

Marta (H) bitter

Maureen (Celt) great — Moreen

Mave mirth

Mavelle (Celt) songbird — Mavie

Meadghbh (MEEV) (Celt) agile — Meaveen, Mabbina

Meara merry

Melva (Celt) chief

Míde (MEE-duh) var. of Ide — Meeda

Moira (Celt) great

Mona noblewoman

Moncha (Gr) adviser — Monika

Mór (MOHR) (Celt) great — Móire, More

Morgan (Celt) sea dweller

Morna (Celt) beloved

Moya (Celt) great

Muireann (MOR-in) of the long hair — Morrin

Muirgheal (MOHR-e-guhl) sea-bright — Murel, Muriel

Nainsi (NAN-see) (H) grace — Nancy, Nance, Nan

Noel (Gr) born at Christmas

Nóra (L) honor — Nora, Honora

Nuala short form of Fionnuala

Odharnait (OHR-nat) pale, olive-colored — Orna, Ornat

Oilbhe (OL-iv) olive — Olive

Oona one

Orghlaith (OHR-e-lath) golden lady — Orlaith, Orla

Ornóra (L) honor — Honor, Honora

Paili (PAHL-ee) (H) bitter — Polly, Poll, Pal

Patricia (L) noble

Pegeen (Gr) a pearl

Philomena (Gr) powerful friend

Proinnséas (PRON-sheh-uhs) (Teut) free — Frances, Fanny

Ranait (RAN-eh) grace; prosperity — Renny

Regan (Celt) royal

Regina (L) queen

Renny grace; prosperity

Richael (RICH-ehl) name of a saint

Ríoghnach (REE-nuh) Irish saint — Riona, Regina

Riona (REE-nuh) saint name

Rita dim. of Margaret (Gr) a pearl

Róise (ROH-shuh) (L) rose — Rose, Róisín (ROH-sheen)

Rosemary comb. of Rose and Mary

Rowena (Celt) white mane

Sadbh (SAYV) goodness — Sive

Sarah (H) princess; or form of Sorcha (Old Irish) clear, bright

Séarlait (SHEHR-let) (Fr) petite and feminine — Charlotte

Seosaimhín (SHOH-sa-veen) (H) God will add — Josephine

Shawn (H) God's gracious gift

Sheelah (L) blind, gray eyes — Sheila, Shelagh, Sheelagh, Shiela, Sheilag

Sheena (H) God's gracious gift — Shena

Sheila (L) blind — Sheela

Síle (SHEE-luh) (L) blind — Cecilia, Cicily, Celia, Selia, Sheila

Sinéad (SHEE-naid) (H) gracious — Jane, Janey, Sine

Siobhán (shuh-VAHN) (H) gracious — Joan, Hannah

Sláine (SLAHN-nuh) health — Slany

Sorcha (SOHR-e-khuh) clear or bright — Sarah, Sally

Steise (STEH-shuh) dim. of Annstas (Gr) resurrection

Súsanna (H) lily

Sybil dim. of Elizabeth — Sibby, Sibi, Siobaigh (shuh-BEH)

Tara (Celt) tower

Tessie pet form of Teresa (Gr) harvester

Toiréasa (toh-REH-suh) (Gr) harvester — Teresa, Tessie

Treasa strength — Treise

Úna (OO-nuh) unity; ancient Irish name — Winifred, Uny, Oona, Unity

Ursula (L) little bear

Vanessa (Gr) butterfly

Yvon (OFr) archer

IRISH MALE NAMES

Abbán (A-bahn) abbot

Adam (H) son of the red earth — Ádhamh (A-thuhv)

Aidan (Celt) flame, fiery — Edan, Aodhan (EH-thahn)

Ailbe (AL-vyuh) (OGer) noble, bright — Ailbhe, Alvy, Albert

Ailín (A-lin) (Gael) handsome — Alan, Allen

Aindréas (AHN-dree-ahs) (Gr) manly — Aindriú, Andrew

Alaois (A-leesh) (Teut) mighty battle — Aloys, Aloysius

Albert (OGer) noble, bright

Alexander (Gr) defender of mankind — Alex, Alick, Alsandair, Alsander

Allister (Gr) defender of mankind

Amhlaoibh (A-leev) (Norse) ancestral relic — Auliffe, Olave

Andrew (Gr) manly

Angus (Gr) unique choice

Annraoi (AHN-ree) (Teut) ruler of an estate — Henry, Harry

Antoine (AN-ton) (L) inestimable — Anntoin, Antoin

Aodh (EH) (Celt) fire — Hugh, Ea

Árdal (OGer) eagle power — Arnold

Artúr (Celt) noble, bear man — Art, Atty

Austin (L) venerable — Águistín (AH-guhs-teen)

Baird ballad singer — Bar, Bard, Barr

Bairrfhionn (BAR-fin) (Celt) good marksman — Barry

Barra (Celt) good marksman — Bearach (BAHR-akh), Bearchan, Barry

Bartel (Aramaic) ploughman — Bartholomew

Bartley (Aramaic) ploughman — Barclay, Berkley, Parthalan

Batt from Bartley (Aramaic) ploughman — Bat

Beacán (BE-kawn) (Celt) small — Becan

Bearnárd (BEHR-nard) (OGer) courage of a bear — Barney

Beartlaidh (BEHRT-lee) (Aramaic) ploughman — Bartley

Beircheart (BEHR-khart) (A.S.) bright-army — Bertie

Benen (L) blessed — Beineón (BEH-non), Bineán (BIN-ahn)

Bevan (Celt) youthful warrior

Bowie (Gael) (BOO-ee) yellow-haired — Bow, Bowen, Boyd

Brasil (Celt) battle — Breasal, Basil

Bréanainn (BREH-neen) (Celt) sword — Brendan, Breandán

Brendan (Gael) raven — Bran, Bram, Broin (bree-AHN), Brennan

Bret (Celt) from Brittany

Brett (Celt) from Brittany — Britt

Brian (Celt) the strong — Brant, Bron, Bryon

Brody man from the muddy place

Cailean (CAL-lan) (Gael) child — Colin

Cairbre (CAHR-bruh) (Celt) charioteer — Carbry

Callaghan (KAL-uh-khahn)name of two Irish saints — Ceallachán (KEL-uh-khahn)

Callough (KAL-uh) bald — Calvagh, Calbhach (KAHL-ahkh)

Caoimhghin (KWEE-ven) (Celt) kind, gentle — Kevin, Kevan

Caolán (KWEE-lahn) slender — Kealan, Kelan

Carlin (Gael) little champion — Carlie, Carling

Carlus (OFr) full-grown, manly

Carney (Celt) warrior — Karney, Kearney, Car

Carroll (Gael) champion — Carly, Carolus

Cassidy (Gael) clever

Cathal (KA-hal) (Celt) battle-mighty — Cahal (KA-hal)

Cathaoir (KAH-heer) (Celt) warrior — Cathair (KA-heer)

Cearbhall (KAHR-e-val) (OFr) full-grown, manly — Carroll

Cecil (L) blind — Siseal (SEE-sil)

Cedric (Celt) chieftain

Chad (Celt) defender

Cian (KEEN) ancient — Céin, Kian, Kean, Cain

Cianán (KEE-nahn) dim. of Cian — Kienan, Kenan

Ciarrai (KEH-ehr-ree) county — Kerry

Cillian (KEEL-yan) war or strife — Keallach, Killian

Cinnéide (kih-NEH-juh) helmeted-head — Kennedy

Coinneach (KUH-nukh) fair one — Canice, Kenny

Coireall (kohr-EE-ahl) (Gr) lord — Kerill, Cyril

Colla ancient Irish name

Colm dove — Colum, Columba, Colman

Comán (KOH-mahn) bent

Comhghan (KOH-gahn, or CO-en) twin — Cowan

Conall (Celt) high-mighty — Connell

Conán (KOH-nahn) (Celt) wisdom — Conn

Conary (KOH-ner-ee) ancient Irish name — Conaire

Conchobhar (KON-kho-var) high will, desire — Conor, Connor, Conny, Cornelius

Conn (Celt) reason, intelligence — Cuinn (KWIN), Con

Connlaoi (KOHN-lee) chaste-fire — Conley, Conleth

Conroy (Celt) wise man — Conn

Conway (Gael) hound of the plain

Corey from the hollow — Cori, Cory

Cormac charioteer

Críostóir (KRIS-ter) (Gr) Christ-bearer — Criostal (Scotland and N. Ireland)

Cú Uladh (koo-ULL-uh) hound of Ulster — Cooley, Cullo

Cullan (Gael) handsome one — Cullin, Cully

Cúmheá (kuhm-EH) hound of the plains — Cooey, Covey

Curran (Gael) hero — Curr, Curney

Daibhéid (DEH-vid, or da-VEECH) (H) beloved — David, Dáibhid (same pronunciation)

Dáire (DEH-ruh) old Irish name — Dary, Darragh

Dáithí (DAH-hee) swiftness, nimbleness — Dahy

Dallas (Gael) wise — Dall

Damhlaic (DAW-lik) (L) like the Lord — Dominic, Doiminic (DOH-min-ic)

Daniel (H) beloved

Daray (Gael) dark — D'aray, Dar, Darce

Darby (Gael) free man

Darren (Gael) great — Daron

David (H) beloved

Declan Irish saint name — Déaglán (DEK-lan)

Delano (deh-LAH-no) (Gael) a healthy black man

Dempsey (DEM-se) (Gael) proud

Dermot free man — Dermod

Derry (Gael) red-haired

Desmond clan name, from South Munster

Devin (Celt) a poet — Dev

Devlin (Gael) brave or fierce

Diarmaid (JEER-mid) (Gael) free man — Dermot, Dermod

Dillon (Gael) faithful

Dominic (L) like the Lord — Damhlaic

Donahue (Gael) dark warrior

Dónal (DON-al) (Celt) world-mighty — Domhnall, Donall, Donald

Donald (Celt) world ruler — Donal, Doughal

Donnán (DUN-ahn) brown

Donnchadh (DUN-uh-khuh) (Celt) strong warrior — Donogh, Donaghy

Donnelly (Celt) brave, dark man

Donovan (Celt) dark-warrior

Dougal dark stranger — Dubhghall (DOO-gal, or DOO-ahl), Douglas

Doyle (Celt) dark stanger — Doy

Duane (Celt) song — Dewain, Dwayne

Dubhán (DUH-ven, or DUH-wen) black — Dowan

Duer (Celt) heroic

Duff (Celt) dark-faced; black-faced

Dunham (Celt) dark man; black man

Ea (EH) (Celt) fire — Hugh

Éamon (EH-mon) (A.S.) wealthy guardian

Earnán knowing, experienced

Edan (Celt) flame, fiery

Egan (EE-gan) (Celt) ardent — Aodhagán (EH-uh-gahn), Egon

Éibhear (EH-ver) meaning unknown, perhaps (OE) strong as a bear — Ever

Éimhin (EH-veen) swift, active — Evin

Énán Irish saint name — Eanan (EH-nahn)

Eoghan (oh-GAHN) (H) God's gracious gift — Eoin (same pronunciation)

Eoghan (YO-wun) (Gr) well-born — Owen

Eóin (OH-en) (H) God's gracious gift — John

Eóin Baiste (OH-en BAHSH-chuh) John the Baptist

Erin (Gael) peace

Evan young warrior — Ewan, Ev

Eveny name used in Derry County — Aibhne

Faolán (FEH-lahn) wolf — Felan

Farrell (Celt) courageous — Fearghal (FAHR-gahl), Farr

Fearghus (FAHR-gus) (Celt) super-choice — Fergus

Felix (L) fortunate, or lucky — Feidhlim (FELL-em)

Feoras (FEE-uh-rus) (Gr) stone — Pierce

Ferris (Gr) the rock — Farris

Fiachra (FEE-uh-khruh) Irish saint name — Feary

Finghin (FIN-jin) fair birth — Fineen, Finnin

Finlay (Gael) little fair-haired soldier — Findlay, Finn

Fionán (FIN-ee-ahn) fair — Finnian, Fionn

Fionnbharr (FIN-ver) fair head — Finbar, Barram, Bairrfhoinn

Flann ruddy — Flainn, Floinn, Flannan

Flynn (Gael) son of the red-haired man — Flin

Forbes (Gael) prosperous or headstrong

Frederick (Teut) peaceful ruler — Feardorcha (fee-ar-e-DOHR-ekh-e)

Gale strange — Gael, Gaile

Galen (Gael) calm

Gannon (Gael) fair-complected — Gannie

Garbhán (GAHR-van) rough — Garvan

Garrett (Teut) with a mighty spear — Garret

Gearóid (GEHR-ed) (Teut) spear-mighty — Garrett, Gerald

Gilchrist servant of Christ — Gil, Gilley

Gilmore (Gael) devoted to the Virgin Mary

Gilvarry servant of St. Barry — Giolla Bhearaigh (GIL-a VER-ee)

Giolla Bhríghde (GIL-a-BREED) servant of St. Brigid — Gilbride

Giolla Chríost (GIL-a KREEST) servant of Christ

Giolla Dhé (GIL-a-DEH) servant of God — Gildea

Glaisne (GLAS-nee) a favored name in Ulster up to modern times — Glasny

Glen (Celt) valley — Glyn, Glenn

Gofraidh (GO-free-y) God's peace — Godfrey, Gorry

Gordan (Gael) hero; a Scotch-Irish name used in Ulster — Gordain

Grady (Gael) noble, illustrious — Gradey

Greagoir (GREG-or) (Gr) vigilant — Gregory

Guy (Celt) sensible

Hannraoi (HAN-ree) (Teut) ruler of an estate — Henry, Einri (EHN-ree)

Hogan (Gael) youth

Hurley (Gael) sea tide — Hurlee

Iarfhlaith (YAR-lath) Irish saint name — Jarlath

Innis (Celt) from the island

Íomhar (YOWR, or YO-ver) (Teut) archer — Ivor

Íoseph (YO-sef) (H) God will add — Iósep, Joseph

Irving (Gael) handsome — Earvin

Jonathan (H) God gives

Joseph (H) God will add

Justin noble judge

Kane (Gael) tribute — Kayne, Kaine

Kearney (Celt) warrior — Carney

Keefe (Gael) cherished, handsome

Keegan (Gael) little and fiery one — Kegan

Keir (KEER) (Celt) dark-skinned

Keiran (Celt) dark-skinned

Kern (Gael) little black one — Kearn, Kerne, Kieran

Kerry (Gael) son of the black one

Kerwin little jet-black one

Kevin (Celt) kind, gentle

Kyle (Gael) handsome; from the strait

Labhrás (LAU-rahsh) (L) laurel — Laurence

Laughlin servant of St. Secundinus — Lanty

Laurence (L) crowned with laurel

Leachlainn (LEKH-len) servant of St. Secundinus — Laughlin, Lanty

Léon (L) lion

Liam from Uilliam (Teut) resolute protector

Lochlain (LOKH-lan) home of Norsemen: Lakeland — Lochlann, Laughlin

Logan (Gael) from the hollow

Lomán (LO-man) bare

Lúcás (LOO-kahsh) (L) bringer of light — Lucan

Lughaidh (LOO-ee) (OGer) renowned warrior — Lewy

Maeleachlainn (MAL-uh-khlin) servant of St. Secondinus — Malachy, Milo, Miles

Maghnus (MAKH-nus) (L) great — Manus

Mahon bear

Mairtin (MAHR-teen) (L) warlike one — Martin, Martain

Maitias (muh-THY-uhs) (H) gift of God — Matthias, Maithias

Maitiú (MATH-yoo) (H) gift of God — Matthew

Mannix monk — Mainchin (MAN-e-kheen)

Maolruadhan (mal-ROO-ahn) servant of St. Ruadhan — Melrone

Meilseoir (MEL-shyahr) (H) king — Melchior

Melvin (Celt) chief — Mal, Malvin, Melvyn

Micheal (mee-HAHL) (H) who is like God? — Michael

Morgan (Celt) sea warrior — Morgun

Morven (Celt) mariner — Morvin

Muireadhach (MUR-e-thekh) sea-lord — Murry

Mundy from Reamonn

Murchadh (MUR-kha) sea-warrior — Murrough, Morgan

Murray (Celt) seaman

Naomhán (NAU-ahn) holy — Nevan

Neal (Celt) champion — Neale, Nealon

Neasán (NESH-ahn) Irish saint name — Nessan

Neil (Celt) champion — Neal, Niall

Nevan holy

Nevin (Gael) worhsipper of the saints — Nevins

Niall (NEE-AL) (Celt) champion — Neal, Neil, Neill, Niallán

Niece (NEES) (Celt) choice — Aonghus, Neese

Nioclás (NEE-klahs) (Gr) victory of the people — Nicholas

Niocol (NEE-col) (Gr) victory of the people — Nicol

Nolan (Gael) famous or noble — Noland

Nyle (Celt) champion

Odhrán (OH-rahn) pale green — Oran, Odran

Oilibhéar (OH-li-vehr) (ONorse) ancestor's relic — Oliver

Oistin (OHS-teen) (L) venerable — Austin

Oscar (Celt) warrior

Owen (Celt) lamb — Ewen, Eoin

Owney old Irish name — Oney

Paddy (L) noble

Pádraig (PAH-dreek) (L) noble — Patrick, Padraic, Padhraig

Parthalán (PAR-ha-lahn) (Aramaic) ploughman — Parlan, Bartholomew, Bartley

Patrick (L) noble — Pat, Patty

Peadar (PA-der) (Gr) stone — Peter, Peadair

Piaras (PEE-a-ras) (Gr) stone — Pierce, Piers

Pilib (Gr) lover of horses — Philip, Filib

Proinnsias (PRON-shee-as) (Teut) free — Francis, Frank

Raghnall (RAN-al) (Teut) wise power — Reginald, Reynald, Randal

Réamonn (RYEH-mon) (Teut) mighty protector — Raymond, Mundy

Riocárd (REE-kard) (OGer) powerful ruler — Richard, Ristéard (REESH-tyard)

Rodhlann (ROH-lan) (L) fame of the land — Roland, Rowland

Roibeárd (ROH-bahrd) (Teut) of shining fame — Robert, Riobart

Roibhilín (ROH-ve-lin) old Irish name — Revelin

Roibín (ROH-bin) dim. of Roibeard — Robin

Rónán (ROH-nahn) old Irish name — Ronan

Rory (Teut) famous ruler — Roderick

Ruaidhri (RWE-e-ree) (Teut) famous ruler — Rory, Roderick

Scully (Gael) town crier

Séafra (SHEE-a-fra) God's peace — Sheary, Geoffrey, Seafraid

Séamas (SHEE-a-mus) (from James) (H) the supplanter — Shemus

Seán (SHAWN) (H) God's gracious gift — Seaghan, Shane, Shawn, Shan

Seanán (SHAH-nan) (H) God's gracious gift — Senen, Sinon

Searbhreathach (SAR-vra-huhkh) noble judge — Justin

Séarlas (SHAHR-las) (OFr) full-grown, manly — Charles, Searlus

Seoirse (SYAHR-sha) (Gr) farmer — George, Seorsa

Seosamh (SHOH-sav) (H) God will add — Joseph, Seosaph

Shane (H) gracious gift of God

Síomón (SHEE-mohn) (H) God is heard — Simon

Siseal (SEE-sil) (L) blind — Cecil

Slevin (Gael) mountaineer

Steafán (STEF-ahn) (Gr) crowned with laurel — Stephen, Stiofan

Tadhg (TAYG) (Gr) honors God (form of Timothy) — Teague, Taidgh, Tiege

Téadóir (TEH-dohr) (Gr) divine gift

Teague poet, philosopher

Thady (Aramaic) praise

Tiarnach (TEEAR-nakh) lordly — Tierney, Tighearnach

Tierney lordly — Tiernan

Tiomóid (TEE-mohd) (Gr) honors God — Timothy, Tim

Tomaisin (TA-ma-seen) dim. of Tomas (H) twin — Tommy

Tomás (TA-mahs) (H) twin

Torin chief

Torrance (Gael) from the knolls

Uaine (OON-yuh) old Irish name — Oney, Owney, Hewney

Uileog (IH-lig) dim. of Uilliam — Ulick

Uilliam (UHL-yahm, or WIL-yam) (Teut) resolute protector — William

Uinseann (WIN-shen) (L) conqueror — Vincent

Úistean (OOSH-tchen, or ISH-tchen) (Teut) intelligence — Euston, Hugh

Vaughn (Celt) small

Wynne (Celt) white, fair

ISRAEL

The first Jewish immigrants were Portuguese Jews who came from Brazil to New Amsterdam (New York) in 1654 to escape religious persecution. Since then, Jewish immigration has been almost continuous, although it was low during colonial times and in the early 18th century.

Between 1830 and 1860 the U.S. Jewish population rose from 6000 to 150,000 and then to 250,000 by 1880. Between 1882 and 1924 an estimated 2.3 million Jews immigrated to the U.S. The restrictive 1924 immigration law and the Depression lowered the immigration considerably; however between 1925 and 1975 another 576,000 Jews immigrated.

Before the Civil War, German Jews were the largest group. They moved west as merchants and assimilated easily into an expanding economy.

Between 1881 and 1924 one-third of the Jews in Eastern Europe left their homes, and over ninety percent of those came to the U.S. A declining death rate and rising birth rate had caused overcrowding in the restricted areas (Pales) in Russia and Poland, outside of which Jews were rarely allowed to live. Restrictive laws increasingly made it difficult for them to make a living, and later, outright violence caused Jews to begin immigrating in numbers that swelled to a peak of 152,000 in 1906.

Most of them were young skilled workers, often in the garment trades. Seventy percent of the 1.5 million Jews who immigrated between 1899 and 1914 stayed on in New York City. Other destinations included large cities along the Eastern seaboard as well as Chicago, Philadelphia and San Francisco.

Since the founding of the Israeli state in 1947 more than 300,000 Jews have immigrated from Israel. Some left to search for wider opportunity or remove themselves from the frequent threat of wars. Among those numbers may be American Jews who went to live for a while in their symbolic homeland and then returned to the U.S.

A Jewish child may be named after any person, friend, or relative, who is deceased. Naming a child after a family member is intended to preserve family memories and maintain a living memorial to that person.

Among the Jews from Central and Eastern Europe (the Ashkenazim) a child is customarily named after a deceased loved one. However, among Sephardim (from Middle Eastern countries), a child is usually named after a living grandparent. Both customs reflect the hope that the good qualities of the namesake will be reborn in the child. Thus similar given names remain in the family for generations.

Because of the dispersion of Jews, the name of the deceased may be translated into the adopted land's language from Hebrew. In America and many European countries a child is often given both a Hebrew name after a relative and one common to the land of the child's birth.

The naming trends in Israel have closely followed the recent history of the Jewish people. Throughout the 1920's, 1930's, and 1940's, as the idea of a Hebrew state gathered momentum, it was very important to name children with purely Hebrew names. After the Holocaust of World War II a wave of Yiddish names occurred, following the Jewish custom of naming a child after a recently deceased relative. Many of the European Jews who were murdered spoke Yiddish, a Middle High German language mixed with Hebrew, Aramaic, and the host culture.

After the 1940's, Hebrew names became popular in the newly formed state of Israel as Jews attempted to put the past behind them and look to the future.

Now Israelis choose names from a variety of sources including Hebrew names, Nature names, place names in Israel, and American-influenced names. Israeli parents are likely to pick a very trendy name (that is, trendy in Israel), or else search diligently for a very unusual Hebrew name.

Although Yiddish names are rarely chosen in Israel today several have been included in the name list for interest.

Pronunciation

a = "ah" as in ball
e = "eh" as in late
i = "ee" as in keep
o = "o" as in go, an abbreviated sound which eliminates the near diphthong sound with which Americans pronounce "o" (oh-oo)

u = "oo" as in moon
ch =a guttural sound pronounced at the back of the throat, roughly estimated with "khh"

ISRAELI FEMALE NAMES

Adah (ah-DAH) (H) ornament — Ada

Adena (ah-deh-NAH) (H) adornment — Adene, Adina, Dena, Dina

Adina (ah-dee-NAH) (H) slender, pliant

Afra (H) female deer

Ahuva (ah-hah-VAH) (H) love, beloved — Ahava, Ahuda

Ailat (eh-LAHT) (H) hind, roe

Akiva (H) protect — Kiva, Kivi, Kiba, Akiba

Aleeza (H) joy — Aliza, Alizah, Alitza, Aleezah

Alona (H) oak tree — Allona, Allonia, Alonia

Alumit (ah-LOO-meet) (H) girl — Aluma

Amira (Y) ear of grain

Ana grace

Anat (H) sing

Arielle (H) lion of God — Ariela, Ariellil, Ariel

Ashira (H) wealthy (old-fashioned)

Atalia (H) the Lord is mighty

Ateret (ah-tah-REH) (H) crown — Atarah, Atara

Atira (H) prayer

Avichayil (ah-vee-KHAH-eel) (H) strong father — Abichail (old-fashioned)

Avigail (ah-vee-GAH-eel) (H) father's joy — Abichail

Avivit (H) fem. Aviv: ear of corn, spring, freshness — Avivi, Aviva

Aya (ah-YAH) (H) bird

Ayalah (ah-YAH-lah) (H) hind, roe

Aziza (H) fem. Aziz

Bat-tseeyon (baht-tsee-ON) (H) daughter of Zion — Bath-Zion

Bathsheba (H) daughter of Sheba — Bathseva, Bathshua, Batshua, Bat-sheba

Batya (H) daughter of God — Bitya

Beruriah (beh-ROO-ree-ah) (H) chosen by God

Blima (BLEE-mah) (Y) flower — Blime

Brachah (BRAH-khah) (H) blessing

Carmela (cahr-MEH-lah) (H) garden

Chanah (KHAH-nah) (H) grace — Hannah

Chasidah (khah-SEE-dah) (H) pious woman (old-fashioned)

Chasya (KHAHS-yah) (Y) to find shelter — Chasye (old-fashioned)

Chava (H) life — Chaya, Haya, Chabah, Eva, Chayka

Chaviva (khah-VEE-vah) (H) beloved — Eva

Chedva (KHEHD-vah) (H) joy

Chephzibah (KHEFH-see-vah) (H) my delight is in her — Hepzibah

Clara (Y) clean

Cochava (ko-khah-VAH) (H) star

Daganyah (H) ceremonial grain — Daganya

Dalit (DAH-leet) (H) draw water — Dalis

Daliyah (DAH-lee-yah) (H) a branch — Daliah

Daniela (H) God is my judge — Danya

Danit (DAH-neet) (H) to judge

Daphnah (DAHF-nah) (H) laurel

Davida (dah-VEE-dah) (H) beloved — Davi, Davita, Davina

Derora (H) freedom — Derorit, Derorice

Devora (H) bee — Deborah, Debora

Diklit palm tree, date tree — Dickla, Diklice, Dikla

Dinah (DEE-nah) (H) adjudged, vindicated — Dina

Divsha (DEEV-shah) (H) honey (old-fashioned)

Dobeh (Y) bee — Dobra

Dorit (do-REET) (H) of this generation

Edna (H) pleasure

Edra (H) mighty — Edrea

Elia (H) Jehovah is God

Eliora (H) God is my light — Eleora

Elisheva (H) consecrated to God

Elka (ehl-KAH) (Y) swear by God — Elke

Emunah (H) faith (old-fashioned)

Enye (EHN-yeh) (Y) grace

Erelah (ehr-EH-lah) (H) messenger, angel

Erith (eh-REET) (H) name of a flower

Ester (H) star — Esther

Etta (Y) light — Ette, Ethel, Itta, Ittke

Frieda (Y) peace

Frumit (FROO-meet) (Y) pious — Fruma

Galia (H) God has redeemed — Gallia, Galya

Galilah (H) name of a place in Israel

Galit (H) fountain — Gali, Galice

Galya (H) God has redeemed

Ganit (GAH-neet) garden — Gana, Ganice

Ganyah (Y) of a garden — Ganye

Gavrila (H) God is my strength — Gavriella

Gazit (H) hewn stone — Gisa, Giza

Gella (Y) yellow — Gelle

Gilah (H) my joy is eternal

Gilit (H) joy — Geela, Gilia, Gila, Gili, Gilal, Gilana, Gilat

Gurit (H) young animals, especially lion cubs — Gurice

Guta (goo-TAH) (Y) good — Gute

Hadar (H) ornament

Hadara (hah-DAH-rah) (H) splendor

Hadassah (hah-DAH-sah) (H) myrtle

Hagar (H) flight

Hentshe (HEHNT-sheh) (Y) grace — Henye

Hessye (HEHS-yeh) (Y) star

Hulda (H) weasel (old-fashioned)

Ilana (H) tree — Ilanit

Ilanit (ee-LAH-neet) (H) tree — Ilana, Elana, Elanit

Inda (een-DAH) (Y) pleasure — Inde

Iris (EE-rees) (H) name of a flower

Jaffa (YAH-fah) beautiful — Jafit (YA-feet)

Jardena (H) to flow downward

Joella (yo-EHL-lah) (H) the Lord is willing — Jola

Jonati (yo-NAH-tee) (H) my dove

Kalanit flower name

Karmia (H) vineyard of the Lord — Karmit, Karmelit, Marmel, Carmel

Kefira (H) young lion

Keren (H) horn — Keryn

Kinneret (KEE-nehr-eht) (H) harp — Kinneret

Lailie (LEH-lee) born at night — Laila, Laili, Laylie

Leshem (H) precious stone

Libbe (LEE-beeh) (Y) love, beloved — Libbie

Lipsha (LEEP-shah) (Y) love, beloved — Lipshe

Lirit poetic, lyrical

Magda (H) woman of Magdala

Malcah (mahl-KAH) (H) queen — Malkah, Milcah

Margalit (mahr-gah-LET) (Gr) a pearl

Marganit (mahr-gah-NEET) flower name (native to Israel)

Masha (mah-SHAH) (Y) brave (old-fashioned)

Mayah from Michaela (H) who is like God?

Mazal (MAH-zahl) (H) luck

Meira (meh-EE-rah) light

Menachemah (meh-NAH-kheh-mah) (H) consolation (old-fashioned)

Micaela (H) who is like God? — Michaila, Michla

Michal (me-KHAHL) (H) small stream

Milcah (H) queen — Malka

Mindel (MEEN-dehl) (Y) sea of bitterness

Minna (MEE-nah) (Y) bitter — Minah, Mintze, Mirel (old-fashioned)

Miriam (H) bitter — Mimi, Miri, Mitzi

Mirit (H) bitter — Mira, Miri

Mirka (MEER-kah) (Y) sea of bitterness — Mirke, Mirtza, Mirtze

Moriah (H) God is my teacher — Morit, Moriel, Morice

Naamah (nah-MAH) (H) pleasant — Namah, Nama

Naamit (H) bird

Naavah (nah-ah-VAH) (H) beautiful

Naomi (H) pleasant

Navit (NAH-veet) (H) pleasant — Naava, Mava

Nechama (neh-KHAH-mah) (H) comfort — Nehama (old-fashioned)

Nedivah (H) generous — Nediva (old-fashioned)

Neomi (H) pleasant — Naomi

Neorah (H) light

Neta (H) plant

Nili (H) Israel's triumph shall not fail

Nira (H) beam of loom

Niria (H) plow

Nirit (H) plant name

Nitzanah (nee-TSAH-nah) (H) blossom — Nizana, Nitza

Noga (H) shining

Noya (H) ornament

Nurit (H) plant name — Nurita, Nuria, Nureet

Odeda (H) strong

Ofra (H) young deer

Ona (H) graceful — Onit

Ophrah (H) dust

Ora (H) light — Orah

Oralee (H) my light — Orali, Orlee

Ornah (H) light, cedar tree — Ornette, Orna

Osna granary — Asna, Isna

Pazit (PAH-zeet) (H) golden — Pazia, Pazice, Paz, Paza

Peninah (H) pearl

Pessa (PAH-sah) (Y) pearl — Pessel, Pessye, Pesha, Peshe, Perril

Raananah (rah-NAH-nah) (H) fresh

Rachel (H) innocence of a lamb

Rada (Y) rose — Rade

Ranit (H) song — Ranita, Ranice

Rashka (Y) innocence of a lamb — Rashke, Rechell

Reba (REE-vah) (H) fourth-born — Rabah

Rebecca (H) binding, servant of God — Rivka, Rebeca, Reba, Becky

Reina (REH-ee-nah) (Y) clean

Rena (REE-nah) (H) song, joy — Rina, Rinna, Rinnah

Rimona (H) pomegranate — Mona

Rivka (REEV-kah) (H) servant of God; binding — Rebecca, Riva, Rive

Ronli (H) joy is mine — Rona, Ronia, Ronit

Roza (Y) rose — Royze, Rosa, Rada

Sarah (H) princess — Sara, Sarita

Sarai (H) quarrelsome

Segulah (H) precious (old-fashioned)

Sela (H) rock — Seleta, Saleet

Semadar (seh-mah-DAHR) (H) berry

Shayndel (Y) beautiful — Shayne

Shifra (H) beautiful (old-fashioned)

Shira (SHEE-rah) (H) song — Shiri, Shirley

Shlomit (SHLO-meet) (H) peace — Shlomit

Shosha (Y) rose

Shoshanah (H) rose

Shulamit (SHOO-lah-meet) (H) peaceful

Silka (sel-KAH) (Y) princess

Sima (Y) incense, treasure — Sime, Simca

Simcha (SEEM-khah) (H) joy

Sirka (Y) princess — Sirke, Silka, Sosya, Sosye

Sobel (Y) sustaining

Talia (H) heaven's dew — Talya, Tal

Talor (H) dew of the morning — Talora

Tamar (tah-MAHR) (H) palm tree — Tamara

Tamma (H) perfect — Teme

Temima (H) perfect (old-fashioned)

Temira (H) tall — Timora

Tikva (TEEK-vah) (H) hope

Tivona (H) lover of nature — Von

Tobit good — Tova, Tovah

Tova (H) good — Toibe, Toba

Tseeli princess

Tsifira (H) crown

Tzilla (TSEE-lah) (H) protection

Tzippa (TSEE-pah) (Y) bird — Tzipporah, Sippora

Tzivia (TSEE-vyah) (H) deer — Zibiah

Tziyona (TSEE-yo-nah) (H) Zion

Tzophiah (tso-FEE-ah) (H) looking towards

Urit (H) light — Urice

Varda (H) rose — Vadit, Vardit

Vered (H) rose

Vitel (vee-TEHL) (Y) life — Vitka, Vitke

Vitka (veet-KAH) (Y) life — Vitke

Ya-akova (H) supplanter

Ya-el (YAH-ehl) (H) mountain goat — Jael (pronounced same)

Yaffa (YAH-fah) (H) beautiful — Jaffa (pronounced same), Yaffit

Yardenah (H) River Jordan

Yarkona (H) green

Yedidah (yeh-DEE-dah) (H) friend — Jedidah (pronounced same)

Yehudit (H) praise — Yuta, Judith, Judit, Judinta, Yehudit

Yenta (Y) genteel — Yente

Yitta (Y) light — Yitte

Yocheved (YO-kheh-vehd) (H) glory of God — Jochebed (old-fashioned)

Yona (H) dove — Yonah, Yonina, Yonita

Yosepha (H) God will add — Josepha

Yovela (H) rejoicing

Zahavah (zah-HAH-vah) (H) golden

Zehava (H) golden — Zahava, Zehuva, Zehavit, Zehavi

Zehira (H) guarded

Zelda (zehl-DAH) (Y) rare — Zelde (old-fashioned)

Zemirah (H) song of joy

Zimra (H) branch, song of praise — Zimria, Zemira, Zemora, Zamora

Ziva (ZEE-vah) (H) splendor, brightness — Zivit

Zohar (H) shine

Zoheret (H) she shines

ISRAELI MALE NAMES

Aaron* (AH-ron) (H) teaching; mountaineer – Aharon

Abir* (H) strong

Adam* (ah-DAHM) (H) earth

Adar* (H) noble

Aderet (ah-dehr-EHS) (H) covering, crown

Adir* (ah-DEER) (H) majestic, noble

Adiv (ah-DEEV) (H) pleasant, gentle

Adon (H) Lord

Aharon* (ah-hah-RON) (H) exalted, lofty

Aitan* (H) strength – Ethan

Akiba* (H) the supplanter – Akub, Akiva

Alon* (ah-LON) (H) oak

Alter (ahl-TEHR) (Y) old one; other one

Ami-el (ah-me-EHL) (H) of the family of God

Amichai* (ah-me-KHAH-ee) (H) my folk is alive

Amiel* (ah-me-EHL) (H) God of my people

Amikam* (ah-mee-KAHM) (H) nation arisen

Amir* (ah-MEER) (H) proclaimed

Amiram* (ah-me-RAHM) (H) lofty people

Amitai (H) truth – Amiti

Ammi* (H) my people

Ammitai* (ah-mee-TAH-ee) (H) truthful

Amnon* (H) faithful – Amon

Amos* (ah-MOS) (H) burdened

Amram* (AHM-rahm) (H) mighty nation

Anshel (AHN-shehl) (Y) blessed; happy – Anshil [df. Asher]

Ari* (AH-ree) (H) lion – Arie

Ariel* (H) (ahr-ee-EHL) lion of God

Arion (H) melodious

Arnon* (ahr-NON) (H) roaring stream

Aryeh* (AHR-yeh) (H) lion – Arye

Asa* (AH-suh) (H) physician or healer – Ase

Asaph* (H) gather – Asaf

Asher* (AH-sher) (H) blessed; happy

Avi* (ah-VEE) father – Avidan, Avidor, Aviel, Avniel

Avichai* (ah-vee-KHAH-ee) (H) my father alive

Avidan* (ah-vee-DAHN) (H) God is just

Avidor* (ah-vee-DOR) (H) father of a generation

Aviel* (ah-vee-EHL) (H) God is my Father

Avigdor* (ah-veeg-DOR) (H) father protector

Avimelech (ah-vee-MEH-lekh) (H) father king – Abimelech

Avinoam* (ah-vee-NO-ahm) (H) pleasant father – Avinoam

Aviram* (ah-vee-RAHM) (H) father of heights – Abiram

Avisha* (H) God's gift – Avishai

Avital* (ah-vee-TAHL) (H) father of dew

Aviv* (H) spring, freshness, youth

Avner* (AHV-ner) (H) father of light – Abner

Avniel (AHV-nee-ehl) my Father is my rock; or my strength

Avraham* (AHV-rah-hahm) (H) father of a multitude – Abraham

Avram* (ahv-RAHM) (H) father of elevation – Abram

Avshalom* (AHV-shah-lom) (H) father of peace – Avsalom

Azaryah* (ah-ZAHR-yah) (H) God helps – Azaria, Azaryahu

Azriel (ahz-ree-EHL) (H) God is my help

Baram* (BAH-ram) son of a nation

Baruch* (bah-ROOKH) (H) blessed

Beinish (BEH-ee-neesh) (Y) son of the right hand

Bela (BEH-lah) (H) destruction (old-fashioned)

Ben* (H) son

Ben-ami* (beh-NAH-mee) (H) son of my people

Ben-aryeh (H) son of lion – Benroy

Ben-tziyon (behn-tsee-YON) (H) son of Zion – Ben-Zion

Bendit (BEHN-deet) (Y) blessed

Ber* (BEHR) (Y) bear – Baer

Berakhiah (H) God blesses

Berg mountain

Betzalel* (BEH-tsah-lehl) (H) in the shadow of God

Binah (BEE-nah) (H) understanding; wisdom (old-fashioned)

Binyamin* (ben-yah-MEEN) (H) son of the right hand – Benjamin

Boas* (BO-ahz) (H) swift and strong – Boaz

Breindel (breh-een-DEHL) (Y) blessing – Breine

Carmel* (KAHR-mehl) (H) garden

Carmi* (H) vine dresser

Chagai (khah-GAH-ee) (H) meditation

Chaim* (KHIGHM) (H) life – Hayyim, Chayim

Chana* (KHAH-nah) (Y) God is gracious – Hannah

Chanan (KHAH-nun) (H) cloud

Chanoch* (KHAH-nokh) (H) initiating

Chavivi (khah-VEE-vee) (H) beloved — Chaviv, Habib

Chiram (H) exalted, noble

Choni (H) gracious

Dagan* (H) corn or grain

Dani* (DAHN-ee) (H) God is my judge

Daniel* (H) God is my judge — Daniyel

Dar* (H) pearl

David* (dah-VEED) (H) beloved

Dekel* (DEH-kehl) palm tree, or date palm

Deron (DEH-ron) (H) bird; freedom

Dor* (H) a generation; a home

Doron* (DO-ron) (H) gift

Dotan* (DO-tahn) law — Dothan

Dov* (DOV) (Y) bear

Dovev (DO-vehv) (H) to whisper; to speak quietly

Eben (H) rock — Eban (old-fashioned)

Efrat* (H) honored

Efrayim* (EH-frah-eem) (H) fruitful — Ephraim

Ehud* (eh-HOOD) (H) Biblical name

Elan* (eh-LAHN) (H) tree

Elchanan* (ehl-KHAH-nahn) God is gracious — Elkan

Eleazar* (EHL-ee-ah-ZAHR) (H) God has helped — Elazaro, Eli, Elie

Elhanan* (H) God is gracious

Eli* (EL-lee) (H) highest

Eliezer* (EH-lee-eh-zehr) (H) God aids — Eleazar

Elijah (eh-LEE-juh) Jehovah is God — El, Elia, Elias, Elihu, Eliot, Ellis

Eliseo (H) God is my salvation — Elisha

Elisha* (eh-LEE-shah) (H) God is salvation

Elishama* (H) God hears

Elisheva* (H) God is my oath — Elisheba

Eliyahu* (eh-lee-YA-hoo) (H) the Lord is God — Elijah

Elkanah* (ehl-KAH-nah) (H) God possessed

Elliott (H) close to God

Elrad* (EHL-rahd) (H) God rules

Elye (ehl-YEH) (Y) the Lord is God — Ellie

Emanual* (H) God is with us — Immanuel, Manual, Eman

Enoch (H) educated, dedicated

Ephraim* (H) doubly fruitful

Eshkol (H) grape cluster

Ethan* (EH-thahn) (H) strong — Etan

Eyov (H) symbol of piety and resignation of the just — Job

Ezer* (EH-zehr) help — Azrikam, Azur, Ezri, Azariah, Ezra

Feivel (FEH-ee-fehl) (Y) God aids

Gad (GAHD) good fortune

Gadi (GAH-dee) (Arabic) my fortune

Gadiel* (gah-dee-EHL) (Arabic) God is my fortune

Gal* (H) wave, mountain

Gavi* (GAH-vee) from Gabriel (H) God is my strength

Gavriel* (gahv-ree-EHL) (H) God is my strength — Gabriel

Gedalya* (geh-DAHL-yah) (H) God has made great — Gedaliah, Gedalyahu

Gershom* (gehr-SHOM) (Y) a stranger there

Gideon* feller of trees

Gil* (GEEL) (H) happiness

Gilad* (GIL-ad) camel hump, man from Giladi

Gili* (H) my joy — Gilli

Gilon* (gee-LON) circle

Givon* (gee-VON) hill; heights

Goel (go-EHL) the redeemer

Guri (H) my lion cub

Gurion (GOO-ree-on) (H) young lion

Guy* (H) valley

Hadar* (ha-DAHR) (H) glory

Hanan (H) grace — Johanan

Hananel* (H) God is gracious

Harel* (H) mountain of God — Harrell

Harrod* (H) heroic conqueror

Henoch (HEH-nokh) (Y) initiating — Enoch

Hersh (HEHRSH) (Y) deer — Hirshel

Hertz (HEHRTS) (Y) my strife — Herzel

Hod* (HOD) (H) vigorous, splendid

Honi (H) gracious — Choni

Hoshea* (H) salvation — Hosheah

Immanu-el (H) God with us

Isaac* (H) laughter

Isaiah* (H) God lends

Isser (EE-sehr) (Y) Israel — Yisra-el

Itai* (H) friendly

Ittamar* (EE-tah-mahr) (H) island of palms

Itzik (EE — Izik

Jael* (YAH-ehl) (H) mountain goat — Yael

Japhet (YAH-fet) (H) youthful, beautiful

Jephtah (H) he will open (first born)

Jocheved (YO-khuh-vehd) (H) God is glorious (old-fashioned)

Joel* (YO-ehl) God is willing

Jonah* (yo-NAH) (H) dove

Joshua* (YO-shua) (H) God saves

Judah (YOO-dah) (H) praise — Jud, Judd, Jude, Judas

Kyle (KIL) (Y) crowned with laurels

Lapidos (LAH-pee-dos) (H) torches — Lapidoth

Lavan* (LAH-van) (H) white — Laban

Lavi* (LAH-vee) (H) lion

Leben (LEH-behn) (Y) life

Leib (Y) lion — Leibel

Leor* (LEE-or) I have light

Leron* (LEE-ron) song is mine — Liron

Lev* (LEHV) (H) heart — Leb

Levi* (H) joined in harmony — Lev, Levey, Lewi

Machum (MAH-khum) (H) comfort — Nahum

Mai-ron (may-RON) (H) name of a holy place

Malachi* my messenger — Mal, Malachy

Marnin (MAHR-neen) (H) one who creates joy — (old-fashioned)

Mayir* (MEH-eer) (H) enlightener — Meir

Menachem* (meh-NAH-khem) (H) comforter — Nachum

Menassah* (H) causing to forget

Mendel (MEHN-dehl) (Y) comforter

Micha* (MEE-shah) (H) who is like God? — Michah

Micha-el* (me-shah-EHL) (H) who is like God? — Michel

Michael* (H) who is like God?

Miron (H) my messenger

Mordechai (MOR-duh-khah-ee) (H) warrior — Mordecai (old-fashioned)

Mosheh (MO-sheh) (H) drawn out (from the water) — Moses (old-fashioned)

Naaman* (nah-MAHN) (H) pleasant

Nachman* (NAKH-mahn) (H) comforter

Nadav* (NAH-dahv) (H) giver

Nadiv* (H) noble

Naftali* (H) wreath — Naftalie

Nahum (H) compassionate, comforted

Namir* (nah-MEER) the leopard

Nechemya* (neh-KHEM-yah) (H) God comforts — Nehemiah

Nissim (nee-SEEM) (H) wonders; miracles

Noach* (NO-ahkh) (H) rest — Noah

Noam* (NO-ahm) pleasant

Nuri (H) my fire

Oded* (O-dehd) (H) encourage

Ofer* (H) young deer

Ophir* (O-fer) (H) Biblical name

Oren* (H) tree — Orin, Oris

Ori* (H) my light

Orneet* (H) light, cedar tree

Ovadiah* (o-vah-DEE-ah) (H) servant of God — Ovadya

Oved* (O-vehd) (H) worshiper, worker

Ozi (H) strong

Palti (pahl-TEE) (H) God liberates — Palti-el

Paz (H) golden

Pessach (PEH-sakh) (H) spared — Pesach

Pinchos (PEEN-khos) (H) mouth of brass; dark complexion

Pinye (PEEN-yeh) (Y) dark complexion

R'phael* (ruh-fah-EHL) (H) God heals — Raphael

Raanan* (RAH-nahn) (H) fresh, luxuriant

Raisa (RAH-ee-sah) (Y) rose — Raysel

Ranit* (RAH-neet) (H) song — Ronit

Ravid* (H) wander — Arvad, Arvid

Razi (Aramaic) secret — Raz, Raziel

Re'uven* (reh-oo-VEHN) (H) behold, a son — Reuben

Rechavia (reh-khah-VEE-ah) (H) breadth

Ron* (RON) (H) sing

Ronit* (RAH-neet) (H) song — Rani, Roni

Saadya* (SAHD-yah) (H) God's helper

Sasson* (SAHS-son) (H) joy

Sha-ul* (SHAH-ul) (H) asked for — Saul

Shachna (SHAHKH-nah) (Y) close to God

Shalom* (shah-LOM) (H) peace

Shamir (shuh-MEER) a rocklike material that can cut through metal

Shelomo* (sheh-LO-mo) (H) peaceable — Solomon

Shet (H) compensation, appointed

Shim'on* (shee-MON) (H) hearing, with acceptance — Simeon, Simon

Shimshon* (sheem-SHON) (H) like the sun — Sampson

Shmaiah* (shmah-EE-ah) (H) God hears

Shmuel* (shmoo-EHL) (H) God hears — Samuel

Shraga* (SHRAG-gah) (Y) Phoebus, sun (old-fashioned)

Simcha* (SEEM-khah) (H) joy

Sinai (H) clay desert

Tal (H) dew or rain — Talor

Tevel (TEH-vehl) (Y) df. David (H) beloved

Tovi (H) good

Tuvya (tuv-YAH) (H) God's goodness — Tuvyahu, Tobiah

Tzadok (tsah-DOK) (H) just — Zadok

Tzefanyah (tseh-FAHN-yah) (H) treasured by God — Tzefanyahu, Zephaniah

Tzion (H) sunny mountain — Zion

Tzuriel (TSOO-ree-ehl) (H) God is my rock

Tzvi (TSVEE) (H) deer — Zevi

Uri (OO-ree) (H) my light

Uriah (OO-ree-yah) (H) light of God

Uriel (oo-ree-EHL) (H) light of God

Uzziel (H) God is strong — Uzziah

Velvel (VEHL-vehl) (Y) wolf

Yaakov (YAH-kov) (H) supplanter; held by the heel — Jacob

Yagil (YAH-gel) (H) he will rejoice

Yair (YAH-eer) (H) he will enlighten — Jair

Yaphet (H) handsome — Japhet

Yardane (yahr-DAH-neh) (H) descendant — Jordan

Yaron (H) singing

Yavin (H) he will understand — Jabin

Yechiel (YEHKH-ee-ehl) God liveth — Jehiel

Yedidyah (yeh-dee-DEE-yah) (H) beloved of God — Jedediah

Yeeshai (yeh-SHAH-ee) (H) wealthy, gift — Jesse

Yehoash (yeh-HO-ahsh) (H) God gave — Jehoash

Yehonadov (yeh-HO-nah-dov) (H) God giveth — Nadab, Jonadab (old-fashioned)

Yehoshua (ye-HO-shoo-ah) (H) God's help — Joshua

Yehudah (yeh-HOO-dah) (H) praised — Judah

Yerachmiel (yehr-AHKH-mee-ehl) (H) whom God loves — Jerahmeel (old-fashioned)

Yerucham (YEH-roo-khahm) (H) loved; finding mercy — Jeruham

Yeshaya (yeh-SHAH-yah) (H) God lends — Yeshayahu

Yeshurun (yeh-SHOO-roon) (H) the right way — Jeshurun (old-fashioned)

Yiftach (YEHF-tahkh) (H) will open — Jephthah

Yigal (yee-GAH-ehl) (H) he will redeem — Yigol

Yisrael (yees-rah-EHL) (H) prince of God; strove with God — Israel

Yissachar (yee-SAH-khahr) (H) there is a reward — Issachar

Yitzchak (YEETZ-khahk) (H) sporting; will laugh — Isaac

Yo-el (yo-EHL) (H) God prevails — Joel

Yoav (YO-ahv) Biblical name — Joab

Yochanan (yo-KHAH-nahn) (H) grace of God — Johanan

Yomtov (YOM-tov) (H) holiday

Yonah (YO-nah) (H) dove — Jonah

Yoram (H) high God — Joram

Yosef (YO-sehf) (H) God will add

Yuval (H) rejoicing

Z'ev (SEHV) (H) wolf — Ze'ev

Zachariah (H) remembered by the Lord — Zachary, Zach

Zaide (SAH-ee-deh) (Y) elder

Zalman (Y) peaceable

Zamir a bird, or a song

Zanvil (SAHN-veel) (Y) God hears — Zanwill

Zayit (H) olive

Zelig (SEH-leeg) (Y) blessed — Zelik

Zevulun (ZEH-voo-loon) (H) habitation — Zebulun

Zimra (ZEEM-rah) (H) song

Zindel (SEEN-dehl) (Y) df. Alexander (Gr) defender of man — Zindil, Zunde

Ziskind (ZEES-keend) (Y) df. Eliezer (H) God aids

Ziv (H) brightness

Zohar (zo-HAHR) (H) brilliance

ITALY

The first Italian in the New World was Christoforo Columbus who arrived in 1492. He was followed in 1502 by the explorer of South America, Amerigo Vespucci, whose name, which means "loving one" (from Latin), graces two continents. However, Italians were slow to immigrate to the U.S. in the early years of the country. By 1850 only 5,000 Italians lived here. Few immigrated before 1880, and most of them were well-educated northerners.

After 1880 huge numbers of illiterate peasants began immigrating from southern Italy (anywhere south of Rome) a region called "mezzogiorno," meaning "the land time forgot," when an unprecedented series of disasters devastated the region's economy. A civil war won in 1860 by northerners failed to bring unification.

Corruption and bungling in the new government caused hardship to peasants because of high rents imposed by absentee landlords, increased taxes on grain, and the expensive price of salt that made it nearly impossible to store food.

The land was barren after centuries of deforestation and erosion. The population of Italy increased by twenty-five percent between 1871 and 1905. In 1881 two-thirds of the population of Naples was without food or employment, according to a government study. In 1906 Mt. Vesuvius erupted near Naples, in 1910 Mt. Etna erupted in Sicily, and many earthquakes and tidal waves also decimated the region. Even today, most of the immigrants from Italy come from the "mezzogiorno."

So strong are family ties in Italy that only the direst conditions could force young men to leave their families. Over one million Italians immigrated to the U.S. between 1880 and 1900, eighty percent of whom were males aged fourteen to forty-five. They came primarily to fill the nearly insatiable demand for labor brought about by the Industrial Revolution. Many of them planned to work until they made enough money to return to Italy to buy land. In fact, more than one-third of them did, spurred in part by prejudice they encountered in the U.S.

Many Italian laborers worked construction during the nine months around summer in the U.S., then sailed home to Italy. Others headed to Argentina, which had one of the fastest growing economies in the world, to work during the winter. Some followed this migratory pattern several times and came to be called "birds of passage" or "golondrinas" (swallows) in Argentina.

Most immigrants of this time period settled in the Northeast, however by 1897, 45,000 Italians lived in California, called "Italy in America" because of its climate. The multi-million dollar Del Monte Company and the Bank of America (formerly the Bank of Italy, now the largest bank in the world) were both started in California by Italian immigrants.

However, by far the largest wave of Italian immigration occurred between 1900 and 1920 when three million moved to the U.S. Again, many of them returned to their homeland as in 1908 when the number of Italians re-migrating soared to 160,000, half the total number of immigrants that year.

Later, more immigrants stayed, often settling in the cities. The 1940 census shows eighty-eight percent of Italian-Americans were urban-dwellers. A total of 4.7 million Italians immigrated to the U.S. between 1890 and 1950. Immigration continued through the 1960's averaging 20,000 per year, then 10,000 annually in the 1970's, and now down to about 4,000 per year.

In Italy the traditional influence is strong, with most native parents selecting Italian names for their babies. This custom is a contrast to other European countries where there is more borrowing from other cultures. It is customary in southern Italy to give the first-born the father's name; if the child is a girl the name is adapted to a female form. The names in this list are all in current use in Italy with the most popular ones noted.

Pronunciation

a = "ah" as in ball
c= "k" as in carry
e = "eh" as in late
c= "ch" as in church (before e, i)
i= "ee" as in keep
ch= "k" as in carry
i = "y" as in yet when before ci=
   "ch" as in church another
   vowel (before a,o,u)
o = "oh" as in hope
gi= "j" as in joke
u = "oo" as in moon

g, gh = "g" as in gun
u = "w" as in well before
g = "j" as in joke (before e,i)
   another vowel
gli= "ly" as in million
gn = "ny" as in onion
h = always silent
sc = "sh" as in ship (before e, i)
sch = "sk" as in skill
z = "ts" as in bets
zz = "dz" as in adze

ITALIAN FEMALE NAMES

Agnese (ah-NYEH-seh) (Gr) gentle, pure

Aida (ah-EE-dah) happy

Alberta (OGer) noble, bright — Berta

Alessandra (Gr) defender of mankind

Allegra happy

Alonza (ah-LON-tsah) (Teut) eager for battle

Andreana fem. Andrew (L)

Angela (Gr) angel

Anna (H) grace — Annabella, Annamaria

Annunziata (ahn-noon-tsee-AH-tah) (Sp) religious holiday

Antonia (L) inestimable

Baptiste (Gr) baptizer — Bautista (old-fashioned)

Barbara (Gr) the stranger

Beatrice (beh-ah-TREE-cheh) (L) she blesses

Benedetta (L) blesses

Benigna (bee-NEEN-yah) (L) kind, blessed

Berta (OGer) bright, glorious

Bianca (L) white

Bruna (Teut) dark-haired

Cara (L) dear — Carina (old-fashioned)

Carlotta (Fr) petite and feminine

Carmelina (H) vineyard

Carolina fem. Carlo (OFr)

Caterina (Gr) pure

Cecilia (L) gray eyes, blind

Cira (CHEE-rah) possibly from Persian for "sun"

Clara (L) bright, clear — Clariss, Clarice

Claudia (L) lame

Concetta (kon-CHEHT-tah) (Span) Immaculate Conception — Conchetta

Constanza (L) constant — Constantia, Constantina

Cristina (L) Christian

Donata (L) gift

Dorotea (L) gift of God

Editta (Teut) rich gift

Elda var. Hilda (Teut) warrior

Elenora (Gr) light — Elena

Elisabetta (H) consecrated to God

Emilia (Teut) industrious

Emma (OGer) universal

Eva (H) life

Fabiana (L) bean grower — Fabia, Fabiola

Fausta (L) fortunate

Fidelia (L) faithful

Filomena (Gr) lover of mankind

Fiorenza (L) flower

Flaminia (L) Roman priest

Flavia (L) blonde, yellow

Florenza (L) flowering

Fortuna (L) goddess of good luck — Fortune

Francesca (frahn-CHEHS-kah) (Teut) free

Fulvia (L) blond

Gabriela (H) God is my strength — Gabriella

Gaetane (gah-eh-TAH-neh) from Gaete in central Italy — Gaetana

Gelsomina (jehl-so-MEE-nah) (Persian) jasmine

Gemma (JEM-mah) (Fr) precious stone

Genevra (OFr) juniper

Ghita (GEE-tah) (Gr) pearl

Giacinta (jah-SEEN-tah) (Gr) hyacinth

Gina (JEE-nah) var. Eugenia (Gr) — Luigina

Ginevra (Celt) white as foam

Giovanna (H) God's gracious gift

Giuditta (joo-DEE-tah) (H) praised

Giulia (JOOL-yah) (L) youth — Juliet, Juliana

Giuseppina (joo-sehp-PEE-nah) (H) God will add

Grazia (GRAH-tsee-ah) (L) graceful

Gulielma fem. Wilhelm — Helmina, Guillelmina, Minna, Helm, Willa

Irene (ee-REH-neh) (Gr) peace

Isabella (H) consecrated to God — Bella, Isabela

Laura (L) crown of laurels — Laurenza, Lorenya

Leonora (Gr) light — Lina

Letizia (leh-TEE-tsee-ah) (L) gladness

Lia (Gr) bringer of good news

Lucia (loo-CHEE-ah) (L) light — Luca, Luciana

Luisa (OGer) famous warrior woman

Manuela (H) God is with us

Margherita (Gr) a pearl

Maria (H) bitter — Mara, Mariana, Marea, Marietta

Marta (Gr) a pearl

Martina (L) warlike (fem. Mark) — Marcia, Marcella

Massima (L) greatest

Maura (OFr) dark-skinned

Melania (Gr) black

Mercede (mehr-CHEH-deh) (L) merciful

Michaela (mee-KAH-ee-lah) (H) who is like God?

Nicia (NEE-chee-ah) (Gr) fem. Nicholas

Nunzia (NOON-tsee-ah) (L) messenger

Olga (Russian) holy

Olimpia (Gr) Olympian

Oriana (L) the East, golden — Oria (old-fashioned)

Ortensia (L) gardener

Ottavia eighth

Paola (pah-O-lah) (L) little

Patrizia (pah-TREET-see-ah) (L) noble, wellborn

Philippa (Gr) lover of horses — Pippa

Pia (L) pious

Rachele (rah-CHEH-leh) (H) innocence of a lamb

Rebecca (H) servant of God, binding

Regina (reh-JEE-nah) (L) queen

Renata (reh-NAH-tah) (L) reborn

Ricarda (OGer) ruler

Roma (L) eternal city (rare)

Rosa (L) rose — Rosina, Rosalba, Roseta, Rosana

Rosalia comb. Rose and Lily

Rosamaria comb. Rose and Mary

Rufina (L) red hair

Ruth (H) beauty, friend

Sabrina (L) from the border

Sancia (SAHN-cha) (Span) holy (old-fashioned)

Sara (H) princess

Sebastiana (Gr) venerable

Serafina seraph

Serena (L) serene

Sigismonda (Teut) conquering protection

Silvana (L) forest — Silvia

Simona (H) God is heard

Sofia (Gr) wisdom — Sophia

Speranza (L) hope

Susana (H) lily — Suzetta

Tecla (Gr) divine fame

Teodora (Gr) gift of God

Teresa (Gr) harvester

Tiberia of the Tiber

Tonia (L) short for Antoinette (L) beyond praise

Trista (L) woman of sadness (old-fashioned)

Valentina (L) strong, brave

Violetta (L) violet

Virginia (L) pure

Vittoria (L) victorious

Viviana (L) lively

ITALIAN MALE NAMES

Abramo (H) father of a multitude

Adriano (L) of the Adriatic

Aldo* (OE) antiquity

Alessandro (Gr) defender of mankind

Alfonso (OGer) noble, ready

Amadeo (L) love God

Amerigo (Teut) industrious

Anastagio (Gr) resurrection

Anatolio (Gr) from the East

Andrea (Gr) manly

Angelo (Gr) messenger

Antonio (L) inestimable

Armanno (Teut) soldier — Armino

Arnaldo (Teut) mighty in battle — Aroldo

Arrigo (Teut) ruler of an estate — Arrighetto, Alrigo, Enrico

Arturo (Celt) noble; bear man

Baldassare Balthazar

Basilio (Gr) kingly

Benedetto (L) blessed

Beniamino (H) son of the right hand

Bernardo (OGer) courage of a bear

Bruno brown-haired — Bruns

Carlo (OFr) strong and manly — Carlino

Carmine (kahr-MEE-neh) (H) vineyard

Cecilio (L) gray eyes, blind

Cesare Caesar — Caseareo

Corrado (Ger) bold, wise counselor

Cristoforo (Gr) Christ-bearer

Daniele (dahn-YEHL-eh) (H) God is my judge

Dante lasting

Dominico (L) of the Lord — Domenico

Donato (L) a gift — Donato, Donatello

Edmondo (OE) prosperous protector

Edoardo (OE) wealthy guardian — Eduardo

Egidio (eh-GEE-dee-o) (Gr) shield-bearer

Enea (Gr) ninth

Enrico (Teut) ruler of an estate

Enzo var. Henry (Teut) ruler of an estate

Ercole (Gr) glorious gift

Ermanno (Teut) warrior

Ernesto (OGer) serious

Ettore (Gr) steadfast

Eugenio (Gr) noble

Fabiano (L) bean farmer — Fabio

Fabrizio (fah-BREET-see-o) (L) craftsman

Fausto (L) fortunate

Federico (Teut) peaceful ruler — Federigo

Felice (feh-LEE-cheh) (L) fortunate, or lucky — Felicio

Fidelio (L) faithful

Filippo (Gr) lover of horses — Pippo, Lippo, Lipp

Flavio (L) blond, yellow

Francesco (frahn-CHEHS-co) (Teut) free — Franco

Gabriele (gah-bree-EH-leh) (H) God is my strength

Gaetano from Gaete in central Italy

Georgio (Gr) farmer — Giorgio

Gerardo (jehr-AHR-do) (OE) spear hard — Gherardo

Geremia (H) God is high

Giacomo (H) the supplanter

Gian (JON) (H) God's gracious gift

Giancarlo comb. of John and Charles

Gilberto (Teut) illustrious pledge

Gino short for Louis

Giorgio (Gr) farmer

Giovanni (jo-VAHN-ee) (H) gracious gift of God

Giuliano (joo-LYAH-no) (L) youth

Giulio (JOO-lee-o) (Gr) youthful

Giuseppe* (joo-SEHP-ah) (H) God will add

Giustino (joo-STEE-no) (L) the just − Giusto

Goffredo (Teut) God's peace − Godofredo, Giotto

Gregorio (Gr) vigilant

Gualtiero (Teut) powerful ruler − Galtero

Guglielmo (goo-lyee-EHL-mo) (Teut) resolute guardian

Guido (GWEE-do) (L) life

Gustavo (Teut) staff of the gods

Ignazio (ee-NYAH-tsee-o) (L) fiery

Ilario (L) cheerful

Innocenzio (ee-no-CHEHN-tsee-o) (Span) innocent, harmless

Lazzaro (lahd-ZAHR-o) (H) God will help

Leonardo (Teut) bold lion

Leone (leh-O-neh) (L) lion − Leonidas

Lorenzo (L) crowned with laurel − Loretto, Renzo

Luciano (loo-chee-AH-no) (L) light − Lucio, Lucan

Lucio (LOO-chee-o) (L) bringer of light − Luca, Lucca, Luciano

Luigi (OGer) renowned warrior − Luigino

Marcello (L) warlike − Marco, Marciano, Marcelino, Martino

Marco (L) warlike − Mario

Marino (L) sea

Mario (L) warlike

Martino (L) warlike

Massimo (L) most excellent − Massimiliano

Matteo (mah-TEH-o) (H) gift of God

Maurizio (L) Moorish

Michele (mee-SHEHL-leh) (H) who is like God?

Nicola (Gr) victory of the people − Cola, Niccolo

Nuncio (L) messenger − Nunzio

Octavio (L) eighth

Orlando (OGer) from the famous land

Ottavio (L) eighth

Paolo (L) little

Pasquale (pahs-QUAH-leh) (Fr) Easter

Patrizio (pah-TREET-see-o) (L) noble

Piero (Gr) stone

Pietro (Gr) stone − Perino, Pero, Piero

Pio (L) pious

Rafaele (H) God has healed − Rafaello

Raimondo (Teut) mighty protector

Renato (L) reborn

Renzo laurel, short for Lorenzo

Riccardo (ree-KAHR-do) (OGer) powerful ruler − Ricciardo (ree-CHAHR-do)

Rinaldo (Teut) wise power

Roberto (Teut) of shining fame

Romano (L) Roman

Ruggero (roo-GEHR-o) (Teut) famous warrior − Rogero

Ruggiero (roo-JEHR-o) (Teut) famous warrior

Salvatore (sahl-vah-TO-reh) (Span) Savior

Sandro short for Alexander (Gr) defender of mankind

Sebastiano (Gr) venerable, revered

Sergio (SEHR-jee-o) (L) the attendant

Sigismondo (Teut) conquering protection

Silvano (L) forest − Silvio

Silvestro (L) from the woods

Stefano (Gr) crown

Tiberio of the Tiber

Tito (Gr) of the giants

Tobia (H) God is good

Tomasso (H) twin

Uberto (oo-BEHR-to) (Teut) bright mind

Ugo (OO-go) (Teut) intelligence, spirit

Valerio (L) strong, brave − Valentino

Vincenzo (veen-CHEHN-tso) (L) conqueror − Vincenzio

Vitale (L) living

Vito (L) short for Vittorio (L) conqueror

Vittorio (L) conqueror

JAPAN

Japan had been isolated for hundreds of years when Commodore Matthew Perry of the U.S. Navy convinced Japan to open its ports to the West in 1869. Not surprisingly, there is no recorded immigration from Japan until 1861, and even then less than 300 Japanese arrivals between 1861 and 1880. Most of them came by by accident, being shipwrecked sailors.

In 1885 the Japanese government passed laws allowing people to emigrate. After that immigration from Japan rose sharply fueled by the Chinese Exclusion Act of 1882 which prohibited Chinese immigration. A severe labor shortage on the West Coast led to an influx of Japanese, most of whom were willing to work for low wages.

Japanese immigration was also encouraged by a law passed by the Japanese government in 1896 allowing a person to emigrate only if he had someone responsible for his financial support should he become ill or unable to work. Because the financial requirements were so strict, few Japanese families could afford an emigrant. However, emigration companies arose in Japan in co-operation with American companies which provided the necessary financial backing in exchange for a work contract.

This system proved enormously successful, and between 1899 and 1904 nearly 60,000 Japanese came to America this way, primarily ending up in California and the territory of Hawaii.

The total immigration between 1891 and 1924 was recorded at nearly 300,000; however many returned to Japan or went back and forth several times. By 1920 about 110,000 Japanese lived in California and an equal number in Hawaii.

West Coast natives began to fear that the Japanese would flood the labor market in a re-run of the earlier panic that led to the Chinese Exclusion Act of 1882. Under pressure from the public the U.S. negotiated the Gentlemen's Agreement with Japan under which Japan agreed to voluntarily restrict emigration of laborers.

Professionals could still immigrate, however, so arrivals continued. Also "picture brides," courted by the families of Japanese immigrants, came to relieve the two to one balance of male to female among the immigrants.

Japanese immigration virtually came to a halt in 1924 when the Immigration Act excluded immigrants who could never become citizens. At the time only whites and Negroes could become naturalized citizens.

After World War II Japanese brides of American soldiers stationed in Japan (an estimated 25,000 by 1960) began to arrive along with other nonquota immigrants. In the 1960's and 1970's the immigration from Japan has remained at about 4,000 per year. Because of their low numbers these new immigrants have been able to assimilate fairly easily into mainstream culture.

Japanese names come from a variety of sources. Some names are made up when parents may take a Chinese character and interpret it in some unique way. They may play with syllables to come up with a new name, but this is more common for girls than boys. Boys and girls may be named for someone in the family or country who has achieved much. Male virtues such as courage, wisdom, power, and tranquility may be a name source. The female virtues embodied in names are such attributes as gentleness, wisdom, purity, and beauty.

Number names are sometimes used. Low numbers denote birth order, and very high numbers such as "chi" (thousand) a wish for the child's long life. Girls may be named for the month flower of the month they were born in; for instance "kiku" means chrysanthemum and is the month flower for November. Foreign names used as Japanese names are possible if they "sound" Japanese. Mari ("Mary") and Mai ("May") are popular now, by coincidence, and each means something in Japanese.

The suffixes -ko, -e, and -yo denote female names, and the suffix -o appears in male names.

Pronunciation

Japanese pronunciation is very consistent.

a = "a" as in ball   o = "oh" as in hope
e = "eh" as in late   u = "oo" as in moon
i = "ee" as in keep
Consonants are the same as in English.

JAPANESE FEMALE NAMES

Ai (ah-EE) love, indigo blue

Aiko little love, beloved

Akako red

Akasuki bright helper

Aki (ah-KEE) born in autumn

Akina very bright spring flower; bright leaves

Anzu apricot

Aoi hollyhock

Asa (AH-sah) born in the morning

Au meeting

Ayako damask pattern

Ayamé iris flower

Azami thistle flower

Chika near – Chikako

Chikako clever; wisdom

Chitose thousand years

Chiyo thousand generations

Chizu a thousand storks – Chizuko

Cho born at dawn; butterfly

Dai great

Den bequest from ancestors

Etsu delight

Fuyu born in winter

Gen source, spring

Gin silver – Gina

Hama (hah-MAH) shore – Hamako

Hanako flower, fair blossom – Hana, Hanae

Haru born in spring

Harué springtime bay

Haruko tranquil, born in spring

Hatsu first-born

Haya quick, light

Hidé excellent

Hidéyo superior generations

Hiro broad

Hiroko magnanimous

Hisa (hee-SAH) long-lasting – Hisako, Hisae, Hisayo

Hisano long plain

Hoshi star – Hoshiko, Hoshie

Iku nourishing

Ima now – Imako

Iné rice

Isamu vigorous, robust

Ishi (ee-SHEE) stone – Ishie

Ito thread

Iwa rock

Jin tenderness

Junko obedient

Kaedé maple leaf

Kagami mirror

Kaiyo forgiveness

Kama sickle

Kamé tortoise (symbol of long life)

Kameko tortoise child (hope for long life) – Kaméyo

Kaméyo generations of the tortoises

Kana a character of the alphabet

Kane (KAH-nee) the doubly accomplished – Kaneko

Kaoru fragrant

Kata worthy

Katsu victorious

Kawa river

Kaya a yew, or a rush

Kazashi hair ornament

Kazu first, or obedient – Kazuko

Kei rapture, reverence – Keiko

Kichi fortunate – Yoshi

Kikuë chrysanthemum branch

Kikuko chrysanthemum (flower for November)

Kikuno chrysanthemum field

Kimi peerless – Kimiko, Kimiyo, Kimie

Kin gold

Kinu silk cloth

Kishi beach

Kiwa born on a border – Kiwako

Kiyo happy generations, pure

Kiyoshi clear, bright

Ko filial piety

Kohana little flower

Koko stork

Koma filly; term of endearment – Komako

Komé rice

Konomi nuts

Koto harp

Kozakura little cherry tree

Kozue branches of a tree

Kukiko snow

Kuma bear

Kumi braid – Kumiko

Kuni country-born – Kuniko

Kura treasure house

Kuri chestnut

Kurva mulberry tree

Kyoko mirror

Leiko arrogant

Machi ten thousand thousand (wish for long life)

Mai brightness

Mari ball – Mariko

Masa straightforward

Masago sand

Masu increase

Matsu pine, strong old age

Matsuko pine tree

Michi the righteous way

Michiko beauty and wisdom

Midori green

Mië triple branch

Mieko bright

Mika new moon

Mikazuki moon of the third night

Miki stem of the family tree

Mikie main branch

Mina south – Miniami

Miné peak — Mineko

Mineko peak; mountain child

Misao fidelity

Mitsu light — Mitsuko

Miwa the far-seeing — Mawako

Miyoko beautiful generation child — Miyo

Miyuki silence of deep snow

Mon gate

Morie bay

Moto source

Mura village

Murasaki purple

Nagisa shore

Nami wave — Namiko

Nani (Polynesian) beautiful

Naoki straight tree

Nara oak (symbol of stability)

Nari thunder peal — Nariko

Natsu born in summer

Nishi west

Nori precept, doctrine — Noriko

Nui tapestry

Nyoko gem treasure

Orino weaver's field — Ori

Rai trust

Raku pleasure

Ran water lily (symbol for purity)

Rei (RAY) gratitude; propriety — Reiko

Ren arranger

Riku land

Roku emolument

Ruri emerald — Ruriko

Ryo dragon

Ryu lofty

Sachi bliss child — Sachiko

Sada (SAH-dah) the chaste — Sadako

Sai talented

Sakaë prosperity

Saki cape

Sakura cherry blossom (symbol of wealth and prosperity)

Sato sugar

Sawa marsh

Sayo born at night

Seiko force, truth — Sei

Seki great

Sen wood fairy

Setsu fidelity — Setsuko

Shigé exuberant

Shiho to maintain original intention

Shihobu perseverance

Shika deer — Shikako

Shina good; virtue

Shino slender bamboo

Shirushi evidence

Shizu quiet, clear — Shizuyo, Shizue, Shizuko, Shizuka

Sugi cedar (symbol of moral rectitude)

Suki beloved

Sumi the clear, or refined

Suté foresaken, foundling

Suzu little bell

Suzuë branch of little bells

Suzuki bell tree

Taka tall; honorable; or falcon — Takako

Takako filial piety

Takara treasure; precious object

Také bamboo

Takeko (tah-KEH-ko) bamboo (symbol of fidelity)

Taki plunging waterfall

Tama jewel

Tamaki armlet; bracelet — Tamako

Tamé unselfish

Tami people — Tamiko

Tanaka dweller in a rice swamp

Tané seed

Tani valley

Taru cask, barrel

Tatsu dragon

Tazu rice-field stork (symbol of long life)

Tetsu iron

Toki time of opportunity

Tokiwa eternally constant

Tomi riches

Tomiju wealth and longevity

Tomo knowledge, intelligence

Tora tiger

Tori bird

Toshi year of plenty — Toshiko

Tsuhgi second child

Tsuna bond

Tsuru stork, wish for long life

Umeko plum blossom child

Uméno plum-tree field

Urano coast

Uta poem — Utako

Utano song field

Wakana plant name

Yachi eight thousand

Yasu the peaceful — Yasuko

Yayoi born in spring (March)

Yei flourishing

Yo positive — Yoko

Yoi born in the evening

Yoko positive child; female

Yoné wealth

Yori trustworthy

Yoshe a beauty

Yoshi good; the respectful — Yoshiko (good child)

Yoshino good, fertile field

Yuki snow — Yukie

Yukiko snow child (born in December)

Yuri lily — Yuriko

JAPANESE MALE NAMES

Akemi beauty of dawn

Akihiko bright male child

Akio (AH-kee-o) bright boy – Akira

Akira – intelligent

Botan (bo-TAHN) peony, the flower of June

Hideaki wisdom, clever person

Hiromasa broad-minded, just

Hiroshi generous

Hisoka scretive; reserved

Isas (ee-SAHS) meritorious

Jiro (jee-RO) the second male

Jo (H) God will increase

Joji (JO-jee) (L) farmer

Jun (JOON) obedient, purity

Kane (KAH-neh) golden

Kazuo man of peace

Ken one's own kind

Kin golden

Kiyoshi quiet

Makoto sincerity

Masahiro broad-minded

Masao righteous

Masato justice

Naoko straight, honest

Raiden (RI-den) thunder god

Ringo apple; peace be with you

Saburo third-born male

Samuru (H) his name is God

Shiro fourth-born son

Takeshi unbending (like bamboo tree)

Taro first-born male

Tomi rich

Toshihiro wise

Toshio (to-SHEE-o) year boy

Yasahiro peaceful, calm, wise

Yasuo tranquility

Yemon guarding the gate

Yukio (yoo-KEE-o) snow boy (i.e., he gets his own way)

Yukio (yoo-KEE-o) snow boy (i.e., he gets his own way)

KENYA

Like Ugandans, Kenyans were too far from the African West Coast to have been part of the forced immigration of slaves to the Western Hemisphere in the 16th-19th centuries. Immigration to the U.S. today is very small, numbering about 600 annually in recent years. This chapter is presented merely to give an example of the great diversity of African cultures.

In many ways African countries that have recently won independence from colonial rule have to contend with a melting pot of their own, one that is even more difficult to deal with than the one in America. This evolved when colonial governments simply carved up Africa, drawing boundaries suiting them rather than regarding tribal boundaries, or the fact they might be throwing together tribes that had been formerly bitter enemies. In modern America, at least, the immigrants have usually voluntarily thrown themselves into "the melting pot."

Kenya won its independence from England on December 12, 1962. It is located on the Indian Ocean on the east side of Africa. About the size of Texas, it borders Tanzania to the south, Ethiopia to the north, and Uganda and Lake Victoria (third largest lake in the world) on the west.

Of the ten million people in Kenya about two percent are Asian and Arabs, and Europeans number less than 50,000. The forty-six tribes in Kenya are divided into four main groups, the Bantu, Nilotic, Nilo-Hamitic, and Hamitic.

The largest groups are the Bantu tribes comprising sixty-five percent of the population. The Kikuyu tribe, which farms around the base of Mt. Kenya, is the largest tribe. Second largest is the Luo, a Nilotic tribe. They farm and fish near the shore of Lake Victoria in one of the most densely populated regions in Africa. The Masai are the best known of the Nilo-Hamitic tribes. They are Nomadic herdsmen who inhabit the Great Rift Valley, a massive chasm that cuts through Kenya from north to south twenty to forty miles wide and in places 2,000 to 3,000 feet below the surrounding area. The largest Hamitic tribe is the Somali, also herdsmen who range over northern Kenya.

The presence of nearly 200,000 Asians is due to the 35,000 East Indians who were recruited by the British at the turn of the century to build a railroad from the seaport of Mombasa to Lake Victoria. The present Indians are their descendants.

Although each tribe speaks its own dialect, the government encourages all to learn to speak Swahili, a Bantu language which developed from a mixture of Arabic, a little Portuguese, Galla (from the Horn of Africa), and several local languages. Swahili is spoken all over Eastern and Central Africa, which includes Kenya, Uganda, Rwanda, Burundi, Tanzania, provinces of the Congo, Malawi, northern Zambia, and Mozambique. There are several dialects of Swahili; however all are mutually intelligible. Thus Swahili names are found under several ethnic groups in eastern and central Africa. Islam has been an important presence and influence in East Africa and has made a considerable contribution to the Swahili vocabulary. In addition to the Bantu language names in Swahili, there are many names that are "Swahilized" forms of Muslim, or Arabic names.

Among Swahili speakers, a child is given a name immediately after birth called his "jina la utotoni" or childhood name by an elderly relative or occasionally by the attending midwife. Somewhat a nickname, it may either describe circumstances at time of the child's birth or the child's appearance.

Seven and sometimes up to forty days later, the child is given his "jina la ukubwani," or adult name, usually of Islamic or Biblical origin and always given by the child's parents or paternal grandparents. The oldest boy in the family usually bears the name of his paternal grandfather; the eldest girl, her paternal grandmother.

Naming ceremonies vary, even among different families in the same immediate area. They are along the same general lines, however, with elders playing a significant role in the proceedings. Considerable attention is paid to the requirements of family and religious traditions.

In recent years when Afro-Americans dropped their "Christian" names in favor of African names they were following ancestral precedent as well as contemporary African custom. Adults might change their names when the individual concerned has acquired a special personal characteristic — physical, intellectual, or moral — or is perceived as being capable of displaying some distinctive quality. In addition, the careful consideration in choosing a name which is an apt description or self-fulfilling prophecy signifies the bearer's spiritual liberation and personal and group identity. Opanin Kwame Nyame declared: "Man came to seek a name, and nothing more."

KENYAN FEMALE NAMES

Abbo (Dama) vegetable

Afiya (ah-FEE-yah) (Swahili, from Tanzania) health

Aisha (Swa) (ah-EE-shah) life

Aluna (Mwera) come here

Arusi (ah-ROO-see) (Swahili) born at the time of a wedding — Harusi

Asha (AH-shah) (Swahili) life

Ashura (ah-SHOO-rah)(Swahili) born during Islamic month Ashur

Asya (AHSS-yah) (Swahili) born at a time of grief

Ayubu (ah-YOO-boo) (Swahili) patience in suffering

Aziza (ah-ZEE-zah) (Swahili) precious

Bahati (bah-HAH-tee) (Swahili) luck

Barika (Swahili) bloom, or be successful

Bimkubwa (beem-KOOB-wah) (Swahili) a great lady

Chausiku (chah-oo-SEE-koo) (Swahili) born at night

Chiku (CHE-koo) (Swahili) chatterer

Chuki (CHOO-ke) (Swahili) born when there was animosity

Dalila (dah-LEE-lah) (Swahili) gentle

Dalili (dah-LEE-lee) (Swahili) sign, omen

Eshe (EH-sheh) (Swahili) life

Faraji (fah-RAH-jee) (Swahili) consolation

Fatuma (fah-TOO-mah) (Swahili) weaned

Fujo (FOO-jo) (Swahili) born after parents' separation

Hadiya (hah-DEE-yah) (Swahili) gift — Hadiyah

Halima (hah-LEE-mah) (Swahili) gentle

Haoniyao (hah-o-nee-YAH-o) (Swahili) born at the time of a quarrel

Hasanati (hah-sah-NAH-tee) (Swahili) good

Hasina (hah-SEE-nah) (Swahili) good

Hawa (HAH-wah) (Swahili) longing, or Eve

Jaha (JAH-hah) (Swahili) dignity

Jamila (jah-MEE-lah) (Swahili) beautiful

Jokha (JO-kah) (Swahili) robe of adornment

Jumapili (joo-mah-PEE-lee) (Mwera) born on Sunday

Kamaria (kah-mah-REE-ah) (Swahili) like the moon

Kanika (Mwera) black cloth

Kesi (KEH-see) (Swahili) born when father was in trouble

Khadija (kah-DEE-jah) (Swahili) born prematurely

Kibibi (kee-BEE-bee) (Swahili) little lady

Kifimbo (kee-FEEM-bo) (Swahili) a very thin baby, literally, twig

Kijakazi (kee-jah-KAH-zee) (Swahili) your life is due to us

Layla (LAH-ee-lah) (Swahili) born at night

Lulu (Swahili) a pearl

Marjani (mahr-JAH-nee) (Swahili) coral

Mashavu (Swahili) cheeks [literally, baby with chubby cheeks]

Masika (Swahili) born during rainy season

Maskini (mah-SKEE-nee) (Swahili) poor

Maulidi (mah-oo-LEE-dee) (Swahili) born during Islamic month Maulidi

Mkiwa ('m-KEE-wah) (Swahili) orphaned child

Mosi (MO-see) (Swahili) the first-born

Msiba ('m-SEE-bah) (Swahili) born during calamity or mourning

Mtupeni ('m-too-PEH-nee) (Swahili) not very welcome

Mwajuma ('m-wah-JOO-mah) (Swahili) born on Friday

Mwaka ('m-WAH-kah)(Swahili) born during the opening of the farming year

Mwamini ('m-wah-MEE-nee) (Swahili) honest

Mwanahamisi ('m-nah-hah-MEE-see) (Swahili) born on Thursday — Mwanakhamisi

Mwanaidi ('m-wah-nah-EE-dee) (Swahili) born during the Idd festival

Mwanajuma ('m-wah-nah-JOO-mah) (Swahili) born on Friday

Mwanatabu ('m-wah-nah-TOO-boo) (Swahili) born at time of trouble

Mwasaa ('m-wah-SAH) (Swahili) timely

Mwatabu ('m-wah-TAH-boo) (Swahili) born at a time of sorrow

Neema (neh-EH-mah) (Swahili) born during prosperous times

Nigesa (nee-geh-sah) (Lumasada) born during harvest season

Nuru (Swahili) light; born during day

Paka (Swahili) pussycat

Panya (PAHN-yah) (Swahili) mouse (a tiny baby)

Pasua (pah-SOO-ah) (Swahili) born by Caesarean operation

Pili (PEE-lee) (Swahili) the second born

Radhiya (rah-THEE-yah) (Swahili) agreeable

Ramla (RAHM-lah) (Swahili) predictor of the future

Rashida (rah-SHEE-dah) (Swahili) righteous

Raziya (rah-ZEE-yah) (Swahili) agreeable

Rehema (reh-HEH-mah) (Swahili) compassion

Rukiya (roo-KEE-yah) (Swahili) she rises on high

Saada (sah-AH-dah) (Swahili) help

Safiya (sah-FEE-yah) (Swahili) clear-minded, pure

Salama (sah-LAH-mah) (Swahili) peace

Salma (SAHL-ma) (Swahili) safe

Sanura (sah-NOO-rah) (Swahili) kitten [baby who looks like a kitten]

Sauda (sah-OO-dah) (Swahili) dark-complexioned

Shani (SHAH-nee) (Swahili) marvellous

Sharifa (shah-REE-fah) (Swahili) distinguished

Shukura (shoo-KOO-rah) (Swahili) be grateful

Sikudhani (see-koo-THAH-nee) (Swahili) a surprise, unusual

Siti (SEE-tee) (Swahili) lady

Siwatu (see-WAH-too) (Swahili) born during time of conflict with other group

Siwazuru (see-wah-ZOO-ree) (Swahili) they are not nice people (conflict)

Subira (soo-BEE-rah) (Swahili) patience rewarded

Taabu (tah-AH-boo) (Swahili) troubles

Tabia (tah-BEE-ah) (Swahili) talents

Tatu (TAH-too) (Swahili) the third born

Zahra (Kiswahili) flowers

Zainabu (zah-ee-NAH-boo) (Swahili) beautiful [eldest daughter of Muhammed]

Zakiya (zah-KEE-yah) (Swahili) intelligent

Zalika (zah-LEE-kah) (Swahili) well-born

Zawadi (zah-WAH-dee) (Swahili) gift

Zuwena (zoo-WEH-nah) (Swahili) good

KENYAN MALE NAMES

Abasi (ah-BAH-see) (Swahili) stern

Abdalla (ab-DAHL-lah) (Swahili) servant of God

Abdu (ab-DOO) (Swahili) worshipper of God

Abubakar (ah-BOO-bah-kar) (Swahili) noble

Ali (ah-LEE) (Swahili) exalted

Ashur (Swahili) month of Ashur

Azizi (ah-ZEE-zee) (Swahili) precious

Bakari (Kiswahili) promise

Beno (BEH-no) (Mwera) one of a band

Bwana Mkubwa (bwah-nah-KOOB-wah) (Swahili) great master

Chane (CHAH-neh) tough leaf for weaving; hence dependability

Chilemba (chee-LEHM-beh) (Mwera) turban

Chitundu (chee-TOON-doo) (Mwera) birds' nest

Chiumbo (chee-OOM-bo) (Mwera) small creation

Darweshi (dahr-WEH-shee) (Swahili) saintly

Daudi (dah-OO-dee) (Swahili) beloved one — Daudy

Habib (Kiswahili) beloved

Haji (HAH-jee) (Swahili) born during month of pilgrimage to Mecca

Hamadi (hah-MAH-dee) (Swahili) praised

Hamidi (hah-MEE-dee) (Swahili) commendable

Hamisi (hah-MEE-see) (Swahili) born on Thursday

Hanif (HAH-neef) (Kiswahili) believer

Haoniyao (hah-o-nee-YAH-o) (Swahili) born at the time of a quarrel

Hasani (hah-SAH-nee) (Swahili) handsome – Husani

Idi (EE-dee) (Swahili) born during Idd festival

Issa (ee-SAH) (Swahili) God is our salvation

Jabari (jah-BAH-ree) (Swahili) brave

Jafari (jah-FAH-ree) creek

Jahi (JAH-hee) (Swahili) dignity

Jela (JEH-lah) (Swahili) father in prison when child was born

Jelani (jeh-LAH-nee) (Swahili) mighty

Juma (JOO-mah) (Swahili) born on Friday

Jumaane (joo-MAH-neh) (Swahili) born on Tuesday

Kamau (kah-MAH-oo) (Kikuyu) quiet warrior

Keambiroiro (keh-am-bee-RO-ee-ro) (Kikuyu) mountain of blackness

Keanjaho (keh-an-JAH-ho) (Kikuyu) mountain of beans

Keanyandaarwa (keh-ah-nee-yan-DAR-wah) (Kikuyu) mountain of hides

Kereenyaga (keh-rehn-YAH-gah) mountain of mystery [i.e., Mt. Kenya]

Khalfani (kahl-FAH-nee) (Swahili) destined to rule

Khamisi (kah-MEE-see) (Swahili) born on Thursday

Kifeda (chee-feh-dah) (Luo) only boy born among several girls

Kifimbo (kee-FEEM-bo) (Swahili) a very thin baby [literally, twig]

Kito (Swahili) jewel; i.e., child is precious

Kitwana (kee-TWAH-nah) (Swahili) pledged to live

Kondo (KON-do) (Swahili) war

Lipapwiche (lee-pap-WEE-chay) (Mwera) torn

Machupa (mah-CHOO-pah) (Swahili) likes to drink

Madaadi (mah-DAH-dee) (Kikuyu) name of an age-group

Makalani (mah-kah-LAH-nee) (Mwera) clerk, one skilled in writing

Masud (mah-SOOD) (Swahili, Arabic) fortunate

Maulidi (mah-oo-LEE-dee) (Swahili) born during the Islamic month Maulidi

Mbita ('m-BEE-tah) (Swahili) born on a cold night

Mbwana (m-BWAH-nah) (Swahili) master

Mhina (m-HEE-nah) (Swahili) delightful

Mosi (Kiswahili) firstborn

Mpenda ('m-PEHN-dah) (Mwera) lover, fond

Mtumwa ('m-TOOM-wah) (Swahili) pledged

Muhammed (moo-HAH-mahd) (Swahili) praised

Musa (MOO-sah) (Swahili) child [cf. Moses]

Mwaka ('m-WAH-kah) (Swahili) born during opening of the farming year (Nairuz)

Mwinyi ('m-WEN-yee) (Swahili) king

Mwita ('m-WEE-tah) (Swahili) the summoner

Nangwaya (nahn-GWAH-yah) (Mwera) don't trifle with me

Njowga ('n-JO-gah) (Mwera) shoes

Nuru (NOO-roo) (Swahili) born in daylight

Omari (Kiswahili) God is highest

Pili (PEE-lee) (Swahili) the second born

Rajabu (rah-JAH-boo) (Swahili) born in the Muslim seventh month

Ramadhani (rah-mah-DHAH-nee) (Swahili) born during the month of Ramadan

Rashidi (rah-SHEE-dee) (Swahili) of good council

Rehema (Kiswahili) second born

Sadiki (sah-DEE-kee) (Swahili) faithful

Safari (Kiswahili) born while on a trip

Salehe (sah-LEH-hee) (Swahili) good

Salim (sah-LEEM) (Swahili) peace

Sefu (SEH-foo) (Swahili) sword

Shaaboni (shah-BO-nee) (Swahili) born in the eighth Muslim month

Shomari (sho-MAH-ree) (Swahili) forceful

Simba (see-'mbah) (Kiswahili) lion; a strong person

Siwatu (see-WAH-too) (Swahili) born during a time of conflict

Siwazuri (see-wah-ZOO-ree) (Swahili) they are not nice people (conflict)

Sudi (SOO-dee) (Swahili) luck

Sultan (sool-TAHN) (Swahili) ruler

Tuwile (too-WEE-leh) (Mwera) death is inevitable

Vuai (voo-AH-ee) (Swahili) savior

Wafula (Samia) rain; or born during the rain

Yahya (YAH-yah) (Swahili) God's gift

Yusuf (yoo-SOOF) (Swahili) he shall add (to his powers) [cf.Hebrew]

Zahur (zah-HOOR) (Swahili) flower

Zuberi (zoo-BEH-ree) (Swahili) strong

KOREA

The Korean immigration to the U.S. began relatively late. Restrictive immigration laws in the late 19th century severely limited the number of Oriental immigrants. But more important, Western influence and information about the West didn't reach Korea in any significant way until the latter half of the 19th century.

The earliest Korean immigrants to America were recruited to come to the territory of Hawaii in the early 1900's. Massive numbers of workers were needed to tend the fields of the burgeoning sugar cane industry.

A total of 7,000 workers, given passage in exchange for a work contract of usually three years, were brought to Hawaii between 1903 and 1905 for this purpose. All but 2,000 remained in Hawaii permanently, often migrating to the cities and setting up their own businesses. In 1905 Japan forced Korea to become its protectorate and prohibited further emigration.

Another 1,000 Korean women immigrated between 1910 and 1924 (when immigration laws were changed) as "picture brides" for the Korean workers. They had courted by exchanging photographs, and if both were agreeable to the marriage the man would send about $100 for traveling money. The couples then married on the docks so the women could enter the U.S. legally.

A small number of Korean women and children came to the U.S. after the Korean War, entering as dependents of U.S. servicemen, and thus without restriction. American soldiers have been stationed in Korea since 1950 (onset of the Korean war), further contributing to this small immigration source.

Another small but significant source is Korean girls under the age of four. Because education is considered paramount in Korea as in most Asian countries, and illegitimate children, especially girls, are not allowed to go to school, unwed mothers of girls sometimes give up their daughters for adoption in hopes of bettering their futures. Many small Korean baby girls have come to the U.S. in this way.

Since new immigration laws took effect in 1968, up to 20,000 Koreans may immigrate each year. An estimated 15,000 a year have done so, settling in large cities such as Los Angeles, San Francisco, Honolulu, New York, and Chicago. Los Angeles is the Korean capital of the U.S., having grown from 5,000 in 1970 to 150,000 in 1980.

In fact, it's estimated that ninety percent of the Koreans living in the U.S. have been here for less than twenty years. Many of the newer immigrants are well-educated and members of the middle class, with managerial and business experience. By the mid-1970's there were at least 1,200 small businesses in the U.S. that had been established by Koreans.

The traditional system used by Koreans for naming children is one of the most fascinating. Each person has a name of two syllables, the first of which is exactly the same as his or her siblings and paternal cousins of the same generation and sex. Both male and female siblings and cousins of a generation may share the same syllable, but this is less common.

That syllable has been predestined for generations and is based on a cycle, which in turn is determined by the family's surname. One family might have a twelve-generation cycle of names while another might have a three-generation cycle.

In one Korean family the three daughters are named Hee Sook, Sook Hee, and Chung Sook. In another, the two sons are named Ja Bong and Ja Yong. However, the trend in Korea is toward Anglo-American names. In Korea people often move out of their clan villages, and the genealogy is not readily available (also families are becoming smaller), so the custom of naming several boys or girls with the cyclic name is becoming less common.

The first list below is a sample of individual syllables that might be combined to form names. Most can be used for either boys or girls but may be expressed by a slight difference in the Chinese character, which in turn sometimes denotes a different meaning, as in the word Young (meaning "flower" for a girl and "unchanging, or forever" for a boy). The second and third lists contain female and male names created by combining the single syllables, and the resulting meanings.

KOREAN NAMES

Bae (BEH) inspiration

Bong eminence; or Phoenix (mythical bird)

Chin precious

Cho beautiful

Chul firmness

Chun spring

Dae great

Doh accomplishment, the way, the past

Dong East

Du head

Eui (uh-ee) righteousness

Eun silver

Gi (JEE) brave, foundation

Goo completeness

Gook nation

Hea (heh-ah) grace

Hee pleasure (for girls; very popular); brightness for boys

Hei (heh) grace; wisdom Hye

Ho goodness, the lake (depth)

Hyo filial duty

Hyun wisdom

Hyun wisdom

Il superiority

In humanity; wise

Ja attraction, magnetism; or to breed

Jin jewel, truth — Gin

Joo jewel

Jung rightness, righteous

Ki arise

Kwan strong

Kyong brightness

Kyu standard

Mee beauty

Min cleverness

Moon learned

Myung brightness

Nam south

Ryung brightness

Sam third or No. 3

Sang (SAHNG) always

Shik planting

Shin belief

So smile

Soo excellence; long life

Sook purity (female); light, clear (male)

Suck hardness

Sun obedience

Sung successor, or winning

U gentleness

Whan enlargement

Woong magnificence

Yeo (ye-ah) mildness

Yon lotus blossom

Yong bravery (often a girl's name)

Yong face

Young flower, forever (girls); unchanging (boys)

KOREAN FEMALE NAMES

Ae-Cha loving daughter

Bong-Cha ultimate girl

Chung-Cha righteous girl

Chin-Sun truth and goodness

Choon-Hee spring girl

Chung-Ae righteous love

Eun-Kyung graceful gem

Hae-Won graceful garden

He-Ran grace and orchid

Hee-Young joy and prosperity

Ho-Sook clear lake

Hwa-Young beautiful flower

Hyo-Sonn filial and gentle

Hyun-Ae clever and loving

Hyun-Ok wise pearl

Jae-Hwa pile of beauty

Kyung-Hu girl in the capital

Kyung-Soon honored and gentle (mild)

Mi-Cha beautiful girl

Mi-Hi beautiful joy

Mi-Ok beautiful pearl

Mun-Hee literate girl

Myung-Hee bright and shiny; clear, pure girl

Myung-Ok bright pearl

Soon-Bok gentle and blessed

Sun-Hi goodness and joy

Young-Il the most prosperous, or #1 prosperity

Young-Soon flowery and mild

KOREAN MALE NAMES

Bon-Hwa utmost glory

Chin-Hae truth – ocean (depth)

Chin-Hwa advanced prosperity

Chul-Moo ironlike weapon

Chung-Ho righteous lake

Dong-Sun goodness of East

Dong-Yul passion of East

Duck-Hwan repeated virtue (virtue to return)

Duck-Young virtue and prospect

Hak-Kun literate root or intelligent root

Hyun-Ki wise foundation

Hyun-Shik rooted cleverness

In-Su preserving the wisdom

Jae-Hwa rich and prosperity

Kang-Dae strong and big

Kwang-Sun wide goodness

Mal-Chin advancement to the last

Man-Shik deep-rootedness

Man-Young ten thousand years of prosperity

Mun-Hee literate and shiny

Myung-Dae right and great

Myung-Suck longlasting rock

Sang-Ook (SAHNG-ook) always well

Suck-Chin unshakable rock

Won-Shik head of the root

Yong-Sun dragon in the first position

Young-Jae pile of prosperity

Young-Soo keeping the prosperity

LATVIA

Latvia is a country about the size of West Virginia and is located on the eastern shore of the Baltic Sea south of Finland and Estonia. Part of northern Europe's coastal plain, Latvia features gently rolling topography. More than half of Latvia's people are farmers, raising grains, potatoes, and flax. About one-fourth of the country is covered with forests.

Latvian immigration in the 19th century was small but steady. The 1900 census showed 4,300 Latvians living in the U.S. Another 5,000 arrived between 1905 and 1913 in the aftermath of the Russian revolution. Many settled in eastern and midwestern states and found work in construction jobs as carpenters, bricklayers, engineers, etc.

From 1918-40, during Latvia's only period of freedom from Russian domination since 1795, immigration dropped to a trickle. Over 40,000 Latvians immigrated as refugees between 1939 and 1951 under the U.S. Displaced Persons Act of 1948, fleeing Nazi and Soviet suppression. Many began their lives in the U.S. by taking jobs as unskilled laborers but in ten years time had re-established themselves in their former professions or had started new ones.

Latvians belong to an almost extinct group of Baltic peoples. Their language (the only related one still spoken is Lithuanian) is most closely related to the ancient Indo-European tongues.

LATVIAN FEMALE NAMES

Agata (Gr) gentle, pure

Albertine (AHL-behr-tee-nuh) (OGer) noble, bright

Anastasija (Gr) resurrection — Nastaska, Stasya, Taska, Nastechka

Ance (H) grace — Aneta, Anka, Asenka, Anyuta, Nyurochka, Nyusya

Eizenija (Gr) well-born, noble

Evelina (H) life

Gizela (Teut) pledge

Helena (Gr) light

Inesa (Gr) gentle, pure

Irisa (Gr) rainbow

Janina (YAH-nee-nuh) (H) God's gracious gift — Jana, Zanna

Julija (L) youthful — Yuliya, Iuliya, Yulinka, Yulka

Kathryn (Gr) pure — Katrina, Trine

Klara (L) bright, clear

Ksenija (Gr) hospitable

Lizina dim. of Elizabete (H) consecrated to God — Lizite, Liza

Lucija (L) light

Marija (H) bitter — Marika, Marika, Mare

Olga (Russian) holy

Tatjana fairy queen

Tereze (Gr) harvester

Urzula (L) little bear

LATVIAN MALE NAMES

Boris (Slavic) a fighter — Boriss

Filips (Gr) lover of horses

Janis (H) God's gracious gift — Jancis, Janka, Zanis, Ansis

Karlis (OFr) strong and manly — Karlens, Karlitis

Labrencis (L) crowned with laurel — Brencis

Mikelis (H) who is like God? — Miks, Mikus, Milkins

Niklavs (Gr) victoy of the people — Nikolajs, Kola

Oleg holy

Oto (Teut) prosperous — Otto, Otokars, Otomars

Pauls (L) little — Pavils

Romans (L) Roman

Stefans (Gr) a crown

Teodors (Gr) gift of God

Valerijs (L) strong and brave

Vilhelms (Teut) resolute protector — Vilis

LITHUANIA

In the 1860's and 1870's small groups of Lithuanians began migrating regularly to find work. They worked on railroad construction projects in Lithuania, on large estates in Prussia and Latvia as agricultural workers, in mines in the Ukraine, and even in Scotland and England as industrial workers.

A phenomenon known as chain migration was common with Lithuanians as well as many other nationalities. As newcomers became established in America they would invite friends and relatives to join them, often sending money and tickets for the trip. They would usually provide temporary housing until jobs could be found. This pattern of informal assistance continued over forty years, producing numerous immigrant chains that left scarcely a Lithuanian village untouched.

Economic pressures (an increasing landless peasant class and a severe famine in the late 1860's) caused the immigration to begin moving further afield to America. An estimated half million Lithuanians arrived between 1868 and 1914, largely settling in coal-mining regions of Pennsylvania and West Virginia and in older urban areas such as New York City and Baltimore. Another 37,000 were admitted after World War II from displaced persons' camps. Some of these immigrants were political refugees from Soviet rule, who had fled westward in 1944-5. Many were concentration camp inmates, soldiers, and laborers conscripted by the Germans in World War II. They tended to be better educated than the peasant immigrants from the 1870-1914 period and often settled in the metropolitan areas of the Northwest and Midwest.

LITHUANIAN FEMALE NAMES

Adelyte (OGer) noble, of good cheer

Angelika (Fr) angel

Anikke (H) grace — Annze, Ona, Onele, Ane

Dorota (L) gift of God

Elzbieta (H) consecrated to God — Elzbute, Elzbietele

Jadvyga (yahd-VEE-guh) (Teut) refuge in battle — Jada

Julija (L) youthful — Julyte

Magdalena (H) woman from — Magdala Magde, Magdute, Magdele

Margarita (Gr) a pearl

Marija (H) bitter — Maryte

Nastusche (Fr) born at Christmas — Naste, Natalija

Sofija (Gr) wisdom — Sofiya

Stanislava (L) star

Viktorija (L) victorious

Zuzane (H) lily

LITHUANIAN MALE NAMES

Alexandras (Gr) defender of mankind — Alexandrukas

Anatolijus (Gr) from the East

Andrius (Gr) manly

Antanas (L) inestimable — Ante, Antanelis, Antanukas

Benejaminas (H) son of the right hand

Danielius (H) God is my judge — Dane, Danukas

Eugenijus (Gr) well-born — Eugeniyus

Jonas (H) God's gracious gift — Jonelis, Jonukas, Jonutis

Jurgis (Gr) farmer

Karolis (OFr) strong and manly

Konstantinas (L) constant

Krystupas (Gr) Christ-bearer

Petras (Gr) stone — Petrukas, Petrelis,

Viktoras (L) conqueror

Vladislava (Slavic) possesses glory

MALAWI

Malawi is a republic in central Africa northwest of Mozambique. Formerly called Nyasaland while a British protectorate, in 1966, when independence was attained, the name of an ancient Bantu kingdom was revived. The country became Malawi — "land of flaming waters" — to connote the fiery sunlight glinting off Lake Nyasa.

Lake Nyasa (or Lake Malawi), covers a quarter of Malawi's 46,000 square mile area. The lake is long and narrow, running north to south, as is Malawi itself, which follows the lake's western shore. Several steamers on the lake serve swimming resorts, especially Monkey Bay, as part of Malawi's rising tourist trade.

In 1869 explorer David Livingstone was the first European to visit Lake Nyasa. He found slave trading and vicious tribal wars. Malawi was ravaged by slave traders until the 1890's when a Mr. (later Sir) Harry Johnson put an end to the slave trade with the help of Indian troops.

Swahili is spoken in northern Malawi (See Kenya chapter for roots of Swahili), however Nyunja and Tumbaka are the most important African languages. Over ninety-nine percent of Malawi's people are black Africans from Bantu tribes. Christianity has spread throughout Malawi as a result of European missions begun in the 1870's.

Immigration to the U.S. from Malawi in the 1970's and early 1980's was less than fifty per year, perhaps because Malawi is a poor country. Many people must seek work as migrant farmers in adjacent countries.

MALAWIAN FEMALE NAMES

Abikanile (ah-bee-kah-NEE-leh) (Yao) listen

Alile (ah-LEE-leh) (Yao) she weeps

Asale (ah-SAH-leh) (Yao) speak

Buseje (boo-SEH-jeh) (Yao) ask me

Chaonaine (chah-oh-nah-EE-neh) (Ngoni) it has seen me

Chimwala (cheem-WAH-lah) (Malawi) stone

Chiwa (CHEE-wah) (Yao) death

Chotsani (chot-SAH-nee) (Yao) take away

Kausiwa (kah-oo-SEE-wah) (Yao) the poor

Kuliraga (koo-lee-RAH-gah) (Yao) weeping

Kwasausya (kwa-sah-OOS-yah) (Yao) troubled

Mesi (MEH-see) (Yao) water

Njemile (njeh-MEE-leh) (Yao) upstanding

Sigele (see-GEH-leh) (Ngoni) left

Teleza (teh-LEH-zah) (Ngoni) slippery

MALAWIAN MALE NAMES

Bomani (boh-MAH-nee) (Ngoni) warrior

Chikosi (chee-KOH-see) (Ngoni) neck

Dulani (doo-LAH-nee) (Ngoni) cutting

Funsani (foon-SAH-nee) (Ngoni) request

Kafele (kah-FEH-leh) (Ngoni) worth dying for

Kwayera (kwah-YEH-rah) (Ngoni) dawn

Ligongo (lee-GOHN-goh) (Yao) who is this?

Mapira (mah-PEE-rah) (Yao) millet

Masamba (mah-SAHM-bah) (Yao) leaves

Mpasa (MPAH-sah) (Ngoni) mat

Ndale (NDAH-lee) (Ngoni) trick

Sabola (sah-BOH-lah) (Ngoni) pepper

Thenga (TEHNG-gah) (Yao) bring him

Useni (oo-SEH-nee) (Yao) tell me

NETHERLANDS

The first immigrants from the Netherlands, sponsored by the Dutch India Company, came in 1621 to Manhattan Island, which they called New Amsterdam. They were primarily traders rather than colonizers, trading freely for beaver pelts with the Algonquin Indians up and down the Hudson River. Their numbers were never great – 1,600 in New Amsterdam and 10,000 in New Netherlands. In 1664 King Charles of England, deciding to re-establish what he considered England's earlier claim to the territory, sent four ships to drive out the Dutch "squatters."

He first offered them the chance to join the English colonies. The Dutch elected to do so because they had become increasingly annoyed with the despotic way Dutch West India Company officials ruled them. The "take-over" occurred without a shot being fired.

Little immigration occurred after that until the 1830's and 1840's. Between 1845 and 1855 more than 20,000 Dutch immigrated to the U.S., often as entire congregations from churches seeking religious freedom or as entire neighborhoods looking for economic improvements.

The U.S. Civil War temporarily halted the flow, and after that period, emphasis shifted to families and individuals rather than large groups. A major agricultural crisis in the Netherlands during the 1880's caused 75,000 to immigrate to the U.S. until the panic of 1893 slowed the flow. Between 1880 and 1928 a total of about 200,000 people immigrated from the Netherlands.

The ravages of the Depression and World War II, which included six years of Nazi occupation, the bombing of Rotterdam, the extermination of most of Netherlands', Jews, the inundation of farm land by salt water, and the loss of the Indonesian empire, left the Netherlands unable to cope with its rising population, which doubled between 1900 and 1950.

Immigration became a government-encouraged policy as a means of coping with these disasters. Unfortunately, the quota laws in the U.S. limited immigration from the Netherlands to 3,000 per year; by 1952 a waiting list of 40,000 developed. As a result nearly a million Dutch emigrants moved to Canada, Australia, and other places.

Special Congressional acts allowed 31,000 Dutch repatriates from Indonesia to settle in the U.S. between 1958 and 1962. In 1953, another 17,000 Dutch immigrants were allowed into the U.S. after a disastrous flood left them homeless.

By the time the quota laws were repealed in the mid-1960's new prosperity had come to the Netherlands, making recent immigration minimal. Fewer than 1,000 immigrate from there each year now.

Dutch names show a bridge between the English and Scandinavian languages. Many of the names are readily recognizable as similar to English (to which Dutch is more closely related), but the Scandinavian influence is still there. As in Germany, French and other European influenced names are enjoying current popularity in the Netherlands, and it is said that the Dutch, in general, do not limit themselves to strictly Dutch names, but borrow freely from other cultures.

DUTCH FEMALE NAMES

Adele (OGer) noble, of good cheer

Adrie (L) of the Adriatic

Agatha (Gr) good

Alida (OGer) noble, kind — Aleida, Adelheid

Aleen alone — Alene, Aline

Alva (AHL-vah) one that is dead and lives in the underworld

Amelia (L) industrious

Andreas fem. of André (Gr) manly

Angelique* (Gr) messenger

Anke (AHN-kuh) (H) grace — Anki, Anika

Annemie comb. Anna and Mae

Annie (AH-nee) (H) gracious

Beatrix (L) she brings joy

Bella dim. for Isabella (H) consecrated to God

Betje (BEHT-yuh) dim. for Elizabeth (H) consecrated to God

Brigitta* (Celt) strength

Carla fem. Charles (OFr) manly — Carolina

Catharina (Gr) pure

Cecilia (L) blind

Christie* (Gr) Christian — Christin, Christina

Clarissa (L) clear

Corrie short for Cornelia (L) horn

Dacie (Fr) from Acy in France

Danielle* (H) God is my judge

Debora (H) a bee

Doortje (DORT-yuh) (L) gift of God

Edda (Scandinavian) mythological figure

Eefje (EEF-yuh) (H) life

Elizabeth (H) consecrated to God — Eliza

Els (H) consecrated to God

Elsje (EHLS-yuh) (OGer) noble, kind

Emilia (Teut) industrious

Engeltje (ehn-GEHLT-yuh) (Gr) messenger (angel)

Eva (L) life

Francisca (Teut) free — Fransje (FRAHNT-syuh)

Freda (Teut) peaceful

Gabrielle (H) God is my strength

Gijs (OE) bright

Grietje (GREET-yuh) (Gr) a pearl — Greta

Gust (Teut) staff of the gods — Gustaaf, Guus

Gusta (L) venerable

Gustha* from Gustava (Teut) staff of the gods

Hendrika (Teut) ruler of an estate — Rika

Henie (Teut) ruler of an estate — Hennie, Hen, Henny

Hortensia (L) gardener

Isabella (H) consecrated to God

Janita (yahn-EE-tah) (H) God's gracious gift

Jansje (YAHNS-yuh) (H) God's gracious gift — Jans, Jaantje

Jetje (YEHT-yuh) (Teut) mistress of the home

Johanna (yo-HAHN-a) (H) gracious

Joka (YO-kah) meaning unknown, poss. from Joakim (H) God will establish

Jose* (yo-SEH) fem. Joseph (H) God will add

Julia (L) youthful

Kaatje (KAHT-yuh) (Gr) pure — Kara, Karen, Kay, Kelly, Ketty, Ka

Katrien (Gr) pure — Kathryn

Klaartje (KLAHRT-yuh) (L) clear — Klara

Klazina (Gr) victory of the people — Klaasje (KLAHS-yuh), Nicola

Leonora (Gr) light — Eleanora

Letje (LEHT-yuh) (L) gladness — Let

Lia (H) dependence

Liesje (LEES-yuh) (H) consecrated to God — (equiv. to Lizzie)

Lijsbet (LEES-bet) (H) consecrated to God

Lilly (L) lily flower

Lina nickname for Carolina (equivalent to "Carrie" in English) — Lien

Loes (Teut) famous holiness

Lotje (LOT-yuh) dim. Charlotte (Fr) petite and feminine

Lucie (L) bringer of light

Lydië (L) ancient province in Asia Minor — Lidia

Magdalena (H) woman of Magdala

Malin (H) woman of Magdala

Marian (H) bitter — Martha

Marie (H) bitter — Maria

Marieke (H) bitter

Maryk (H) bitter — Marek

Mathilde (Teut) brave in battle

Mies (H) bitter (Molly) — Mietje (MEET-yuh)

Mina dim. Wilhelmina

Nel (Gr) light

Olivia (L) olive tree

Orseline (L) bear

Petra (Gr) stone

Pia* (L) pious

Ria (Span) a river mouth

Riet (Gr) a pearl

Sanne (H) lily

Saskia unknown, perhaps dim. of Alexandra

Sonja (SON-yah) (Gr) wisdom

Sophia (Gr) wisdom — Sophie, Sofia

Tjitske (TYEETS-kuh) (H) God's grace

Tryn (Gr) pure

Victoria (L) victorious

Virginië (L) pure

Wigburg the young woman

Wilhelmina fem. of Wilhelm (Teut) resolute protector

Wilna (VIL-nuh) fem. Wilhelmus (Teut) resolute protector

Winfreda (Teut) friend of peace

Zefanjua (H) protected by the Lord

* Popular

DUTCH MALE NAMES

Aart (A.S.) eagle-like

Abram (H) father of a multitude

Alarik (Ger) ruler of all

Alexander (Gr) defender of mankind — Alex

André (Gr) manly

Andries (Gr) manly

Ansgar (Celt) warrior

Arend (OGerm) eagle, power — Arnall

Barend firm bear

Bart (Aramaic) ploughman — Bartel

Bastiaan (Gr) venerable, revered

Ben (H) son of the right hand

Berg mountain

Bert (BEHRT) from Albert (OGer) courage of a bear

Bram short for Abraham (H) father of a multitude

Carel (OFr) full-grown, manly

Carolus* (OFr) full-grown, manly

Carsten (L) Christian — Kersten

Chris (Gr) Christ-bearer — Christoffel

Christiaan (L) Christian

Claus (Gr) victory of the people — Klaas

Dane a form of Daniel (H) God is my judge — Deen

Daniël (H) God is my judge — Danny

David (H) beloved

Deman man

Dewitt (duh-WIT) white — Dwight, Wit

Dick (OGer) powerful ruler

Dirk (DEERK) (Teut) dagger

Eduard (OE) wealthy guardian

Erik* (ONorse) ever powerful

Everhard (OE) strong as a bear

Flip (Gr) lover of horses — Pip

Franciscus (Teut) free

Frank* (Teut) free

Frits (Teut) peaceful ruler — Fritz

Gabe (H) God is my strength

Gabriël (H) God is my strength

George* (Gr) farmer

Georgius (Gr) farmer — Jons

Gijs (GEES) (OE) bright (equiv. to Bertie)

Gilles (GIL-uhs) (L) shield-bearer

Gilpin (OE) trusted

Godfried (Teut) God's peace

Gotthard (Teut) divine firmness

Govert (Teut) heavenly peace

Gregoor (GREH-gor) (Gr) vigilant

Gunnar (GUHN-nahr) (Teut) bold warrior

Hank from Hendrik (Teut) ruler of an estate

Hans (H) God's gracious gift

Harm from Harry (Teut) ruler of an estate

Harry* (Teut) ruler of an estate

Hendrik (Teut) ruler of an estate — Henk

Hermann (Teut) warrior

Jaap (YAHP) (H) supplanter (equiv. to Jim)

Jacob (YAH-kob) (H) the supplanter — Jaap

Jan (YAHN) (H) God's gracious gift — Hans

Jantje (YAHNT-yuh) (H) God's gracious gift (equiv. to Johnny)

Jeroen (Gr) holy

Jilt (YILT) money

Jim (YIM) (H) the sup-planter

Johan (YO-hahn) (H) God's gracious gift — Johannes

Joop (JOP) nickname for Josephus (H) God will add — Jopie

Joost (JOST) (L) just

Jordaan (H) descendant

Joris (YO-ris) (Gr) farmer

Josephus (H) God will add

Josua (H) God saves — Jozua

Jules (L) youth — Juliaan

Jurrien (H) God will uplift — Jurre, Jore

Karel (OFr) full-grown, manly

Kasper (Persian) treasure-master

Kees (CASE) from Cor-nelius (L) horn

Kerstan (L) Christian

Klaas from Nicolaus (Gr) victory of the people

Kleef (KLEHF) (OE) from the cliff

Koenraad (KAHN-rahd) (OGer) honest counselor — Koen

Konstanz (L) Constantine

Krelis (L) horn

Kris (Gr) Christ-bearer — Kit

Leorad (Teut) patriotic — Leopold

Lucas (L) bringer of light

Lucianus (L) bringer of light

Marten (L) warlike — Mat-tin

Martijn (MAHR-teen) (L) warlike — Marten

Matheu* (H) gift of God

Maurids (L) dark-skinned (Moorish) — Maurits

Michiel (H) who is like God?

Narve (NAHR-veh) the healthy and strong

Nicolaus (Gr) victory of the people

Niklaas (Gr) victory of the people — Klasse

Olivier (L) olive tree — Noll

Otto (Teut) prosperous — Ode

Paul* (L) little

Piet** (Gr) stone

Pieter (Gr) stone — Pietr

Pippin (Teut) father

Ramone* (Teut) mighty protector

Rob* (Teut) shining fame — Bob*

Rudi* (Teut) famous wolf

Samson (H) the sun's man

Schuyler (SKY-ler) shelter

Simen (H) God is heard

Tom (H) twin

Valentijn (VAL-en-teen) (L) strong, brave

Van from Vander

Vandyke from the dyke

Victor (L) conqueror

Vincentius (L) conqueror

Wies (VEES) (Teut) renowned warrior

Wilhelmus (vil-HEHLM-us) (Teut) resolute pro-tector — Willem, Willy

Willem (Teut) resolute pro-tector — Wilhelmus, Willy

Wim (Teut) resolute protec-tor

Wouter (Teut) powerful warrior

Zacharia (H) remembered by the Lord

---

* Popular
** Very popular

NIGERIA

Of the 650,000 Africans who were brought to the mainland of North America approximately half have been estimated as coming from Angola and southern Nigeria. Thus the number of Nigerian immigrants between the peak slaving years of 1741 to 1807 might have been 160,000 to 200,000. (See also chapter on Ghana.)

The two largest tribes in southern Nigeria then and now are the Ibo and the Yoruba. It took years for the American slaves to begin to call themselves "blacks" or "Africans" rather than members of their tribes. Striking cultural differences remain; the Yoruba people tend to be artistic, and in slave times had built city-states of upwards of 20,000 people.

The Ibos lead quiet, pastoral lives with close family ties. Northern Nigeria is inhabited by the Hausa tribe. In build, they resemble Arabs and many are Moslem, as well as another tribe of the north, the Fulani. It is unlikely that many Hausa were taken as slaves since they lived far-removed from the coast.

The slave trade is a bleak chapter for not only North America and Europe, from which the slave ships originated, but for Africa because the collecting of slaves was done primarily by black chieftains and other black slave traffickers. In most cases the white ship captains did not venture into the interior. They merely picked up the slaves from forts and "factories" along the coast, and were allowed to dock only with the permission of the local chieftains.

It must be assumed that those who sold fellow Africans into slavery had no idea of the brutal treatment they would endure, and the traffic certainly couldn't have been sustained without the insatiable demand for it in the "civilized" nations.

It is seldom realized that much of the credit for building the southern United States should go to the African slaves. It should also be recognized that it was through their barter that the basis for northern Europe's prosperity was laid. There are still ties between the U.S. and Nigeria. Immigration from Nigeria in recent years has gradually increased from 700 in 1972 to 2,000 in 1982.

Naming customs among the Yoruba people are as follows: A boy is named on his ninth day, a girl on her seventh and twins on their eighth. Until then, the child is simply called Ikoko Omon or "newborn child." A naming ceremony is held at the parents' house. Guests include the entire immediate family and members of the community.

The baby's mouth is touched with various substances to signify hopes for the future: water for purity of body and spirit; red pepper for a resolute character; salt for power like that of royalty; honey and oil for happiness and prosperity; kola nut for good fortune. After the child's name is announced feasting and dancing may last until the early hours of the next day.

Thus a new baby is welcomed into the Yoruba community; a human being in his or her own right and known by its own name. The name consists of three parts; the first of which describes family circumstances at child's birth (called the "oruko," personal name), the second of which expresses a hope for what the child will become (called the "oriki," praise name), and the third (called "orile") which tells the child's kinship group's origin.

As in most African tribes Ibo children are prized and treated as welcome guests favored with much affection. When a child is given an unpleasant sounding name like Chotsani ("take it away"), it is often an attempt by the family to hide its joy so ancestors or divinities will not take back the infant.

An Ibo child is given several names. The choice may be based on observations about the child such as its health or birthmarks present, or some remarkable characteristic. A name may be associated with a particular divinity, or the child may be named after the market day on which it was born.

Hausa babies are each given a Muslim name, and a nickname referring to an object, physical trait, sequence of birth, or event coinciding with time of birth. The nickname may be expressive of wishes for good health and fortune.

ABBREVIATIONS USED:
Yor = Yoruba

NIGERIAN FEMALE NAMES

Abayomi (ah-BAH-yo-mee) pleasant meeting

Abebi (AH-beh-BEE) (Yor) we asked for her and got her

Abeje (ah-beh-JEH) (Yor) we asked to have this one

Abeke (ah-beh-KEH) we begged for her to pet her

Abeni (ah-beh-NEE) (Yor) we asked for her, and behold she is ours!

Abeo (ah-beh-O) (Yor) her birth brings happiness

Abidemi (ah-bee-deh-ME) (Yor) born during father's absence

Abimbola (ah-BEEM-bo-lah) (Yor) born to be rich

Adamma beautiful child

Adebola (ah-DEH-bo-lah) (Yor) comer met honor

Adebomi (ah-deh-bo-MEE) (Yor) crown covered my nakedness

Adedagbo (ah-DEH-dah-bo) (Yor) happiness is a crown

Adedoja (ah-DEH-do-jah) (Yor) crown becomes a thing of worth

Adeleke (ah-DEH-leh-keh) crown achieves happiness

Adeola (ah-deh-o-LAH) (Yor) crown has honor

Adesimbo (ah-deh-SEEM-bo) (Yor) noble birth

Aina (ah-ee-NAH) (Yor) delivery had complications

Aiyetoro (ah-YEH-to-ro) (Yor) peace on earth

Akanke (ah-kahn-KEH) (Yor) to meet her is to love her

Alaba (ah-lah-BAH) (Yor) second child born after twins

Alake (ah-lah-KEH) (Yor) one to be petted and made much of

Amadi (ah-MAH-dee) (Ibo) general rejoicing

Amonke (ah-mon-KEH) (Yor) to know her is to pet her

Asabi (ah-sah-BEE) (Yor) she is of choice birth

Ayo (AH-yo) (Yor) joy

Ayobami (ah-yoh-BAH-mee) (Yor) I am blessed with joy

Ayobunmi (ah-yo-BOON-mee) (Yor) joy is given to me

Ayodele (ah-yo-DEH-leh) (Yor) joy comes home

Ayofemi (ah-yo-FEH-mee) (Yor) joy likes me

Ayoluwa (ah-yo-LOO-wah) (Yor) joy of our people

Ayoola (ah-YO-o-lah) (Yor) joy in wealth

Baderinwa (bah-day-REEN-wah) (Yor) worthy of respect

Bayo (BAH-yo) (Yor) joy is found

Bejide (beh-JEE-deh) (Yor) child born in the rainy time

Bolade (BO-lah-deh) (Yor) honor arrives

Bolanile (baw-lah-NEE-leh) (Yor) the wealth of this house

Bunmi (BOON-mee) (Yor) my gift

Chinue (CHEEN-weh) (Ibo) God's own blessing

Dada (DAH-dah) (Yor) child with curly hair

Dayo (DAH-yo) (Yor) joy arrives

Ebun (eh-BOON) (Yor) gift

Edenausegboye (eh-deh-nah-oo-seh-BO-yeh) (Benin) good deeds are remembered

Ekaghogho (eh-kah-HO-ho) (Benin) born on an important day

Enomwoyi (eh-nom-WO-yee) (Benin) one who has grace, charm

Fabayo (fah-BAH-yo) (Yor) a lucky birth is joy

Fayola (fah-YO-lah) (Yor) good fortune walks with honor

Femi (FEH-mee) (Yor) love me

Fola (FAW-lah) (Yor) honor

Folade (faw-lah-DEH) (Yor) honor arrives

Folami (faw-LAW-mee) (Yor) respect and honor me

Folashade (faw-lah-shah-DEH) (Yor) honor confers a crown

Folayan (faw-LAH-yahn) (Yor) to walk in dignity

Hembadoon (HEM-bah-doon) (Tiv) the winner

Idowu (ee-DO-woo) (Yor) first child born after twins

Ifama (ee-FAH-mah) (Ibo) everything is fine

Ife (ee-FEH) (Yor) love

Ifetayo (ee-feh-TAH-yo) love brings happiness

Ige (EE-geh) (Yor) delivered feet first

Ikuseghan (ee-KOO-seh-han) (Benin) peace surpasses war

Irawagbon (ee-rah-WAH-bon) (Benin) enemy's attempt to kill her

Isoke (ee-SO-keh) (Benin) a satisfying gift from God

Ityiarmbiamo (ee-tee-arm-bee-AH-mo) (Tiv) I am against war

Iverem (ee-VEH-rem) (Tiv) blessing and favor

Iyabo (ee-YAH-bo) (Yor) mother has returned

Izegbe (ee-ZEH-beh) (Benin) long expected child

Jumoke (joo-MO-keh) (Yor) everyone loves the child

Kehinde (keh-heen-DEH) (Yor) second born of twins

Kokumo (KO-koo-mo) (Yor) this one will not die

Limber (Tiv) joyfulness

Mbafor ('m-BAH-for) (Ibo) born on a market day

Mbeke ('m-beh-KEH) (Ibo) born on the first day of the week

Mhnonum ('m-HOH-num) (Tiv) mercifulness

Modupe (mo-DOO-peh) (Yor) I am grateful

Monifa (MO-nee-fah) (Yor) I have my luck

Morihinze (mo-ree-hin-ZEH) (Tiv) child of either sex is good

Nayo (NAH-yoh) (Yor) we have joy

Ngozi ('n-GO-zee) (Ibo) blessing

Nneka ('n-NEH-kah) (Ibo) her mother is prominent

Nnenia ('n-NAH-nee-ah) (Ibo) her grandmothers look alike

Nourbese (noor-BEH-seh) (Benin) a wonderful child

Nwakaego ('n-wah-kah-EH-go) (Ibo) more important than money

Ode (o-DEH) (Benin) born along the road

Olabisi (o-LAH-bee-see) (Yor) joy is multiplied

Olabunmi (aw-lah-BOON-mee) (Yor) honor has rewarded me

Olaniyi (o-lah-NEE-yee) (Yor) there's glory in wealth

Olubayo (o-loo-BAH-yo) (Yor) highest joy

Olubunmi (o-loo-BOON-mee) (Yor) this highest gift is mine

Olufemi (o-LOO-feh-mee) (Yor) God loves me

Olufunke (o-loo-FOON-keh) (Yor) God gives me to be loved

Olufunmilayo (o-loo-FOON-mee-LAH-yo) (Yor) God gives me joy

Oluremi (o-loo-REH-mee) (Yor) God consoles me

Omolara (o-MO-lah-rah) (Benin) born at the right time

Omorenomwara (o-mo-reh-nom-WAH-rah) (Benin) meant not to suffer

Omorose (o-mo-RO-seh) (Benin) my beautiful child

Omosede (o-MO-seh-deh) (Benin) a child counts more than a king

Omosupe (o-MO-soo-peh) (Benin) a child is the most precious thing

Oni (o-NEE) (Benin) desired

Oni (AN-nee) (Yor) born in a sacred abode

Osayiomwabo (o-sah-yohm-WAH-bo) (Benin) God will help us

Oseye (o-SEH-yeh) (Benin) the happy one

Shiminege (shee-mee-NEH-geh) (Tiv) let's see the future

Taiwo (TAH-ee-wo) (Yor) first born of twins

Titilayo (tee-tee-lah-YO) (Yor) happiness is eternal

Torkwase (tor-kwah-SEH) (Yor) queen

Uchefuna (oo-cheh-foo-NAH) (Ibo) I have my wits about me

Urbi (OOR-bee) (Benin) princess

Yahimba (yah-him-BAH) (Tiv) there is nothing like home

Yejide (yeh-jee-DEH) (Yor) the image of her mother

Yetunde (yeh-TOON-deh) (Yor) mother comes back

NIGERIAN MALE NAMES

Abegunde (ah-beh-GOON-deh) (Yor) born during holiday

Abejide (ah-beh-JEE-deh) (Yor) born during winter

Abiade (ah-bee-ah-DEH) (Yor) born of royal parents

Abidugun (ah-BEE-doo-goon) (Yor) born before the war

Abimbola (ah-BEEM-bo-lah) (Yor) born rich

Abiodun (ah-BEE-o-doon) (Yor) born at the time of a festival

Abiola (ah-BEE-o-lah) (Yor) born in honor

Abiona (ah-BEE-o-nah) (Yor) born during a journey

Abioye (ah-BEE-o-yeh) (Yor) born during coronation

Ade (ah-DEH) (Yor) royal

Adeagbo (ah-DEH-ag-bo) (Yor) he brings royal honor

Adebamgbe (ah-DEH-bam-beh) (Yor) royalty dwells with me

Adebayo (ah-DEH-bah-yoh) (Yor) he came in a joyful time

Adeboro (ah-DEH-bo-ro) (Yotuba) royalty comes into wealth

Adedapo (ah-DEH-dah-po) (Yor) royalty brings the people together

Adegoke (ah-DEH-go-keh) (Yor) the crown has been exalted

Adejola (ah-DEH-jo-lah) (Yor) the crown feeds on honors

Adelabu (ah-DEH-lah-boo) (Yor) the crown passed through deep water

Adelaja (ah-DEH-lah-jah) (Yor) the crown settles a quarrel

Ademola (ah-DEH-mo-lah) (Yor) a crown is added to my wealth

Adesola (ah-DEH-so-lah) (Yor) the crown honored us

Adetokunbo (ah-DEH-to-koon-boh) (Yor) honor came from overseas

Adewole (ah-DEH-wo-leh) (Yor) royalty enter the house

Adeyemi (ah-deh-yeh-MEE) (Yor) the crown suits me well

Adigun (ah-dee-GOON) (Yor) righteous

Adio (ah-dee-O) (Yor) be righteous

Adisa (ah-dee-SAH) (Yor) one who makes his meaning clear

Adunbi (ah-doon-BEE) (Yor) born to be pleasant

Afiba (ah-FEE-bah) (Yor) by the sea

Agu (ah-GOO) (Ibo) leopard

Ajagbe (ah-jahg-BEH) (Yor) he carries off the prize

Ajamu (ah-jah-MOO) (Yor) he fights for what he wants

Ajani (ah-JAH-nee) (Yoruban) one who takes possession after a struggle

Ajayi (ah-JAH-yee) (Yor) born face-down

Akanni (ah-KAHN-nee) (Yor) our encounter brings possessions

Akin (ah-KEEN) (Yoruban) hero, strong man

Akinkawon (ah-keen-KEH-won) (Yor) bravery pacified them

Akinlabi (ah-KEEN-lah-bee) (Yor) we have a boy

Akinlana (ah-keen-LAH-nah) (Yor) valor

Akinlawon (ah-keen-LAH-won) (Yor) bravery sustains them

Akins (ah-KEENS) (Yor) brave boy

Akinsanya (ah-KEEN-sahn-yah) (Yor) the valor avenges

Akinshegun (ah-kwen-sheh-GOON) (Yor) valor conquers

Akinsheye (ah-KEEN-shee-joo) (Yor) valor acts honorably

Akinshiju (ah-KEEN-shee-joo) (Yor) valor awakes

Akinwole (ah-KEEN-wo-leh) (Yor) valor enters the house

Akinwunmi (ah-KEEN-woon-mee) (Yor) valor is pleasing to me

Akinyele (ah-keen-WEH-leh) (Yor) valor benefits this house

Akono (ah-KO-no) (Yor) it is my turn

Alonge (ah-LON-geh) (Yor) a tall and skinny boy

Amadi (ah-MAH-dee) (Benin) seemed destined to die at birth

Animashaun (AH-nee-mah-shon) (Yor) generous

Aondochimba (ah-on-do-HEEM-bah) (Tiv) God is above all things on earth

Apara (ah-PAH-rah) (Yor) child that comes and goes

Aren (AIR-en) eagle

Atuanya (ah-TOO-ahn-yah) (Ibo) son was born when daughter was expected

Ayinde (ah-yeen-DEH) (Yor) we gave praises and he came

Ayo (AH-yo) (Yor) happiness

Ayodele (ah-YO-deh-leh) joy enters the house

Azagba (ah-ZAH-bah) (Benin) born out of town

Azi (ah-ZEE) the youth, (energy)

Azikiwe (ah-ZEE-kee-weh) (Ibo) vigorous

Babafemi (bah-BAH-feh-mee) (Yor) father loves me

Babatunde (bah-bah-TOON-deh) (Yor) father returns (image of grand-father)

Babatunji (bah-bah-TOON-jee) (Yor) father returns again

Balogun (bo-lo-GOON) (Yor) warlord

Bandele (ban-DEH-leh) (Yor) born away from home

Banjoko (BAN-jo-ko) (Yor) stay with me and go no more

Bankole (BAN-ko-leh) (Yor) help me to build the house

Bem (BEHM) (Tiv) peace

Boseda (beh-SEH-deh) (Tiv) born on a Sunday

Chi (CHEE) personal guardian angel — Cis

Chijioke (CHEE-jee-o-keh) (Ibo) God gives talent

Chike (CHEE-keh) (Ibo) power of God

Chinelo (CHEE-neh-lo) (Ibo) thought of God

Chinua (CHEE-noo-ah) (Ibo) God's own blessing

Chioke (CHEE-o-keh) (Ibo) gift of God

Chukwueneka (choo-kwoo-eh-NEH-kah) (Ibo) God has dealt kindly with us

Dada (DAH-dah) (Yor) child with curly hair

Danjuma (dan-joo-MAH) (Hausa) born on Friday

Danladi (dan-LAH-dee) (Hausa) born on Sunday

Daren (DAH-rehn) (Hausa) born at night — Dare

Dumaka (Ibo) help me with hands

Dunsimi (doon-SEE-mee) (Yor) don't die before me

Durojaiye (doo-ro-jah-YEH) (Yor) wait and enjoy what the world offers

Eberegbulam (eh-BEH-reh-boo-lam) (Ibo) my kindness shall not destroy me

Ekundayo (eh-KOON-dah-yo) (Yor) sorrow becomes happiness

Enobakhare (eh-no-bah-KAH-reh) (Benin) the king's word

Ewansiha (eh-wan-see-HAH) (Benin) secrets are not for sale

Foluke (fo-LOO-keh) (Yor) placed in God's hands

Gowon (GO-won) (Tiv) rainmaker

Ibrahim (EE-brah-hem) (Hausa) my father is exalted

Idogbe (ee-do-BEH) (Yor) second born after twins

Idowu (ee-DO-woo) (Yor) born after twins

Ilom (ee-LOM) (Ibo) abbrev. of Ilomerika: my enemies are many

Imarogbe (ee-MAH-ro-beh) (Benin) child born to a good family

Iniko (Efek, Ibibio) time of trouble

Iroagbulam (ee-RO-eh-boo-lam) (Ibo) let enmity destroy me

Iyapo (ee-YAH-po) (Yor) many trials

Jaja (JAH-jah) (Ibo) honored

Jibade (jee-bah-DEH) (Yor) born close to royalty

Jumoke (joo-MO-keh) (Yor) everyone loves the child

Kayin (kah-YEEN) (Yor) celebrated (long-hoped-for child)

Kayode (KAH-yo-deh) (Yor) he brought joy

Kehind (keh-HEEN-deh) (Yor) second born of twins

Kosoko (ko-SO-ko) (Yor) no hoe to dig a grave

Kunle (KOON-leh) (Yor) home is filled with honors

Madu (MAH-doo) (Ibo) people

Mazi (MAH-zee) (Ibo) sir

Modupe (mo-DOO-peh) (Yor) thank you

Mongo (MON-go) (Yor) famous

N'namdi ('n-NAHM-dee) (Ibo) father's name lives on

N'nanna ('n-NAHN'-ah) (Ibo) grandfather

Ngozi ('n-GO-zee) (Ibo) blessing

Nmerigini ('n-MEH-reh-ghee-nee) (Ibo) what have I done?

Nosakhere (no-SAH-keh-reh) (Benin) God's way is the only way

Nwabudike (NWAH-boo-dee-keh) (Ibo) son is the father's power

Oba (AW-bah) (Yor) king

Obadele (aw-bah-DEH-leh) (Yor) the king arrives at the house

Obafemi (ah-bah-FEH-mee) (Yor) the king likes me

Obahnjoko (ah-ban-JO-ko) (Yor) the king is enthroned

Obaseki (aw-BAH-seh-ke)(Benin)the king's influence goes beyond the market

Obataiye (aw-bah-TAH-ee-yeh) (Yor) king of the world

Obawole (aw-bah-WO-leh) (Yor) the king enters the house

Obayana (aw-bah-YAH-nah) (Yor) the king warms himself at the fire

Ode (o-DEH) (Benin) one born along the road

Odimkemelu (o-deem-KEH-meh-loo) (Ibo) I have done nothing wrong

Odion (O-dee-on) (Benin) first of twins

Ogbonna (o-BON-nah) (Ibo) image of his father

Ogonna (o-GO-nah) (Ibo) father-in-law

Ogunkeye (o-GOON-keh-yeh) (Yor) the god Ogun has gathered honor

Ogunsanwo (o-GOON-shahn-wo) help comes from Ogun, god of war

Ogunsheye (o-GOON-sheh-yeh) (Yor) the god Ogun had acted honorably

Ojo (o-JO) (Yor) a difficult delivery

Okafor (o-KAH-for) (Ibo) born on Afor market day

Okanlawon (o-kahn-LAH-won) (Yor) son born after several daughters

Okechuku (o-keh-CHOO-koo) (Ibo) God's gift

Okeke (o-KEH-keh) (Ibo) born on the market day

Oko (o-KO) (Yor) god of war

Okonkwo (o-KONG-kwo) (Ibo) born on Nkwo market day

Okorie (o-KO-ree-eh) (Ibo) born on Oryo market day

Okpara (ok-PAH-rah) (Ibo) first son

Ola (AW-lah) (Yor) wealth, riches

Oladele (aw-lah-DEH-leh) (Yor) honors, wealth arrive at home

Olafemi (aw-lah-FEH-mee) (Yor) wealth, honor favors me

Olamina (aw-lah-MEE-nah) (Yor) this is my wealth

Olaniyan (o-lah-NEE-yahn) (Yor) honors surround me

Olatunji (aw-lah-TOON-jee) (Yor) honor reawakens

Olu (O-loo) (Yor) pre-eminent

Olubayo (o-loo-BAH-yo) (Yor) highest joy

Olufemi (o-loo-FEH-mee) (Yor) God loves me

Olugbala (o-LOO-bah-lah) (Yor) savior of the people

Olugbodi (o-LOO-bo-dee) (Yor) child born with extra finger or toe

Olujimi (o-loo-JEE-mee) (Yor) God gave me this

Olukayode (o-loo-KAH-yo-deh) (Yor) my lord brings happiness

Olumide (o-loo-MEE-deh) (Yor) my lord arrives

Olumiji (o-loo-MEE-jee) (Yor) my lord awakens

Olushegun (o-loo-SHEH-goon) (Yor) God is the victor

Olushola (o-LOO-sho-lah) (Yor) God has blessed me

Olutosin (o-loo-TO-seen) (Yor) God deserves to be praised

Oluwa (o-LOO-wah) (Yor) our lord

Oluyemi (o-loo-YEH-mee) (Yor) fulfillment from God

Omolara (o-MO-lah-rah) (Benin) child born at the right time

Omorede (o-mo-REH-deh) (Benin) prince

Omoruyi (o-mo-ROO-yee) (Benin) respect from God

Omotunde (o-mo-TOON-deh) (Yor) a child comes again

Omwokha (on-WO-kah) (Benin) second of twins

Onipede (o-nee-PEH-deh) (Yor) the consoler will come

Onuwachi (o-noo-WAH-chee) (Ibo) God's world

Onyebuchi (on-yeh-BOO-chee) (Ibo) who is God?

Onyemachi (on-yeh-MAH-chee) (Ibo) who knows God's will

Orji (OR-jee) (Ibo) mighty tree

Orunjan (Yor) mid-day sun

Osagboro (o-SAH-bo-ro) (Benin) there is only one God

Osahar (o-SAH-har) (Benin) God hears

Osakwe (o-SAH-kweh) (Benin) God agrees

Osayaba (o-sah-YAH-bah) (Benin) God forgives

Osayande (o-sah-YAHN-deh) (Benin) God owns the world

Osayimwese (o-sah-eem-WEH-seh) (Benin) God made me whole

Osaze (o-SAH-zeh) (Benin) whom God likes

Ottah (o-TAH) (Urhobo) child thin at birth

Owodunni (o-wo-DOON-nee) (Yor) it is nice to have money

Shangobunni (shang-go-BOON-nee) (Yor) a child given by Shango

Sowande (sho-WAHN-deh) (Yor) the wise healer sought me out

Taiwo (TAH-ee-wo) (Yor) first born of twins

Teremun (TEH-reh-moon) (Tiv) father's acceptance

Tor (TOOR) (Tiv) king

Tyehimba (tah-eh-heem-BAH) (Tiv) we stand as a nation

Uche (oo-CHEH) (Ibo) thought

Wafor (WAH-for) (Ibo) born on Afor market day

Weke (WEH-keh) (Ibo) born on Eke market day

Worie (WO-ree-eh) (Ibo) born on Afor market day

Yohance (yo-HAHN-seh) (Hausa) God's gift [cf.John]

NORTH AMERICAN INDIAN

The first immigrants to North America probably crossed the Bering Strait of Alaska, (then a land bridge) from Asia between 10,000 and 20,000 years ago. Later groups may have sailed across the Pacific. Little else is known about the North American Indians until European explorers and settlers began arriving in the 16th century.

The population at that time in the area of the future United States has been roughly estimated between 900,000 and 1.5 million. Firearms and European diseases, especially smallpox, malaria, tuberculosis, typhus, and cholera, took their toll on the Indian population. By 1880 the native Indian population was down to 250,000.

Before that the pressure of the European presence caused the Sioux and Apache tribes, among others, to change their lifestyles. The Chippewas (Ojibwa is the native term) who lived in the northern Great Lakes region responded to the French demand for furs by pushing west in search of additional hunting grounds. This migration displaced the Sioux tribes causing them to head west, where they became buffalo hunters with the aid of the European horse and weaponry.

The Apache, the last Indians conquered by the U.S. Cavalry, had migrated south from Canada even before the Spaniards arrived in the 1500's. They developed a raiding way of life, which more than any other image, has influenced the American perception of the stereotypical "American Indian."

In fact, Indians lived many different ways of life, ranging from simple groups of food-gatherers to farmers living in city-states (such as the Pueblos) to organized political confederacies.

Despite the myth of the vanishing Indian, the population of Indian or part-Indian ancestry now numbers over 800,000. More than half of them live on reservations across the country. Of the estimated 200 cultures or "nations," as they were called by the early Europeans, at least 170 existing tribes maintain a cultural identity.

In the 1970 census fifty-nine percent of the Indian population belonged to only fifteen tribal groups with the largest numbers reported in the Navaho, Cherokee, Dakota Sioux, Chippewa, Pueblo, Lumbee, Choctow, Houma, Apache, and Iroquois.

Many of the Indian languages had vocabularies of 7,000 to 10,000 words. Although this seems small compared to the total English vocabulary of 130,000 words, most English-speaking people have a vocabulary of only about 10,000 words.

Because the Navaho language is so complex it is almost impossible to counterfeit or learn as an adult. The same syllables, given different pronunciations have entirely different meanings. During World War II a group of 420 Navahos were trained as code talkers. They were able to transmit communications about Pacific troop movements without the time-consuming step of encoding and deciphering the messages and fear of the messages being intercepted. The code was never broken by the enemy.

The naming traditions among American Indians were as varied as the cultures. Many were conceptual names which were passed down through many generations. If a baby was given a name of a living relative, the name might be changed slightly. Thus, Little White Bear might be named after Walking Bear.

In some tribes, notably the Kiowas, it was taboo to name a child after a recently deceased relative. In fact, when a relative died, entire families had to change their names and all terms suggesting the name of the dead person were dropped from the language for several years.

In many cultures it was believed that everyone and everything had a name which might remain long unknown to all, even to the owner, and which perfectly expressed one's inmost nature. The name might be revealed to the person confidentially at some point, but the name always had such a sacredness to it, that it was considered a discourtesy to directly address the person by it.

Sources for names included totems — animal, plants, objects or values revered by the tribe (Navaho names often reflect events of war). Other names evolved from a noticeable characteristic of the baby (not given until sufficient time had passed to discern the characteristic), an image revealed to the father in a dream, or an event or object that impressed the mother at the time of the birth.

Realizing that roughly one million Indians inhabited the United States before the white man came to a land that now houses 240 million people, it is not hard to see the overwhelming part that Nature played in the culture of the Indians and their choices of names. Many reflect the beauty and power of the untamed land, such as the Miwok names Pakuna, meaning "deer jumping while running downhill," Namid, meaning "star dancer" and Lupu, meaning "silvery quality of an abalone shell."

NORTH AMERI-CAN INDIAN FEMALE NAMES

Abedabun (Chippewa) peep of day

Abequa (Chippewa) she stays home

Abeque (Chippewa) she stays at home

Abetzi (Omaha) yellow leaf

Abey (Omaha) leaf

Abeytu (Omaha) green leaf

Adoette (ah-do-AY-tuh) big tree

Adsila (Cherokee) blossom

Aiyana eternal bloom

Alameda cottonwood grove

Alaqua (ah-LAH-quah) sweet gum tree

Aleshanee (Coos Indian) she plays all the time

Algoma valley of flowers

Alkas (Coos Indian) she is timid

Altsoba (Navaho) all are at war

Amadahy (Cherokee) forest water

Amayeta (Miwok) big manzanita berries

Amitola rainbow

Anaba (Navaho) she returns from war

Anevay superior

Angeni spirit

Anpaytoo (Sioux) day; radiant

Aponi butterfuly

Aquene peace

Atepa (Choctaw Indian) wigwam

Awanata (Niwok) turtle

Awenasa (Cherokee) my home

Awendela early day

Awenita a fawn

Awinita (Cherokee) young deer

Ayashe (Chippewa) little one

Ayita the worker

Ayita (Cherokee) first in the dance

Bena pheasant

Bly high, tall

Chapa (Sioux) beaver

Chapawee (Sioux) industrious

Chenoa white dove

Chilali snowbird

Chimalis bluebird

Chitsa fair one

Cholena bird

Cholena (Delaware) bird

Chumani (Sioux) dewdrops

Cocheta (sho-CHAY-tah) the unknown

Dena a valley

Dezba (Navaho) going to war

Doba (Navaho) there was no war

Doli (Navaho) bluebird

Donoma (Omaha) visible sun

Dowanhowee (Sioux) singing voice

Dyani a deer

Ehawee (Sioux) laughing maid

Elu (Zuni) beautiful, fair

Enola alone

Etenia the wealthy

Eyota the greatest

Fala (Choctaw) crow

Flo like an arrow

Gaho mother

Galilahi (Cherokee) amiable, attractive

Haloke (Navajo) salmon

Halona of happy fortune

Hantaywee (Sioux) cedar maid; faithful

Hateya (Miwok) to press with the foot

Helki (Miwok) to touch

Hiti (Eskimo) hyena (a totem name)

Hola (Hopi) a ceremonioal instrument

Honovi (Hopi) strong deer

Huata (Miwok) carrying seeds in burden basket

Humita (Hopi) shelled corn

Huyana (Miwok) rain falling

Ilia meaning unknown

Imala disciplinarian

Isi (Choctaw) deer

Istas snow

Ituha the strong, sturdy oak

Iuana blowing backward as the wind blows over the water of a stream

Izusa white stone

Jesusita (Zuni) Virgin Mary — Chucha, Chuchita

Kachina sacred dancer

Kai (Navaho) willow tree

Kaliska (Miwok) coyote chasing deer

Kamata (Miwok) a gambling game

Karmiti (Eskimo) trees

Kasa (KAH-sah) (Hopi) fur-robe dress

Kaya (Hopi) my elder sister

Keezheekoni (Chippewa) fire briskly burning

Kimama (Shoshone) butterfly

Kimimela (Sioux) butterfly

Kineks rosebud

Kirima (Eskimo) a hill

Kiwidinok (Chippewa) woman of the wind

Koko (Blackfoot) night

Kolenya (Miwok) fish coughing

Kulya (Miwok) sugar pine nuts burned black

Kwanita (Zuni) (H) God is gracious

Lenmana (Hopi) flute girl

Leotie (leh-o-TEE-eh) prairie flower

Liluye (Miwok) chicken hawk singing when soaring

Liseli (Zuni) unknown meaning

Lissilma be thou there

Litonya (Miwok) hummingbird darting

Lolotea (Zuni) (L) gift from God

Lomasi pretty flower

Lulu rabbit

Luna (Zuni) (Span) the moon

Lusela (Miwok) bear swinging its foot when licking it

Lusita (Zuni) (Span) bringer of light

Luyu the wild dove

Macawi (Sioux) generous, motherly

Macha (Sioux) aurora

Magaskawee (Sioux) swan maiden; graceful

Magena the coming moon

Mahal woman

Mai coyote

Maka (Sioux) earth

Makawee (Sioux) earth maiden, generous, motherly

Malia (Zuni) (H) bitter

Malila (Miwok) salmon going fast up a rippling stream

Manaba (Navaho) war returned with her coming

Mankalita (Zuni) (Gr) a pearl

Mansi (Hopi) plucked flower

Mapiya (Sioux) sky; heavenly

Maralah child born near time of an earthquake

Masalina (Zuni) unknown

Mausi plucking flowers

Meda prophet

Meli (Zuni) (H) bitter

Memdi a henna plant

Meoquanee (Chippewa) clothed in red

Meriwa (Eskimo) thorn

Miakoda power of the moon

Migina (Omaha) returning moon

Migisi (Chippewa) eagle

Mika the knowing racoon

Miliya (Miwok) hitting farewell-to-spring seed on a bush

Mimiteh (Omaha) new moon

Minaku (Blackfoot) berry woman

Minal fruit

Minowa moving voice

Minya (Osage) elder sister

Misae (Osage) white sun

Mitena (Omaha Indian) born under coming or new moon

Mituna (Miwok) wrapping a salmon in willow leaves after catching it

Muna (Hopi) freshet

Nahimana (Sioux) mystic

Namid (Chippewa) the star dancer

Nara place name

Nascha (Navaho) owl

Nashota twin

Nasnan (Carrier) surrounded by a song

Nata speaker or creator

Nata-akon (Chippewa) expert canoeist

Natane (nah-TAH-neh) (Arapaho) daughter

Niabi (Osage) fawn

Nida (Omah) mythical being

Nidawi (Omaha) fairy girl

Nina mighty

Ninita (Zuni) (Span) little girl

Ninovan (Cheyenne) our home

Nita (Choctaw) bear

Nituna my daughter

Nova (Hopi) chasing a butterfly

Nuna land

Odahingum (Chippewa) ripple one the water

Odina (Algonquin) mountain

Ogin (o-GEEN) the wild rose

Ojinjintka (Sioux) rose; queen of flowers

Olathe (o-LAH-tah) beautiful

Ominotago (Chippewa) pleasant voice

Omusa (Miwok) missing things when shooting with arrows

Onatah (Iroquois) corn spirit; daughter of the earth

Onawa wide-awake one

Onida the looked-for one

Opa (Choctaw) owl

Orenda (Iroquois) magic power

Oya (Miwok) naming or speaking of, the jacksnipe

Pakuna (Miwok) deer jumping when running downhill

Papina (Miwok) a vine growing on an oak tree

Pati (Miwok) to break by twisting

Pazi (Ponca) yellow bird

Pelipa (Zuni) (Gr) lover of horses

Peni (Carrier) mind

Peta (Blackfoot) golden eagle

Poloma (Choctaw) bow

Posala (Miwok) fare-well to spring flower

Ptaysanwee (Sioux) white buffalo; queen of the herd

Rozene (ro-ZAY-nuh) the rose

Sadzi (sahd-ZEE) (Carrier) sun heart; clock

Sahkyo (Navaho) mink

Salali (Cherokee) squirrel

Sanuye (Miwok) red cloud coming with sundown

Satinka magic dancer

Sedna (Eskimo) goddess of food

Shada pelican

Sheshebens (Chippewa) little duck

Shuman (Hopi) rattlesnake girl

Sibeta (see-BAY-tah) (Miwok) pulling white sucker fish from under a rock

Sihu a flower or bush

Sinopa (Blackfoot) kit fox

Sisika a thrush or swallow

Sitala (Miwok) display memory

Snana (Sioux) jingles (like little bells)

Suletu (Miwok) to fly around

Suni (Zuni) means Zuni

Sunki (Hopi) overtake

Taci (TAH-shee) (Zuni) washtub

Tadewi (Omaha) wind

Tadita (Omaha) a runner

Taigi (Omaha) returning new moon

Taima crash of thunder

Taini (Omaha) coming new moon

Taipa (Miwok) to spread wings

Takala (Hopi) corn tassel

Takchawee (Sioux) doe; loving

Tala wolf

Talasi (Hopi) corn tassel flower

Talula (Choctaw) leaping water

Talutah (Sioux) scarlet

Tama thunderbolt

Tansy (Hopi) flower name

Tasida (Sarcee) a rider

Tateeyopa (Sioux) her door; happy hostess

Tayanita (Cherokee) young beaver

Tehya precious

Tiwa (Zuni) onions

Tolikna (Miwok) coyote's long ear flapping

Toski (Hopi) squashbug

Totsi (Hopi) moccasins

Tusa (Zuni) prairie dog

Tuwa (Hopi) earth

Una (Hopi) remember

Urika (Omaha) useful to all

Utina woman of my country

Wachiwi (Sioux) dancing girl

Waitilanni (Laguna) wonder water

Wakanda (Sioux) inner magical power

Waneta the charger

Wasula (Sioux) little hailstorm; stormy, impulsive

Wauna (wah-OO-nah) (Miwok) snow geese calling as they fly

Weeko (Sioux) pretty girl

Wenona first-born daughter

Wicapi wakan (Dakota) holy star

Wihakayda (Sioux) youngest daughter; little one

Wihunahe (Cheyenne) chief woman

Winona (Sioux) eldest daughter; charitable

Witashnah (Sioux) virgin; untouched

Wyanet beautiful

Yamka (Hopi) flower budding

Yanaba (Navaho) she meets the enemy

Yepa snow maiden

Yoki (Hopi) rain; bluebird on the mesa

Yoluta farewell-to-spring flower

Yoomee (Coos) star

Zaltana high mountain

Zihna (Hopi) spinning

Zitkala (Dakota) bird

Zonta (Sioux) trustworthy

NORTH AMERICAN INDIAN MALE NAMES

Adahy (Cherokee) in the woods

Agna-iyanke (Dakota) runs beside (horse)

Ahanu he laughs

Ahmik the beaver, a symbol of skill

Akando (ah-KAHN-do) ambush

Akecheta (ah-KEE-chee-tah) (Sioux) warrior

Akule (ah-KOO-lee) he looks up

Anoki actor

Apenimon (ah-PEE-ni-mon) trusty

Apiatan (Kiowa) wooden lance

Awan (AH-wahn) somebody

Bedagi (Wabanaki) big thunder

Bemossed the walker

Biminak slick roper

Bimisi slippery

Bodaway (bo-DAH-way) fire maker

Chankoowashtay (Sioux) good road

Chash-chunk-a (Winnebago) wave

Chayton (Sioux) falcon

Chesmu gritty

Ciqala (Dakota) little

Dasan (DAH-san) (Pomo) leader of the bird clan

Delsin he is so

Demothi (deh-MO-tee) he talks walking

Dichali (dee-CHAL-lee) he speaks often — Dishaly

Dohosan (do-HO-suhn) small bluff

Dyami (di-AHM-ee) an eagle

Elan (EH-lahn) friendly — Elangonel

Elia (Zuni) from Spanish Elias (H) Jehovah is God

Elki (Miwok) to hang on top of

Elsu falcon flying

Enapay (EE-nap-ay) (Sioux) comes out (appears bravely)

Enli (Dene) that dog over there

Enyeto (en-YEH-to) the bear's manner of walking

Etu (EH-too) the sun

Ezhno (EHZH-no) solitary; a loner

Gomda (Kiowa) wind

Gosheven (go-SHAY-ven) the great leaper

Guyapi candid

Hache-hi (Arapaho) wolf

Hahnee a beggar

Hakan fiery

Halian (hah-lee-AHN) (Zuni) from Spanish Julian (L) youthful

He-lush-ka (Winnebago) warrior

Helaku (heh-LAH-koo) sunny day

Helki (Miwok) to touch

Hesutu (Miwok) lifting a yellow jacket's nest out of the ground

Hiamovi (Cheyenne) high chief

Hinto (Dakota) blue

Hinun (hee-NOON) god of clouds and rain

Honon (Miwok) bear

Honovi strong

Hotah (Sioux) white

Hototo the whistler

Howahkan (Sioux) mysterious voice

Howi (HO-wee) (Miwok) turtle-dove

Huhuseca-ska (Dakota) white bone

Hute (HOO-teh) star in the Big Dipper

Igasho a wanderer

Inteus (en-TEH-oos) he shows his face; he is not ashamed

Istu (ES-too) sugar-pine sugar

Iye (EE-yeh) smoke

Jacy (Tupi-Guarani) the moon (creator of all plant life)

Jolon valley of the dead oaks

Kaga (KAH-gah) tribe "writer," or chronicler

Kangee (Sioux) raven

Kele (KEH-lee) (Hopi) sparrow hawk — Kelle

Kibbe (KEEB-eh) (Nayas) the night bird

Kijika (kee-YEE-kah) walks quietly

Knoton (K'NO-ton) the wind — Nodin

Kohana (Sioux) swift

Kono (Miwok) a tree squirrel biting through a pine nut

Kosumi (Miwok) fishing for salmon with a spear

Kuruk (Pawnee) bear

Kuzih (KOO-zhi) (Carrier) great talker

Kwam (KWAHM) (Zuni) from Spanish Juan: (H) God's gracious gift — Kwan

Langundo peaceful

Lanu (Miwok) refers to tribal custom

Len (LEHN) (Hopi) flute

Lenno man

Lesharo (Pawnee) chief

Leyati (Miwok) shape of an abalone shell

Lise (LEE-suh) (Miwok) salmon's head just coming out of the water

Liwanu (li-WAN-oo) (Miwok) bear growling

Lokni (Miwok) rain coming through a small hole in the roof

Lonan (Zuni) cloud

Lonato flint

Lootah (Sioux) red

Lusio (Zuni) (L) bringer of light

Luyu (LOO-yoo) (Miwok) to shake the head

Mahkah (Sioux) earth

Mahpee (Sioux) sky

Makya (Hopi) eagle hunter

Manipi (mah-NEE-pee) a walking wonder

Maona (Winnebago) earthmaker (name of omnipotent deity)

Maska powerful

Masou (mah-SO-oo) fire deity

Mato (MAH-to) brave

Mato-nazin (Dakota) standing bear

Matoskah (Sioux) white bear

Maza blaska (Dakota) (piece of) flat iron

Melvern great chief

Metikla (Miwok) reaching a hand under water to catch a white sucker fish

Mika (Ponca) raccoon

Mikasi (Omaha) coyote

Milap he gives

Mingan (MEEN-gahn) gray wolf

Misu (MEE-soo) (Miwok) rippling water

Mojag (MO-yahg) never quiet (baby who cries a lot)

Molimo (Miwok) bear going into shade of trees

Momuso (Miwok) yellow jackets piled up in their nest in winter

Mona (Miwok) gathering jimson weed seed

Motega (mo-TEH-gah) new arrow

Muata (Miwok) yellow jackets in the nest

Muraco (MOO-rah-cho) white moon

Nahele (nah-HEH-leh) forest or grove of trees

Nahios-si (Cheyenne) three fingers

Nahma (NAH-mah) the sturgeon

Nakos (Arapaho) sage

Nalren (Dene) he is thawed out

Namid (NAH-meed) (Chippewa) the star dancer

Nantai (Navajo) chief

Nantan (Apache) spokesman

Napayshni (nah-PAY-shnee) (Sioux) he does not flee (courageous)

Nashashuk (Sauk, Fox) loud thunder

Nashoba (Choctaw) wolf

Nawat (NAH-waht) left hand

Nawkaw (Winnebago) wood

Nayati (nah-YAH-tee) the wrestler

Neka the wild goose

Nibaw I stand up

Nigan ahead

Nikiti round and smooth like an abalone shell

Nitis (NEE-tes) friend − Netis

Nodin the wind − Noton

Notaku (Miwok) growling of a bear as someone passes by

Odakota (Sioux) friendly

Ogaleesha (Sioux) red shirt

Ogima (Chippewa) chief

Ohanko reckless

Ohanzee (Sioux) shadow (comforting)

Ohitekah (Sioux) brave

Otadan (o-TAH-dahn) plenty

Otaktay (Sioux) kills or strikes many

Otu collecting sea shells in a basket

Ouray (o-RAY) the arrow

Oya (Miwok) naming, or speaking of the jacksnipe

Paco (PAH-cho) bald eagle

Pallaton (PAHL-lah-ton) fighter

Pat (PAHT) fish

Patakasu (Miwok) small ant biting a person hard

Patamon raging

Patwin man

Payat he is coming

Paytah (Sioux) fire

Pilan (pee-LAHN) supreme essence

Pinon (pee-NON) (Tupi-Guarani) a god who became the constellation Orion

Quanah (Commanche) fragrant

Raini (Tupi-Guarani) a god who created the world

Sahale (sah-HAH-leh) falcon

Sakima king

Sakuruta (Pawnee) coming sun

Sewati (Miwok) curving of the bear's claws

Sipatu (see-PAH-too) (Miwok) to pull out

Siwili long tail of the fox

Skah (Sioux) white

Skiriki (Pawnee) coyote

Son star

Songan (SON-gahn) strong

Tadi (TAH-dee) (Omaha) wind

Tadzi (Carrier Indian, Canada) the loon

Taima crash of thunder; born during storm

Takoda (Sioux) friend to them all

Talli (Lenape) a legendary hero, who led the tribe after the great flood

Täpko (Kiowa) antelope

Tasunke (Dakota) horse

Tatanka-ptecila (Dakota) short bull

Tate (TAH-teh, or TAYT) windy; great talker

Teetonka (Sioux) big lodge

Telutci (Miwok) bear making dust as it runs

Tiimu (Miwok) black-and-white caterpillar coming out of the ground

Tokala (Dakota) fox

Tooantuh (Cherokee) spring frog — Dústú

Tuari (Laguna) young eagle

Tuketu (Miwok) bear making dust as it runs

Tukuli (Miwok) caterpillar travelling down a tree

Tumu (Miwok) deer thinking about going to eat wild onions

Tupi (Miwok) to pull up

Tyee chief — Tyonek

Uzumati (Miwok) grizzly bear

Viho (Cheyenne) chief

Waban the east wind

Wahchinksapa (Sioux) wise, clear-headed

Wahchintonka (Sioux) patient

Wahkan (Sioux) sacred

Wahkoowah (Sioux) charging

Wakiza desperate fighter

Wamblee (Sioux) eagle

Wambleeska (Sioux) white eagle

Wambli-waste (Dakota) good eagle

Wanageeska (Sioux) white spirit

Wanahton (Sioux) charger

Wanikiya (Sioux) savior

Wapi lucky

Weayaya (Sioux) setting sun

Wehinahpay (wee-HIN-ah-pay) (Sioux) rising sun

Wemilat child born to wealthy parents

Wenutu sky clearing after being cloudy

Wicasa (Dakota) man

Wichado willing — Wingi

Wilanu (Miwok) pouring water on acorn flour

Wilny (WEEL-nee) eagle singing while flying

Wilu (Miwok) chicken hawk calling "wi"

Wuliton to do well

Wunand God is good

Wuyi (Miwok) turkey vulture soaring

Wynono first-born son

Yahto (Sioux) blue

Yakecen (Dene) sky on song

Yancy Englishman

Yoskolo breaking off sugar pine cones

Yotimo yellow jacket carrying pieces of meat from a house to its nest

Yuma son of a chief

Yutu (Miwok) to claw

NORWAY

Small Norwegian immigrant colonies began near Rochester, New York in 1825, the Fox River in Illinois in 1834, and Milwaukee, Wisconsin in 1839. Glowing reports about life in America began to entice a rising tide of immigrants starting in 1843. There were never less than 1,000 immigrants per year after the mid-19th century until the 1930's.

Large-scale immigration to the United States from Norway began in earnest in the late 1860's, for several reasons. The social system of Norway kept the land in the same families for centuries, and those who were not landed had little hope of becoming so.

For the first time in centuries, Norway was not at war, and the young men were staying home and beginning to raise families. With improved living conditions, the population began to increase significantly above levels that could be supported by Norway's agricultural system. Only about four percent of the land is tillable, the rest being either mountain, dense woodland, bog, or icefield.

Norwegians began to immigrate in record numbers in the 1860's (total of 98,000). The pace slowed slightly in the 1870's and 1890's, but in the 1880's (peak decade for all northern European immigration) Norwegian immigrants numbered 186,000 and in the first decade of the 20th century, 190,000.

Most settled in Wisconsin, Minnesota, and North Dakota, where the largest Norwegian populations continue to live. Many also moved to the Northwest and did very well in fishing, lumbering, and shipbuilding industries. In 1900 Seattle had the largest urban Norwegian population.

The biggest urban population today, however, is in Brooklyn, New York, where an estimated 40,000 Norwegians compose an area formerly called the fourth largest Norwegian city in the world. Norwegian is one of the languages that can be studied in some of the high schools there.

Altogether, over 855,000 Norwegians have immigrated since 1820, a number equal to the population of Norway in 1820. No other country except Ireland has sent a larger proportion of its native population to America.

Norwegian names of both Biblical and pagan origin date back more than a thousand years. The ancient Norwegians honored their dead in the hopes that the good traits of the deceased would be reborn in their children. In Norse mythology, dead fighting heroes were brought to feast in the castle Valhalla. Valkyries (battle maidens) brought them there to a vast dining hall line with walls of gold and pillars of gleaming spears.

Many of the old Norse names reflect the glory given to warriors. Around 1000 A.D. King Olaf Haroldson brought Christianity to Norway along with the Biblical names of Greek, Latin, and Hebrew origins that have taken parallel forms in most countries of the Western World. It is these Biblical names that dominate the current list of most popular names for babies, although Old Norse names are also popular. The starred names in the list below are the top ten names for 1985. Pronunciation is included for most of the entries.

NORWEGIAN FEMALE NAMES

Ågot (AW-got) (Gr) good

Alvar (OGer) elf army

Andras (ONorse) breath

Anette* (H) grace, mercy — Annette

Anne* (AHN-neh) (H) grace, mercy — Anna

Arna eagle

Åse (AW-seh) tree, tree-covered mountain — Asta

Åshild (AWS-hil) god-fighting woman

Aslaug (AHS-laug) god-consecrated

Astrid (AHST-ree) god-lovely, divine strength — Astra

Asvoria (Teut) divine prudence

Aud prosperity, happiness

Audhild (AUD-hil) prosperity, fighting woman

Audny new prosperity

Audun deserted or desolate

Beate (beh-AH-teh) (L) happy

Bente (BEHN-teh) (L) blessed

Bera (Teut) bear

Berit (BEH-rit) (Celt) magnificent

Birgit (Celt) magnificent — Berta, Brit(a), Birgitte, Birte

Bodil (BO-dil) penance-fighting woman

Borgny (BORG-nee) "help-new"

Brenda flame, sword

Brita from Britain — Brit

Brynhild (BRIN-hil) "coat of mail-fighting woman"

Camilla* (L) ceremonial attendant

Cathrine* (Gr) pure — Katrine

Dagmar (Teut) Dane's joy

Dagny (dahg-NEE) day, or brightness

Dale (ONorse) valley

Disa active spirit

Dordi (Gr) (from Dorothy) gift from God — Dorte, Dordei, Dora, Tea

Dorte (Gr) God's gift

Edit (EH-diht) (A.S.) wealth

Eldrid (EHL-dre) fire-lovely

Eli (EH-lee) (Gr) the illustrious — Elin, Eline, Ellen, Lene, Line

Elise (eh-LE-seh) (H) consecrated to God — Ellisif, Else, Lisbet, Lise

Erica (ONorse) ever powerful — Erika, Ricci

Eva (EH-vah) (H) life

Freya noble woman

Frida lovely

Frøydis (FRUY-dis) Frøy-goddess. Frøy was a Norse god.

Gerd (GEHRD) protection

Greta (GREH-tah)(Gr) a pearl — Margit, Marit, Magrit, Marte, Merete, Mette, Rita

Gro (GRO) she who makes things grow

Gudrun (GUHD-ruhn) divine wisdom — Guro

Guri gods-lovely

Gyda (GID-ah) gods

Haldis stone-help

Hanne* (HAHN-uh) (H) grace, mercy

Hedda (HED-dah) (Ger) vigorous fight

Hege (HEH-geh) holy

Helle from Hilde, a Valkyrie, battle maiden in Norse mythology

Herdis (HEHR-dis) group of warriors-goddess

Hilde a Valkyrie — Hild, Hilda, Helle, Hildur (Iceland)

Hildegunn (HIL-deh-guhn) fighting woman

Hulda hidden, Hulder was a beautiful netherworld woman with a cow's tail

Ida (EE-dah) (OGer) she who is active

Idun (EE-duhn) active-love

Inga (IHNG-ah) (Teut) hero's daughter ("ing" as in singer)

Ingeborg (IHNG-eh-borg) Frøy-help

Ingjerd (IHNG-yerd) Frøy-protection

Ingrid (IHNG-red) Frøy-lovely

Ingunn (IHNG-uhn) Frøy-love

Jorunn (YOHR-uhn) chief-love

Kaia (KAH-ee-ah) (Gr) from "Gaia" (earth)

Karen (KAH-rehn) (Gr) pure — Kari, Karine, Katinka, Trine

Kelsey (ONorse) from the ship's island — Kelci, Kelda

Kristin* (Gr)the anointed — Kirsten, Kristine, Kirsti, Kjersti, Stina, Christine

Kristine* (Gr) Christian — Christine

Laila (Finnish) meaning unknown

Lene (LEH-neh) the illustrious

Linda* (Span) beautiful

Line (LEE-neh) short form of names ending with -ina. Short for Eline.

Liv (LEEV) life — Live (LEE-vuh)

Magna (MAHGN-ah) strength

Magnhild (NAHGN-nil) strength-fighting woman

Maren (MAH-rehn) (H) bitter

Marete (meh-REH-teh) (Gr) a pearl

Margit (Gr) a pearl

Marianne* see Marie and Anne

Marie (ma-REE-ah) (H) bitter — Maren, Maria

Marit (MAH-riht) (Aramaic) mistress, lady

Marta (Gr) a pearl

Mathea (mah-TEH-ah) (H) gift of God

Mildri (MIL-ree) mildlovely

Mona (Gr) solitary

Nina short form of Annina, a Russian nickname for Anna

Nora (Gr) light

Oda (OO-dah) short form of names starting with Aud- or Odd-

Oddny point-new

Oddveig (OD-vey) pointwoman

Ola (OO-lah) descendant or reminder or ancestor

Olaug (OO-laug) ancestorsconsecrated

Olga (Russian) holy

Ragna (RAHN-nah) short form of names starting with Ragn-, gods

Ragnfrid (RAHGN-freed) gods-lovely — Ragni, Randi

Ranveig house-woman

Reidun (REYD-uhn) nestlovely

Rona mighty power

Rønnaug (RUN-aug) house-woman

Runa (ROON-ah) short form of female names ending with -run; secret

Sara (SAH-rah) (H) princess

Selma (Celt) beautiful

Silje* (SIL-yeh) (form of Cecilia) (L) blind

Sissel (form of Cecilia) (L) blind

Siv (SEEV) kinship, also the name of the wife of Norse god, Thor

Solveig (SOL-vey) housewoman

Sonja (SON-yah) (Gr) wisdom

Sunniva (A.S) sun-gift — Synne, Synnove

Svanhild (SVAHN-hil) swan-fighting woman

Synnove (SIH-nuh-veh or sihn-UH-veh) (A.S) sungift

Tone (TO-neh) Tor-new — Torny

Tora short form, names ending with -tora, female form of -tor, thunder

Tordis Tor-goddess

Toril Tor-fighting woman

Torunn Tor-love

Tove (TO-veh) (H) good

Trine (TREE-neh) (from Karen) (Gr) the pure

Trude (TROO-deh) strength

Unn (UHN) love, or she who is loved

Vera (VEH-rah) (L) true

Vibeke (VEE-beh-keh) (Low German) little woman

Vigdis battle goddess

*** Most popular**

NORWEGIAN MALE NAMES

Åge (AW-geh) ancestors — Ake, Ove

Aksel (AHK-sel) (H) father of peace

Alf (AHLF) one that is dead and lives in the netherworld

Amund (AH-mun) bridal gift

Anders* (Gr) strong and manly

Anton (L) inestimable

Aren (AH-rehn) eagle, rule

Aricin the eternal king's son

Arild (AH-ril) war chief

Arkin the eternal king's son

Arne (ARH-neh) (OGer) eagle — Are, Adne, Arnt

Arnljot (ARN-lyawt) he who frightens the eagle

Arve (AHRV) inheritor of property; heir — Arvid

Arvid (AHR-ved) eagle-tree — Arve

Åsgeir (AWS-gayr) godspear. Later forms are Eske, Ansgar, Oscar

Audun (AU-dun) friend of prosperity

Axell (H) father of peace

Balder god of light — Baldur

Bard fight-lovely

Baste (Gr) (from Sebastian) reverenced

Bendik (L) blessed — Bent, Bengt

Birger (BIHR-gehr) rescue

Bjarne (BYAHR-neh) from older names featuring "bjorn," (bear)

Bjørn (BYUHRN) bear

Bodil commanding

Borg from the castle

Brede (BREH-deh) broad; the glacier

Canute knot – Knute, Cnute

Carr from the marsh – Karr, Kerr

Cort short – Cortie, Kort

Dag (DAHG) day

Dana from Denmark – Dain, Dane

Darby from the deer estate

Davin (DAH-vin) the brightness of the Finns

Denby from the village of the Danes – Danb, Den, Denny

Derby from the village of the Danes – Danby, Den, Denney

Donalt (Celt) world ruler

Dreng young man, brave man, or hired farmhand

Dyre (DIH-reh) uncertain meaning, either dear or deer

Egil (EH-gihl) awe-inspiring – Eigil

Einar (I-nahr) warrior, leader

Elvis all wise – Alvis, El

Erik (EH-rik) ever powerful – Eirik (AY-rik)

Erlend (EHR-lehn) "chief-turned"

Erling chief-descendant

Eskil (EHS-kil) modern form of Askjell, "god-vessel"

Espen Danish form of Asbjorn, "god-bear"

Eystein (EY-steyn) turned toward luck

Faste (FAHS-teh) firm

Filip (Gr) lover of horses

Finn Laplander

Frans (Teut) free man – Franzen

Fredrik (Teut) peaceful ruler – Fredek

Frode (FROO-deh) wise

Gale (GAH-leh) (OE) to sing

Galt (OE) high ground

Garth (ONorse) garden, grounds-keeper – Garrett

Gaute (GAU-teh) great man

Geir (GAYR) spear

Gerhard (OE) spear-hard

Gjest (GYEST) guest, stranger

Gregor (Gr) vigilant

Gudbrand (GOOD-bran) gods-weapon

Håkon (HAH-kon) of the chosen race – Haaken

Halvdan (HAHLF-dahn) half-Danish

Halvor (HAHL-vor) rock-protection

Hans (HAHNS) (H) God's gracious gift – Johan, Jon, Jens

Harald (HAHR-ald) (ONorse) war chief

Hauk hawk

Havelock sea battle

Hrorek (Teut) famous ruler

Hugo (Teut) intelligence, spirit

Ivar (EE-vahr) Frøy-warrior. Frøy was a Norse god; archer

Jan* (YAHN) (H) God's gracious gift

Jens (YEHNS) (H) God's gracious gift

Jon (YOON) (H) God's gracious gift

Jorgen (YUHR-gehn) (Gr) farmer

Kare (KAW-reh) tremendous

Karl (OFr) strong and manly

Kelsey (ONorse) from the ship's island

Kleng he with the claw

Knut (KNUHT) knot – Canute, Cnut

Krist (Gr) anointed one

Kristian (Gr) Christian – Christian

Lamont lawyer

Lang (ONorse) tall man

Lars* (LARSS) (L) laurel – Lavrans, Lasse, Laurits, Lorens

Laurens (L) crowned with laurel – Lorens, Larse

Leif (LAYF) the one who remains, descendant

Lorens (L) crowned with laurel – Laurans, Larse, Lars

Magnar (MAHGN-ahr) strength-warrior

Magne (MAHGN-eh) strength

Martin (L) warlike

Mikkel (MIK-el) who is like God?

Morten* (L) warlike

Nels (Celt) chief

Nils (Gr) victory of the people – Niklas, Nikolai, Nick, Nial, Nels

Odd point

Oddvar (ODD-vahr) point-able

Ola (OO-lah) ancestors-descendants – Olin, Olen

Ole* (OO-leh) ancestors-descendants – Olav (OO-lahv)

Ottar (O-tahr) point-warrior or fright-warrior

Øystein (OY-stayn) happiness-rock – Ostein, Osten

Pal (PAUL) little

Peder (Gr) stone – Peder, Petter

Per (PEEHR) (Gr) stone

Ragnar (RAHG-nahr) gods-warrior – Raynor, Rainer

Reidar (RAY-dahr) nest-warrior

Roald (RO-ahl) (OGer) famous ruler

Roar (RO-ahr) praise-warrior

Rolf praise-wolf

Sigurd (SIH-guhr) victorious guardian – Sjur, Syver

Skipp shipmaster

Skule (SCOO-leh) hide

Steinar (STI-nar) rock-warrior

Stian* (STEE-an) one who takes large steps, or "quick on his feet"

Sutherland southern land

Svein (SVAIN) young man — Sven

Tait (TIGHT) cheerful

Terje (TEHR-yeh) Tor-spear

Theodrekr (Gr) gift of God

Thomas* (H) twin — Tomas, Tom, Tommy

Thorbjorn (THOR-byuhrn) Tor-bear

Tor (TOOHR) thunder — Thor

Torgeir (TOR-gayr) — Tor-spear; newer forms are: Terje, Torger, Tarjei

Torgny (TOHRG-nee) Tor-clamor of weapons

Trond (TRON) growth-turned

Trygve (TRIG-ve) brave-victor

Ulf wolf

Vegard (VEE-gahr) sanctuary-protection

Vidar (VEE-dahr) tree-warrior or wide-warrior

---

* Most popular

PHILIPPINES

About 113,000 Filipinos immigrated to Hawaii between 1909 and 1931 to work on pineapple plantations and in sugar cane fields and mills. Of these 55,000 remained in Hawaii, 39,000 returned home, and 19,000 moved on to the west coast of the U.S.

The election of President Ferdinand Marcos in 1972 coincided roughly with the liberalization of immigration laws in the U.S. As Marcos moved to acquire dictatorial powers and suspend civil rights Filipino immigration took a sudden upturn, from 6,000 in 1966 to 32,000 in 1974. An estimated one-half of the 500,000 Filipinos now living in America are foreign-born.

Over eighty dialects are spoken in the Phillipines; the three languages most used by Filipino-Americans are Visayan, Tagalog, and Ilocano. Names have a Spanish influence because of the colonization by Spain that lasted three centuries, until the end of the Spanish-American War. Filipino babies are traditionally given their mother's maiden name as a middle name.

FILIPINO FEMALE NAMES

Amalia (L) industrious

Asuncion ascension of Christ into heaven

Aurora (L) dawn

Candida (L) pure white

Consuelo consolation

Corazon heart

Duvata (Filipino) nymph

Filemon (Gr) loving friend

Honorina (L) honor

Isabello (H) consecrated to God

Julita (L) youth

Kristina (Gr) Christian, or Christmas

Mahal (Filipino) love

Malaya (Filipino) free

Maria (H) bitter

Mayuni (Filipino) timid

Milagros miracles

Mutya (Filipino) pretty

Paz (L) peace

Pilar Virgin Mary (pillar of the Catholic Church)

Rosario rosary

Soledad health

Victoria (L) victory

FILIPINO MALE NAMES

Ambrocio (Gr) the divine, immortal one

Arturo (Celt) noble — Art

Bayani (Filipino) hero

Bienvenido welcome

Cenon (Gr) hospitable

Cipriano from the island of Cyprus

Florencio (L) flowering

Gabriel (H) God is my strength (in honor of the Archangel Gabriel)

Gregorio (Gr) vigilant

Honesto (L) honest

Jose (H) God will add, in honor of St. Joseph

Juan (H) God's gracious gift (in honor of St. John)

Lauro (L) laurel

Manuel (H) God is with us

Matalino (Filipino) bright

Modesto modest

Pacifico (L) peaceful

Renato (Fr) king

Rosito (L) rose

POLAND

In the first half of the 19th century the nature of Polish emigration was primarily political. At that time Poland as a separate country hardly existed because it had been partitioned three times in the 18th century by its powerful neighbors. Most of Poland was under Russian rule by 1815; Prussia controlled the smaller western part of Poland; and Austria, the poor and populous territory of Galicia.

In 1830 a nationalist insurrection was suppressed by Czar Nicholas I of Russia. Many revolutionaries, who considered the U.S. a model liberal society, emigrated from Poland, settling in New York and Chicago (at least 1,000 came to America) as well as London, Paris, and Geneva. Another uprising in 1863 failed to achieve independence for Poland, but swelled the ranks of emigrants.

Poland experienced the same woes that accumulated in other countries of northern Europe in the last half of the 19th century. Massive population growth worsened the problem of family farms subdivided among descendants to below subsistence levels. In Galicia the effect was worst because no industry developed to provide jobs for the increasing numbers of landless peasants.

Thus, the Polish immigrants from the second half of the 19th century were much more concerned with basic survival. In Poland they were called "za chlebem" (for-bread) emigrants, and from the German section they numbered an estimated 380,000 between 1850 and 1898. Another 50,000 arrived before 1914.

The tide of emigration gradually shifted to the east. In the 1890's 400,000 Galician Poles immigrated to the U.S. with an equal number arriving between 1900 and 1914. The bulk of Russian Poles arrived after 1900 (635,00 from 1900 to 1914, 170,000 before 1900).

A significant aspect of the Polish immigration were the support networks of previous immigrants in the U.S., which eased the entry of the newcomers into American life. Most immigrants also came armed with plenty of information about American customs from a voluminous flow of letters to and from Poland.

Most Polish immigrants of this time made their way to rapidly developing cities of the Midwest and Middle Atlantic states, especially Chicago, taking jobs in mills, slaughterhouses, refineries, and foundries. Very few became farmers.

After World War I Polish emigration resulted mainly from discouragement about the unstable political situation, which went through many rocky transformations including Nazi occupation during World War II and culminating in the establishment of a pro-Soviet government in 1945.

As occurred before the War, most Poles immigrated to industrial areas of the Midwest. The total number of Americans of Polish heritage is estimated at between five and six million, making it one of the largest ethnic groups.

The majority of Polish people, including the immigrants, have been Roman Catholic since their forebears, a tribe of Western Slavs converted to Christianity in 966 A.D. Saint names are common in the Polish name calendar, as well as names of early Polish kings such as Kazimeirz, Stanislaus, and Wladyslaw. It is customary in Poland to celebrate a person's birthday on the first day that the person's name appears on the name calendar. Many of the most common names repeat themselves several times a year. Someone named Tomasz, for instance, born in late May would celebrate his birthday on September 22, the first name day after that. Polish children are usually known by nicknames or diminutives.

POLISH FEMALE NAMES

Adelajda (AH-deh-LAH-ee-dah) (OGer) noble, kind

Agata (Gr) good, or kind

Albinka (L) blond, white

Aldona (OGer) old

Alina bright, beautiful

Alka noble, brilliant

Amelia (L) industrious, persuasive — Amalia

Anastazja (ah-nah-STAZ-yah) (Gr) resurrection

Anieli meaning unknown, perhaps fem. of Aniol (Gr) manly

Anna (H) grace — Ania, Hania, Anka, Hanka, Hanna

Antonina (L) inestimable

Balbina (L) stammerer

Barbara (Gr) the stranger

Basha (Gr) the stranger (dim.)

Beata (L) she blesses

Bodgana God's gift — Bohdana

Bogna God's gift

Brygid (Celt) strength

Cecilia (tseh-TSEE-lyuh) (L) blind, gray eyes

Celina (tseh-LEE-nah) (Gr) mythological figure — Celestyn, Cela, Celek, Celinka, Cesia, Inok, Inka

Diana (Gr) goddess of the moon

Dominika (L) of the Lord

Dorota (L) gift of God

Edyta (eh-DEET-ah) (Teut) rich gift

Elwira (Sp) white, fair — Ela, Wira, Wiera, Wirke

Elzbieta (H) consecrated to God — Eliza, Liza, Elka

Emilia (Teut) industrious

Eufemia (Gr) well-known

Euzebia (Gr) pious

Ewa (EH-vah) (H) life

Felcia (FEHL-shah) (L) fortunate, or lucky — Felka, Fela, Felicia

Filipina (Gr) lover of horses

Filomena (Gr) lover of mankind

Florentyna (L) flowering

Franciszka (frahn-SHEESH-ka) (Teut) free — Frania, Fraka

Gizela (Teut) pledge

Grazyna (H) grace

Gutka good

Halina (Gr) light

Helena (Gr) light

Henka (Teut) ruler of an estate — Henia, Heniuta, Henrieta

Hilaria (L) cheerful

Honorata (L) honor

Hortenspa (L) gardener — Tesia

Inga (Teut) hero's daughter

Irena (Gr) peace

Iwona (ee-VO-nah) (Scand) archer

Izabel (H) consecrated to God — Iza

Jadwiga (yahd-VEEG-ah) (Teut) refuge in battle

Jana (YAH-nah) (H) God's gracious gift — Janina, Janecska, Jasia, Joasia

Joanka (YO-ahn-kah) (H) God's gracious gift — Nina, Joanna, Janka, Zanna

Joanny (yo-AHN-nee) (H) God's gracious gift

Jolanta (yo-LAHN-tah) (Gr) violet blossoms — Jola

Julia (YOO-lyah) (L) youthful

Julita (L) youthful

Justyna (L) just

Kamilla (L) ceremonial attendant — Mila, Kamilka

Karin (Gr) pure

Karolin fem. Karol

Kassia (Gr) pure — Kasia, Kasin, Kasienka, Kaska

Katarzyna (kah-tarzh-EE-nah) (Gr) pure — Kasia, Kaska, Kasienka

Katrine (Gr) pure — Katrin, Katine, Kati, Katya

Klara (L) bright, clear

Klaudia (L) lame

Kleopatra (Gr) glory of the father

Krysta (Gr) Christian — Krystka, Krysia, Krystynka

Krystyn (KRIS-tin) (Gr) Christian

Ksena (H) praise to God

Kunegundy meaning unknown

Laura (Gr) crown of laurels

Lechsinska woodland spirit

Lidia (Gr) ancient province in Asia Minor

Lilianna (L) pure as a lily

Lilka famous warrior-maiden — Ludka, Iza, Lodoiska, Lucwika, Luisa

Lucja (LOOTS-yah) (L) bringer of light

Lucyna (LOOT-sih-nah) (L) light-bringer

Ludmila (Russian) loved by the people

Madde (Gr) woman from Magdala

Malgorzata (mahl-gor-ZHAH-tah) (Gr) a pearl

Marcelina (L) warlike — Marzena

Margarita (Gr) a pearl — Margisia, Gita, Rita

Maria (H) bitter — Mania, Marysia, Macia, Manka

Marianna (H) rebellious; form of Mary

Marta (H) bitter — Masia, Macia (MAH-tsee-ah)

Marysia (H) bitter

Matyidy unknown, perhaps Matilda (Teut) brave in battle

Mela pet form of Melania: black, or dark — Melka, Ela

Melania (Gr) black — Ela

Melcia (MEHLT-shuh) (Teut) ambitious — Amalia

Michalin (H) who is like God?

Minka (Teut) strong, resolute

Monika (L) advisor

Morela apricot

Nadzia (Slavic) hope — Natka

Nata hope — Natia

Natalia (Fr) born at Christmas

Nelka nickname for Petronela (Gr) the stone — Nela, Petra, Ela

Olesia (Gr) defender of mankind — Ola

Olga (Russian) holy

Olimpia (Gr) Olympian

Otylia (OGer) lucky heroine

Paulina (L) little

Pelagia (Gr) sea-dweller

Pelcia (PEL-shuh) nickname for Penelopa (Gr) weaver — Pela, Lopa

Petronela (Gr) stone

Rahel (H) innocence of a lamb

Rasia queen

Rasine rose

Reginy (L) queen

Rita (Gr) a pearl

Roch (Ger) glory

Roza (L) rose — Rozyczka (ro-ZEESH-kuh)

Rozali comb. of Rose and Lily

Rozalia (L) rose

Sabina (L) Sabine woman (ancient tribe of central Italy)

Sabiny (L) Sabine woman (ancient tribe in central Italy)

Sylwia (SIL-vyah) (L) from the forest

Tamary (Russian) palm tree

Tekli (Gr) divine fame

Teodory (Gr) gift of God

Teodozji (teh-o-DOZ-yee) (Gr) God-given

Teresa (Gr) harvester — Czeslaw (CHEHS-lahv)

Tesia (Gr) loved by God — Teofila, Fila

Tosia nickname for Antonina (L) inestimable — Anta, Nina, Tola

Truda (OGer) warrior woman — Trudka, Giertruda, Gerta

Urszuli (uhr-SHOO-lee) (L) little bear

Valeska (Russian) glorious ruler

Vanda (OGer) wanderer

Wandy (VAHN-dee) (OGer) wanderer

Weronikia (L) true image

Wioletta (vee-o-LEH-tuh) (L) violet

Wisia (VEE-shuh) (L) victory — Wicia, Wikitoria, Wiktorja, Wikta

Wladyslawa (vlah-dis-SLAH-vah) (Fr) petite and feminine (from Charlotte)

Yachne (YAKH-nee) (H) gracious

Zefiryn (Gr) like the zephyr

Zenobia (Gr) stranger

Zofia (Gr) wisdom

Zuzanny (H) lily

Zyta dim. Teresa (Gr) harvester

Zytka nickname to Rosita, and Brigita — Zyta

POLISH MALE NAMES

Adam (H) son of the red earth

Adok (L) dark one

Adolf (OGer) noble wolf

Adrian (L) of the Adriatic

Albin (L) white

Aleksandr (Gr) defender of mankind

Aleksy (Gr) defender of mankind

Alfred (OE) wise counselor

Anatol (Gr) from the East

Andrzej (AHND-zheh) (Gr) manly

Aniol (Gr) strong and manly — Jedrus, Jedrik

Antoniy (L) inestimable — Antonin

Anzelm (Teut) divine helmet

Apoloniusz (ah-po-LON-yoosh) (Gr) Apollo

Aron (H) lofty or exalted

Artur (Celt) noble; bear man

Augustyn (L) venerable — August

Aurek (AW-rek) golden-haired — Aureli, Elek

Barnaby (Aramaic) ploughman

Bazyli (bah-ZIH-lee) (Gr) kingly

Bendek (L) blessed — Benek, Benedykt

Beniamin (H) son of the right hand

Bernard (OGer) courage of a bear — Bernardyn

Bialy (BYAH-lee) white-haired boy — Bialas

Bogdan (H) God's gift — Bohdan

Bogumil God's peace

Boguslaw (BO-goo-slahv) (Slavic) God's glory

Bonifacy (L) well-doer

Borys stranger

Boryslaw stranger-glory

Bronislaw (BRON-is-lahv) (Slavic) weapon of glory

Brunon (Ger) brown

Casimir (kah-SEE-muhr) he announces peace

Celestyn (L) heaven

Cyprian (SHIH-pree-an) (L) from Cyprus

Cyryl (Gr) lordly one — Cyrek

Czeslaw (CHEHS-lahv) (L) fortress

Damian (Gr) taming

Daniel (H) God is my judge

Dionizy (Gr) god of wine

Dobieslaw (DO-bee-slav) (Gr) god of wine

Dobry (DO-bree) good

Dodek noble hero — Adek, Adolph

Dominik (L) of the Lord

Donat (Celt) world ruler

Dorek gift of God

Dymitr (Gr) belonging to Demeter, goddess of the harvest

Edward (EHD-vahrd) (OE) wealthy guardian — Eduard

Elek from Aurek: "golden-haired"

Emanuel (H) God is with us

Emilian (Teut) energetic

Erek lovable

Ernest (OGer) serious

Eryk (ONorse) ever powerful

Eustachy (Gr) fruitful

Felicjan (feh-LEETS-yahn) (L) fortunate, or lucky

Feliks (L) fortunate, or lucky

Feodor (Gr) gift of God — Fedor, Tolek, Teos, Teodor, Dorek

Ferdynand (Teut) adventurous

Fidelis (L) faithful

Filip (Gr) lover of horses — Fil

Flawiusz (FLAH-vee-oosh) (L) blond, yellow

Florentyn (L) flowering

Florian (L) flowering

Franciszk (frahn-TSEESHK) (Tuet) free

Fryderyk (Teut) peaceful ruler — Fredek

Gabriel (H) God is my strenth

Gerard (OE) spear hard

Gerik (GEHR-ik) prosperous spearman — Edek

Gerwazy (gehr-VAH-zee) (Teut) warrior

Grzegorz (GZHEG-orzh) (Gr) vigilant

Gwidon (GVEE-don) (L) life

Henryk (Teut) ruler of the home

Heromin (hehr-oh-MEEN) (Teut) ruler of an estate

Hieronim (Gr) sacred name

Hilary (L) cheerful

Hipolit (Gr) letting horses loose

Holleb like a dove

Innocenty (L) innocent

Izak (H) laughter — Icek

Izydor (Gr) a gift of ideas

Jack (yahk) (H) God's gracious gift

Jakub (YAH-koob) (H) the supplanter

Jan (YAHN) (H) God's gracious gift — Janek

Jarek (YAH-rek) born in January — Janiusz, Janiuszck, Januarius

Jedrik (YED-rik) strong and manly — Jedrus

Jerzy (YEHR-zee) (Gr) farmer

Joachim (yo-ah-KEEM) (H) God will establish

Josep (YO-sehp) (H) God will add — Josef

Juliusz (YOO-lee-oosh) (L) youthful — Julian

Justyn (YOOS-tin) (L) just

Kajetan (kah-yeh-TAHN) (It) from Gaete in central Italy

Karol (OFr) strong and manly — Karolek

Kazimierz (kah-see-meerzh) declare peace

Klemens (L) merciful

Konrad (OGer) honest counselor

Konstancji (kon-STAHNT-syee) (L) constant — Konstanty

Kornel (L) horn

Kosmy (Gr) order, universe

Krzysztof (KZHIS-tof) (Gr) Christ-bearer

Laiurenty (L) crowned with laurels

Leon (L) lion

Liuz (LOOZ) (L) light

Lubomir peace-loving

Luboslaw loving glory

Lucjan (LOOTS-yahn) (L) bringer of light

Ludoslaw love of glory

Ludwik (LOOD-vik) (OGer) renowned warrior

Lukasz (LOO-kahsh) (L) bringer of light

Maksym (L) greatest — Makimus, Maksymilian

Mandek (MAHN-dek) army man — Armand, Armandek, Arek

Marcely (mar-SHEH-lee) (L) warlike

Marek (MAH-rek) (L) warlike — Marcin, Marcinek

Marian (MAHR-yahn) (L) warlike

Mark (L) warlike — Marek

Mateusz (mah-TOOSH) (H) gift of God — Matyas

Maury (L) Moorish

Maurycy (mo-REET-see) (L) Moorish, dark-skinned

Melchior (H) king

Michal (H) who is like God?

Mikolaj (MEE-ko-lah-ee) (Gr) victory of the people Milosz, Milek, Mikolai

Miron peace

Miroslawy (MEE-ro-slah-vee) (Slavic) peace-glory

Nelek pet form of Kornelek (L) horn — Kornel, Kornek

Nestor (Gr) traveler; wisdom

Niki (NEE-kee) nickname for Dominik (L) like the Lord

Nikodem (Gr) conqueror of the people

Olaf (Norse) descendants

Oles form of Alexandr (Gr) defender of mankind

Onufry unknown meaning

Paschalis (paht-chahl-is) (Fr) Easter

Patryk (L) noble

Pawel (PAH-vel) (L) little — Paulin, Pawelek, Inek

Pawl (L) little

Piotr (Gr) stone — Piotrek, Pietrek

Placyd (PLAH-tsid) (L) serene

Prokop unknown meaning

Radoslaw love of peace — Radzmir, Mirek, Slawek

Rafal (H) God has healed

Rajmund (RAH-y-moond) (Teut) mighty protector

Renat (L) reborn

Robert (Teut) of shining fame

Roman (L) from Rome

Rudolf (Teut) famous wolf

Rufin (L) red-haired

Ryszard (RIH-shard) (OGer) powerful ruler

Serafin (H) seraph

Sergiusz (SEHR-goosh) (L) the attendant

Seweryn (SEH-ver-in) (L) severe

Stanislav (Slavic) stand of glory

Stasio (Slavic) stand of glory

Stefan (Gr) crown

Szczepan (zh-CHEH-pahn) (Gr) crown

Szymon (SHIH-mon) (H) God is heard

Telek iron cutter

Teodor (Gr) gift of God

Teofil (Gr) divinely loved

Tomasz (TO-mahsh) (H) twin

Tomek (H) twin — Tomcio, Tomislaw, Slawek

Tycjan (tee-TSYAHN) unknown meaning

Tymon (TEE-mon) (Gr) honoring God — Tymek

Tymoteusz (tim-o-TEH-oosh) (Gr) honoring God

Urban (L) of the city

Valentyn (L) strong, brave — Waleran

Waldemar (OGer) mighty and famous

Walerian (vah-LEHR-yan) (L) strong, brave

Walter (Teut) powerful warrior

Wicent (VEE-tsent) (L) conqueror — Wicek, Wicus, Wicenty, Wincenty, Vincenty

Wienczyslaw (VEEN-sis-lahv) wreath, garland

Wiktor (VIK-tor) (L) conqueror — Viktoryn

Wilhelm (VEEL-helm) (Teut) resolute protector — Wilek, Wilus

Wincenty (veen-TSEHN-tee) (L) conqueror

Wit (VEET) (L) life

Wojciech (VOY-tseech) (Gr) farmer

Yusef (H) God will add

Zarek (ZAH-rek) (Gr) may God protect the king — Baltek

Zenon (Gr) hospitality

Ziven (ZI-ven) (Slavic) vigorous and alive — Ziv, Zivon

Zygmunt (Teut) conquering protection

PORTUGAL & BRAZIL

Although Portuguese sailors were exploring America as early as 1492 (in Columbus' entourage), the first recorded Portuguese settlement in North America was of a group of Jewish refugees who came to New Amsterdam in 1542.

They had left Portugal 150 years earlier to escape religious persecution, settling first in Holland, then in Recife, Brazil, and finally in America after the Portuguese conquered Brazil. These refugees were the founders of the American Jewish community.

Portugal colonized the Azores and Madeira islands in the fifteenth century. These islands are located approximately one-third of the way from Portugal to the North American mainland and had been explored by Portuguese sailors as early as the sixth century. From these islands have come many of the Portuguese immigrants to America, including large numbers of Azorean sailors who were recruited in the 1830's and 1840's to man whaling ships.

By 1880 some 15,000 Portuguese lived in America, split about evenly between California, Massachusetts, and Rhode Island. At that time the discovery of oil led to the decline of the whaling industry. Many Portuguese who had settled in the East went into fishing, farming, or factory work. In New England especially, there was a huge demand for textile mill workers.

Between 1880 and 1920 another 200,000 Portuguese arrived, settling mainly where other Portuguese had settled before them. There were large concentrations of Portuguese in New Bedford, Fall River, Massachusetts; Providence, Rhode Island; and Oakland, California.

In 1878 a group of 120 Portuguese from Madeira migrated to the Hawaiian Islands in search of work, beginning a mass migration that totaled 13,000 in the following twenty years. By 1930 the Portuguese-American population in Hawaii made up over seven percent of the total population.

The 1924 immigration law drastically decreased the Portuguese immigration to 440 per year, and no more large scale immigration from Portugal occurred until the 1950's. Some 20,000 immigrated, mainly from the Azores, because of a disastrous submarine eruption off one of the Azores Islands. Most of these immigrants were agricultural workers who couldn't speak English, and many became construction workers.

In the 1960's military efforts to repress independence movements in Portugal's colonies of Angola, Mozambique, and Portuguese Guinea drained the economy of Portugal. It had already suffered under thirty-five years of the dictatorship of Antonio Salizar which had kept Portugal underdeveloped and one of the poorest nations in Europe.

This led many Portuguese to immigrate permanently to America, looking for better economic opportunity. More than 100,000 came to America in the late 1960's and early 1970's, bringing the total immigration to over 400,000 between 1820 and 1975. These new immigrants, like earlier Portuguese immigrants, came to America, not to seek their fortunes and return home, but to stay here for good.

Most Portuguese are Roman Catholics, which reflects itself heavily in the choosing of baby names. One Portuguese source pronounced half-humorously that probably ninety-five percent of the Portuguese baby girls are named Maria (after the Virgin Mary) with some other name added on such as Maria Elena, Maria Luisa, or even Maria Jose (Mary Joseph). Similarly a baby boy might have a double name beginning with Jose. Jose Maria is popular.

The list below includes the most popular Portuguese names.

Pronunciation

Pronunciation is similar to Spanish, with the exception of "j" which is pronounced as "zh" as the "z" in azure.

a = "ah" as in ball
e = "eh" as in late
i = "ee" as in keep

o = "oh" as in hope, or "oe" as in work
u = "oo" as in moon

PORTUGUESE FEMALE NAMES

Adelaide (OGer) noble, kind

Albertina (OGer) noble, bright

Alda (OGer) rich, old

Alexandrina (Gr) defender of mankind

Alice (OGer) noble, kind

Amalia (Teut) industrious; persuasive

Amanda (L) beloved

Ana* (H) grace

Anabela comb. of Ana and Bella

Angelina (Gr) messenger

Antonia (L) inestimable

Barbara (L) the stranger — Babette, Barbaria, Berberia

Bibiana (L) lively

Brites (BREE-tehs) (Celt) strength

Caozinha literally means "little dog"

Carla (OFr) fem. Charles

Carlota* (Fr) petite and feminine

Catia (Gr) pure

Conceisão (kon-SAY-sao) Conception — Connie

Constancia (L) constant

Constantina (L) constant — Tina

Daniela (H) God is my judge

Debra (H) bee

Deolinda (deh-o-LEEN-dah) beautiful God

Eduarda (OE) wealthy guardian

Elvira (ehl-VEE-rah) (Sp) white, fair

Elzira (ehl-SEE-rah) (H) consecrated to God

Emilia (Teut) industrious

Estrela (H) star — Estrelinha

Eugenia (Gr) well-born

Eva (H) life

Fatima* name for Virgin Mary, Our Lady of Fatima — Fatinha

Felisberta comb. of Felisa (L) fortunate, and Alberta (OGer) noble, bright

Fernanda (Teut) adventurous, brave

Francisca (Teut) free

Fryda (Teut) peaceful ruler

Gabriela (H) God is my strength

Germana (Fr) from Germany

Gilberta (Teut) illustrious pledge

Gilda (OE) gilded

Gloria (L) glorious

Graca (GRAH-sah) (L) graceful — Gracinha

Helena (Gr) light

Horacia (L) timekeeper

Ilda (Teut) heroine

Ines (EE-nehs) (Gr) gentle, pure — Inez

Isabela (H) consecrated to God — Isabel

Joana (zho-AHN-uh) (H) God's gracious gift — (common in Brazil)

Julia (ZHOO-lyah) (L) youthful

Laudalina praise — Lina

Laurinda (Gr) crowned with laurel

Lidia (Gr) ancient province in Asia Minor

Linda (Span) beautiful

Lizete (H) consecrated to God

Lucia* (loo-SEE-ah) (L) bringer of light — Lucille

Luisa (OGer) famous warrior woman

Mae (H) bitter

Manuela (H) God is with us

Margarida (Gr) a pearl — Guidinha

Maria*** (H) bitter

Mariana comb. of Mary and Ana

Marta (H) bitter

Mel honey

Natalia (L) born at Christmas

Olga (Russian) holy — Olginha

Olimpia (Gr) Olympian

Olivia (L) olive tree — Olivinha

Patricia (L) noble, well-born

Paula* (L) little — Paulina

Rita (Gr) a pearl

Roberta (Teut) of shining fame

Rosa* (L) rose

Sonia (Gr) wisdom

Tereza (teh-REH-suh) (Gr) harvester (used in Brazil)

Terezinha* (teh-reh-SEEN-ah) (Gr) harvester

Trindade (treen-THAH-theh) — Trinity

Vidonia vine branch

Zenaide (Gr) daughter of Zeus

---

* Most popular

PORTUGUESE MALE NAMES

Albano (L) white

Alberto (OGer) courage of a bear

Alexio (Gr) defender of mankind

Alfredo (OE) wise counselor

Alvaro (L) white

Andres (Gr) strong and manly — Andre

Angelo (AHN-geh-lo) (Gr) messenger

Antonio* (L) inestimable — Antos

Armando (Teut) soldier

Arnaldo strong

Artur (Celt) noble, bear man

Augusto (L) venerable

Baltasar Balthazar

Belmiro meaning unknown, possibly "beautiful view"

Benedicto (L) blessed

Benjamin (BEHN-zhah-meen) (H) son of the right hand

Bernardo (OGer) courage of a bear

Braz (L) stammerer

Carlos* strong and manly

Daniel (H) God is my judge

David (H) beloved

Dinis (Gr) god of wine

Duarte (Teut) rich guard

Edmundo (OE) prosperous protector

Eduardo (OE) wealthy guardian

Enrique (ehn-REE-keh) (Teut) ruler of an estate

Estevao (Gr) crowned with laurels

Fernando* (Teut) adventurous, brave

Francisco* (frahn-SEES-co) (Teut) free

Gabrielo (H) God is my strenth

Germano (gehr-MAHN-o) (Fr) from Germany

Gil (Gr) shield-bearer

Gilberto (Teut) illustrious pledge

Godofredo (Teut) God's peace

Gregorio (Gr) vigilant

Guilherme (geel-HEHR-meh) (Teut) resolute soldier

Horacio (o-RAH-see-o) (L) timekeeper

Huberto (Teut) bright mind

Hunfredo (oon-FREH-do) (Teut) peaceful Hun

Isidoro (Gr) a gift of ideas — Isidro

Jacinto* (zhah-SEEN-to) (Gr) hyacinth

Jacob (HAH-kob) (H) the supplanter — Jayme, Diogo

Jaime (ZHAH-ee-meh) (H) supplanter

Januario (zhah-nyoo-AHR-yo) January

Jesús (zheh-SOOS) Jesus

João* (JWO) (H) God's gracious gift

Joaquim (zhwah-KEEM) (H) God will establish

Jordão (zher-DA-o) (H) descendant

Jorge (Gr) farmer

Jose* (joo-ZEH) (H) God will add

Julio (ZHOOL-yo) (L) youthful

Laudalino (L) praise — Lino

Laurencho (L) crowned with laurel

Leonardo (Teut) bold lion — Leonaldo

Liberio liberation

Lidio (Gr) ancient province in Asia Minor

Lorenco (L) crowned with laurel — Lourenco

Lucas (L) bringer of light

Luis* (OGer) renowned warrior

Manuel (H) God is with us (from Emanuel)

Marcos (L) warlike — Marco, Martial, Mario, Martins

Mario (L) warlike

Mauricio (L) dark-skinned, Moorish

Miguel (H) who is like God?

Moises (H) saved from the water

Nicolao (Gr) victory of the people

Oliverio (L) olive tree

Paulo* (L) little

Pedro* (Gr) a stone

Ramiro (Sp) great judge

Ricardo (OGer) powerful ruler

Roberto (Teut) of shining fame

Rogerio (Teut) famous warrior

Rolando (Teut) fame of the land

Ronaldo (Teut) wise power

Rosario the Rosary

Rui (OFr) king

Serafim (H) seraph

Silvino (L) forest

Simao (H) God is heard

Tomas (to-MAHS) (H) twin — Tome, Tomaz

Tonio short for Antonio (L) inestimable

Vincente (L) conqueror

---

* **Most popular**

ROMANIA

Immigration totaled 66,000 from Romania between 1900 and 1920, spurned by mounting political and economic upheavals. In the early 1920's, 60,000 more Romanians immigrated, until 1924 when the immigration quota system went into effect.

Numbers of Romanian immigrants may be underestimated as over eighty-five percent of Romanian immigrants were from Transylvania, Bukovina, or Banat territories, part of the Romanian kingdom until 1948. Though ethnically Romanian, many were classified as Hungarians, Austrians, or Russians.

Before 1895 Romanian immigrants tended to be tradesmen or artisans; after that time ninety-seven percent were unskilled. From 1900-20 two-thirds of Romanians who came to the U.S. returned home after making enough money to buy land or improve their economic status in their native villages.

By World War II the Romanian-American population stood near 116,000 according to the census, with most living in the mid-Atlantic and Great Lakes states.

The Romanian language is descended directly from the Romans, with influences from several tribes that successively invaded the country.

ROMANIAN FEMALE NAMES

Ana (H) grace — Anicuta, Anica

Brigita (Celt) strength

Ecaterina (Gr) pure — Caterina

Elena (Gr) light

Elica (OGer) noble, kind Alicia

Elisabeta (H) consecrated to God (dim.) Beti, Elenuta

Ioana (yoh-AH-nah) (H) God's gracious gift

Irini (Gr) peace

Iulia (YOO-lyah) (L) youthful

Lucia (loo-CHEE-ah) (L) light

Magdalena (H) woman from Magdala

Maria (H) bitter — Maricara

Reveka (H) binding, servant of God

Suzana (H) lily

Tereza (Gr) harvester

ROMANIAN MALE NAMES

Andrei (Gr) manly — Dela

Anton (Gr) inestimable

Carol (OFr) strong and manly

Cristofor (Gr) Christ-bearer

Danila (H) God is my judge Daniel

Frantisek (Teut) free

Gheorghe (GEH-urg) (Gr) farmer

Ioan (H) God's gracious gift — Iancu, Ionel

Iosif (YOH-sif) (H) God will add — Yousef

Mihas (H) who is like God? Mihail

Petru (Gr) stone — Petar

Robin (Teut) of shining fame

Stefan (Gr) a crown

Toma (H) twin

Vilhelm (Teut) resolute protector

RUSSIA

Russia is a federation of sixteen republics, each of which is inhabited by various ethnic group with diverse languages, customs and histories. They are much more different from each other than people from various states in the U.S.

The first Russian immigrants to the U.S. established themselves as fur traders in the Aleutian Islands off Alaska in the 1740's. They gradually developed many trading posts in the mainland of Alaska, even venturing briefly as far south as San Francisco. In 1857 Russia sold Alaska to the U.S. for $7.2 million, but Congress took no interest in establishing a civilian government there. Lawlessness became rampant, and most of the Russian settlers returned to Russia.

Meanwhile, Russian peasants began immigrating to the U.S. in large numbers, during the 1870s. Many were illiterate and desperately poor under the Russian czar. When the serfs had been freed in 1861 it was estimated that eighty-five percent of the population had been in bondage under that system. After receiving their freedom, they were often forced to support themselves on narrow strips of land from two to ten yards wide, which was owned by the community and could be re-distributed routinely.

Between 1871 and 1900, more than 750,000 people immigrated from Russia. Over fifty percent of them ended up in New York and Pennsylvania, working in coal mines and textile mills. Their illiteracy and ignorance of the English language caused tremendous hardships because often they could only apply for the most backbreaking jobs, which were little or no improvement over their lot in Russia.

Those who became farmers fared better, although language was still a barrier. They settled in the Western plain states, especially the Dakotas, and Wisconsin, New York, and Massachusetts.

Between 1920 and 1940 more than two million people fled the Soviet regime in Russia. Many found homes in France, Germany, and other east European countries, but about 30,000 immigrated to the U.S. In 1969 a change in Soviet policy enabled over 200,000 to emigrate. Many were Jews who went to Israel, but there were 24,000 Soviet Jews in the U.S. by 1979. Over 75,000 Russians have immigrated to the U.S. since 1971. A total of 3.4 million Russians have immigrated to the U.S. since 1820. Most of them were Jews; many were Poles, Ukraines, and Lithuanians.

The most remarkable aspect about Russian names is the immense popularity of nicknames and diminutives. At birth a child is given a formal name known as the "passport name." Throughout childhood, and often adulthood the child is called by an affectionate name derived from the formal name. The suffix "-ka" used to denote that the person was a serf. Today, it denotes extreme familiarity and is often used between children. Parents are more reluctant to use these "-ka" nicknames, wishing to avoid the stigma of serfdom on their children. Instead they might use these names for a pet.

When a child is sixteen the name known as the "patronymic" is bestowed. It denotes entry into adulthood and carries connotations of age and respect. The patronymic consists of the passport name plus the father's first name taken as a middle name. For a boy the suffix "-ovich" or "-evich" is added to the father's name; for a girl the suffix is "evna" or "-ovna." Thus, Piotr's daughter Natasha would become Natalia Petrovna, and his son Alyosha would become Alexii Petrovich. Within the family the child may continue to be known by the nickname. Business colleauges would be more likely to use the patronymic.

Pronunciation

The pronunciation Russian is much tighter than American English. The sounds are similar, but the mouth is not opened as wide. Note that the accent is often on the first syllable, which sometimes runs counter to an American's attempt to pronounce it. Thus, Pashenka is "PAH-shen-ka," not "pah-SHEN-ka."

a = "ah" as in ball   o = "oh" as in hope
e = "eh" as in late   u = "oo" as in moon
i = "ee" as in keep

RUSSIAN FEMALE NAMES

Agafia (Gr) good — Agafon

Agrafina (L) born feet first

Akilina (L) eagle

Alena (Gr) light

Alexandra* (Gr) defender of mankind — Sasha, Sashenka, Shura, Shurochka

Alina bright, beautiful

Alla* meaning unknown — Allochka

Alma name of river

Amalija (Teut) industrious

Anastassia* (Gr) of the Resurrection — Tasya, Tasenka, Stasya, Nastya

Anna* (H) grace — Anya, Anechka, Asya

Antonina* (L) inestimable — Tonya, Tonechka

Asenka (H) graceful

Bruna (Teut) dark-haired

Dasha (Gr) gift of God

Devora (H) bee — Debora

Dina nickname for Dinah (H) judged

Dominika (L) born on Sunday; belonging to the Lord — Mika

Doroteya (Gr) God's gift — Dosya, Dasha

Duscha (DOOSH-hah) soul, term of endearment

Ekaterina* (Gr) pure — Katya, Katyenka, Katyuska

Elena* (Gr) pure — Lena, Lenochka

Elizaveta (H) consecrated to God — Liza

Eva (H) life

Evelina (H) life

Evgenia* (yv-jeen-yah) (Gr) well-born — Zenya, Zenechka (ZHEHN-ech-ka)

Feodora (Gr) gift of God

Galina* (H) God has redeemed — Galya, Galochka, Galenka

Ilia (H) God is the Lord

Inessa (Gr) gentle, pure

Irina (Gr) peace — Ira (EE-rah)

Irisa (Gr) rainbow

Ivana (H) God's gracious gift

Karolina (Fr) petite, feminine

Katerina (Gr) pure — Ekaterina, Katya, Katinka, Kiska, Katuscha

Kira (L) light — Kirochka*

Kisa pet name meaning kitty or pussycat

Kiska nickname for Katerina

Kostya pet name for Konstantin (Gr) constant — Kostenka, Kotik, Kostyusha

Lada mythological goddess of beauty

Lara (L) famous

Larisa* (L) cheerful — Lara, Larochka

Lenora (Gr) light

Lenusya pet form of Yelena: lily flower — Liolya

Lida (Gr) happy — Lidiya, Lidochka

Liza dim. Elizabeth (H) consecrated to God — Lizette, Lisil, Lisilka

Lubmila loving

Lyudmila* people's love — Lyuba, Lyubochka, Lyubonka, Luda, Mila, Milena

Manya dim. Mara (H) bitter

Mara (H) bitter — Marya, Masha, Marusya, Manechka, Mashenka, Mura

Margarete (Gr) a pearl — Margo, Margosha, Rita

Maria* (H) bitter — Masha, Mashenka

Marianna (H) rebellious; form of Mary — Masha

Marina* (L) sea maid — Marinochka (mah-REE-nosh-ka)

Marisha pet name for Mara (H) bitter

Mavra (L) Moorish

Nadezhda* (Slavic) hope — Nadya, Nadyenka, Nadyuiska

Nadia (NAH-dee-ah) hope — Nadiya, Nadya, Nadenka, Nadysha, Dusya

Narkissa (Gr) daffodil

Nastassia (Gr) resurrection

Natalia* (Fr) born at Christmas — Natalya, Natasha, Natashenka, Tasha

Nessa pet form of Agnessa (Gr) gentle, pure — Nesha, Netia

Nika belonging to God — Domka, Mika

Nina* (H) grace — Ninockha (NEE-nosh-ka)

Oksana* (H) praise be to God — Ksana, Ksanochka, Oksanochka

Olena (Gr) light — Lenusya, Lila, Lyalechka, Lyalya, Alena, Alenka

Olga* holy — Olya, Olenka, Olechka

Orlenda female eagle

Panya dim. for Stephania (L) crowned with laurel

Parasha born on Good Friday

Pasha (Gr) Easter

Pheodora (Gr) divine gift

Rahil (H) innocence of a lamb

Sabina (L) Sabine woman (ancient tribe of central Italy)

Sacha pet form of Alexandra — Sasha

Sashenka (SASH-ehn-kah) pet form of Alexandra — Shuroshka

Sinovia (Gr) stranger

Sonya (Gr) wisdom — Sofia, Sofiya, Sonechka, Sonyuru, Sonyusha

Stesha dim. of Stephania (Gr) crowned with laurel

Svetlana* star, bright — Sveta, Svetochka (SVEH-tosh-ka)

Tanya fairy queen — Tania, Tanechka

Tasya dim. Anastassia (Gr) resurrection

Tatyana* fairy queen — Tanya, Tanichka (TAHN-eech-kuh)

Theodosia (Gr) gift of God — Theda, Feodora

Tonya pet name for Antonina (L) inestimable

Ursola (L) little bear — Ursula

Valentina (L) strong, brave — Tina

Vanya pet form of Anna (H) grace — Vania

Varinka (Gr) stranger

Varvara (VAHR-vahr-ah) (L) the stranger — Varya, Varenka, Varyusha

Velika great

Vera* (L) true — Verochka (VEH-rosh-ka)

Vilma (Teut) resolute protector

Yalena (Gr) light — Lenusya, Liolya

Yelizaveta (H) consecrated to God — Liza, Betti, Lizanka, Lizabeta

Yuliya* (L) youth — Yulenka

Zenaida* (Gr) daughter of Zeus — Zena, Zenochka

Zenevieva (Celt) white wave — Zinerva

Zoya* (Gr) life — Zoyenka, Zoyechka, Zoia

***** **Most popular**

RUSSIAN MALE NAMES

Adrik (L) of the Adriatic — Andrian

Alek (Gr) defender of mankind — Lyaksandr, Sanya, Shurik

Alexandr* (Gr) defender of mankind — Sasha, Sashenka, Shura, Shurochka

Alexei* (Gr) defender of mankind — Alyosha, Alyoshenka

Anatolii* (Gr) from the East — Tolya, Tolenka (TO-lehn-ka)

Andrei* (AHN-dray) (L) manly — Andrusha

Andrian (L) dark one — Adrik

Anton* (L) inestimable — Antosha, Antinko, Tosya, Tusya

Arman (ahr-MAHN) (Teut) army man

Artur (ahr-TOOR) (Celt) noble, bear man

Berdy (BEHR-dee) (OGer) brilliant mind or brilliant spirit

Bohdan (Ukrain) given by God — Bogdan, Bogdashka, Danya, Bohdan

Boris* (bo-REES) fight, warrior — Borya, Boryenka

Brencis (BREN-tsis) (Latvian, L) crowned with laurel

Brody man from Brody

Burian (Ukrain) he lives near the weeds

Cheslav (CHEHS-lav) lives in a fortified camp

Danya (Ukrain) given by God — Bohdan, Dania

Denis* (Gr) god of wine — Deniska

Dima (DEE-muh) powerful warrior — Vladimir

Dimitri (Gr) from Demeter, goddess of the harvest — Dima, Mitya

Donat (L) a gift

Edik (EH-dek) wealthy guardian

Eduard (OE) wealthy guardian — Edik

Egor* (Gr) farmer — Yurik, Yuri, Yura, Zhorah, Gorya, Georgy, Egorushka, Igor, Jeorgif, Jurg

Evgenii* (yev-GEH-nee) (Gr) well-born, noble — Zhenya, Zhenechka

Fabiyan (L) bean grower — Fabi

Fadey (fah-DAY) (Ukrain) courageous — Faddei, Fadeyka, Fadeyushka

Fedor (Gr) gift of God — Fedya

Feliks (fey-LEEKS) (L) fortunate, or lucky

Filip (Gr) lover of horses

Fredek from Frederick (Teut) peaceful ruler

Fyodor* (Teut) divine gift — Fedya, Fedyenka

Garald (gah-RAHLD) (Teut) spear brave — Garold, Gerald, Garolds

Gavril (gav-REEL) man of God — Ganya, Gav, Gavrel

Georgii* (geh-OR-gee) (Gr) farmer — Gorya, Yurik, Yura, Yuri, Egor, Zhorz

Grigori (Gr) vigilant — Grigor, Grisha

Hedeon (heh-DEH-on) (Ukrain) destroyer; tree cutter

Igor* (EE-gor) (Gr) farmer — Igoryok

Ioakim (ee-o-AH-keem) (H) God will establish — Akim, Jov, Iov, Yov

Ivan* (ee-VAHN) (H) God's gracious gift — Vanya, Vanyusha, Vanechka

Jermija (yehr-MEE-ah) (H) God will uplift

Jov (YOV) pet form of Iokaim (H) the supplanter

Karol (OFr) manly or strong — Karolek

Kiril (Gr) lordly one — Kiryl

Kliment (L) kind, gentle

Kolya pet form of Nikolos: (Gr) victorious army

Kostantin* (L) constant — Kostya, Kostenka

Laurentij (lo-REHN-tee) (L) crowned with laurel

Leon (L) lion — Leonid, Lev, Leonide

Leonid* (leh-o-NEED) (L) lion — Lyonya, Lyonechka

Lev (LEF) (L) lion — Levka, Levushka

Lukyan (loo-kee-YAHN) (L) bringer of light — Lukasha, Luka

Maksim (mahk-SEEM) (L) greatest in excellence — Maks

Martyn (L) warlike

Matvey (H) gift of God — Matyash, Motka

Mendeley (men-de-LEH) (Y) comforter; (L) of the mind

Michael* (mee-khah-EHL) (H) who is like God? — Mishe, Mishenka

Michail (mee-khah-EHL) (H) who is like God? — Mikhail, Misha, Mishenka

Moriz (L) dark-skinned (Moorish)

Nicolai* (Gr) victory of the people — Kolya, Kolenka, Nikita

Oleg* (o-LEHG) holy — Oleg, Olezka

Pavel* (L) little — Pasha, Pashenka, Pavlusha, Pavlushenka

Pyotr* (Gr) stone — Petya, Petenka

Roman* (ro-MAHN) (L) Roman — Roma, Romochka

Serguei* (SEHR-gay) (L) the attendant — Seriozha, Seriozhenka

Slavik pet name for Stanislav (Slavic) stand of glory

Stanislav (Slavic) stand of glory — Stas, Slavik

Stephan (ste-PAHN) (L) crown — Stefan, Stepka

Tomas (H) twin — Foma

Valerii* (vah-LEH-ree) (L) strong, brave — Valera, Valerik

Vasilii* (Gr) royal — Vasya, Vasyenka, Vasilik

Viktor* (L) conqueror — Vitya, Vitenka

Vladimir* (Slavic) possess peace — Dimka, Vimka, Volodya, Vova, Bolodenka

Vladislav* (Slavic) possesses glory — Vladik, Vladya

Vyacheslav* (Slavic) possesses glory — Slava, Slavochka (SLAH-vochka)

Yakov (H) supplanter — Jasha (YAH-sha)

Yerik (H) appointed by God — Yarema, Yaremka

Yurii* (Gr) farmer — Yura, Yurochka

Ziven (ZEE-ven) (Slavic) vigorous and alive — Ziv, Zivon

---

* **Most popular**

SCOTLAND

Although over 800,000 Scots immigrated to America between 1820 and 1975, the Scottish presence was felt in America long before immigration records were kept.

During the late 1600's and early 1700's a significant proportion of Scottish immigrants were transported to America as punishment for participating in rebellions against the British government or tenaciously maintaining their Presbyterian beliefs in an officially Episcopalian country.

In 1707 parliamentary union between Britain and Scotland was achieved and voluntary immigrants from Scotland became one of the earliest groups to immigrate in large numbers. Thousands of soldiers stayed in America after being discharged from the Seven Years War (1754-1761) between British and French forces in this country. It is said that of 12,000 Highlanders who had enlisted only seventy-six returned to Scotland.

Many had joined the army to escape the severe economic hardships common in Scotland at that time. By royal proclamation at the end of the war they were able to obtain cheap land. New York Province and Prince Edward Island were the most common settlement points.

Another colony began in 1767 in North Carolina in which settlers could be granted 100 acres per person — man, woman, or child. A family of six could receive a square mile of land, where they had been forced to live on perhaps ten to twelve acres in Scotland.

More than 200,000 Scotch-Irish (Scottish people who had been encouraged to settle in northern Ireland by the British government in the first half of the 17th century), approximately one-third of the Protestant population there, emigrated to America during the first half of the 18th century because of economic pressures and religious persecution.

Scotch-Irish immigrants settled in western Pennsylvania, then farther south preferring to be as far from government taxes and influence as possible. Later immigrants included large numbers of skilled textile and machinery workers.

The Scotch-Irish supported the revolutionary cause in the American war for independence, while the Scots from Scotland remained loyal to the British crown (except for people like Patrick Henry and John Paul Jones). Many Scots filled positions of importance in government and commerce after the war. Their influence then was the greatest it has ever been.

A disproportionate number of Scottish immigrants came from the Highlands and eastern islands of Scotland during the 1600's and 1700's, whereas Lowlanders predominated after 1815. The greatest period of Scottish immigration came in the 1920's when unemployment forced more than 390,000 people to immigrate during that decade. So great was the emigration out of Scotland that the population actually dropped by 40,000.

Gaelic, the ancient language of Scotland, was an import from Ireland in the sixth century when a Celtic tribe called Scots migrated to Caledonia (now Scotland). The similarity to Irish can be seen in the Irish chapter of this book. Gaelic is spoken today by only about 80,000 people (fifteen percent of the population) and mainly in the Highlands and islands.

A separate list of Gaelic names has been included for interest, although parents in Scotland today select primarily Anglicized names for their children. Tradition remains a staunch ally in choosing a Scottish baby name, as many of the popular names are the same as those appearing in a name book that was published over 100 years ago!

SCOTTISH FEMALE NAMES

Agnes (Gr) gentle, pure

Aileen* (Gr) light

Aili (OGer) noble, kind — Alison, Allie

Ailsa (form of Elsa from Elizabeth) (H) consecrated to God

Alice (OGer) noble, kind

Amy (Fr) beloved

Angela (Gr) messenger

Anne* (H) grace

Annot (H) light

Audrey (OE) noble strength — Audra, Audie

Barbara (Gr) the stranger

Becky (H) binding, servant of God

Bonnie (L) sweet and beautiful — Bonny

Bridget (Celt) strength — Bride

Caroline fem. Charles — Carol

Catherine (Gr) pure

Christine (Gr) Christian

Coleen (Gael) girl

Constance (L) constant — Connie

Deborah (H) bee

Diana (L) goddess of the moon

Edith (Teut) rich gift

Eileen (Gr) light

Elspeth (H) consecrated to God — Elsbeth, Elizabeth, Elsie

Emily (Teut) industrious

Felicia (L) fortunate, or lucky

Fiona* (Celt) white, fair

Gail (Gael) strong

Gillian (JILL-ee-an) (L) youth — Jill, Jillian

Glen (Gael) valley — Glenna

Glynis (Gael) valley

Heather* (OE) heather

Helen (Gr) light — Ellen

Isobel (from Elizabeth) (H) consecrated to God

Jean (H) God's gracious gift — Janet, Joan

Jennifer* (Celt) white wave

Julia (L) youthful

Kirstie (nickname for Christine) (L) Christian

Laurie (L) crowned with laurel — Laura

Lorna* (L) crowned with laurel

Mae (H) bitter — May

Maggie (from Margaret) (Gr) pearl — Maisie (old-fashioned)

Margaret* (Gr) a pearl

Marion (H) bitter — Mae, May

Maureen (Celt) great

Megan* (A.S.) strong

Moira* (Celt) great

Molly (H) bitter

Morag (MOR-ack) (Gael) (form of Sheila) (L) blind

Myra (Gr) myrtle

Nancy (H) grace

Patricia (Gr) noble

Rachel (H) innocence of a lamb

Rebecca (H) binding, servant of God

Robena robin — Robina

Rowena (Celt) white mane

Sarah (H) princess

Sheila (L) blind (from Cecilia)

Sophia (Gr) wisdom

Susan (H) lily

Winnifred (Welsh) white wave

---

* Popular

SCOTTISH MALE NAMES

Adam* (H) man of the red earth

Alan (Gael) handsome

Alastair (Gr) defender of mankind — Alister, Alexander

Alec* (Gr) defender of mankind

Andrew (Gr) manly

Angus (Gr) unique choice

Arth (A.S.) eagle-like — Arthur

Baird (Gael) poet — Bard (old-fashioned)

Balfour pasture land

Birk birch tree

Blair (Gael) child of the fields

Brian (ONorse) strong

Bruce (Fr) woods

Busby village on woodlands

Calum (Celt) dove

Camden from the winding valley — Camdin, Camdan

Cameron* (Celt) crooked nose — Camero, Camey

Campbell (KAM-bel) crooked mouth — Cam, Camp

Carey (Welsh) stony, rock island

Charles (OFr) full-grown, manly

Christopher (Gr) Christ-bearer

Colin (Gael) (KAW-lin) child — Cailean, Colan, Collin, Coll

Connell (Celt) high and mighty

Corey (Gael) ravine — Cori, Cory

Craig (Celt) crag dweller — Craggie

David (H) beloved

Davis David's son — Dave

Derek (OGer) people's ruler — Dirk, Derrick

Donald (Celt) dark or brown — Donnee

Dougald* (DOO-gald) (Celt) dark stranger

Duncan dark-skinned warrior — Dune, Dunn

Edward (OE) wealthy guardian

Erskine* from the height of the cliff — Kinny, Kin

Ewen (Celt) youth

Fergus (Gael) strong man

Finlay (Gael) fair hero

Gavin white hawk — Gawain, Gawen, Gaven

Geordie (Gr) farmer — George

Gleann (Gael) valley — Glen, Glendon

Gordon (A.S.) from the cornered hill — Gordie, Gordy

Gow (Gael) a smith

Graham (A.S.) warlike; or (L) grain — Graeme, Gram

Grant* (L) great

Gregory (Gr) vigilant

Hugh (Teut) intelligence, spirit

Ian* (EE-an) (H) God's gracious gift — Iain

James* (H) supplanter

Jamie* (H) the supplanter

Jock (H) the supplanter (older name)

John* (H) God's gracious gift

Keith the battle place

Kenneth (Celt) handsome — Ken

Kirk church — Kerk

Laird wealthy landowner

Lawrence (L) crowned with laurel — Lawren

Leith river

Leslie (Gael) from the gray fortress — Lesley

Mac son of — Mack, Max

Malcolm (Celt) servant of St. Columbia

Michael (H) who is like God?

Murdoch sea protector (old-fashioned) — Murdo

Nicholas (Gr) victory of the people — Nicol

Niels (Celt) champion — Niel

Nigel (L) dark, or black

Patrick (L) noble

Paul (L) little

Payton dim. Patrick (L) noble — Paton, Peyton

Peter (Gr) stone

Robert* (Teut) of shining fame

Ronald (Teut) wise power

Ronan (Irish) seal — Ronat, Renan

Ryan (Gael) little king; strong

Scott Scotsman

Stewart* (A.S.) steward — Stuart

Thomas (H) twin — Tamlane (old)

Wallace (A.S.) stranger — Wallis

William* (Teut) resolute protector

---

* Popular

GAELIC FEMALE NAMES

Anna (AN-na) (Ann) (H) grace

Baraball (BA-ra-bul) (Barbara) (L) the stranger

Beathag (BEH-hack) (Becky) (H) servant of God

Cairistìona (KAR-ish-tchee-unna) (Christine) (L) Christian

Catrìona (KAT-ree-unna) (Catherine) (Gr) pure

Deirdre (JEE-ur-druh) (Deirdre) (Celt) mythological heroine; young girl

Dìorbhail (JIR-ivil) (Dorothy) (L) gift of God

Ealasaid (YALL-u-satch) (Elizabeth) (H) consecrated to God

Eìlidh (EH-lee) (Helen) (Gr) light

Flòraidh (FLAW-ree) (Flora) (L) flower — Fionnghal (FYOON-u-ghal)

Iseabail (EE-sha-bal) (Isobel) (H) consecrated to God

Màili (MA-lee) (Molly, May) (H) bitter

Mairead (MA-ee-rat) (Margaret) (Gr) a pearl

Màiri (MA-ree) (Mary) (H) bitter

Marsaili (MAR-sally) (Marjory) (Gr) a pearl

Mòrag (MAW-rack) (Marion) (H) bitter; Sarah (H) princess

Oighrig (EU-ee-rick) (Effie) (Gr) pleasant speech (Euphemia)

Peigi (PAEG-ee) (Peggy) (Gr) a pearl

Raonaid (REUN-eetch) (Rachel) (H) innocence of a lamb

Seonag (SHAW-nack)
(Joan) (H) God's gracious
gift

Seònaid (SHAW-natch)
(Janet) (H) God's gra-
cious gift

Sìleas (SHEE-luss) (Julia)
(L) youth; (Celia) (L)
blind

Sìne (SHEE-nuh) (Jane,
Jean) (H) God's gracious
gift

Siùsaidh (SHOO-see)
(Susan) (H) lily

Una (OO-na) (Winnifred)
(Celt) (Welsh) white
wave

GAELIC MALE NAMES

Alasdair (ALL-us-tir) (Alexander) (Gr) defender of
mankind

Anndra (AH-oon-drah)
(Andrew) (Gr) manly

Aonghas (EUN-eu-uss)
(Angus) (Gr) unique
choice

Artair (AHRSH-tar)
(Arthur) (A.S.) eagle-like;
high, noble

Cailean (CAL-lan) (Colin)
(Gael) child

Calum (CAL-lum)
(Malcolm) (Celt) dove

Coinneach (KON-yokh)
(Kenneth) (Celt) hand-
some

Daibhidh (DA-ee-vee)
(David) (H) beloved

Dòmhnal (DAW-ull) (Donald) (Celt) dark, or brown

Donnchadh (DON-ah-
choo) (Duncan) (Gael)
dark-skinned warrior

Dùghall (DOO-ull) (Celt)
dark stranger

Dùghlas (DOOG-lass)
(Douglas) (Celt) dark
stranger

Eachann (EU-chun)
(Hector) (Gr) steadfast

Eideard (AE-jard) (Edward)
(OE) wealthy guardian

Eòghann (YOE-wun)
(Ewan) (Celt) youth

Fearchar (FER-a-char)
(Farquhar) (Gael) super-
dear one

Fearghus (FER-ra-ghuss)
(Fergus) (Gael) strong
man

Fionnlagh (FYOON-ee-
loo) (Finlay) (Gael) fair
hero

Frang (FRANG-G) (Frank)
(Teut) free

Gilleasbuig (GEEL-yes-
pick) (Archibald) (OGer)
genuine, bold

Gordon (GOR-dan)
(Gordon) (A.S.) from the
cornered hill

Iain (EE-an) (H) God's gracious gift — Ian

Iomhair (EE-uh-var) (Ivor)
(Teut) archer

Lachlann (LAKH-lunn)
(Lachlan) (Gael) from
Scandinavia

Màrtainn (MAHRSH-teen)
(Martin) (L) warlike

Micheil (MEECH-yell)
(Michael) (H) who is like
God?

Murchadh (MOOR-uh-
choo) (Murdo) sea pro-
tector

Niall (NYEE-all) (Celt)
champion

Pàdraig (PAH-dreek)
(Patrick) (L) noble

Peadair (PED-dur) (Peter)
(Gr) the stone

Pòl (PAWL) (Paul) (L) little

Raghnall (REU-ull)
(Ronald) (Teut) wise
power

Raibeart (RAB-burt)
(Robert) (Teut) of shining
fame

Ruairidh (RO-urree) (Roderick) (Teut) famous ruler

Seòras (SHAW-russ)
(George) (Gr) farmer

Seumas (SHAE-muss)
(James) (H) the sup-
planter

Tearlach (TCHAR-lokh)
(Charles) (OFr) full-
grown, manly

Tòmas (TO-mass) (Thomas)
(H) twin

Tormod (TOR-ro-mot)
(Norman) (Teut) from the
north

Uilleam (OOL-yam)
(William) (Teut) resolute
soldier

Uisdean (OOSH-jan)
(Hugh) (Teut) intelli-
gence, spirit

SPAIN
& SOUTH AMERICA

Since 1820 only 300,000 people have immigrated to the U.S. directly from Spain, although hundreds of thousands of Spanish-speaking people have immigrated from Puerto Rico, Mexico, and Cuba.

During the 1900-1920 period millions of Spaniards emigrated; however many more of them went to South and Central America, primarily Cuba and Argentina, where language would not be a barrier. Of the 174,000 who immigrated to the U.S. between 1900 and 1924, 70,000 returned to Spain.

In northern Spain the system of dividing plots of inherited land among relatives led to smaller plots, until some families didn't have enough land to cultivate profitably. Most Spanish immigrants came from the Galicia province and the Basque region of northern Spain (see Basque chapter). Many settled around New York City.

Spaniards from Andalusia in southern Spain were recruited to work on sugar cane plantations in Hawaii between 1903 and 1907. By 1920 most had moved to California. Cigar makers from the northern Spanish province of Asturias settled in Key West and Tampa after immigrating to Cuba. Other Spaniards took manufacturing jobs in the Midwest and coal mining jobs in Virginia.

During the 1880's many Mexicans worked for the Southern Pacific and Sante Fe Railroads constructing them or running them. Small communities of shacks often sprung up along the rail lines to house permanent workers, which were the basis of many of today's Mexican-American communities.

However, the large-scale influx of Mexican laborers into the Southwest did not begin until the period between 1910 and 1925. Before that time, labor needs had been filled by slaves (until slavery was abolished in 1865) or by Chinese and Japanese (whose immigration was restricted by agreements in 1882 and 1902).

During 1910-25 a bloody civil war in Mexico killed over one

million people. Homes and farms were destroyed, and many Mexicans fled north to escape the horror and poverty. California, Texas, New Mexico, and Arizona employed vast numbers of Mexican workers to raise cotton, fruits, and vegetables. Mines in New Mexico, Colorado, and Arizona employed many Mexican immigrants.

The 1924 immigration laws did not place quotas on immigrants from Mexico or any other country in the Western Hemisphere, in the interests of diplomatic deference to America's neighbors.

However, during the economic hardship years of the 1930's some 89,000 Mexican aliens were "re-patriated" whether voluntarily or not, to Mexico, because the natural disasters of those years had caused a shortage of agricultural jobs, and many displaced Anglos from the Dust Bowl states now competed for the low-paying jobs that had been previously held by Mexicans. Altogether nearly 2.4 million legal immigrants have entered the U.S. since 1820 from Mexico.

Some immigration from Puerto Rico occurred after 1900 but large numbers did not begin immigrating until the 1920's when jobs were plentiful in the U.S. After World War I a severe depression in Puerto Rico along with a rising birth rate and a falling death rate brought crowding and unemployment to Puerto Rico. Many Puerto Ricans immigrated to New York as well as Miami, New Orleans, Chicago, and Boston.

Puerto Ricans enjoyed U.S. citizenship after 1917, and could move to the mainland without any restriction. Since immigration laws of 1924 sharply reduced the numbers of European immigrants, Puerto Ricans had no trouble finding jobs, both skilled and unskilled, in New York and elsewhere.

During the Depression immigration slowed considerably since jobs were as scarce in the U.S. as in Puerto Rico and the cost of boat fare was more than most Puerto Ricans earned in a year. During World War II, immigration all but halted, though there were jobs available, because submarine warfare in the Caribbean made the crossing very hazardous.

Immigration rose after World War II, reaching a peak of 69,000 in 1953. A total of some 570,000 Puerto Ricans (net migration) moved to the mainland between 1945-1956. The vast majority lived in New York City. After that immigration slowed as automation took over many jobs they had previously filled, and economic conditions improved in Puerto Rico.

Because the Roman Catholic faith is so important in Spain, and especially the adoration of the Virgin Mary, most girls are given the name Maria as part of their names, or have some name that signifies a religious event, such as Concepcion or Milagros (miracles). They may have a name which is the short form of a reference to the Virgin Mary, such as the name Luz which stands for Maria de la Luz (Mary of the Light).

A boy may be named Salvator (savior) or Jesus (pronounced "heh-SOOS"), but names from other sources are popular, too. Nicknames and pet forms, especially of the male and female versions of Joseph and Francis are common in Spain. The most popular names in Spain have been noted in the list, as well as a few names which would be found only in particular regions of Spain (denoted N, S, E, or W).

In Puerto Rico names for girls tend to be very trendy. Many girls a few years ago were named Diana, after Princess Diana of England. Before that the name Marisol (Mary/sun) was popular when a young Puerto Rican woman of that name won the Miss Universe contest. Right now the most popular girls' names are heavily European-influenced and include names like Vanessa, Lisette, Cecilia, Christine, Nicole, and Melissa.

Boys in Puerto Rico are usually named after their fathers, with Jose and Javier being the most popular names. Among Mexican-Americans, older names with a definitely Hispanic flavor are gaining popularity as are authentic ethnic names in many other American immigrant groups.

Pronunciation

a = "ah" as in ball
e = "eh" as in late
i = "ee" as in keep
o = "oh" as in hope
u = "oo" as in moon
j = "h" as in hope

g = "h" as in hope before e or i,
   "g" as in go before a,o,u,iu,ue
d = a sound halfway between
   "d" and "th" as in there
b = a sound halfway between
   "b" and "v"
ll = "y" as in yarn

SPANISH FEMALE NAMES

Adelina (NW) (OGer) noble, kind — Adela, Adelita

Adoración adoration

Adriana (L) of the Adriatic

Africa (Gael) pleasant

Agata (Gr) good or kind — Agace, Agacia, Aggie, Agueda

Agnese (ahg-NEH-seh) (Gr) gentle, pure

Agueda (ah-GWAY-duh) (Gr) good

Aida help (rare)

Albertina (OGer) noble, bright — Elberta, Berta, Elbertina

Aldonza sweet

Alegria (ah-leh-GREE-ah) happiness — Allegria

Alejandrina (ah-leh-hahn-DREE-nah) (Gr) defender of mankind — Drina

Alicia* (Gr) truthful

Alita (OGer) noble — Adelina, Adelita, Dela, Lela

Alma soul, spirit

Almira woman from Almeira

Almudena ref. to the Virgin Mary

Alonsa (OGer) noble, ready

Amalia (L) industrious; persuasive

Amanda (L) lovable

Amaranta flower name

Amor love

Andeana going ("a walker")

Andrea fem. Andrew (Gr) manly

Angelina (Fr) angel — Angela

Anica (H) graceful

Anna (H) grace — Ana, Maria, Anita, Ninor, Nanor, Nina, Nita

Antonia (L) inestimable — Antonina

Anunciación Annunciation of the Virgin Mary

Aquilina (L) eagle

Araceli (L) altar of heaven

Arcadia (L) adventurous woman

Arcelia (ahr-SEH-lee-ah) (L) treasure chest

Arnalda (OGer) eagle, power

Artemisia perfect

Ascención Ascension of Christ into heaven

Asunción feast of the Assumption

Aurelia (L) gold — Aureliana, Aurita

Bárbara (Gr) the stranger

Beatriz* (BEH-ah-treess) (L) she blesses — Beatrisa, Trisa

Belinda pretty (popular in South America)

Bella (L) beautiful

Benigna (N) (beh-NEEN-yah) kind, blessed — Benita

Berta (OGer) bright, glorious

Bibiana (L) lively

Bienvenida welcome

Blanca (L) white

Brigida (bree-GEE-dah) (Celt) strength, protecting

Camila (L) ceremonial attendant

Candida (L) pure white — Candi

Carlota (Fr) petite and feminine

Carmen (S) song — Carmina

Carolina fem. Carlos

Casta (Gr) purity

Catalina (Gr) pure

Cenobia (Gr) stranger — Zenobia

Charo* (CHAH-ro) short for Rosario

Cipriana (N) (Gr) from the island of Cyprus

Clara (N) (L) bright, clear — Clarissa

Clareta (L) brilliant — Clarita

Clementina (L) gentle, merciful

Clotilda (OGer) heroine

Concepción (kon-sehp-SYON) Immaculate Conception — Concha, Conchita

Conchita (N) dim. Concepcion — Chita

Consolación consolation — Consolata, Consuela, Chela

Constanza (L) constant — Constanta, Constantia, Constantina

Corazon (kor-ah-SON) heart

Cristina* (L) Christian

Dalila (H) delicate

Daniela (H) God is my judge — Danita

Desideria (N) (Fr) desire

Digna (L) worthy — Dinya

Dolores* (S) sorrow of the Virgin Mary — Doloritas, Dolorcitas, Lolita, Lola

Dorotea (L) gift of God — (rare)

Dulce sweet — Dulcie

Dulcinea sweet, character in *Don Quixote*

Eldora golden

Elena* (Gr) light

Elisa* (Gr) consecrated to God — Belita, Ysabel (ee-sah-BEL)

Elsa (Gr) truthful

Ema (Teut) grandmother

Emilia (Teut) industrious — Emiliana, Emilienna

Encarnación Incarnation of Christ

Engracia* graceful

Enriqueta (ehn-ree-KAY-tah) (Teut) ruler of an estate

Erendira Mexican princess

Esperanza* (Fr) hope

Estella (eh-STEH-yah) (Gr) star – Estrella

Esteva (Gr) crowned with laurels

Estrella* (ehs-TREH-yah) (L) star

Eva* (H) life – Evita

Evelina (H) life

Evita (H) life

Exaltación ref. to Holy Cross

Fabiana (N) (L) bean grower – Fabiola (rare)

Fausta (L) fortunate – Faustina

Fé (L) trust, faith

Felisa (L) fortunate, or lucky

Fina short for Josefina (H) God will add

Flor (L) flower

Florencia (L) flowering

Francisca* (frahn-SEES-kah) (Teut) free

Gala (L) from Gaul – (rare)

Ginebra (geen-EH-vrah) (Celt) white as foam – Ginessa (rare)

Gracia (GRAH-see-ah) (L) graceful – Grata, Gratia, Graciana, Engracia

Gregoria (Gr) watchful

Guadalupe* name for the Virgin Mary – Lupe, Lupita, Pita

Herminia (ehr-MEEN-yah) daughter of Venus and Mars

Honorata (o-no-RAH-tuh) (L) honor (rare)

Iluminada illuminated (rare)

Immaculada* Immaculate Conception

Ines* (ee-NEHS) (Gr) gentle, pure – Inez, Ynes, Nessa, Neysa, Inesita

Inocencia (N) (een-o-SEHN-see-ah) innocence – Inocenta

Irene (ee-REH-neh) (Gr) peace

Isabel* (H) consecrated to God – Isa, Elisa, Belita, Ysabel, Isabelita, Belicia

Isolda (OGer) ice rule (rare)

Jacinta* (hah-SEEN-tah) (Gr) hyacinth

Jesusa (heh-SOO-sah) short form of "Mary de Jesus"

Jimena (hee-MEH-nah) (H) heard (rare)

Joaquina (hwah-KEE-nah) (H) God will establish – Joaquine

Josefina (ho-seh-FEE-nah) (H) God will add

Juana* (HWAH-nah) (H) God's gracious gift – Juanita, Nita

Judit (HOO-deet) (H) praised

Julia* (HOO-lyah) (L) youthful – Juliana, Julita, · Julieta

Laura* (L) crown of laurels – Laurenzia, Laurana, Larunda, Laurencia

Leonora (Gr) light

Leticia (L) gladness

Liana (L) youth (rare)

Liliana (L) pure as a lily

Lina (Gr) light

Linda beautiful

Liseta (H) consecrated to God

Lola dim. Carlota, Dolores

Lolita pet form of Dolores

Loretta pure

Lourdes shine of the Virgin Mary

Lucita ref. to the Virgin Mary: "Mary of the Light"

Lucrecia (loo-KREH-syah) (L) brings light

Luisa* (OGer) famous warrior woman – Luella, Louella, Lulu, Lois, Lulita

Luz* (LOOS) short form of Maria de la Luz: (of the light)

Manuela* fem. Emmanuel (H) God is with us

Margarita* (Gr) a pearl – Marga

Maria*** (H) bitter – Mariana, Marietta, Marea, Mara

Marina (N) sea maid

Mariquita (S) form of Maria (H) bitter – Maria, Mariquilla

Marisa* comb. Maria and Luisa

Marisol (S) comb. Maria and sol (sun) popular in Puerto Rico

Marita (H) bitter – Marta

Melosa honeylike, sweet

Mercedes* (mehr-SEH-dees) name for Virgin Mary: "mercies" – Mecha

Miguela (H) who is like God? – Micaela, Miguelita

Milagros* miracles – Mila, Milagritos, Miligrosa (miraculous)

Miranda (L) admirable – Marenda

Mireya miraculous

Modesta modest

Monica* (L) advisor

Mora little blueberry

Narcisa (Gr) daffodil

Natividad* Nativity

Nelia yellow – Amelia

Neva (NEH-vah) snow

Nevada snowy

Olimpia (Gr) Olympian

Olinda (OGer) protector of property – Yolanda

Olivia (L) olive tree

Orquidea (or-kee-DEH-ah) orchid

Paciencia (L) patience

Palmira city of palms

Paloma dove

Paquita (L) free (from Francisca)

Pastora (Teut) shepherd

Paula (L) little – Paulita

Paz (PAHS) peace

Pepita (H) God will increase (from Joseph)

Pia (L) pious

Piedad* (pee-eh-THAHTH) ref. to Virgin Mary

Pilar* (pee-LAHR) pillar; (refers to Virgin Mary, pillar of the Church)

Placida serene

Presentación ref. to the Virgin Mary

Prudencia (N) (L) purdent

Pureza* (poo-REH-suh) purity

Purificación* Purification

Purisima purest — Pura

Ramona (Teut) mighty protector

Raquel* (N) (H) innocence of a lamb

Rebeca (N) (H) servant of God, binding

Regina (reh-GEE-nah) (L) queen

Reina (reh-EE-nah) (L) queen

Remedios* (S) (reh-MEH-thee-os) remedy

Ricarda (OGer) powerful ruler

Rita from Margarita (Gr) a pearl

Rocío* (S) (ro-SEE-o) dewdrops

Romana (L) Roman

Rosa* (L) rose — Rosina, Rosalba, Roseta, Rosana

Rosamariá comb. Rose and Mary

Rosalía comb. rose and Lily

Rosalind comb. of Rose and Linda

Rufina (L) red hair

Ruth (H) beauty, friend

Sabina (L) Sabine (ancient tribe of central Italy)

Salvadora Savior

Sancha holy

Sara* (H) princess — Sarita

Serafina seraph

Serena (L) serene

Silvia (L) forest

Simona (H) God is heard

Socorro* help

Sofia (Gr) wisdom

Solana sunshine (rare)

Soledad (so-leh-THAHTH) solitary — Sole, Chole

Suelita pet form of Consuela: Consolation — Chela

Susana* (H) lily

Teresa* (Gr) harvester

Urbana (L) of the city (rare)

Ursulina (L) little bear

Valentina (L) strong, brave

Verdad (vehr-THAHTH) true

Verónica (L) true image

Violeta* (L) violet — Violante

Virginia (L) pure

Vittoria (L) victorious

Viviana (L) lively — Vivina, Bibiana

Yolanda (OFr) violet

Zita (SEE-tah) little rose — Rosita

---

* Currently popular

SPANISH MALE NAMES

Abrahan (H) father of a multitude

Adriano (N) dark one

Agustin* (ah-goos-STEN) (L) the exalted one

Alano handsome

Alberto* (OGer) noble, bright

Alejandro* (Gr) defender of mankind — Alejo

Alfredo* (OE) wise counselor — Alfeo

Alonso (Teut) eager for battle — Alonzo

Amado (L) loving God

Anastasio (Gr) resurrection

Andrés (ahn-DREHS) (Gr) strong and manly

Angel (AHN-hehl) (L) messenger

Anibal (Gr) grace of the Almighty

Anselmo (Teut) divine helmet

Antonio* (N,S,W) (L) inestimable

Aquilino (L) eagle

Armando (Teut) soldier

Arturo* (Celt) noble, bear man — Turi

Aurelio (L) gold

Bartolo (S) son of the earth — Bartoli, Toli, Bartolome

Basilio (Gr) kingly or magnificent

Benedicto (L) blessed

Benjamin (behn-hah-MEEN) (H) son of the right hand

Bernabé (H) son of prophecy

Bernardo (OGer) courage of a bear

Berto (BAIR-to) bright and distinguished — Veto

Bienvenido (byehn-vehn-EE-tho) welcome

Blas stammerer

Bonifacio (L) welldoer

Camilo (L) ceremonial attendant

Carlomagno Charlemagne

Carlos (OFr) strong and manly

Casimiro (Polish) he announces peace

Cesar (SAY-sar) long-haired or hairy

Che (CHEH) pet form of Joseph (H) God will increase — Chepe, Chepito

Ciceron (see-see-RON) (L) chickpea

Cipriano* from the island of Cyprus

Cirilo (Gr) lordly one — Ciro, Cirio

Ciro (SEE-ro) the sun

Claudio (L) lame

Clemente (L) merciful

Colon (ko-LON) (L) dove

Conrado (kon-RAH-do) (OGer) honest counselor

Constantino (L) constant

Cornelio (L) horn

Cristiano (L) Christian

Cristóbal (krees-TO-vahl) (Gr) Christ-bearer

Curcio (N) (OFr) (KOOR-see-o) courteous (rare)

Dagoberto (OGer) bright day

Damián* (Gr) taming

Daniel* (H) God is my judge

Dario (DAHR-ee-o) wealthy

David* (H) beloved

Delmar (L) mariner

Desiderio (N) desired

Diego (S) (H) the supplanter — Iago, Diaz, Jago

Domingo born on Sunday

Edmundo (OE) prosperous protector

Eduardo (OE) wealthy guardian — Eduards

Elias (H) Jehovah is God

Eloy (eh-LOY) (OGer) renowned warrior

Elvio (L) yellow, blond

Emilio* flattering or winning one

Eneas (Gr) (eh-NEH-uhs) praised one — Aneas

Enrique* (ehn-REE-keh) (Teut) ruler of the home

Erasmo (Gr) amiable

Ernesto (OGer) serious

Esteban* (ehs-TEH-vahn) (Gr) crown — Stefano

Eugenio* (Gr) noble

Fabio (L) bean grower

Farruco (from Francisco) free — Frasco, Paco, Frascuelo, Pacorro, Pancho

Fausto (L) fortunate

Federico* (Teut) peaceful ruler

Felipe (feh-LEP-eh) (Gr) lover of horses

Félix (L) fortunate, or lucky — (rare)

Fermin (fair-MEEN) firm and strong

Fernando* (Teut) adventurous, brave, strong

Fidel (fee-DEHL) (L) faithful — Fidele

Flaminio (L) Roman priest

Flavio (L) blond, yellow — Flaviano

Florentino (L) flowering — Florinio

Francisco* (frahn-SEES-co) (Teut) free — Chicho, Chico, Chilo, Currito, Curro, Pancho, Quico

Gabriel (H) God is my strength — Gabino, Gabrio

Galeno (gah-LEH-no) little bright one

Garcia (Teut) mighty with the spear

Gaspar (gahs-PAHR) (Persian) master of treasure

Generoso (hehn-ehr-O-so) generous

Gerardo* (OE) spear hard

Germán (hehr-MAHN) (Teut) warrior

Gervasio (Teut) warrior

Gil (Gr) shield bearer

Gilberto (Teut) illustrious pledge

Godofredo (Teut) God's peace — Gofredo

Gregorio (Gr) vigilant

Gualterio (Teut) powerful ruler — Galtero

Guido (GWEE-do) (L) life

Gustavo (Teut) staff of the gods

Hector (Gr) defender, steadfast

Heriberto (Teut) bright warrior

Hernando (ehr-NAHN-do) (Ger) adventuring life

Hilario (N) (ee-LAHR-ee-o) (L) cheerful

Honorato (N) (L) honor

Horacio (or-AH-see-o) (L) timekeeper

Hugo (OO-go) (Teut) intelligence, spirit

Humberto (Teut) bright mind

Ignacio* (L) fiery

Inocencio (N) innocent, harmless — Inocente

Isidoro (S) (Gr) a gift of ideas — Isidro

Ivan (Teut) archer

Jacinto (he-SEEN-to) (Gr) hyacinth

Jacobo (hah-KOB-o) (H) supplanter — Santiago

Jaime (HAH-ee-meh) (H) supplanter — Diego

Javier (hah-vee-EHR) (Fr) January — Xavier

Jeremias (hehr-eh-MEE-as) (H) God will uplift

Jerónimo (hehr-O-nee-mo) (L) holy name — Jeromo

Jesus (heh-SOOS) Jesus

Joachim (hwah-KEEM) (H) God will establish — Joaquin (used in Catalina)

Jonas (ho-NAHS) (H) dove

Jorge (HOR-heh) (Gr) farmer

José (HO-seh) (H) God will increase — Che, Chepe, Joselito, Pepe, Pepillo, Joseito

Josué (ho-SWEH) (H) God saves

Juan (HWAHN) (H) God's gracious gift — Juanito

Julián (hoo-LYAHN) (L) youthful — Julio

Lazaro (H) God will help — Lazarillo (lah-sah-REE-yo)

Leandro (Gr) courage of a lion

Leon (leh-ON) (L) lion — Leonidas

Leonardo (Teut) bold lion

Lorenzo (L) crowned with laurel

Lourdes shrine of the Virgin Mary

Lucas (LOO-kahs) (L) bringer of light — Lucio, Lucero

Luis* (OGer) renonwed warrior — Luduvico

Macario (Gr) happy blessed

Manuel* (S) (mahn-oo-EHL) (H) God is with us

Marcos (L) warlike — Mario, Marco, Martial, Martins

Mario (L) warlike — Marcos, Martin, Mariano

Martin (mahr-TEEN) (L) warlike

Mateo (mah-TEH-o) (H) gift of God — Matro, Matias

Mauricio (L) dark-skinned (Moorish) — Mauro

Miguel (mee-GEHL) (H) who is like God?

Moises (mo-ee-SEHS) (H) saved from the water

Natal (nah-TAHL) born at Christmas — Natalio

Nemesio (L) justice

Neron (L) strong, stern

Nestor (Gr) traveler; wisdom

Neto earnest — Ernesto

Nicanor (nee-keh-NOR) victorious army

Nicolás (Gr) victory of the people

Noé (no-EH) (H) quiet peace

Norberto (ONorse) hero

Oliverios (L) olive tree

Orlando (OGer) from the famous land

Pablo (L) little — Paulo

Paquito (pah-KEE-to) (from Francisco) (Teut) free — Panchito, Quico

Pastor (L) shepherd, spiritual leader

Patricio (L) noble

Pedro (Gr) stone

Pirro (PEER-ro) (Gr) with flaming hair

Placido (N) serene

Platon (plah-TON) broadshouldered

Ponce (PON-the) fifth son

Porfirio (N) (Gr) purple stone

Próspero (L) fortunate

Quintin (keen-TEEN) fifthborn child

Rafael (H) God has healed

Raimundo (Teut) mighty protector — Ramón

Ramiro great judge

Raul (Teut) strong, wise counsel — Rulf, Rodolf

Rey (Fr) king

Reyes kings (Magi)

Ricardo (OGer) powerful ruler

Rico (OGer) noble ruler

Roberto (Teut) of shining fame — Ruperto

Rodas (Gr) place of roses

Rodolfo (OGer) famous wolf

Rodrigo (Teut) famous ruler

Rogelio (Teut) famous warrior

Roldan (Teut) fame of the land

Román (L) Roman

Ruben (H) behold, a son

Rufo red-haired (nickname)

Sabino (N) (L) Sabine (ancient tribe in central Italy)

Salomon (H) peaceful

Salvador Savior — Salvatore, Salvadore, Xavier

Samuel (H) God hears

Sancho holy — Sanz

Sanson (sahn-SON) (H) the sun's man

Santiago St. James

Santos saints

Saturnin Saturn

Saül (H) longed for

Sebastiano (Gr) revered

Segundo (N) (L) second

Senon (SEH-non) living

Serafin (H) seraph

Tadeo (Aramaic) praise

Tajo (TAH-ho) (Teut) day

Teodoro (Gr) gift of God

Tino short for Augustino (L) son of the exalted one

Tito (Gr) of the giants

Tobias (H) God is good

Tomas (to-MAHS) (H) twin

Tulio (L) lively

Urbano (L) of the city

Vicente (vi-SEHN-teh) (L) conqueror — Victor

Virgilio (L) strong, flourishing

Vito (L) vital — Vital

Xavier (zah-vee-EHR)(Basque) owner of the new house — Javier

Yago (H) supplanter

Zacarias (H) remembered by the Lord

Zenon (seh-NON) (Gr) hospitable

---

* Currently popular

SWEDEN

An early colony was established by a Swedish mercantile company in Delaware in 1638, but the settlers were later driven west when Peter Stuyvesant, the new governor of the Dutch colony of New Amsterdam, took over the Swedish colony by force in 1655. Although their early numbers were very small, Swedish and Finnish immigrants left an indelible mark on the American pioneering way of life. It was they who introduced the construction of the log cabin.

Record numbers of Swedes did not begin immigrating again until the the 1850's. As in other areas of Scandinavia the combined effects of a prolonged peacetime, the development of the smallpox vaccine, and the successful propagation of the potato as a food crop resulted in a dramatic population increase.

Fifteen to twenty years later there were enormous numbers of young men looking for work, beyond what Sweden could support. A severe crop failure in the late 1860's caused over two percent of Sweden's population to starve to death, and it was this blow which gave the first big impetus to the Swedish exodus. Between 1868 and 1873 nearly 100,000 Swedes immigrated to America.

Unlike other immigrant groups very few Swedes remained in the port of entry, New York City. Instead they sought areas which had similar climate and topography to Sweden, settling in upstate New York, Illinois, Michigan, the Dakotas, Nebraska, and especially Minnesota. The draw of cheap land was enormous to a people that had become progressively more landless (forty-eight percent of the farm population by 1870) as the total population grew.

But immigration reached even greater numbers later on as crises in the manufacturing and mining industries in north Sweden cost many their jobs. Between 1879 and 1893 over 500,000 immigrated, and the tide continued at a lesser but still significant pace until the Depression in the U.S. brought the Swedish immigration to a halt. Since then, immigration has ranged from averages of one to two thousand per year, never reaching the quotas set in 1924.

The total Swedish immigration has numbered about 1.4 million since records were first kept in 1820. This number represents one-fourth of Sweden's population in the late 19th century.

The most popular names for babies in Sweden now come from a variety of sources. Old Scandinavian names such as Sven and Inga are favored, as well as Swedish versions of Biblical names such as Eva and Johan, and names borrowed from other countries. Jennifer was the most chosen girl's named in 1981 in the U.S. and is now enjoying popularity in Sweden, though it is pronounced the Swedish way: "YEHN-i-fer." Combined or hyphenated names are also much used, with Anna and Inga being the favorite forms for girls, and Jan and sometimes Olof for boys.

Pronunciation

Pronunciation of Swedish names is very difficult to generalize because each of the vowels and some of the consonants have at least two ways of being pronounced and, as in English, it's not always possible to tell from the surrounding letters which is the correct one. Also there are several sounds that have no direct equivalent in English.

The pronunciation of some Swedish names has been approximated in the list and the following consistencies are presented:

dj, gj, hj, j = "y" as in yes

gn = "ng" as in sing when at the end of a syllable

kj, tj = "ch" as in child

ng = "ng" as in singer, but not as in finger (See what I mean!)

rs = "sh" as in shoe

s,z = soft "s" as in so, but not as in his

sj, skj, stj = "sh" as in shoe

SWEDISH FEMALE NAMES

Adrian (L) of the Adriatic

Agata (Gr) good or kind — Agaton

Agda meaning unknown

Agneta* (Gr) gentle, pure — Agnek, Agne

Aina (ah-EE-nah) (Celt) joy

Albertina (OGer) noble, bright

Alexandra (Gr) defender of mankind

Algot meaning unknown

Alicia (Gr) truthful

Alma (L) loving, kind

Amalia (Teut) industrious

Amanda (L) loving

Anna* (H) grace — Ann

Anna Cristina comb. name

Annalina comb. name; — Anna and Lena, or Carolina

Annika* (ah-NEE-kah) (H) grace — Annette, Anita, Annie, Annike

Antonetta (L) inestimable

Astrid (ONorse) divine strength

Barbro (Gr) the stranger — Barbara

Beata (beh-AH-tah) (L) blessed

Berit* (OGer) bright, glorious — Berta

Blenda heroine

Botilda (Norse) commanding heroine

Brigitta* (brih-GEE-tah) (Celt) strength — Birget, Birgit, Birgitta

Britt* (Celt) strength — Brite

Britta* (Celt) strength

Carina (Gr) pure — Caren, Carin, Karen, Cary, Carine

Cecilia (L) gray eyes, blind

Charlotta* (shahr-LO-tah) (Fr) petite and feminine

Dagmar (Norse) Dane's joy

Dorotea (L) gift of God

Ebba (OGer) strong — Ebbe

Edit (EH-deet) (Teut) rich gift

Eleonora (Gr) light

Elin (Gr) light

Elisabet* (eh-LEE-sah-beht) (H) consecrated to God — Lisa, Elsa

Elsa (Gr) truthful

Emilia (Teut) industrious

Emma (OGer) universal

Erika* (ONorse) powerful — Erica

Ester (H) star

Eugenia (yoo-HEH-nyah) (Gr) well-born

Eva** (EH-vah) (H) life

Evelina (H) life

Fanny (L) free

Filippa (Gr) lover of horses

Fredrika (Teut) peaceful ruler

Freya mythological goddess of love

Frida (Teut) peaceful

Frideborg (Teut) peaceful helper — Fritjof

Gabriella (H) God is my strength

Gala (ONorse) singer

Gerda (GEHR-da) (Norse) protection — Gerd

Germund protect the world

Gertrud (Teut) fighter

Göta (GER-tuh) meaning unknown — Göte, Götilda

Greta short for Margareta (Gr) a pearl

Guda divine

Gudny divine freshness

Gudrun divine wisdom — Gudruna

Gunilla* (OGer) battle-maid — Gunnel

Gunnel gun

Gustava (Teut) staff of the gods

Håkan (Norse) noble

Hanna (H) gracious

Harriet (Teut) mistress of the home

Hedwig (HEHD-veek) (Teut) refuge in battle

Helena (Gr) light — Lena

Helga (Russian) holy

Henrika (Teut) ruler of an estate

Hilda (Teut) warrior — Hildegard

Hulda (Norse) hidden

Ida (EE-dah) (OGer) she who is active

Inga* (Teut) hero's daughter — Inge, Inger*, Ingrid*

Ingalill* comb. Inge and Lillian

Ingeborg (ONorse) daughter-helper — Ingegerd

Ingemar (ONorse) daughter of the sea

Ingrid* (Teut) hero's daughter — Ingriet

Isabella (H) consecrated to God

Jennifer* (YEHN-i-fer) (Celt) white wave — Jenny

Jenny* (YEHN-nee) (Celt) white wave

Johanna (yo-HAHN-ah) (H) gracious

Josefina (yo-seh-FEE-nah) (H) God will add

Judit (YOO-deet) (H) praised

Julia (YOO-lyah) (L) youthful

Karin* (KAH-rehn) (Gr) pure

Karla fem. Karl

Karolina fem. Karl

Katarina* (Gr) pure — Karin, Katrina

Kaysa (KAH-ee-sah) (Gr) pure — Kolina

Kerstin* (KEHR-sten) (L) Christian — Kristina

Klara (L) bright, clear

Kolina (Gr) pure

Kristina* (krees-TEE-nah) (Gr) Christian

Lage (LAHG-uh) meaning unknown; may be (Gr) the sea

Laura (L) crown of laurels

Lena* (Gr) light

Linnea (ONorse) lime tree

Lisbet* dim. Elisabeth (H) consecrated to God

Lotta* dim. Charlotte (Fr) petite, feminine

Lovisa (OGer) famous warrior woman

Lucia (loo-SEE-ah) (L) bringer of light

Lydia (Gr) ancient province in Asia Minor

Magdalena (H) woman of Magdala

Maj* (MAHY) (Gr) a pearl — Mai, Maja

Malena dim. Magdelena — Malin

Margareta* (Gr) a pearl — Margit, Greta, Mag, Meta

Maria* (H) bitter — Marta, Mariana, Marita

Marianne (mahr-ee-AHN-e) (H) rebellious; form of Mary

Marja (MAHR-yah) (H) bitter

Märta (H) bitter — Marta

Martina (L) warlike — Märten

Matilda (Teut) brave in battle

Mikaela (mee-KAH-ee-lah) (H) who is like God?

Monika (L) advisor — Mona*

Nanna (H) grace — Nina

Olga (Russian) holy

Olivia (L) olive tree

Ottilia (OGer) lucky heroine

Paula (L) little — Paulina

Petra (Gr) a stone — Petronella

Pia* (L) pious

Quenby (Teut) womanly

Quinby from queen's estate

Ragnar (RAHNG-ahr) (Norse) god's-lovely — Ragnhild (RAHNG-eeld)

Rakel (RAH-kehl) (H) innocence of a lamb

Rebecka (H) servant of God

Regina (reh-GEE-nah) (L) queen

Rigmor (REEG-mor) name of a Danish queen

Rosa (L) rose

Rut (H) beauty, friend

Sabina (L) Sabine (ancient tribe of central Italy)

Sara (H) princess

Sibylla (Gr) the prophetess

Signe (SING-uh, soft g) unknown meaning; possibly "victory" — Signild

Sigrid (ONorse) victorious counselor

Silvia (L) forest

Solveig (SOL-vehg) (Norse) house-woman

Sonya (Gr) wisdom — Sonja, Sonia

Stella (Gr) star — Ester

Stina nickname for Kistina

Susanna (H) lily

Svante meaning unknown; possibly from "svan" (swan)

Svea (SVEE-ah) location

Sylvia (L) from the forest

Tekla (Gr) divine fame

Teresia (Gr) harvester — Teresa

Tilda (Teut) heroine

Tora short for Viktoria

Trind (Gr) pure

Ulla will — Ulrika

Ulla* (OO-lah) will

Ulrika (OGer) ruler of all

Vedis forest nymph

Vega (L) star

Viktoria (Gr) victorious

Vilhelmina (Teut) resolute protector

Vilma (Teut) resolute protector

Viola (L) violet

Virginia (L) pure

Viveka (Scand) living voice; or (German) little woman

Vivianne (L) lively

Yvonne (Teut) archer

---

* Popular
** Very popular

SWEDISH MALE NAMES

Adam (H) son of the red earth

Åke (ONorse) ancestors

Albert (OGer) courage of a bear

Alexander (Gr) defender of mankind

Alfred (OE) wise counselor − Alf

Alrik (OGer) ruler of all

Alvar a dwarf shrub native to Sweden

Anders** (AHN-dersh) (Gr) strong and manly

Ansgar (Celt) warrior

Anton (L) inestimable

Arne (OGer) eagle − Arnold

Aron (H) enlightened

Artur (Celt) noble; bear man

Arvid man of the people

Augustin (L) venerable − August

Axel (H) father of peace

Beck brook

Bengt* (L) blessed

Benjamin (BEHN-ya-meen) (H) son of the right hand

Berg mountain

Bergren mountain stream − Bergron

Bernhard (OGer) courage of a bear − Bern

Bertil* bright

Birger (ONorse) rescue

Björn (BYUHRN) bear

Bo* commanding − Bodil

Borg (ONorse) from the castle

Börje (BUHR-yeh) (ONorse) castle

Burr (BOOR) youth

Daniel (H) God is my judge

David (H) beloved

Davin (DAH-vin) the brightness of the Finns

Eddy unresting

Edmund (OE) prosperous protector

Edvard (OE) wealthy guardian

Elias (H) Jehovah is God

Emil (Teut) energetic

Enar (EH-nahr) (ONorse) warrior, leader

Erik (ONorse) ever powerful

Erland (ONorse) stranger − Erling (old name)

Ernst (OGer) serious (old name)

Esbjörn (ONorse) god-bear

Eskil (ONorse) god-vessel

Eugen (YOO-gyen) (Gr) noble

Evert (OE) strong as a bear

Fabian (L) bean-grower

Felix (L) fortunate, or lucky

Filip (Gr) lover of horses

Fisk the fisherman − Fiske

Folke (Teut) people's guard

Frans (Teut) free man − Franzen (FRAHN-sen)

Fredrik (Teut) peaceful ruler − Fredek

Gabriel (H) God is my strength

Garth (ONorse) enclosure, protection

Georg (GYORG) (Gr) farmer

Gerhard (OE) spear-hard

Goran (YO-ran) (Gr) farmer

Greger (Gr) vigilant

Gunnar* (Norse) battle-army

Gustav (Teut) staff of the gods − Gustaf

Hadrian dark one

Halvard (Norse) rock-protection

Hans* (H) God's gracious gift

Hansel (H) gift from God

Harald (HAH-rahld) (ONorse) war chief

Harry (Teut) ruler of an estate

Helmer (Teut) warrior's fury

Hemming unkown meaning, perhaps from Henrik

Henning (Teut) ruler of an estate

Henrik* (Teut) ruler of an estate − Hendrik

Herbert (Teut) bright warrior

Hermann (Teut) army man

Hillevi unknown meaning

Hilmar famous noble

Hjalmar (HYAHL-mer) unknown meaning

Hugo (Teut) intelligence; spirit

Ingmar* famous son − Ingemar

Ingvar* famous warrior

Isak (H) laughter

Ivar (EE-vahr) yew-bow army; archer

Jakob (YAH-kob) (H) supplanter

Jan* (YAHN) (H) God's gracious gift

Jens (YEHNS) (H) God's gracious gift − Jonam

Jesper (YEHS-per) (OFr) jasper stone

Joakim (YO-ah-keem) (H) God will establish

Joel (YO-ehl) (H) Jehovah is God

Johan* (YO-hahn) (H) God's gracious gift

John (YON) (H) God's gracious gift − Johan

Jonas* (YO-nahs) (H) dove, God gives

Jonatan (H) God gives

Josef (YO-sef) (H) God will add

Julius (L) youthful

Justus (L) just

Kalle** (KAHL-uh) (OFr) strong and manly

Karl* (OFr) strong and manly

Kjell* (SHELL) unknown meaning, perhaps form of Karl

Klas (Gr) victory of the people

Klemens (L) merciful

Knut (K'NOOT) (ONorse) the knot

Kolbjörn black bear

Konrad (OGer) honest counselor

Konstantin (L) constant

Krister (KREE-ster) (Gr) Christian — Kristar, Krist

Kristian (KREE-stee-ahn) (Gr) believer in Christ

Kristofer (Gr) Christ-bearer

Lang (ONorse) tall man

Lars** (L) laurel — Laurentius

Leif beloved, descendant

Lennart* (Teut) brave as a lion

Leo (L) lion — Leon

Lorens (L) crowned with laurel

Lucio (L) bringer of light

Lukas (L) bringer of light

Lunt (LOONT) from the grove

Magnhild (ONorse) strong, warrior

Magnus** (ONorse) strength

Malin (H) woman of Magdala

Malkolm (L) dove

Malte unknown meaning

Manfred (Teut) man of peace

Markus (L) warlike

Marten (L) warlike — Martin

Mats** (H) gift of God

Matteus (H) gift of God — Mattias

Maurits (L) Moorish

Max (L) greatest

Melker (H) king

Mikael (mee-KHAHL) (H) who is like God?

Nansen son of Nancy

Natanael (H) gift of the Lord

Nels* (Celt) chief

Nicklas (Gr) victory of the people — Nikolaus

Nils* (NEELS) (Celt) champion

Olof (ONorse) descendant

Oskar (Celt) warrior

Otto (Teut) prosperous

Ove (OO-veh) unknown meaning, perhaps from (L) egg

Pal (L) little — Paulo, Paulus

Patrik (L) noble

Per* (Gr) stone — Peder, Petrus, Petter

Pol (L) little — Poul

Ragnar (RAHNG-ahr) mighty army

Ragnvard mighty warrior

Reinhold (Teut) wise power

Rickard (OGer) powerful ruler

Roald (OGer) famous power

Robert (Teut) of shining fame

Roland (Teut) fame of the land

Rolf (Teut) swift wolf

Rudolf (Teut) famous wolf

Rune (ROON-e) (Ger) secret

Rurik (Teut) famous ruler

Rutger (ROOT-yer) (Teut) famous warrior

Samson (H) the sun's man

Samuel (H) God hears

Saul (H) longed for

Set (H) compensation

Sigurd (SEE-gerd) (ONorse) victorious guardian

Sigvard (ONorse) victorious warrior — Siv

Simon (H) God is heard

Sören unknown meaning; perhaps from sorel (OFr) reddish-brown hair

Staffan (Gr) crowned with laurels — Stefan

Sten (Teut) stone

Stig* (Teut) mount

Sture unknown meaning

Sven*** youth — Svend, Svens

Svenbjorn young bear

Sylvester (L) from the woods

Tage (TAHG-e) (Teut) day

Tait (TIGHT) cheerful

Teodor (Gr) gift of God

Tobias (TO-byas) (H) God is good

Tomas** (TO-mas) (H) twin

Tor (TOR) thunder god — Tore

Torbjörn thunder bear — Torborg (thunder mountain)

Torgny (ONorse) Torclamor of weapons

Torkel (Teut) Thor's cauldron

Torsten (Teut) Thor's rock

Ture (TOO-reh) unknown meaning

Ulf** (ONorse) wolf

Urban (OOR-bahn) (L) of the city

Valborg mighty mountain

Valdemar famous power

Valentin (L) strong, brave

Valfrid strong peace

Valter (Teut) powerful ruler

Verner (Teut) protecting friend

Vilhelm (Teut) resolute protector

Yngve (ING-ve) ancestor, lord, master

---

* Popular
** Very popular

TANZANIA

Tanzania is located midway along the southeast coast of Africa. Although it's substantially an inland country rather than a "coastal" area, nearly one-half of Tanzania's borders are water. The Indian Ocean forms the eastern coast; Lake Victoria lies along the northern border with Kenya and Uganda; Lake Tanganyika forms Tanzania's western boundary with Zaire; and Lake Nyasa (Lake Malawi) stretches along part of its southern border (with Malawi). These large lakes, which rival the Great Lakes in size, are part of the great Rift Valley, which extends from Jordan in the Middle East to south-central Africa. In places the walls of the Rift Valley rise a thousand feet or more above the valley floor.

Despite its distance form the U.S. it is possible slaves were transported from there in the 18th and 19th centuries, until the efforts of Dr. David Livingstone (who traveled extensively in eastern and central Africa in the 1860's and 1870's) brought the slaving to a halt. Because of the strength of the Masai and other northern tribes in protecting themselves against slaving attacks, few of these tribes fell under the yoke of the slavers. Along southern slave routes, because of the brutal conditions (the forced march to the coast took up to two years) as many as five slaves may have died for each one who survived.

Repressive German colonial rule, from the late 1880's until World War I, was replaced by British colonial rule (as part of German surrender), then independence in 1961.

Many Tanzanians speak three languages: the language of their ethnic group (there are 120 tribes in Tanzania); Swahili (which refers to the combination of Arab and African cultures) with a person from another ethnic group; and English for business.

TANZANIAN FEMALE NAMES

Afiya (ah-FEE-ah) (Swahili) health

Bupe (BOO-peh) (Nyakyusa) hospitality

Doto (DOH-toh) (Zaramo) second of twins

Kizuwanda (kee-zu-WAHN-dah) (Zaramo) last born child

Kulwa (KOOL-wah) (Zaramo) first of twins

Kyalamboka (kee-ah-lam-BOH-kah) (Nyakyusa) God save me

Mwanawa (mwah-NAH-nah) (Zaramo) first born child

Mwanjaa (Mwah-nan-JAAH) (Zaramo) born during famine

Ngabile (ngah-BEE-leh) (Nyakyusa) I have got it

Sekelaga (seh-keh-LAH-gah) (Nyakyusa) rejoice

Sigolwide (see-gol-WEE-deh) (Nyakyusa) my ways are straight

Suma (SOO-mah) (Nyakyusa) ask

Tulinagwe (too-lee-NA-gweh) (Nyakyusa) God is with us

Tumpe (TOOM-peh) (Nyakyusa) let us thank God

Waseme (wah-SEH-meh) (Swahili) let them talk

Zahra (ZAH-rah) (Swahili) flower

TANZANIAN MALE NAMES

Ambakisye (am-bah-KEES-yeh) (Ndali) God has been merciful to me

Ambokile (am-bo-KEE-leh) (Nyakyusa) God has redeemed me

Andwele (ahn-DWEH-leh) (Nyakyusa) God brought me

Asukile (ah-soo-KEE-leh) (Nyakyusa) the Lord has washed me

Badru (BAH-droo) (Swahili) born at full moon

Ipyana (eep-YAH-nah) (Nyakyusa) grace

Maskini (mah-SKEE-nee) (Swahili) poor

Mosi (MOH-see) (Swahili) first born

Mposi (MPOH-see) (Nyakyusa) blacksmith

Mwamba (MWAHM-bah) (Nyakyusa) strong

Nassor (NAH-sohr) (Swahili) victorious

Nikusubila (nee-koo-soo-BEE-lah) (Nyakyusa) hopeful

Suhuba (soo-HOO-bah) (Swahili) friend

Tuponile (too-poh-NEE-leh) (Nyakyusa) we are afraid

Watende (wah-TEHN-deh) (Nyakyusa) there shall be no revenge

THAILAND

Thailand, whose name means "free nation," has been independent for seven centuries. Nearly seventy-five percent of Thailand's fifty-three million people are Thais, a fairly homogeneous group that has occupied the area for an estimated 5,000 years. About fourteen percent are Chinese. Other minority groups, especially refugees, are growing. Ninety-five percent of Thais are Buddhists, and ninety percent speak Thai, a language originally like Chinese but influenced by the Cambodian and Indian languages. Thai has a Roman alphabet.

The northern mountains are logged, using trained elephants, of teak and other woods. Many houses are built on stilts as protection against snakes in the June to October rainy season. A central plain where most Thais live is heavily cultivated with rice fields. A southern appendage where rubber tree plantations and tin mines are common reaches into the Malay Peninsula. Thailand is a tropical country, and the southern area is hot thoughout the year.

About 5,000 Thais have immigrated to the U.S. since the mid-1970's. In the late 1970's women (many had married U.S. servicemen during the Vietnam War), outnumbered men three to one. Most male Thai immigrants have been professional or white-collar workers.

THAI FEMALE NAMES

Daw stars
Kanok (kan-OHK) design
Kanya (kan-YAH) young lady
Lawan (lah-WAHN) pretty
Mali jasmine (flower)
Mayuree beautiful
Phailin (pah-ee-LEEN) sapphire
Ratana (ra-ta-NAH) crystal
Solada (soh-lah-DAH) listener
Sopa very pretty
Suchin (soo-CHEEN) beautiful thought
Sumalee beautiful flower
Sunee good thing
Tasanee beautiful view
Tida (tee-DAH) daughter

THAI MALE NAMES

Aran forest
Aroon dawn
Asnee lightning
Atid (ah-TEED) the sun
Decha (deh-CHAH) power
Kasem (ka-SEHM) happiness
Kiet honor
Kovit (koh-VEET) expert
Lek small person
Niran (nee-RAHN) eternal
Pravat (PRAH-vaht) history
Pricha (pree-CHAH) clever
Runrot (roong-ROT) prosperous
Sum (SOOM) appropriate
Virote (vee-roh-TEH) power

TURKEY

An estimated 36,000 Turks immigrated to the U.S. between 1820 and 1950. During 1899-1924 roughly eighty-six percent returned to Turkey. Turks often found it difficult to adjust to American life because their numbers were not large enough to form cohesive communities, and because they came from substantially different cultural and religious backgrounds than other Americans (virtually all Turks are Muslims).

Ottoman Sultans ruled Turkey and a varying-sized empire for over 500 years, until they were overthrown by the Allies in World War I. Mustafa Kemal, later called Atatürk, organized a revolt against Allied occupation in the 1920's and drove the Allies out. He became president of the Republic of Turkey and instituted many reforms, including five years of mandatory primary education for girls as well as boys, separation of church and state, and simplifying the process of learning to read and write by changing the Turkish written language system from an Arabic to a Roman alphabet.

After the many years of war and internal strife Turkey had experienced, the male population was seriously depleted, so Turks living abroad were encouraged to return through loans and sometimes grants for returnees.

Since 1940 Turkish immigration has been mostly a "brain drain." More than 2,000 engineers and 1,500 physicians have come to the U.S. From earliest times Turkish immigrants settled mostly in urban areas, especially around New York City.

TURKISH FEMALE NAMES

Ahu (AH-hoo) bright and beautiful

Aysen (AYE-soon) beautiful like the moon

Canan (JAH-nahn) beloved

Cemal (JEH-mahl) beauty

Deniz (DEHN-nees) sea

Dilek (DEEL-'k) wish

Emel (EH-muhl) ambitious

Fusun (FEU-suhn) charming, fascinating

Gonul (GOO-nuhl) desire

Gulsen (GUHL-sen) joyous rose

Harika a miracle or wonder

Havva (H) life

Hulya daydream

Huri (HOO-ree) heaven's maiden

Melek angel

Meryem (MEH-ryem) (H) bitter

Ozlem (EUZ-lem) longing, ardent desire

Reyhan sweet-smelling flower

Sevgi love

Zerrin made of gold

TURKISH MALE NAMES

Adem (AH-dehm) (H) son of the red earth

Aydin (AYE-dun) bright, intelligent

Baki enduring, everlasting

Baris (BAHR-'sh) peace

Cengiz (JEN-g's) strong

Coskun (JOSH-koon) enthusiastic

Emre brother

Enver very bright and very handsome

Erol may you be strong and courageous

Eyup (EH-uhp) the patient one

Husamettin (heu-suh-MET-tin) sharp sword

Ihsan compassion

Kahraman hero

Kemal (KEH-mahl) the highest honor

Mesut (MEH-soot) happiness

Murat (MOO-raht) a wish that has come true

Onur honor

Ozturk pure, genuine Turk

Sener (SHEN-er) one who brings happiness or joy

Sukru (SHRUH-kruh) gratitude

Umit (EU-mit) hope

Zeki (ZEH-kee) clever and intelligent

Uganda

Although slaves possibly numbering in the thousands may have been taken in the 19th century from Uganda, their destination was most likely French and English colonial islands southeast of Africa, or seaports around the Red Sea, the Persian Gulf, or the Arabian Sea (India).

It is very unlikely that Ugandan slaves were ever brought to the U.S., because American slaves were taken primarily from the much closer west African countries. This chapter is presented, therefore, only to give an idea of the wide variety of African names and cultures.

Beginning in about 1500 A.D. powerful independent kingdoms established themselves in Uganda, remaining undisturbed until the 19th century. The largest and most powerful of these dynasties was the Buganda kingdom, whose Baganda people are the largest ethnic group in Uganda today. Their language, Luganda, is also the most widely spoken.

For several hundred years Arabs had traded with east Africans for ivory and slaves along the seacoast. By 1840 they established trading posts as far in the interior as Uganda, bringing with them the Moslem religion. Arabic names are common among those who continue to hold the Moslem faith.

Beginning in 1879 Protestant and Catholic missionaries worked in Uganda. Today about fifty percent of Ugandans are Christians, a relatively high ratio for an African country, and an indication of the success of the early missionaries. Colonial rule by the British was being felt by 1890. They chose to rule indirectly in Uganda by allowing local leaders who followed the wishes of the colonial government to stay in power.

Although Uganda is landlocked, it is bordered on the south by the enormous Lake Victoria (third largest in the world). The British colonial government began a railroad at the seaport city of Mombasa, Kenya in 1896, and by 1901 it had been constructed to the eastern side of Lake Victoria. Trains could then carry cargo gathered from around the Lake via ships.

Colonial rule was gradually phased out by 1962. Because foreigners had not been allowed to take over land in Uganda as they had in other British colonies, Uganda's population was still mainly black when it became independent. Thus the struggles between blacks and whites over control of the land was not such a problem as in some colonial nations.

However, the transition was not entirely smooth, in view of the number of strong independent kingdoms that still existed at that time. The dictatorial regime of Idi Amin between 1971 and 1979 did nothing to foster Uganda's democratic growth.

Since the 1970's immigration from Uganda has remained at a fairly constant rate of about 300 each year. It might be guessed that many of them are students, and that possibly a larger number emigrate to Canada or England, since Uganda was once a British protectorate.

In Uganda as in other African countries great importance is given to a child's name. It may indicate the child's birth order, current circumstances of the family, or specific hope for the child's future. A child's name may be amended up to ten years later. If, for instance, it turns out he or she was born before twins the word signifying that may be added later.

A child's name may reflect his or her clan's "totem," a plant, animal, or object that serves as an identifying emblem for the clan. Especially common in the large kingdoms of East Africa, such as Buganda, Bunyoro, Ankole, and Tooro, the totem served as a method of dividing labor. The people of a particular totem were given exclusive right to perform a particular function in the society and the totem identifies the clan's role.

UGANDAN FEMALE NAMES

Abbo (AH-bo) (Mudama) vegetable

Abothi (Jopadhola) thought to be not too useful, but turns out different

Acanit (ah-chah-nit) (Ateso) hard times

Achen (Ateso) one of the twins

Adongo (ah-do-'ngo) (Ateso) first of the twin sisters

Afiya (Kiswahili) health

Ajaruva (Alur) unfortunate

Apio (ah-pee-o) (Ateso) the second to be born of the twin sisters

Babirye (Luganda) first of the twins

Bacia (bah-chee-ah) (Lugbara) family deaths have ruined the home

Bagamba (Rutooro) let them talk (ignore ill-talk of enemies)

Baingama (bah-een-gah-mah) (Runyoro) people are equal

Balikuraira (Rutooro) people will take ages to mature in their mentality

Bategeka (bah-teh-jeh-kah) (Runyoro) people plan

Beesigye (be-see-jeh) (Rukiga) they have trust in God

Birungi (bee-roon-jee) (Luganda) something nice, pretty

Byaitaka (bia-ee-tah-kah) (Rutooro/Runyoro) born to die

Dembe (dehm-beh) (Lug) peace

Ekellot (eh-keh-lot) (Ateso) a girl born after twins

Emojung (EH-mo-yong) (Karamojong) the old one

Gonza (gon-zah) (Rutooro) love

Jendyose (jehn-dio-seh) (Luganda) I have done good to produce this child

Kabonero (Runyankore) sign

Kabonesa (Rutooro) a baby who caused a lot of trouble being born

Kajuga (Runyankore) a baby that cries a lot

Kenyangi (kehn-yahn-jee) (Rukiga) white egret

Kibibi (chee-bee-bee) (Runyankore) beautiful fat girl

Kigongo (chee-go-'ngo) (Luganda) one who comes before twins

Kiho (chee-ho) (Rutooro) fog, or a child born on a foggy day

Kijai (ke-jah-ee) (Ateso) the first girl born in a family

Kisembo (kee-sehm-bo) (Rutooro) the gift; i.e. baby is gift from God

Kissa (kiss-AH) (Luganda) born after twins

Komuntale (koo-moon-tah-leh) (Rutooro) born in a lion country

Komushana (Runyankore) born when the sun was shining

Kugonza (Rutooro) love

Kulabako (Luganda) take a quick look—a pretty girl

Kusmemererwa (koo-seh-meh-rehr-oo-ah) (Runyoro) happiness

Kutaaka (Lugisu) child who follows one that died

Kwehangana (kueh-hahn-gahn-ah) (Rukiga) endurance

Kyagaza (Luganda) what makes an ugly person loved is her good work

Kyaligonza (Rutooro) whatever God decides to do

Lwango (Runyankore) hatred; jealousy

Mangeni (man-GHEH-nee) (Musamia) fish

Masani (Luganda) has gap between teeth

Masiko (Runyankore) the invincible

Mbaziira ('mbah-zee-rah) (Luganda) a tailor

Mirembe (Luganda) peace

Mugaba (Runyankore) given by God

Mugamba (Runyoro) name given to people who talk too much

Mugisa (Rutooro) luck

Mugisha (Rukiga) luck

Muhairwe (moo-hah-ee-rueh) (Runyankore) God-given child

Muhenda (Rutooro) child who caused much pain to the mother at birth

Muhumuza (Runyankore) one who brings peace, calm, and consolation

Mukhwana (Lugisu) the first of the twins to be born

Nabaasa (nah-bah-sah) (Runyankore) omnipotent

Nabirye (nah-beer-YEH) (Luganda) one who produces twins

Nabossa (Luganda) sheep totem

Nabukenya (Luganda) antelope totem

Nabukwasi (nah-boo-KWAH-see) (Luganda) bad housekeeper

Nabulungi (nah-boo-long-GHEE) (Luganda) beautiful one

Nafula (nah-foo-LAH) (Abaluhya) born during rainy season

Nafuna (nah-foo-NAH) (Luganda) delivered feet first

Nagesa (nah-geh-sah) (Lugisu) born during harvest season

Najja (Luganda) second born

Nakagwa (Luhya) following twins

Nakakande (Luganda) jungle

Nakamya (Luganda) a third born after twins

Nakato (Luganda) the second of the twins

Nakimera (nah-kee-meh-rah) (Luganda) a gift to God

Nalongo (nah-long-GO) (Luganda) mother of twins

Nalunga (nah-loo-'ngah) (Luganda) a mushroom totem

Nalwanga (Luganda) a fist totem

Namakula (nah-mah-koo-lah) (Luganda) very pretty girl

Namata (Luganda) milk; given to those whose totem is milk

Namataka (Luganda) the only survivor

Namazzi (Luganda) water

Nambogo (Luganda) buffalo or a girl whose clan is a buffalo

Namirembe (nah-mee-rehm-beh) (Luganda) peace

Namono (NAH-mo-no) (Luganda) younger of twins

Namukasa (Luganda) a goddess

Namusisi (Luganda) baby's mother was pregnent when an earthquake occurred

Namusobiya (nah-moo-so-BEE-yah) (Musoga) one who has offended

Nangoma (Luganda) drum or throne; a princess

Nanjala (Lugisu) born during famine

Nankunda (Runyankore) someone loves me

Nantale (Luganda) clan totem is a lion

Nantumbwe (Luganda) a girl with big legs

Nanziri (Luganda) clan totem is a fish (perch)

Nasiche (nah-SEE-cheh) (Musoga) born in the locust season

Nasikye (nah-seek-yah) (Lumasaba) born when locust swarms were passsing through

Nassuna (Luganda) clan totem is a fish (perch)

Natukunda (Runyankore) God loves us

Nsungwa ('nsoo-'nguah) (Rutooro) a girl following twins

Nyangoma (Rutooro) one of the twins

Onzia (Lugbara) bad

Sabiti (Rutooro) born on Sunday

Sanyu (Luganda) happiness

Tibyangye (te-biahn-jeh) (Runyankore) everything belongs to God

Tukesiga (Rukiga) hopeful

Tumushabe (Rukiga) we pray to God

Tumusiime (too-moo-see-meh) (Rukiga) we thank God

Turyahumura (Rukiga) we will see God

Tusuubira (too-soo-bee-rah) (Rukiga) we have hope

Twesigye (tweh-see-jeh) (Rukiga) let's trust in God

Twinamaani (tween-a-mah-nee) (Rukiga) we are powerful

Wesesa (weh-seh-SAH) (Musoga) careless

Zesiro (ZEH-see-ro) (Luganda) elder of twins

UGANDAN MALE NAMES

Adroa (Luganda) God's will

Akello (Alur) I have bought

Akia (Ateso) first born

Akiiki (ah-kee-EE-kee) (Runyankole) friend

Alanyo (Luo) born while wife was temporarily separated from her husband

Allopu (ah-lo-poo) (Ateso) born after a period of great famine

Angorit (ah-'ngo-ret) (Ateso) last born

Anjait (ah-'njah-it) (Ateso) born on grass

Asea (ah-seh-ah) (Luganda) first twin to be born

Bagamba (Rutooro) let them talk

Bagenda (bah-geh-'ndah) (Lusoga) they went

Bahemuka (bah-heh-moo-kah) (Runyoro) resembles his father

Baingana (bah-ee-ngah-nah) (Runyoro) people are equal

Balikuraira (bah-lee-koo-rah-ee-rah) (Rut.) people take ages to mature mentally

Balinda (bah-lee-'ndah) (Rutooro) fortitude, patience, and endurance

Balondemu (bah-lon-DEH-moo) (Musoga) chosen one

Bategeka (bah-teh-jeh-kah) (Runyoro) people plan

Batte (bah-teh) (Luganda) boy whose totem is an elephant in Kiganda tradition

Bbale (bah-leh) (Luganda) legendary home of the Mutima (Heart) clan

Beesigye (beh-see-jeh) (Rukiga) they have trust in God

Begumisa (beh-goo-mee-sah) (Runyankore) the indefatigable

Bikutwala (bee-koo-tua-lah) (Luganda) problems drive you to seek help

Birungi (be-roo-'njee) (Luganda) something nice, pretty, perfect

Bitalo (bee-TAH-lo) (Luganda) finger-licking

Brahma (brah-MAH) (Hin) the Creator

Bwambale (bua-'mbah-leh) (Rukonjo) second male born

Bwire (bui-reh) (Bakedi/Samia) born at night

Byaitaka (bia-ee-tah-kah) (Rutooro/Runyoro) born to die

Byangireeka (bia-'njee-reh-kah) (Rutooro) doomed to failure

Byarugaba (bia-roo-gah-bah) (Rukiga) For, by, or of God

Byaruhanga (bia-roo-hah-'ngah) (Rutooro) for, by, or of God

Byembandwa (bieh-mbah-'nduah) (Runyoro) for a God

Damba (Luganda) a boy of peace

Dembe (deh-'mbeh) (Luganda) peace

Ejau (eh-jah-ooh) (Ateso) we have received

Enani (eh-nah-nee) (Lugbara) being bewitched when pregnant

Engemu (eh-'ngeh-moo) (Ateso) eats small quantities of food

Galabba (Lugwere) talking

Gonza (go-'nzah) (Rutooro) love

Gwandoya (gwan-DO-yah) (Luganda) met with misery

Hiryagana (hee-ria-gah-nah) (Lunyole) innocent and susceptible to harm

Irumba (ee-room-bah) (Rutooro) follow twins in the immediate family

Isabirye (ee-sah-bee-rieh) (Lusoga) he who gives birth to twins

Isingoma (ee-see-'ngo-mah) (Rutooro) the first of twin boys

Jimiyu (JEE-mee-yoo) (Abaluhya) born in a dry season

Kabiito (kah-bee-to)(Rutooro) born while foreigners are visiting the area

Kabonero (Runyankore) sign

Kabonesa (kah-bo-neh-sah) (Rutooro) baby who caused lots of trouble being born

Kacancu (kah-chah-'nchoo) (Rukonjo) first born

Kadokechi (kah-do-KEH-chee) (Mudama) bitter soup

Kaikara (kah-ee-kah-rah) (Runyoro) name of God in Banyoro people tradition

Kakuru (kah-koo-roo) (Runyankore) the first of the twins to be born

Kakyomya (kah-kio-miah) (Runyoro) ancient God of a group of Banyoro (peas)

Kamirakwo (kah-mee-rah-kuo) (Runyankore) born during famine

Kamoga (Luganda) ancestral name in royal family of Baganda people

Kamuhanda (Runyankore) born during a trip or on the way to the hospital

Kamukama (Runyankore) protected by God

Kamya (kah-mia) (Luganda) a son born after twin brothers

Kariisa (kah-ree-sah) (Runyankore) herdsman, or whose father is one

Karutunda (Runyankore) a little person

Karwana (Rutooro) born during war time

Kasozi (Luganda) mountain

Kasumba (Luganda) a servant

Kato (kah-to) (Runyankore) second of the twins to be born

Katungi (kah-too-'njee) (Runyankore) rich person

Katuramu (Rutooro) born after a pregnancy which seems longer than usual

Kayonga (Runyankore) ash; name of a great warrior of the Ankole clan

Kibuuka (che-boo-kah) (Luganda) name of a brave warrior in Buganda Kingdom

Kigongo (kee-GON-go) (Luganda) born before twins

Kiho (chee-ho) (Dutooro) fog; or child born on a foggy day

Kiintu (kee-'ntoo) (Luganda) name of a man who first came to Buganda kingdom

Kizza (keez-SAH) born after twins

Kugonza (koo-go-'nzah) (Rutooro) love

Kusemererwa (koo-seh-meh-reh-rua) (Runyoro) happiness

Kutaaka (koo-tah-kah) (Lugisu) child who follows one who died

Lutalo (LOO-tah-lo) (Luganda) warrior

Luzige (loo-zee-GEH) (Mugwere) locust

Madongo (mah-DON-go) (Luganda) uncircumcised

Magomu (mah-go-MOO) (Luganda) younger of twins

Mawagali (mah-wah-GAH-lee) (Abaluhya) numerous

Mayanga (Luganda) a sailor of lakes

Mbabazi ('mbah-bah-zee) (Rukiga) mercy

Mbazira ('mbah-zee-rah) (Luganda) a tailor

Mirembe (mee-reh-'mbeh) (Luganda) peace

Mori (Madi) born before father finished paying loan he had on dowry

Mpagi ('mpah-gee) (Luganda) brave person; or pillar of the community

Mpoza ('mpo-zah) (Luganda) tax collector

Mubiru (moo-bee-roo) (Luganda) totem is an eel

Mugaba (moo-gah-bah) (Runyankore) given by God

Mugamba (Runyoro) name given to people who talk too much

Mugisa (Rutooro) luck

Mugisha (Rukiga) luck

Muhairwe (moo-hah-ee-rueh) (Runyankore) God-given child

Muhangi (moo-hah-'njee) (Runyankore) for, by, or of the Creator

Muhenda (Rutooro) child who caused much pain to mother at birth

Muhindo (moo-hee-'ndo) (Rukonjo) given to boy, if first-born

Muhoozi (moo-ho-zee)(Rukonjo) one who takes revenge, on behalf of wronged

Muhumuza (Runyankore) he who brings peace, calm, and consolation

Mukasa (Luganda)God's chief administrator, according to Kiganda doctrine

Mukhwana (moo-KWAH-nah) (Abaluhya) born as a twin

Mukhwana (Lugisu) the first of twins to be born

Mukiibi (moo-kee-bee) (Luganda) one who enters through back door

Mukisa (Luganda) good luck

Mulindwa (moo-lee-ndua) (Rutooro) the protected one

Mulogo (MOO-lo-go) (Musoga) a wizard

Mulumba (Luganda) one who attacks

Munanire (moo-nah-nee-REH) (Luganda) has more than his share

Munyiga (moon-YEE-gah) (Mukiga) one who presses others

Musaazi (moo-sah-zee) (Luganda) a joker; one who jokes

Musabingo (moo-sah-bee-ngo) (Lukonjo) savior

Musembwa (moo-see-mbua) (Luganda) given to boys whose clan totem is a monkey

Musisi (Luganda) mother was pregnant at time earthquake occured

Musoke (moo-so-KEH) (Muganda) cannot be introduced

Musoke (moo-so-keh) (Rukonjo) rainbow; born while rainbow was in sky

Musubaho (Rukonjo) baby who survived after several others died

Mutebi (Luganda) boy whose clan totem is a fresh water perch called Mamba

Mutongole (Luganda) clan totem is a heart

Muwanga (Luganda) the Creator; a traditional God in Ganda culture

Muwemba (Luganda) sorghum; people of the sorghum clan

Muyingo (Luganda) clan totem is a cow

Mwaka (Luganda) born on New Year's Eve

Mwanje (Luganda) leopard

Mwesige (mue-see-geh) (Rutooro) trust

Najja (NAHJ-jah) (Muganda) born after

Nakisisa (nah-kee-SEE-sah) (Muganda) child of the shadows

Nangila (NAN-ghee-lah) (Abaluhya) born while parents were traveling

Natukundo (Runyankore) God loves us

Ndahura ('ndah-hoo-rah) (Runyankore) savior

Nkalati (Luganda) a very hard tree

Nkalubbo ('nkah-loo-bo) (Luganda) hard times

Nkunda (Runyankore) I love those who hate me

Nsubuga ('nsoo-boo-gah) (Luganda) clan totem is a fish (perch)

Ntege (Luganda) clan totem is a skunk

Nuwamanya (Runyankore) omniscient

Nyakoojo (Rutooro) fifth boy in a row

Nyatui ('n-YA-too-ee) (Abaluhya) tiger fighter

Ocan (o-chan) (Luo) hard times

Ochen (Ateso) one of the twins

Ochieng (O-chee-eng) (Luo) born in the daytime

Ochola (Luo) one of the twins

Odongo (Luo) born after twins

Ogwambi (o-GWAHM-bee) (Luganda) always unfortunate

Oidu (Ateso) sharp-eyed person

Ojore (o-jo-REH) (Ateso) a man of war

Okello (Ateso) one who follows twins in birth

Okoth (o-KOTH) (Luo) born when it was raining

Okware (o-kuah-reh) (Ateso) born at night

Okwayi (Ateso) God

Okwonga (o-kuo-'ngah) (Alur) a curse

Olupot (o-loo-pot) (Ateso) one following a brother who has died

Omoit (Ateso) stranger

Oneka (Luo) born to die

Onyait (Ateso) grass or born on grass

Onyango (Lusamia) born in the morning

Onzi (Lugbara) bad

Opio (Ateso) the first of the twins boys to be born

Otem (o-tem) (Luo) born away from home

Othiamba (o-tee-ahm-BAH) (Luo) born in the afternoon

Othieno (o-tee-EH-no) (Luo) born at night

Othieno born in the evening

Ouma (o-oo-MAH) (Luo) born through Caesarian surgery

Owole (Madi) one not expected to live long

Rokani (Madi) parents who have lost all their children

Ruhakana (roo-hah-kah-nah) (Rukiga) an argumentative person

Rwakaikara (Runyoro) a traditional god of the Banyoro people

Sabiti (Rutooro) born on Sunday

Sadiki (Kiswahili) faithful

Sanyu (Luganda) happiness

Sebowa (Luganda) born at a place called Bowa in Uganda

Semanda (Luganda) clan is a cow

Sempala (Luganda) born at a time of prosperity

Senyange (Luganda) white egret

Sera (seh-rah) (Lugisu) goddess in Lugisu tradition

Setimba (Luganda) named after river in Uganda called Setimba

Taamiti (tah-mee-tee) (Lunyole) bravery

Tayebwa (Runyankore) God never forgets

Tibyangye (tee-biah-njeh) (Runyankore) everything belongs to God

Tombe (to-'mbeh) (Kakwa) named after a village in northern Uganda

Tukesiga (Rukiga) hopeful

Tumushabe (Rukiga) we pray to God

Tumusiime (Rukiga) we thank God

Tusuubira (too-soo-bee-rah) (Rukiga) we have hope

Twesigye (tweh-see-jeh) (Rukiga) let's trust in God

Twinamaani (tween-a-mah-nee) (Rukiga) we are powerful

Waarwe (wah-rueh) (Runyankore) born to die

Waloga (Lunyole) bewitched

Wamukota (WAH-moo-ko-tah) (Abaluhya) left-handed

Wanzala (Lugisu) born during famine

Wasswa (Luganda) given to twins

Wemusa (weh-moo-SAH) (Luganda) never satisfied with his possessions

Zesiro (zeh-SEE-ro) (Luganda) elder of twins

Zilaba (Luganda) born while sick

Zilabamuzale (zee-lah-bah-moo-ZAH-leh) (Luganda) sickly child

UKRAINE

Although Ukrainian names appear in the army rolls of the Revolutionary War and the first U.S. Census (1790), large-scale immigration didn't occur until the 1880's. Approximately 250,000 Ukrainians immigrated to the U.S. between 1880 and 1914. Another 85,000 arrived between 1947 and 1955, displaced by World War II. By 1980 an estimated 488,000 Ukrainians and their American-born descendants lived in the U.S. One limited study showed eighty-six percent of them speak only Ukrainian at home. As a result of this and the large influx of immigrants since 1945, Ukrainian is the foreign language with the largest percentage increase in number of speakers in the U.S.

The Ukrainian territory covers nearly 300,000 square miles, which until 1945 was split between the Austro-Hungarian Empire and the Russian Empire. At various times sections of the Ukraine were parts of Poland, Czechoslovakia, and Romania. The Ukrainian dialects are East Slavic.

UKRAINIAN FEMALE NAMES

Aleksandra (Gr) defender of mankind — Lesya, Olesya, Lyaksandra

Alisa (OGer) noble, kind

Anastasiya (Gr) resurrection — Nastasiya, Nastunye

Aneta (H) grace — Anichka, Asya, Nyura, Anku

Iryna (Gr) peace — Yaryna, Orynko

Ivanna (H) God's gracious gift — Ioanna

Katerina (Gr) pure —Katrya, Karina

Klara (L) bright, clear — Klarissa, Klarysa

Lavra (L) crown of laurels

Marynia (H) bitter — Maryska

Pavla (L) little

Sabina (L) Sabine woman — Savina

Yelysaveta (H) consecrated to God — Lizaveta

Yeva (H) life — Yevtsye, Yevunye

Zofia (Gr) wisdom — Sofiya, Sofiyko

UKRAINIAN MALE NAMES

Aleksander (Gr) defender of mankind — Oleksandr, Les, Lyaksandro, Olesko

Bohdan given by God — Bohdanko

Borysko (Slavic) a fighter

Danylko (H) God is my judge — Danylo, Danylets

Dominik (L) of the Lord

Dymtro (James) (H) the supplanter — Dymtrus

Ewhen (Gr) noble — Yevheniy, Yevhen

Ivan (G) God's gracious gift — Ivanets, Ivanko, Ivasenko, Vanko

Khrystiyan (Gr) Christian

Matviy (H) gift of God — Matyash, Matviyko

Mihailo (H) who is like God? — Mychajlo, Mykhas, Mykhaltso

Osip (H) God will add — Yosyf

Petro, UKM, (Gr) stone — Petruno, Petruso

Vasyl (Gr) royal — Vasylko, Vasyltso

Yure (Gr) farmer — Djorgi, Heorhiy, Yehor

VIETNAM

Because the trickle of Vietnamese immigrants was so small before 1966, they were classified as "other Asians" by the U.S. Immigration and Naturalization Service. Between 1968 and 1971 an estimated seventy-five percent of Vietnamese immigrants were wives and children of U.S. citizens, usually American servicemen.

In April 1975 fear of reprisals from rebel forces advancing on Saigon caused a tremendous exodus of South Vietnamese. Between April 21 and April 29 the departure of over 60,000 Vietnamese was arranged by the American embassy. Another 70,000 organized their own departure. They were sent to receiving stations in Guam and the Philippines. Later refugees went to Hong Kong and Thailand. They waited for permission to move to other countries and most came to the U.S.

Approximately forty percent of this group of refugees was Catholic, compared to ten percent of the total population in Vietnam. Many of them had earlier fled the Communist takeover of North Vietnam from the French in 1954.

Virtually all of the refugees spent time in four U.S. resettlement camps, located in California, Arkansas, Florida, and Pennsylvania, until sponsors could be found to help them make the transition to American life. There they attended classes to learn English as well as basic skills such as shopping, applying for a job, and renting an apartment.

One impressive hurdle in finding sponsors for Vietnamese families was the fact that they traditionally include not only grandparents, parents and children, but aunts, uncles, and other relatives. A household may contain up to twenty-five people. Most sponsors were only willing to accept responsibility for five to seven people and considerable resistance was shown to dividing the families into smaller groups.

Since the spring of 1975 the U.S. has allowed an additional 60,000 refugees from Indochina, mainly Vietnam, to enter the country. Many of the later refugees escaped on small, unseaworthy boats; nearly half may have died at sea.

Many refugees settled in the states where the resettlement camps were located, but large numbers settled in Virginia, Texas, Mississippi, Washington, and other states. The largest numbers are in California. The Vietnamese immigrants face many of the same hardships that other immigrants faced, but they tend to become self-supporting very quickly, and within five years have the same employment rate as all Americans.

Like the Japanese, Vietnamese people take Chinese characters and interpret them in their own way for baby names, giving them Vietnamese pronunciation. Because Vietnamese pronunciation is much more subtle, and relies heavily on diphthongs, some Vietnamese immigrants have trouble with the hard consonant sounds of English. Names may be taken from Nature or celebrate values esteemed by Vietnamese such as a respectful attitude towards parents, dignity, and high moral stature.

Pronunciation

The pronunciation of most of the names has been included in the name list. Keep in mind that the pronunciations are approximate. Some sounds have no equivalent in English, and the names that have been transliterated as two syllables should be pronounced as one. The division attempts to describe the sounds of the diphthongs.

VIETNAMESE FEMALE NAMES

Ai (AH-EE) beloved, gentle (sentimental love)

Am lunar

An peace, safety

Anh (AHNH) brother

Be (BEH) doll

Bian (BEE-AN) to be hidden

Bich (BIT) jade, jewelry

Bua hammer, amulet

Cai female

Cam orange fruit, sweet

Cara diamond, precious gem

Choy rainbow

Ha (HA) river

Hang (HANG) angel in the full moon (mythological)

Hanh (HAN) faithful, beautiful, moral

Hoa (HWAH) flower, peace

Hong (HA-ONG) pink

Hue (HWEH) old-fashioned

Huong flower

Hyunh (HYOON) yellow, gold — Hoang

Kim needle

Lan flower name

Lang flower

Le (LE-AH) pearl

Mai flower

Mieu salt

My pretty

Ngoc jade

Nguyet moon

Nu girl

Ping peace

Tam ((TH)-AM) (pronounce "th" softly) heart

Tao peach

Thanh (TAN) brilliant

Thao (TA-OH) courtesy, respectful attitude towards parents

The (TOO-AY) promised, sworn

Thu (TOO) autumn — Tu

Thuy (TU-EE) gentle

Ti (TO-EE) common middle name

Trang (DJA-OMH) serious, intelligent, beautiful, generous

Trinh (DJIN) virgin

Truc (DJUKE) wish

Tuyet ((TH)OO-EE) snow

Ut last

Viet destroy

Xuan spring

VIETNAMESE MALE NAMES

An (ANH) peace, safety

Antoan (AN-twan) safe or secure

Bay seventh-born child, or born in July, seventh lunar month; on Saturday

Binh (BEUN) piece

Buu (BUH-OO) principle, guide

Cadao (ka-DA-o) folk song

Cham hard worker

Chan true

Chim (KIM) bird

Dan (VUNG) yes

Din (VIN) settle down

Dong east

Duc (YUKE) moral

Duy (VEE) moral

Gan to be near

Gia family

Hai (HAH-EE) sea — Han

Hieu (HUH-OO) respect

Hoang (HWANGH) finished

Hoc (HOWK) study

Hung (HONG) spirit of hero, brave

Hy (HEE) hope

Kim gold; metal

Lap (LAP) independent

Long (LAH-ONG) hair

Minh bright

Nam scrape off

Ngai (NGAH-EE) worn, herb

Nghi (NGEE) suspected

Nghia forever

Ngu (NGO) sleep

Nien year

Phuoc good

Pin faithful boy

Son mountain

Tai (TA-EE) talent

Tam (TAM) the number eight

Tan ((TH)-AN) (pronounce "th" softly) new

Teo (TEH-O) a nickname like Tom

Thai (TIE) many, multiple

Thang (TAHNG) victory

Thanh (TANH) finish

Thian (TWANH) smooth

Thuc (TOKE) aware

Tin ((TH)IN) think

Tong (TA-OM) fragrant

Tu'ong (TWONGH) all

Tu tree

Tuan (TUNG) goes smoothly

Tung (TOHNG) tree, calmness, dignity, seriousness

Tuyen (TUING) angel

WALES

Wales has always had a fairly small population, so immigration has been small. Between 1820 and 1976 only 95,000 immigrated to the U.S. from Wales; eighty percent arriving after 1880. Early settlers in the late 18th century were drawn to areas similar to Wales with many hills and valleys, such as Appalachian counties in New York, Pennsylvania, and Ohio.

In Wales, the Industrial Revolution began in about 1760 when coal mines, iron, copper, and tin works, and slate quarries opened in the mountainous areas of Wales. Thus Welsh industrialization had a fifty year headstart on the U.S. and plenty of skilled workmen were available for each American advance; iron workers after 1815, coal miners after 1830, slate quarrymen after 1840, and tin platers in the 1890's. Some employers actively recruited in Wales and workers were often attracted by higher U.S. wages even when times were good in Wales.

Welsh are descended from tall, red-complected Celtic invaders of about 500 B.C. and Romanized Britons. Welsh is related to Cornish and Gaelic; and of the three it is the language most determinedly kept alive. One-fifth of the Welsh people speak Welsh (as well as English) — a lilting, musical language.

WELSH FEMALE NAMES

Anghard (AHN-hahr-ahd) greatly loved one

Bethan (H) consecrated to God

Blodwen white flower

Bronwen dark and pure

Gladys (L) gradiolus, sword

Glenda of the glen

Gwendolen white brow

Gwyn white, fair

Mair (H) bitter

Myfanawy (mih-FAN-uh-wee) my fine one

Olwen white footprint

Rhiannon pure maiden

Rhianwen fair maiden

Rowena white-haired

Sian (SHAWN) (H) God's gracious gift

WELSH MALE NAMES

Alwyn from the river Alwyn

Aneirin unknown meaning, old Welsh name

Arthur bear hero

Arvel wept over

Cadwallen battle-scatterer

Carey from the castle — Cary

Culhwch (COOL-oo) old Welsh name

Dafydd (DAF-eth) (H) beloved

Dewey prized — Dew

Dylan (DIL-un) the sea — Dilan, Dillie

Emyr name of a Welsh saint

Evan a youth

Gareth (A.S.) powerful with the spear

Gavin hawk of the battle

Geraint old Welsh name

Griffin strong in faith

Gwilym (GWILL-em) (William) (Teut) resolute protector

Gwyn fair

Huw (Teut) intelligence, spirit

Ifor (Teut) archer

Kynan chief

Lloyd gray-haired one

Morgan sea dweller

Taliesin radiant brow

Vaughn small one

ZIMBABWE

Zimbabwe (formerly Southern Rhodesia) is a landlocked country in southern Africa just north of South Africa. About two percent of the people are whites, one percent are Asian or people of mixed descent, and the remainder are black Africans. The main groups are the Shona in the north and the Ndebele in the south.

Zimbabwe gained independence in 1980. The country (as Rhodesia) was named for Cecil Rhodes, a British financier who had been granted mineral rights by the Matabele tribe in 1888. British colonial rule followed until 1965, when Rhodesia became the first country to rebel against England and declare itself independent since the U.S. did in 1776. England had refused to grant independence until Rhodesia's ruling white minority guaranteed more representation to the African majority.

In modern times immigration from Zimbabwe, as with most other interior African nations, has only numbered a few hundred per year. Preferential approval for immigration is given to those immigrants who are members of technical professions, or who have relatives already living in the U.S.

Since Africa desperately needs to *keep* rather than give up its very scarce trained professional people, and since tracing relatives is virtually impossible, the difficulties African immigrants face is particularly poignant. As one would-be immigrant put it, "Why can't we immigrate for the same reasons people did in the past, simply to build a better life for ourselves?"

ZIMBABWE
FEMALE NAMES

Arantzasu (ah-rahn-tsah-soo) ref. to the Virgin Mary

Chemwapuwa (chem-WAH-poo-wah) (Shona) that which you are given

Chipo (CHEE-poh) (Shona) gift

Dorleta ref. to the Virgin Mary

Japera (jen-DAH-yee) (Shona) give thanks

Jendayi, give thanks

Kambo (KAM-boh) (Shona) unlucky

Maiba (MAH-ee-bah) (Shona) grave

Mudiwa (moo-DEH-wah) (Shona) beloved

Muzwudzani (mooz-woo-DZAH-nee) (Shona) whom should we tell

Mwaurayeni (mwah-OO-rah-YEH-nee) (Shona) what have you killed?

Mwazwenyi (mwah-WEN-yee) (Shona) what have you heard?

Rufaro (roo-FAH-roh) (Shona) happiness

Sangeya (san-GEH-yah) (Shona) hate me

Shoorai (shoh-oh-RAH-ee) (Shona) broom

Sibongile (see-bon-gee-LEH) (Ndebele) thanks

Sitembile (see-tem-bee-LEH) (Ndebele) trust

Sukutai (soo-koo-TAH-ee) (Shona) squeeze

ZIMBABWE
MALE NAMES

Banga (BANG-gah) (Shona) knife

Chenzira (chen-SEE-rah) (Shona) born on the road

Dakarai (dah-KAH-rah-ee) (Shona) happiness

Gamba (GAM-bah) (Shona) warrior

Goredenna (go-reh-deh-NAH) (Shona) black cloud

Hondo (HOHN-doh) (Shona) war

Jabulani (jah-boo-LAH-nee) be happy

Kokayi (koh-KAH-yee) (Shona) summon the people

Mashama (mah-SHAH-mah) (Shona) you are surprised

Petiri (PEH-tee-ree) (Shona) where we are

Runako (roo-NAH-koh) (Shona) handsome

Sekayi (seh-KAH-yee) (Shona) laughter

Sifiye (see-fee-YEH) (Ndebele) we are dying

Tichawonna (tee-CHAH-oh-nah) (Shona) we shall see

Zuka (zoo-KAH) (Shona) sixpence

ETHNIC ORGANIZATIONS

Arabic-speaking Countries
Association of Arab-American
   University Graduates
P.O. Box 7391
North End Station
Detroit, MI 48202

National Association of Arab
   Americans
2033 M Street, N.W. Suite 900
Washington, DC 20036

Basque
Basque Studies Program
University of Nevada Library
Reno, NV 89557-0012

China
Chinese Culture Assoc. of San
   Francisco
750 Kearney Street
San Francisco, CA 94108

Chinese Cultural Center
159 Lexington Avenue
New York, NY 10016

Denmark
Danish Brotherhood in America
3717 Harney Street
Omaha, NB 68131

France
Club Francais D'Amerique
4051 Divisader Street
San Francisco, CA 94115

Committee of French-Speaking
   Societies
11 West 42nd Street
New York, NY 10036

Germany
German American National
   Congress
Professional Councourse C006
999 Elmhurst Road
Mt. Prospect, IL 60056

The Society for German American Studies
204 Franklin Dr.
Berea, OH 44017

Greece
Greek American Progressive
   Association
3600 Fifth Avenue
Pittsburgh, PA 15213

Hungary
Magyar Tarsasag
Hungarian Association
1450 Grace Avenue
Cleveland, OH 44107

Ireland
Irish American Cultural Assoc.
10415 S. Western
Chicago, IL 60643

Irish Heritage Foundation
2123 Market Street
San Francisco, CA 94114

Israel
National Foundation for Jewish
   Culture
122 E. 42nd Street
New York, NY 10017

Italy
Italian Cultural Institute
686 Park Avenue
New York, NY 10021

Japan

Japanese American Citizen's
    League
1765 Sutter Street
San Francisco, CA 94115

Korea

Korean American Coalition
3921 Wilshire Boulevard
Los Angeles, CA 90010

Netherlands

The Dutch-American Historical
    Commission
Calvin Theological Seminary
3233 Burton Street S.E.
Grand Rapids, MI 49506

North American Indian

National Congress of American
    Indians
1346 Connecticut Avenue,
    N.W.
Washington, DC 20036

American Indian Historical
    Society
1451 Masonic Avenue
San Francisco, CA 94117

Norway

Sons of Norway International
1455 West Lake Street
Minneapolis, MN 55408

Poland

Kosciuszko Foundation
15 E. 65th Street
New York, NY 10021

Polish American Information
    Bureau
55 West 42nd Street
New York, NY 10036

Portugal/Brazil

Luso-American Educational
    Foundation
P.O. Box 1768
Oakland, CA 94604

Portuguese Society Queen St.
    Isabel
3031 Telegraph Avenue
Oakland, CA 94609

Scotland

Sons of Scotland Benevolent
    Association
90 Eglinton Avenue, East
    7th Floor
Toronto, ON
Canada M4P 2Y3

Scottish Heritage U.S.A.
281 Park Avenue
Fifth Floor
New York, NY 10010

Spain and Spanish-speaking Countries of South America

The Hispanic Society of
    America
613 W. 155th Street
New York, NY 10032

(Museum and reference library
of Spanish and Portuguese art,
literature and history.)

Sweden

Swedish Institute
2600 Park Avenue
Minneapolis, MN 55407

Swedish Information Service
825 Third Avenue
New York, NY 10022

Vietnam

Vietnam Foundation
6713 Lumsden Street
McLean, VA 22101

Many other ethnic organizations are listed in the publi-
cation *Encyclopedia of As-
sociations* available in larger
libraries.

FEMALE NAME EQUIVALENT CHART

English Name:	Ann Anne	Christine Kristin	Elizabeth	Emily Amelia	Helen Ellen
Armenia	Anie, Anna		Yeghisapet	Emelia, Melia	Heghine
Basque	Ane		Elizabete Elisa	Milia	Nora
Bulgaria	Anna	Khrustina	Elisveta	Emiliia	Elena
Czecho-slovakia	Anna, Anca Anicka	Kristina	Alzbet Bozena	Emilie Milka	Helena Elenka
Denmark	Anne Hanne	Kirsten, Stinne Kristina	Elisabet Helsa, Lisbet		Ellen Elna
England	Ann Anne	Christine Chris	Elizabeth Betsy	Emily	Helen Ellen, Elaine
Finland	Annikki	Kristina	Elli, Elisa Liisa		Helli Laina
France	Anne	Christine Christele	Elisabeth Lise	Emilie Amalie	Helenore Leonore
Germany	Anna Hanna	Christiana Kirsten	Elisabeth Elsbeth	Emilie	Helena
Greece	Anna Nani	Christina	Elisavet	Aimilios	Elena Helena, Lena
Hawaii	Ana	Kilikina	Elikapeka	Emele Emalia	Helena Elionora
Hungary	Aniko Anna	Krisztina	Erzebet Elizabeth	Amalia	Ilona Ilka
Ireland	Anna	Christin	Elizabeth	Eimile Aimiliona Emily	Helen Aileen
Israel	Ana, Enye		Elisabeth		Eliora
Italy	Anna	Cristina	Elisabetta	Emilia	Lina Elena
Latvia	Ance Ansenka	Kristine Krista	Elizabete Lizina	Amalija	Helena
Lithuania	Anikke Annze, Onele		Elzbieta Elzbute	Emilija	Elena, Ale Aliute
Nether-lands	Anke	Christina Christie	Elizabeth Els, Liesje	Emilia	Leonora
Norway	Anne	Kristin Kjersti Stina	Ellisif Lise Elise		Eli Lene
Poland	Anna Hanka	Krystyn	Elzbieta Elka	Emelia Amalie	Helena Haliana
Portugal	Ana Anicuta	Cristina	Elzira Isabela	Emelia	Helena
Romania	Ana		Elisabeta	Emilia	Elena
Russia	Anna Anechka	Khristina Khrysta	Elisaveta Yelizaveta Liza	Amalija	Elena Leonora
Scotland	Anne	Cairistiona Kirstie	Elsbeth Ealasaid	Emily	Helen Eilidh
Spain	Anna, Nina Nanor	Cristina	Elisa Belita	Emilia Amalia	Elena Leonora
Sweden	Anna	Kristina Kolina	Elisabet Lisa, Elsa	Emilia Amalia	Helena Eleonora
Ukraine	Aneta Nyura	Khristina	Yelysaveta Lisaveta	Emilya	Galena Olena

FEMALE NAME EQUIVALENT CHART

English Name:	Jean Jane	Julia	Karen Katherine	Lucy	Margaret
Armenia	Ohanna	Yulia	Garine	Lucia, Lusia	Markarid
Basque	Jone Yoana	Yulene Julene	Katalin Catalin	Lukene	Margarita Errita, Irta
Bulgaria		Iulia	Katerina	Lucine	Marketa
Czecho- slovakia	Jana	Julie Julka	Katerina Katka	Lucie	Margita Marka, Gitka
Denmark	Johanna		Karen Kasen		Margarethe Grette, Mette
England	Jane Jean, Joanne	Julie Julia	Katherine Cathy, Kate	Lucy Lucie	Margaret Marjory, Peg
Finland	Janne		Kaarina Katrie, Kaisa		Marjatta
France	Jeanne Janine Jacqueline	Julie Juliette	Catharine	Lucille Lucienne Lucie	Marguerite Margaux
Germany	Johanna	Julia	Katharina Kaethe, Katja	Lucie	Margarete Gretchen
Greece	Ioanna	Ioula Ioulia	Katherine Kolina	Lucia	Gryta
Hawaii	Io'ana	Iulia	Kakalina Kalena	Luke	Makaleka
Hungary	Janka Zsanett	Juliska Juliana	Katarina Katalin, Kati	Lucia Lucza, Luca	Margit Margo
Ireland	Sinead Siobhan Sheena, Shawn	Juliane Gillian	Kathleen Caitrin	Lucy Luighseach	Margaret Maggi Pegeen
Israel					Margalit
Italy	Giovanna	Giulia	Catarina	Lucia	Margharita Ghita
Latvia	Janina Jana, Zanna	Julija Iuliya	Kathryn Trine	Lucija	Grieta Margarita
Lithuania	Janina Janyte	Iulija	Katerina		Margarita
Nether- lands	Jansje Jaantje		Katrien Kaatje, Tryn	Lucie	Grietje Greta
Norway		Julia	Catherine Katrine Karen		Margit Marete
Poland	Jana Joanka	Julia Julita	Kataryzna Kassia	Lujca	Margarita Malgorzata
Portugal	Joana	Julia	Catarina	Lucia	Margarida Guidinha
Romania	Ioana	Iulia	Ecaterina Caterina	Lucia	Margareta
Russia	Ivana	Yuliya	Katerina Kiska Katya	Luzija	Margarete Margosha Margo
Scotland	Jean, Janet Seonag, Sine	Julia Sileas	Catharine Catriona	Lucy	Margaret Mairead
Spain	Juana Juanita	Julia Julita	Catalina	Luz	Margarita Marga
Sweden	Johanna	Julia	Katarina Karin	Lucia	Margareta Margit
Ukraine	Ioanna Ivanna	Yulia Ulyana	Katerina Karina		Margaryta

FEMALE NAME EQUIVALENT CHART

English Name:	Mary Maria	Sarah Sally	Sophie	Stephanie	Victoria
Armenia	Maro, Meroom		Sona		
Basque	Mari Miren				Bixenta Bittore
Bulgaria	Maria	Sara	Sofia		Viktoria
Czecho-slovakia	Marie Marenka	Sara	Zofie Sofia	Stefania Stefka	Viktorie Viktorka
Denmark	Marianne		Saffi		
England	Mary Marie	Sarah Sally	Sophia Sonia	Stephanie	Victoria Vicky
Finland	Maija Maikki				
France	Marie Manon	Sarah	Sophie	Stephanie	Victoire
Germany	Marie Maike, Mia	Sara	Sophie	Stefanie	Viktoria
Greece	Maria	Zaharia	Sophia Sofronia	Stefania	Nike
Hawaii	Malia Mele	Kala	Kopia	Kekepania	Wikolia
Hungary	Maria Marcsa	Sari Sasa	Sofia		Viktoria
Ireland	Mairead Maire Mallaidh	Sorcha Sarah	Sophia Sadhbh		
Israel	Mirit, Miriam	Sarah			
Italy	Maria Mara	Sara	Sofia	Stefania	Vittoria
Latvia	Marija Mare		Sofiya		Viktorija
Lithuania	Maria		Sofja Sofiya	Stefanija Stefanute	Viktorija
Nether-lands	Marike Maryk, Mies		Sophia Sonja		Victoria
Norway	Maren	Sara	Sonja		Viktoria
Poland	Maria, Macia Marysia	Sara	Zofia	Stefania Stefa, Stefcia	Wikitoria Wisia
Portugal	Maria Marta	Salomea Sala, Salcia	Sonia	Estefania Estefana	Vitoria
Romania	Maria Maricar	Sara	Sofia		Victoria
Russia	Maria Marisha Masha	Sara Sarka Sarochka	Sonya Sofia	Stephania Stesha Panya	Viktoria Vika, Viktor-ushkca
Scotland	Marion, Mae Maili, Mairi	Sarah Morag	Sophia	Stephanie	Victoria Vicky
Spain	Maria Mariquita	Sara Sarita	Sofia	Setefania Estefania	Victoria Toya, Viqui
Sweden	Maria Marja	Sara	Sonya		Viktoria
Ukraine	Marynia Maryska	Sara	Zofia Sofiya	Stepanyda Stekha, Stepa	Viktoria

MALE NAME EQUIVALENT CHART

English Name:	Alexander	Andrew	Benjamin	Christopher	Daniel
Armenia	Alexan			Kristapor	
Basque		Ander	Benkamin		Danel
Bulgaria	Aleksandur	Andrei, Andres	Veniamin	Hristofor	Danil
Czecho-slovakia	Alexander	Andrej Ondro	Benjamin	Kristof	Daniel Dano
Denmark		Anker			
England	Alexander Alistair	Andrew Andy	Benjamin Ben	Christopher Chris, Kit	Daniel Dan
Finland		Antti	Benjamin Beni	Risto	Taneli
France	Alexandre	Andre	Benjamin	Christopher	Daniel
Germany	Alexander Alex, Axel	Andreas	Benjamin	Christoph	Daniel
Greece	Alexander	Andreas Evagelos	Verniamin	Christophoros Khristos	Daniel
Hawaii	Alika	Analu	Peniamina Peni	Kilikikopa	Kanaiela Kana
Hungary	Sandor Elek	Andor	Benjamin	Kristof	Daniel
Ireland	Alexander Alsander	Aindreas Andrew	Beircheart Benjamin	Criostal Criostoir	Daniel
Israel	Aleksander		Beinish		Daniel, Dani
Italy	Alessandro Lissandro	Andrea	Beniamino	Cristoforo	Daniele
Latvia	Aleksandrs	Andrejs	Benjamins	Kriss Kristaps	Daniels
Lithuania	Alexandras	Andrius	Benejaminas	Krystupas	Danielus
Nether-lands	Alexander	Andries Andre		Christofel Chris	Daniel
Norway	Alexander	Anders	Benjamin	Kristoffer	Daniel
Poland	Aleksandr Aleksy	Andrzej	Beniamin	Krysztof	Daniel
Portugal	Alexio	Andres	Benjamin	Cristovao	Daniel
Romania	Alexsandru	Andrei	Beniamin	Cristofor	Danila
Russia	Alexandr Alexei Sashenka	Andrei	Veniamin	Christofer Khristofor	Danila
Scotland	Alaisdair Alec, Alastair	Andrew Anndra	Benjamin	Christopher	Daniel Danus
Spain	Alejandro	Andres	Benjamin	Cristobal	Daniel
Sweden	Alexander	Anders	Benjamin	Kristofor	Daniel
Ukraine	Aleksander	Andriuy	Veniamin	Khrystofor	Danylko

MALE NAME EQUIVALENT CHART

English Name:	David	James	John	Joseph	Matthew
Armenia	Tavit, Tavid		Ohari, Hovan	Hovsep, Yousef	Mateos
Basque	Dabi	Jacobe	Jon	Joseba	Matai
Bulgaria	David		Ioan, Ivan	Iosif, Yosif	Matei
Czecho-slovakia	David		Ivan Jan	Iosif	Matej Mates
Denmark		Jakob	Jens John		Mads Matthew
England	David	James	John	Joseph	Matthew
Finland	Taaveti	Jaakko Jaakoppi	Jani Jukka	Jooseppi Joosef	
France	David	Jacque Coco	Jean	Joseph	Matthieu
Germany	David	Jakob	Johann Jan	Josef	Mathias
Greece	David	Iokovos	Ioannes, John Ioannikios	Joseph	Matthias
Hawaii	Kavika Havika	Kimo	Keaka Keoni	Iokepa Keo	Makaio
Hungary	David	Zsaki Dzimi	Janos Jancsi	Jozsef	Matyas
Ireland	Daibheid	Seamas Shemus	Seghan Sean Shawn	Seosamh	Maitiu Maitias
Israel	David, Tevel	Yaakov, Jacob	Yochanan	Yosef	
Italy	Davide Davidde	Giacomo	Giovanni Gian	Giuseppe	Matteo
Latvia	Davids	Jekabs Jeska	Janis	Jazeps	Matas Matiss
Lithuania	Dovidas		Jonas Jonelis	Juozapas Juozas	Motiejus
Nether-lands	David	Jacob Jaap	Jan Jantje	Josephus	Matheu
Norway	David		Jan Jens Hans	Josef	Matteus
Poland	David Davi	Jakub	Jan	Josep	Mateusz
Portugal	David	Jacob	Joao	Jose	Mateus
Romania	David	Iocob	Ioan Iancu	Iosif Yousef	Matheiu
Russia	Daveed Danya	Yakob	Ivan	Iosif Osip Yusif	Matvey
Scotland	David Daibhidh	James, Jamie Jock, Seumas	Ian, Iain John	Joseph	Matthew
Spain	David	Jaime Diego	Juan	Jose	Mateo
Sweden	David	Jakob	Jan Jens	Josef	Mattias Matteus
Ukraine	David	Dymtro	Ivan	Osip Yosyf	Matviy

MALE NAME EQUIVALENT CHART

English Name:	Michael	Nicholas	Peter	Stephen	Thomas
Armenia		Nigoghos	Bedros	Panos	
Basque	Mikel	Mikolas	Pello Peru		
Bulgaria	Mihail	Nikolas, Nikita	Piotr	Stefan	Foma
Czecho-slovakia	Michal	Nikulas Niki	Petr Petrik	Stefan Stepka	Tomas Tomik
Denmark	Mikkel Michael	Nicolaus Klaus	Peder Preben		
England	Michael	Nicholas Nick	Peter	Stephen Steve	Thomas Tom
Finland	Mikko	Lasse	Pekka	Tapani Teppo	Tuomas
France	Michel	Nicolas Nicole Colas	Pierre	Etienne Tiennot	Thomas
Germany	Michael	Nikolas Claus	Peter	Stefan	Thomas Thoma
Greece	Michael	Nikolos Nikos	Peter	Stefans	Thomas
Hawaii	Mika'ele	Nikolao	Pekelo	Kiwini	Koma
Hungary	Mihaly	Miklos	Peter	Istvan	Tamas
Ireland	Micheal	Nioclas Niocol	Peadar	Steafan	Tomas Tomaisin
Israel	Micha-el, Micha			Tzefanyah	
Italy	Michele	Nicola, Cola Niccolo	Piero Pietro	Stefano	Tomasso
Latvia	Mikelis	Niklavs	Peteris Peter	Stefans	Toms
Lithuania	Mikas Mikelis	Nikolajus	Petras	Steponas	Tomas Tomelis
Nether-lands	Michiel	Nicolaus Klaas	Piet		Tom
Norway	Mikkel	Niklas Nils	Peder Per	Steffen	Tomas
Poland	Michal	Nikodem Mikolaj, Milosz	Piotr	Szczepan	Tomasz
Portugal	Miguel	Nicolao	Pedro	Estefania	Tomas
Romania	Mihail Mihas	Nicolae	Petru Petar	Stefan	Toma
Russia	Michail Michael	Nicolai Nikolos Kolya	Pyotr Petya	Stephan	Tomas
Scotland	Michael Micheil	Nicholas	Peter Peadair	Stephen	Thomas Tomas
Spain	Miguel	Nicolas	Pedro	Esteban	Tomas
Sweden	Mikael	Nicklas Klaus	Petter Per	Staffan Stefan	Tomas
Ukraine	Mahailo	Mikolai Mykola	Petro	Stepan Stetsko	Foma Khoma